ADVENTURES

IN THE

APACHE COUNTRY:

ADVENTURES

IN THE

APACHE COUNTRY:

A TOUR THROUGH ARIZONA AND SONORA,

WITH

NOTES ON THE SILVER REGIONS OF NEVADA

J[OHN] ROSS BROWNE

New York · 1974

Published by Promontory Press, New York, N.Y. 10016

Library of Congress Catalog Card No.: 73-92644
ISBN: 0-88394-023-X

Printed in the United States of America

———————————

Library of Congress Cataloging in Publication Data

Browne, John Ross, 1821-1875.
    Adventures in the Apache country.

    Reprint of the 1871 ed.
    1. Southwest, New--Description and travel.
2. Arizona--Description and travel. 3. Sonora,
Mexico--Description and travel. 4. Silver mines
and mining--Nevada. I. Title. II. Series.
F786.B87 1973   917.9

ADVENTURES

IN THE

APACHE COUNTRY:

A TOUR THROUGH ARIZONA AND SONORA,

WITH

NOTES ON THE SILVER REGIONS OF NEVADA.

BY J. ROSS BROWNE,

AUTHOR OF

"YUSEF," "CRUSOE'S ISLAND," "AN AMERICAN FAMILY
IN GERMANY," "THE LAND OF THOR," ETC.

Illustrated by the Author.

NEW YORK:

HARPER & BROTHERS, PUBLISHERS,

FRANKLIN SQUARE.

1871.

CONTENTS.

WASHOE REVISITED.

BODIE BLUFF.

THE DEAD SEA OF THE WEST.

THE WALKER RIVER COUNTRY.

THE REESE RIVER COUNTRY.

LIST OF ILLUSTRATIONS.

A 2

ADVENTURES

IN THE

APACHE COUNTRY.

CHAPTER I.

THE GADSDEN PURCHASE.

I HAVE almost forgotten through what uncomfortable part of the world the obliging reader and myself performed our last exploit in the way of a pleasure trip. A foggy remembrance comes over me that it was over the barren fjelds of Norway, and through the treacherous bogs of Iceland. Assuming that we parted on friendly terms, and that we still entertain a kindly recollection of each other, I have now to offer a new programme of exploration and adventure, very different indeed from our last, but possessing peculiar charms in the absence of accommodation for travellers, and extraordinary advantages in the way of burning deserts, dried rivers, rattlesnakes, scorpions, Greasers, and Apaches; besides unlimited fascinations in the line of robbery, starvation, and the chances of sudden death by accident. From the borders of the Arctic circle to Arizona the transition will at least afford us a new sensation of some sort; and if we fail to make the trip remunerative either in novelty of scenery or incident it will be our own fault.

Years ago the romance of Spanish history was the great passion of my life. The grand old viceroys of Mexico, from the days of Cortéz downward, were such a splendid set of marauders—so fired with chivalry, lust, and fanaticism; so wildly visionary to conceive, and so daring to execute—that, upon a general review of their exploits, which so long furnished food for my imagination, it is a matter of the most profound astonishment to myself that I have never turned my attention to piracy or highway robbery. No stronger proof of innate rectitude could possibly exist. At the least calculation I should have arisen to the dignity of an original explorer, instead of rambling over the trodden paths of the western world as I now do, a mere every-day tourist, in the footsteps of those giant old freebooters whose histories have shed such a glorious lustre upon the country that gave them birth. Especially do I remember the peculiar fascination that hung around that wild region far away to the north of Mexico, wherein it was said great cities of marvellous wealth existed and wonderful rivers were found, " the banks of which were three or four leagues in the air." *   The very name of "Arizuma"† was fraught with the rarest charms of romance. Here it was that gold and silver existed in virgin masses ; here were races of highly-civilized Indians and beautiful women, fair as alabaster, living an Acadian life ; here were the magnificent cities of Civola and Chichiticala, and the great river called the Tezon. It was through the wild and mystic region to the north of the Gila that Marco de Niça made his famous expedition under direction of the Viceroy, Mendoza, in 1535 ; and here, over thousands of miles of desert and mountain, roamed those daring adventurers Coronado, and Pedro de Tohar, and Lopez de Cardenas and Cabeza de Vaca—he of the cow-head but lion-heart—and the famous guide Estevan, the blackamoor, who was put to death by the Moquis for making love to their women—a natural though unpardonable offense in that region even unto the present day.

Of a later date were the explorations and adventures of the brave old Jesuit Missionary Padre Eusebius Francis Kino, to whom all honor is rendered by Vanega, the early historian of California. Father Kino, inspired

---

* Expedition of Don Garcia Lopez de Cardenas, under direction of Coronado, in 1540.   † The old Spanish name of Arizona.

by religious motives, left his mission of Dolores in 1698, and journeyed north as far as the Gila River, battling with the perils of the wilderness and Christianizing the Indians. During the years 1699 and 1704 he made numerous journeys equally long, difficult, and dangerous, solving many interesting problems in regard to the newly-discovered countries, erecting missions, and collecting vast treasures of information about the wonderful people whom he encountered in his travels. The peaceful conquests of Father Kino and his followers over the barbarous races of Sonora and Arizuma are among the most curious records of history; and to this day may be seen, in the ruined missions and vestiges of Christian faith among the Yaqui, Opoto, and Papago Indians, the noblest monuments of their works. From the discontinuance of the Jesuit Missions the progress of discovery was chiefly toward the development of the vast silver deposits known to exist in Northern Sonora, which at that time comprised an indefinite extent of territory north of the Gila. Nothing in the pages of romance can equal the marvellous stories that were told of the mineral wealth of Arizuma. Borne out by facts sufficiently wonderful to dazzle the imagination, it is not surprising that the credulity of men was stretched to its utmost limit. Even at that early date there were speculators in " wild cat," and foolish people to listen to them, and mankind was bought and sold just as it is at the present day.

But who could resist such proofs as were presented in the form of solid masses of virgin silver actually dug out of the earth ? Neither you nor I, reader, nor Baron Humboldt who tells us about them, nor Mr. Ward, the British Ambassador, who furnishes corroborative testimony ; nor the laborious Mr. Wilson, who writes a history of Mexico to disperse the mists of fancy cast over that country by the magic pen of Prescott; nor any body else with an eye for the needful, to say nothing of the picturesque or the beautiful. Only conceive the sensations of a poor wretch who stumbles over such a lump of silver as that upon which Don Diego Asmendi paid duties to the Spanish Government! The official report made by the Custom-house officer—and we don't know what percentage of treasure went into his pocket —states that Don Diego paid duties on a virgin lump weighing 275 pounds. The aggregate weight of several other pieces upon which the king's attorney brought suit for duties was 4033 pounds; and the same officer also sued for the possession of a piece of pure silver weighing 2700 pounds, on the ground that it was a curiosity, and therefore rightfully belonged to his majesty the king, which every body must admit was good logic if not very good law.

Nearly three thousand pounds of virgin silver, the heaviest mass ever found in the world! Oh, lovely virgin! effulgent, fascinating, glittering virgin! Who would not worship such a virgin as that? Who would not join me in a visit to the joyous land of Arizuma where such precious virgins exist?

But why is it, you cunningly ask, if the silver mines of Arizona are as rich as they are represented to be, that they are now deserted? Why have they failed to attract a mining population? Why has Arizona made no progress within the past ten years, while Washoe and Idaho have made such rapid strides within three or four years?

Let me answer these inquiries by a brief reference to the past and present condition of Arizona. It is true that the silver mines of Washoe attracted a population of ten thousand during the first year of their discovery; also true that Idaho now boasts a population of twenty thousand; while the melancholy fact can not be denied that Arizona has never yet had an American population of over three thousand, and not a very good one at that.

The Territory of Arizona was acquired by purchase from Mexico, under the Gadsden treaty made in September, 1853, and confirmed by Congress during the session

ROCKY MESA ON THE GILA.

of 1853–4. Prior to its purchase it formed a part of the Mexican State of Sonora. The cession was contained within certain parallels and boundaries, embracing some forty thousand square miles of land, with a length of four hundred and sixty miles and an extreme width of a hundred and thirty. In negotiating for the purchase of this territory Mr. Gadsden made strenuous efforts to secure a strip of country as far south as Guyamas, but he was not sustained by Congress, and thus the most important feature in the treaty was omitted—a port on the Gulf of California. The United States found itself in possession of a country which it was impracticable to reach except across extensive and inhospitable deserts, and over vast ranges of mountains, many of them covered with perpetual snow. It is possible some vague notion prevailed in the halls of Congress that the difficulty might be remedied by a port at Fort Yuma or the Pimo villages. There being, during seasons of drought, from six to ten inches of water in the Colorado, and from four to six in the Gila, except at the two points above-named, where the navigation is further impeded by fluctuating sand-bars, it must be conceded that there is some ground for the idea. A port at either of these places would be of great benefit to the country if it had a bottom to it that would hold water, or a top that would prevent evaporation.

At the period of its purchase Arizona was practically a *terra incognita*. Hunters and trappers had explored it to some extent; but their accounts of its resources and peculiarities were of a vague and marvellous character, according well with their wild habits of life. Few people in the United States knew any thing about it, save the curious book-worms who had penetrated into the old Spanish records. An impression prevailed that it was a worthless desert, without sufficient wood or water to sustain a population of civilized beings. Mr. Gadsden was ridiculed for his purchase, and it was very generally believed that Congress, in expending ten millions of dollars for such an arid waste, had in view some ulterior project of extension, based upon the balance of power between the Northern and Southern States. It was even hinted that this was to be a grand reservoir for disappointed office-seekers, who could be effectually disposed of by means of Territorial appointments. It was inhabited almost exclusively by savage tribes of Indians, from whose ravages the Texans and Mexicans had long suffered; and now, if our surplus of adventurous politicians could only be sent there, the more valuable of our possessions would no longer be subject to their injurious machinations. With this view Mr. Jefferson Davis did one of the few good things he ever did in his life. He organized various expeditions, and caused the newly-acquired territory to be explored. It is possible he contemplated living in it himself upon his retirement from the Presidency of the slave Republic which even then he must have had in his eye. The reports of Lieutenants Whipple and Ives are among the most valuable of the contributions made to our knowledge of this interesting region. In 1853–4, Lieutenant Williamson made a survey of the country north of the Gila, in view of a route for a railway from the Atlantic to the Pacific States. Lieutenant A. B. Gray, in 1854, made a survey from Marshall, Texas, to El Paso, and thence across the country to Tubac, from which point he made branch surveys—one to Port Lobos, on the Gulf of California, and the other to Fort Yuma and San Diego. Mr. Bartlett, of the Boundary Commission, also made some very important surveys, and added materially to our knowledge of the topographical peculiarities of the country, its climate and productions. His report is replete with interesting details of life, scenery, and adventure in Arizona. Few persons, save those who are familiar with the country, will complain of the minutiæ of his camp experiences. Lieutenant Parke, in 1854–5, made a survey of a route from San Diego to Fort Yuma, the Pimo villages, Tucson, El Paso, and into Northern Texas. Lieutenant Edmund F. Beale

SILVER MINES IN THE SANTA RITA MOUNTAINS.

made numerous surveys and explorations through Northern Arizona, the reports of which have been published from time to time by Congress. They are valuable for the information they contain in reference to the availability of the different routes proposed, as well as for the important discoveries made by Mr. Beale himself. In 1854 Mr. Charles D. Poston, a private citizen, landed at Navachista, on the Gulf of California, and explored the country as far as Western Sonoita, and thence through the Papagoria to the Big Bend of the Gila, Fort Yuma, and San Diego. In 1855 the Boundary Survey was completed by Major Emory and Lieutenant Michler. In August, 1856, an exploring party outfitted at San Antonio, Texas, and after a perilous journey through the Apache Pass arrived at Tubac, and proceeded, under the direction of Mr. Poston, to examine the silver mines reported to exist in the Santa Rita, Cerro Colorado, and Arivaca Mountains; and in 1857 companies were formed for the purchase and development of these mines. In August and September, 1857, the San Antonio and San Diego semi-monthly stage-line, under the direction of I. C. Woods, was established, James Burch acting as contractor. This continued till the Butterfield semi-weekly line was put upon the route, in August, 1858, under a contract of six years with the Postmaster-General, at $600,000 a year. An enterprise of greater importance than this had never been undertaken by any private citizen. It was one of the grand achievements of the age to span the continent by a semi-weekly line of stages, under bonds to perform, by the sole power of horse-flesh, a trip of nearly two thousand five hundred miles within the schedule time of twenty-five days. Few believed it could be done; and when the vast deserts through which the route lay, and the hostile tribes of Indians that inhabit them, are taken into account, it is a marvel that it was not only a success but a triumph. There was no failure from the beginning to the end—from St. Louis to San Francisco. The usual time was from twenty to twenty-two days; and on the occasion of the transmission of a Presidential Message, the entire trip was actually made within sixteen days! All praise to Butterfield! and all praise to that enterprising Postmaster-General who put him through!

From 1857 to 1860 a large amount of capital was ex-

HARDY ADVENTURER.

pended in transporting and erecting machinery and developing the silver mines south of Tucson; but in consequence of the inaccessible nature of the country, and the
high rates of duties levied upon all importations through
Sonora, these enterprises were carried on at great expense and under extraordinary difficulties. Boilers
weighing six thousand pounds and heavy engines had to
be transported in wagons from Lavaca in Texas to the
Rio Grande, and thence across the continent to the silver regions—a distance of twelve hundred miles. The
roads were almost as nature had made them—rough and
rocky, abounding in ruts and pitfalls and heavy sands,
and every mile of the way from the Rio Grande was beset with dangers. Fierce and barbarous Indians lurked
behind the rocks and in the deep arroyas, ever on the
alert to plunder and murder the little bands of white men
who toiled wearily through the inhospitable deserts.
The sufferings of these hardy adventurers were almost
without a parallel in the history of human enterprise.
Hunger and thirst and burning suns and chilling nights
were among the least of the trials to which they were
subject; sudden death from hidden foes, or cruel and
prolonged torture, stared them in the face at every step.
The wayside was lined with the bleached bones of unfortunate men who had preceded them, straggling parties who had fallen victims to the various perils of the
journey. When, after weary months of toil and suffering, the jaded teamsters arrived in Arizona with their
precious freight—now literally worth its weight in silver—they found no established homes, no prosperous
communities of families to greet them, but a country as
wild as that through which they had passed, almost desolated by the ravages of Apaches. For three centuries
these Bedouins of the desert had continued their depredations upon stock, robbing the ranches, killing the
rancheros, and harassing emigrant parties. No industry
could prosper under their malign influence. The whole
State of Sonora was devastated, and the inhabitants in a

starving condition. Arizona possessed at least the pretense of military protection. It soon became infested
with the refuse population of Sonora—the most faithless
and abandoned race, perhaps, on the face of the earth.
What the Apaches left undone in the way of murder and
robbery they seldom failed to complete, and indeed were
regarded with more distrust by respectable citizens than
even the barbarous Indians.

Nor was this all. The most desperate class of rene-
gades from Texas and California found Arizona a safe
asylum from arrest under the laws. The Vigilance
Committee of San Francisco did more to populate the
new Territory than the silver mines. Tucson became the
head-quarters of vice, dissipation, and crime. It was
probably the nearest approach to Pandemonium on the
North American Continent. Murderers, thieves, cut-
throats, and gamblers formed the mass of the population.
Every man went armed to the teeth, and scenes of bloodshed were of every-day occurrence in the public streets.
There was neither government, law, nor military protection. The garrison at Tucson confined itself to its legitimate business of getting drunk or doing nothing. Arizona was perhaps the only part of the world under the
protecting ægis of a civilized government in which every
man administered justice to suit himself, and where all
assumed the right to gratify the basest passions of their
nature without restraint. It was literally a paradise of
devils. Under such circumstances it is not a matter of
surprise that the progress of the country was slow. It
was not a place for honest working-men or for families.
Good people feared to go there. The newspapers were
filled with accounts of bloody affrays, robberies, and
Apache raids. Yet, despite all these drawbacks, men of
enterprise began to learn the great natural resources of
the Territory; the silver mines of Santa Rita and Cerro
Colorado attracted attention as they became developed;
and in 1860 Arizona seemed in a fair way of receiving a
rapid increase of population, and obtaining through Con-

gress what it had long needed—a Territorial form of government. Efforts had been made to effect this object as early as 1857, when Mr. Gwin, of California, introduced a bill in the Senate to organize the Territory of Arizona; but there were jealousies on the railroad question which resulted in the defeat of the bill. Mr. Green, of Missouri, in 1860, introduced a bill to provide a "temporary government for the Territory of Arizuma," which also failed. Various other attempts were made, none of which were successful. Disaffection between the advocates of the different railroad routes, agitations on the slave question, and jealousies among the adventurers who sought political preferment, prevented the recognition of a great principle which should always govern a civilized nation in its councils—never to acquire territory until it can extend over it the protection of law. While these questions so vital to the interests of Arizona were pending, public attention was suddenly attracted in another direction. The rich mineral discoveries in Washoe created a sensation throughout the length and breadth of the land. The rush from California to that region was unparalleled in the history of mining excitements. Of that memorable exodus, some few readers of this narrative may remember the description given in a series of articles under the title of "A Peep at Washoe." Gold discoveries in California had become an old story. The placers were beginning to fail; surface digging no longer paid extraordinary profits; the honest miners had passed through so many excitements that the ordinary pursuits of industry no longer possessed a charm for them; and they, in common with the mass of the citizens, were well prepared for the new field of enterprise and speculation. The results of investments in silver stock were immediate, if the silver itself was tardy of appearance. A few fortunes, rapidly made by adroit purchases and speedy sales, inspired thousands of enterprising speculators with the most extravagant hopes of success. Even sober business-men lost their balance, and suffered themselves to be drawn into the whirl of excitement. Silver mining was a novelty. The surplus energy of the American people had never found a vent in that direction. It was an untried experiment, and promised to realize the fabulous stories of Spanish discovery in Mexico. There was no difficulty in reaching the newly-discovered region of boundless wealth. It lay on the public highway to California, on the borders of the State. From Missouri, from Kansas and Nebraska, from Pike's Peak and Salt Lake, the tide of emigration poured in. Transportation from San Francisco was easy. I made the trip myself on foot almost in the dead of winter, when the mountains were covered with snow. Stages laden with passengers inside and out crossed the Sierra Nevadas in twenty-eight hours from Sacramento to Virginia City. A telegraph line speedily followed, and speculation in stocks could be carried on between San Francisco and the Comstock metropolis by the shock of a battery. In the full tide of the excitement Arizona, neglected, suffering, and almost forgotten, received the heaviest blow of all. The rebellion broke out in April, 1861. The Butterfield overland mail line was stopped at the same time, in view of the dangers that threatened it; and an act of Congress was passed changing the route. During the month of July the only Federal troops in the Territory shamefully and without cause abandoned it, and marched from Forts Breckenridge and Buchanan to Cook's Springs, where they heard the Texan rebels were coming. Without waiting to ascertain the number or prepare for any defense, they burned all their wagons, spiked their cannon, and packed their provisions on mules over the mountains to Fort Craig. There were four companies, numbering altogether four hundred and fifty men. They had heard of the surrender of Fort Fillmore toward which they were marching, and this caused them to take a different route. At Fort Fillmore five hundred Federal troops of the regular army surrendered to about two hundred and fifty renegade

Texans, ragged, undisciplined, poorly armed, and badly equipped. A scattered company of these roving bandits, under the command of the guerrilla chief, Captain Hunter, numbering about one hundred, reached Tucson on the 27th of February, 1862, and took possession of the place. Most of the inhabitants had fled to Sonora for safety, or stood ready to join the rebels. It was a secession stronghold, composed almost entirely of Southern outlaws, whose sympathies were naturally opposed to the existing Government. Hunter and his party held possession of the Territory, advancing as far as the Pimo villages and even threatening Fort Yuma, till the advance of the California column in May, when they retreated to the Rio Grande. The few citizens and traders who remained loyal to the Government, and the managers and workmen employed at the mines being thus left at the mercy of lawless desperadoes, roving bands of Apaches and Sonoranians, fled from the country as fast as they could procure the means of escape. Many of them were imprisoned, and some were murdered. The hostile Indians, ignorant of our domestic disturbances, believed they had at length stampeded the entire white population. On the public highways they fell upon small parties and slaughtered them. It was their boast, and is still their belief, that they had conquered the American nation. The Sonoranians, greedy for plunder, rushed in from the borders by hundreds, and commenced ransacking the mines, stealing the machinery, and murdering the few employés that remained. At Tubac, the head-quarters of the Arizona Mining Company, the Apaches besieged the town on one side, while the Sonoranians lurked in the bushes on the other. Twenty men held it for three days, and finally escaped under cover of night. There was nothing left. The troops had burned all the stores, provisions, and groceries, public and private, that they could lay hands upon; tore down the mill at Tucson; burned the Canoa; and destroyed government stores at Breckinridge and Buchan-

B

an worth probably half a million of dollars.   Treason, cowardice, or incompetency must have been the cause of these disgraceful proceedings.   There was no sat-isfactory reason, that can now be seen, why they should have so precipitate-ly evacuated the Territory, and yielded peaceful pos-session to the enemies of the Federal Government.

APACHES.

From that date until the last session of the Thirty-seventh Congress, Arizona remained without a Terri-torial organization.   Few people were left in the country, and there was no protection to the mines. They were all abandoned to the plundering Sonora-nians, who stole the ore and destroyed the machinery. The ranches were in ruin; south and east of Tucson there was not a single inhabited spot within the bound-ary lines.

I have thus at some length attempted to account for the tardy growth of this interesting Territory.   It will be admitted that there is good reason why Arizona has failed to attract a population.   With wonderful re-sources and a climate equal to that of Italy, it has suf-fered a series of misfortunes unparalleled in the history of our territorial possessions.   Two great obstacles to the prosperity of the country still exist: difficulty of access, which can only be remedied by a port on the Gulf of California; and the hostility of the Apache Indians, for which there is no remedy short of extermi-nation.

CHAPTER II.

BUT let us not anticipate the course of our travels. You shall see for yourself the deserts and the mines and the wondrous things of that wondrous land, my gentle friend, if you will patiently follow me. Only don't expect me to be lively in such a wild region. It is not a jolly country. The graves of murdered men, and boundless sand deserts, and parched mountains, and dried-up rivers, and scenes of ruin and desolation are profoundly interesting; but they are not subjects for the indulgence of rollicking humor. It is only serious and reflecting men, like you and myself, who can appreciate them.

We have thus followed up our intended beat from the time of the early Spaniards to the passage of the act of Congress, of the 20th of February, 1863, establishing the Territorial government. And here, by way of making certain that there is no deception in the matter, let us take a look at the official seal of the Territory, designed by Mr. Secretary M'Cormick: An honest miner stands with his left hand in his pocket feeling for the profits of his day's labor. The expression of his countenance is indicative of a serious frame of mind. He gazes into the future, and sees gold and silver a long way off. His spade stands ready to dig it, and his wheelbarrow to wheel it. As yet he has struck nothing very rich—but it will come by and by. In the background you see the two prominent peaks of Bill Williams's Mountain, where he contemplates prospecting next year; or possibly these may be the dirt-piles which he has already thrown up and not yet washed for lack of water. The motto is appropriate, " Ditat Deus."

Although it was my intention to visit Arizona some time or other, as it is to visit every part of the habitable globe, I had no more idea on Saturday morning, December 5, 1863, of starting on such an important expedition at 4 P.M. of the same day, than I had of going on a prospecting tour through the Mountains of the Moon. Yet who can say what an hour may bring forth? A man's fate, as the Arabs say, is written upon his skull, and I suppose it was mine to leave on that day for Arizona. At all events it so chanced in my peregrinations about San Francisco that I fell in with my old friend, Charles D. Poston, the Arizona Pioneer, who had just arrived from the East by the overland route through Salt Lake. He was now Superintendent of Indian Affairs for the new Territory; held various commissions as director of mining companies; was full of the romance and fascinations of Arizona. The best years of his life had been spent there. He knew every foot of the country; talked Spanish like a native; believed in the people; believed in the climate; had full faith in the silver; implicitly relied upon the gold; never doubted that Arizona was the grand diamond in the rough of all our Territories. He looked and talked and acted like a man perfectly sane; and when he confidently assured me that if "feet" chimed with my aspirations, I could have as many as I pleased by accepting a seat in his ambulance from Los Angeles to the Promised Land, cooks and teamsters and vaqueros were all projected; and for military escorts he held the documents in his hand. We would have a grand time; we would feast and hunt and hold pow-wows with the Indians, and do up the whole country even to the Moqui villages, which he informed me, on the authority of an English missionary, were inhabited by a race of Welshmen who made a voyage to the Continent of North America in ancient times. Could flesh and blood stand such a proposition as that? Here was a chance for locomotion on a grand scale; and fortune smiled in the distance.

"Poston," said I, "consider me a partner. At 4 P.M. this memorable day I'm on hand. Should the Apaches get my scalp, you, my venerable friend, and you alone, are responsible to my family and to mankind!"

Over to Oakland—a hurried explanation—a parting glance at the pleasant homestead, the garden, the wife, and the little ones—ah me! how often the same insatiable spirit of adventure has driven me blindly and recklessly through the same trying ordeal! Is there no help for it in this world? Must a man when he has travelled for thirty years never more taste the sweets of content, but keep drifting uneasily along till he drifts into the final haven of rest?

There was no trouble about getting ready. A knapsack, as usual, was my only baggage. The contents were soon packed; a few coarse shirts, a box of pencils and paints, a meerschaum and a plug of tobacco, these were the indispensable parts of my outfit. At 4 P.M. I stood upon the deck of the good steamer *Senator*, fully equipped and prepared for the important enterprise on hand. Poston was true to time. We were favored with the company of Mr. Ammi White, an Indian Agent and trader, on his return to the Pimo villages, and two of his wards, Antonio Azul, chief of the Pimos, and Francisco the interpreter. I was glad to make the acquaintance of Ammi White. He had seen all the ups and downs of Arizona life; had been a prisoner among the Texans, and knew as much of the country as any man in or out of it. Besides, he was a quaint, original man, a native of Maine; long, lank, and leathery; brimful of wild reminiscences, and of that genial turn which promised much in the way of future enjoyment. All hail to our good friend and travelling companion, Ammi White! Slow of speech he may be, and prejudiced against the luxuries of civilization, but a jewel of a White is he in his native element of sage-deserts and

Indians, pork and beans, adobe hovels and pinole.   Antonio Azul, chief of the Pimos, and son of the illustrious Cool Azul, was in the full tide of a triumphant return to his native village.   He had paraded the streets of San Francisco with his illustrious friend Iretaba, chief of the Mojaves, who has since created such a sensation in New York and Washington; had seen the great elephant, civilization; had heard the negro minstrels, and visited the Mint and Custom-house; and now he was about to return laden with treasures of knowledge to the bosom of his virtuous wife and family, and spend the remainder of his days, sitting bare-legged in front of his wigwam, telling his people of the wondrous sights he had seen.   Especially was he prepared to give them

PIMO INDIAN.

a lucid account of the fiery horses that pulled the public with lightning speed along iron roads, and the big canoe that paddled over the briny deep by means of a great kettle of hot water that was always kept boiling down in the hold. Francisco, his official interpreter, was resplendent with badges of distinction given him by the ladies; which he wore on his head, and on his breast, and on his back, and on every available spot of his body from top to bottom; being, as I should have said, a handsome youth, much given to destruction of the female sex. Never for a moment from the time he stepped on board till we got well out of the harbor did the joyous grin of gratified ambition leave his countenance, save when we crossed the bar, and then he went precipitately below, and turned in on a pile of freight. When he came up next morning his face was painted a grim yellow, to disguise the effects of those internal emotions which are apt to disturb the digestion of the bravest warriors; for Francisco was a warrior, too, and scorned weakness of digestion as a disgrace to manhood. He looked as grim as the Sphinx, and frowned from time to time as if nothing on earth, or on the waters of the earth, or on the steamships that plough the waters, could disturb his stolidity; and then, upon the occasion of a sudden lurch or two, rushed to windward with both hands firmly pressed over his mouth, doubling himself up and vainly endeavoring to conceal the horrible contortions of his countenance. But it was no use. Old Neptune got the best of him at last. I was only surprised that he did not follow the example of some of our army officers who become sick of the war—throw up his commission.

Of the voyage I have only to say that it was smooth and pleasant—a mere Lake Como trip, with the addition of a finer climate, a greater extent of scenery, and a much more commodious boat than any to be found on the waters of Como. The change from the chilling fogs of San Francisco to the balmy atmosphere of the South is one of the luxuries of a winter's trip. Few of those

unfortunate beings who dwell upon the shores of the
Atlantic have any conception of the delightful climate
with which we are blessed on the Pacific coast. Bright
sunshine sparkles over the sea and nestles among the declivities of the mountains; the earth rejoices in the
generous flood of light poured down upon it from morning till night; the birds of the air and the beasts of the
field revel in the groves and pastures that stretch back
from the rock-bound shores; nothing in life or in nature
seems wanting in the measure of a joyous future; all is
rich and glowing and full of beauty and promise. A
voyage along the shores of California is a feast of soul
for all the years to come. The mountains, barren as
they appear at the first sight, are strangely fantastic in
form and wonderfully rich in coloring. The full swell
of the ocean, unobstructed for thousands of miles, falls
like the majestic peal of a mighty organ upon the embattlements of solid rock that line the main. Beyond the
Point of Conception the beautiful islands of Santa Barbara loom up over the bright sparkling sea, barren of
foliage yet wonderfully picturesque in the glowing tints
of the southern horizon. What a luxury of lights and
shades; what a balmy, ecstatic atmosphere; what broad
blue fields of water and infinite distances of landscape!
Could it be that a grand mistake was made in Mo-
hammedan history — that Paradise is nothing more
than a faint attempt to delineate the beauties of California?

The old town of San Pedro had not improved since my
last visit in 1860. It then consisted of an ancient adobe
building, in which Mr. Banning carried on his staging
and teaming operations, and a few warehouses and miscellaneous shanties under the bank. It now consists
of the same, in other hands, and somewhat dilapidated by
the lapse of time. The principal inhabitants are wild
geese, sea-gulls, and dead cattle. The steamer lies out
by Deadman's Rock—a little island supposed to be the
burial-place of an unfortunate mariner who came to an

SAN PEDRO.

B 2

untimely end in that vicinity. A cross marks his grave, and sea-gulls and wild sea-waves sing his lullaby.

Banning—the active, energetic, irrepressible Phineas Banning—has built a town on the plain about six miles distant, at the head of the sloo. He calls it Wilmington, in honor of his birthplace. In order to bring Wilmington and the steamer as close together as circumstances will permit, he has built a small boat propelled by steam, for the purpose of carrying passengers from the steamer to Wilmington, and from Wilmington to the steamer. Another small boat of a similar kind burst its boiler a couple of years ago, and killed and scalded a number of people, including Captain Seely, the popular and ever-to-be-lamented commander of the *Senator*. The boiler of the present boat is considered a model of safety. Passengers may lean against it with perfect security. It is constructed after the pattern of a tea-kettle, so that when the pressure is unusually great the cover will rise and let off the superabundant steam, and thus allow the crowd a chance to swim ashore.

Wilmington is an extensive city, located at the head of a slough, in a pleasant neighborhood of sand-banks and marshes. There are not a great many houses in it as yet, but there is a great deal of room for houses when the population gets ready to build them. The streets are broad and beautifully paved with small sloughs, ditches, bridges, lumber, dry-goods boxes, and the carcasses of dead cattle. Ox-bones and the skulls of defunct cows, the legs and jaw-bones of horses, dogs, sheep, swine, and coyotes, are the chief ornaments of a public character; and what the city lacks in the elevation of its site it makes up in the elevation of its water-lines, many of them being higher than the surrounding objects. The city fathers are all centred in Banning, who is mayor, councilman, constable, and watchman, all in one. He is the great progenitor of Wilmington. Touch Wilmington, and you touch Banning. It is his specialty—the offspring of his genius. And a glorious genius has

WILMINGTON.

Phineas B. in his way! Who, among the many thousands who have sought health and recreation at Los Angeles within the past ten years, has not been a recipient of Banning's bounty in the way of accommodation? His stages are ever ready—his horses ever the fastest— his jovial face ever the most welcome on the beach! Big of heart, big of body, big of enterprise, is Phineas— the life and soul of Los Angeles county. The people know it—the public acknowledge it; for he is now a delegate to the National Convention, and will, I venture to assert, make an honorable mark in that body. Long life to Banning! May his shadow grow larger and larger every day! At all events, I trust it may never grow less. I retract all I said about Wilmington—or most of it. I admit that it is a flourishing place compared with San Pedro. I am willing to concede that the climate is salubrious at certain seasons of the year, when the wind does not blow up the sand, and at certain other seasons when the rain does not cover the country with water; and then again at other seasons, when the earth is not parched by drought and scorching suns.

Within a mile of this charming city stands a quadrangular series of houses, well built and commodious, with a large square in the middle, called Camp Drum. Here, in virtue of certain documents from head-quarters, we were provided with an escort of five soldiers and a sergeant, to secure us against the attacks of Greasers, savages, and other disreputable natives, on the road to the Colorado River. We were also furnished with mules for our ambulance and rations for our military forces. The officers of the camp were exceedingly kind and polite, and made our sojourn there an agreeable episode in our journey.

At Camp Drum we heard a good deal about the lively condition of society in and around Los Angeles. It was not considered safe for a man to travel about, even within a few miles of camp, without a double-barrelled shot-gun, a revolver, a bowie-knife, and two Derringer

pistols. Of course in these war times, when thousands
of lives are lost every day, the mere killing of a few citizens now and then must seem ridiculously tame to people on the Atlantic side; and I only speak of it as a
common characteristic of the country through which I
was travelling. At any point on the road between Los
Angeles and Camp Drum, bullets in the back of the head
were to be expected. The recent acts of the Vigilance
Committee in breaking into the jail and hanging Boss
Danewood and four of his fellow-prisoners—three of
whom were Spaniards—had aroused the resentment of
every American outlaw and native Greaser in the country, and assassinations were of frequent occurrence. In
passing through the narrow lanes and between the willow hedges, where the vineyards are located, it was
deemed a necessary precaution to travel with a knife
ready drawn, so as to cut the lassoes that were likely
to be thrown around one's neck. A gentleman of my
acquaintance, connected with the military department,
seemed to relish this state of affairs exceedingly, as it
afforded him an opportunity of indulging his propensity
for hunting. Ducks and geese had long since ceased to
afford him any diversion. He now amused himself by
jumping into his buggy, and starting off with his double-
barrelled shot-gun after Greasers, murderers, and the
like, of whom he generally bagged, or otherwise disposed
of, two or three every week. In fact, he rather prided
himself upon his skill in man-hunting. I was a little
shocked at first when I heard of man-hunting as a recreation, but after a few days' sojourn in Los Angeles
found it was quite a common amusement. Running
down, catching, shooting, and hanging suspicious characters was esteemed the very best kind of sport, being
dangerous as well as exciting. During our stay a party
of the Vigilants went down from Los Angeles to Wilmington, got on board Banning's little steamboat, and
while it was *en route* for the *Senator*, took a prisoner
bound for San Quentin out of the hands of the sheriff

and hanged him by the neck till he was dead. The unfortunate man was a native of California, and was believed to be the murderer of John Raines, an American
ranchero. Since that exploit, performed in full view of
Camp Drum, they pursued and captured the murderer
of Mr. Sandford, another victim of the barbarous condition of society, and strung him up in the same summary
manner. Whether the country will be permanently benefited by these acts remains to be seen. I hope it will,
for it certainly needs reformation of some sort. Putting
this and that together, and throwing in Idaho and Montana by way of good measure, it seems to me that Italy
can no longer claim distinction for her banditti. We
can do as much murdering, robbing and stabbing as any
other people, and a great deal more catching and hanging than ever was done in Europe.

Several days were required to complete our outfit at
Los Angeles. My friend Poston, as already stated, had
travelled through Arizona before, and his notions of the
physical necessities of man in that region were somewhat extravagant. Not that he was unreasonably addicted to comfort, but he delighted in a species of practical satire which usually cost him a considerable sum
of money, not to say an endless amount of trouble.
Arizona, he said, was an extensive country, prolific in
reptiles and the precious metals, but painfully destitute
of every thing for the convenience of civilized man.
His favorite advice to all who contemplated visiting the
Territory was to take with them plenty of mules and
horses; fire-arms, ammunition, clothing, tobacco, cigars,
pipes, pen-knives, pencils, medicines, and whisky; not to
forget an abundant supply of coffee, sugar, flour, and
beans; to be sure and start with a full outfit of acids,
blow-pipes, and green spectacles; and by no means to
omit boots, shoes, handkerchiefs, combs, and percussion
caps—especially the latter—and such other articles as
might be purchased in bulk at the selling out of any extensive variety store. It was not that the traveller him-

self would need all these items of luxury, but there were others in the country who would—fellow-travellers gathered up on the public highways by the cohesive attraction of whisky and provisions; the people throughout the territory generally, and such casual parties and lonely pilgrims as might be encountered on the way to and from the mines. A few extra mules and jacks to lend to intimate friends going on prospecting tours, some spare saddles and *apparejos,* and, if possible, a few thousand dollars in gold or silver coin of various denominations to accompany the prospecting parties, but never to be seen again in any shape whatever, would also be advisable. The articles to be given away, consumed, devoured, and wasted, continued my friend, with a grim ferocity, must be of the very best quality, or woe betide the unhappy donor. Be he Superintendent of Indians, or Special Agent, or what not, his doom, morally and politically, will at once be sealed. Never on earth can he be elected Delegate to Congress from the Territory of Arizona! I rather suspected Poston of a leaning that way, and was surprised at the rashness of his remarks.

In due time the outfit was completed. We had every thing above specified, and a great many things more, including a guard of five soldiers and a sergeant to fight for us, if necessary, on the way over to Fort Yuma. Our baggage-wagon was filled to the utmost limit of its capacity, and even then our little ambulance and four mules groaned under their precious loads. On the day of starting the expedition stood as follows: Poston, commander-in-chief; myself, principal hunter and scribe; a supernumerary friend as general assistant; Jim Berry, cook; and "George," the driver; with the addition of Ammi White and his Pimo Indians, and one Major Stick, a Southern gentleman, recently from Alcatraz Island, where he had been spending a portion of the summer. This was our *corps de reserve.* Jim Berry was a dandy contraband from Maryland, of whose many virtues and peculiar traits of character I shall have occasion to speak hereafter. " George "—I don't know his other name ; in fact, don't think he had any, for I never heard him called any thing but " George "—was a stout, good-natured young fellow from Pike County, Missouri, or thereabouts, or, at all events, from some county in which people grow up to a succulent maturity. If " George" was a little verdant and rude of speech, he had good material in him, and was by no means destitute of a dry, Pike-ish sort of wit that occasionally and at very remote intervals burst upon us like a bomb-shell. I was sorry to discover, before he had been three days with us, that he labored under a dreadful and overwhelming affliction, which seemed to rack him to the very core. It might have been remorse for a murder recently committed, or grief for the loss of all his family connections by a stroke of lightning, or the throes of a benighted mind laboring under conviction ; whatever it was, it caused him to indulge in some startling exhibitions of emotion. Often, as we rattled along the road, " George," after belaboring the mules till he was tired, and telling them to " git " till he was hoarse, would lean back in his seat and think. He thought fearfully. I never saw thinking go so hard with a poor fellow in my life. In the midst of it all he would start up with a sudden yell of anguish, whirl his black-snake and let fly at the mules, misery, passion, ferocity depicted in every feature. " Now git, dodrot ye !" was the climax of these uncontrollable bursts of wretchedness, followed by groans so deep and pathetic that they fairly went to my heart. At night, when we spread our blankets around the camp and lay down to pleasant dreams, our unhappy driver discharged his accumulated miseries in a series of groans and sighs that manifested a speedy dissolution. All night long, at intervals of two or three hours, he gave vent to these heart-rending expressions of woe. Poston offered him pills, but he said he wasn't sick. On the occasion of one of his paroxysms I went over to where he lay and asked

him, kindly, what was the matter. "Nothin'," said he;
"why?" "You groan so, I thought something troubled
you." "Reckon I was dreamin'," muttered George;
and with that he turned over to groan again. Thus it
continued night after night, until the dreadful secret was
revealed by a singular circumstance. The truth is, I
could not sleep. George's groans disturbed me. Loss
of rest was preying upon my system. I was getting thin.
As a desperate remedy I secretly gathered around me,
one night, before turning in, all the clods, chips, sticks,
and pebbles I could find, and having taken the bearings
of George's head, lay down as usual. On this occasion
his groans were especially varied and pathetic. He
sometimes groaned like a horse, and sometimes like a
sheep or a goat, and then varied the note by groaning
hysterically, like a mule. When it came to that I hurled a clod at his head, which stopped him for a little
while. Presently he fell to groaning again. I hurled
sticks and stones at him, and stopped him again. After
a long pause he resumed his doleful laborings of woe,
when I let fly another clod with such dexterous aim that it
must have hit him plumb on the back of his head. "Oh,
Gosh!" he cried, in tones of the bitterest anguish. "I
didn't think that of you, Mary Jane! I know'd you
didn't love me; but I didn't think you'd throw taters at
me!" The dreadful mystery was solved; the secret was
out; George was the victim of unrequited love. Mary
Jane was the cruel fair one who had destroyed his peace
of mind, and driven him with the lash of her scorn, as
he was driving mules with a black-snake, to seek the
chances of life in the deserts of Arizona.

After our departure from the Monte we travelled
slowly, in order that we might keep company with our
provisions and escort. All along the route we heard
vague rumors of one Ramon Castillo, a native bandit
around whose career were centered all the charms of romance. He was represented to be a prodigy of strength
and valor, an irresistible gallant among the ladies; a ter-

ror to his enemies, and a very dangerous character to the public. He had sworn vengeance against the American race, had assassinated many of his pursuers, and declared his determination never to be taken alive. Some supposed he was in the mountains with a band of thirty desperadoes; others thought he was lurking by the road with a few of his *servientes* for the purpose of waylaying travellers. All agreed upon one point—that Ramon Castillo was a man greatly to be admired. Of course he had many friends—such men always have in California—and there were few persons of respectable standing in Los Angeles County who would not have felt pride and pleasure in protecting him from arrest. I almost hoped we would meet Don Ramon, that we might enjoy the romance of a tilt with such an accomplished bandit.

The country through which we travelled for several days was not altogether new to me. I had passed through it before during a tour of exploration among the Southern Indians in 1860. But how different was it now! In former years the magnificent valleys, stretching all the way from Los Angeles to the borders of the Colorado Desert, were clothed in the richest verdure. Vast herds of cattle roamed over them rampant with life. The hill-sides were covered with flowers; the air was laden with sweet perfumes; it was the paradise of rancheros. Now, after two years of drought, all was parched, grim, and melancholy. The pastures scarcely showed the first faint tinge of green, and the higher grounds were barren as the road over which we travelled. For hundreds of miles the country was desolated for want of rain. At the Chino, and through the Temeculo, Warner's Ranch, San Felippe, and Vallecito the effects of the drought were fearfully apparent. Thousands of cattle lay dead around the black, muddy pools. A sickening effluvia from the carcasses filled the air. At least two-thirds of all the cattle on these ranches must have perished from starvation. Vaqueros were ever on the watch to strip each fallen animal of its skin. It was a grand carnival for the buzzards and coyotes. No more pitiable sight ever disturbed the eye of a traveller in this lovely region than the dreary waste of dead and dying animals. Thousands drawn to the pools by thirst were unable to extricate themselves from the mud; and the road was sometimes blocked by the gaunt,

CANON OF SAN FELIPPE.

shrunken bodies of still living animals unable to get out
of the way.

At the Santa Ana River, ten miles beyond the Chino,
we had the usual lively time in crossing. Travellers who
have had occasion to pass this river at certain stages of
the water can not easily forget their experience of its
quicksands and currents. The surrounding country is
weird and desolate. A few Spanish rancherias, with
their dilapidated corrals and littered fronts, occupy the
neighboring sand-banks. Below the crossing is a rugged cañon stretching to the vicinity of Annaheim, the
German colony of wine-makers, whose vineyards have already acquired a high reputation on the Pacific coast.
Immense undulating plains, bounded in the distance by
barren ranges of mountains, lie above and beyond, and
patches of sand-deserts, with a scrubby growth of willow and cotton-wood, lie along the banks of the river.
The water is of a sickly, milky color, and is impregnated
with alkali. Innumerable flocks of geese and ducks
cover the green flats, and the wild croaking of the groo-
jas, or sand-hill cranes, falls mournfully on the ear.
There is something fierce and scathing in the blaze of
the sun; and the unobstructed sweep of the wind across
the deserts, the immensity of the distances and towering ranges of mountains, fill the mind with awe. All the
associations of the wilderness are impressive; and the
traveller instinctively feels that he is in a region of robbery and assassination, where the bones of the dead are
seldom left to tell the tale.

We made a halt upon the bank of the river, and sent
in our cavalry to tramp down the quicksands. By repeatedly crossing they made a tolerably safe road for our
wagons. The next half-hour was occupied in urging in
our mules, which seemed to have a mortal dread of the
treacherous sands. At length the blows and shouts of
our cavalry and the yells and whips of the teamsters,
with volleys of stones hurled at the heads of the mules
from various directions, prevailed, and the plunging, rear-

ing, and strangling of the poor animals as they struggled through the surging waters were exciting in the extreme. Now they halt and begin to sink; now the shouts, and yells, and blows start them up again; now the harnesses are tangled up, and the wagons reel and sway upon their wheels as they sink in the sand; the current sweeps over the hubs of the wheels, and all seems lost. Our ambulance is in advance, our guns and ammunition are in imminent danger, our lives balanced on the slender chances of a struggle amid the wreck of matter, when George rises to the sublimity of the occasion. His black-snake whizzes through the air and down on the back of the lagging wheeler. "You, Mary Jane!" he roars in a wild frenzy. "Git!" And Mary Jane got. She plunged, she reared, she kicked; but out of the quicksand she dragged us, and the baggage-wagon followed, and we were all safely landed on the firm earth. "Oh, Gosh!" groaned George, wiping the sweat from his brow and sinking back dismally in his seat. "Oh, Jeeminy Gosh!" But it was not of the river or its quicksands or troubles he was thinking; his spiritual eye saw other quicksands than those of the Santa Ana. His vision was turned inward; it saw but the cruel fair one, the inexorable Mary Jane, whose magic name had inadvertently escaped his lips in time to save us. Oh, Mary Jane, little did you know that salvation to us was lingering death to your devoted but unhappy George!

Of our journey along the picturesque shores of the Laguna, and through the beautiful but now barren valleys of Temecula, Warner's Ranch, San Felippe, and Vallecito, I must necessarily make short work. It was a continued feast for the soul of an artist; but as I come only incidentally under that head, I can not undertake to delineate it to the exclusion of the more important objects of the expedition. All the way along the road we saw great quantities of geese, ducks, and quail. I had my shot-gun always ready, and generally succeeded, by random shots from the ambulance, in getting a good supply of game by the time we reached camp, to which our cook, Dr. Jim Berry, did ample justice in the line of culinary preparation.   We laughed and ate and slept and grew fat, day after day, till we reached Cariso, the last inhabited station on the road to the Desert.   Here was the jumping-off place.   Beyond this, for a hundred miles, we were at the mercy of the sands and storms and burning suns of Colorado.

CHAPTER III.

THE COLORADO DESERT.

I SCARCELY remember to have seen a wilder country than the first eight miles beyond Cariso. Barren hills of gravel and sand-stone, flung up at random out of the earth, strange jagged mountain-peaks in the distance; yellow banks serrated by floods; sea-shells glittering in the wavy sand-fields that lie between; these overhung by a rich, glowing atmosphere, with glimpses of Indian smokes far off in the horizon, inspired us with a vague feeling of the wonders and characteristic features of the desert region through which we were about to pass. I could not but think of the brave old Spaniards and their heroic explorations across the Colorado. Here was a glowing and mystic land of sunshine and burning sands, where human enterprise had in centuries past battled with hunger and thirst and savage races; where the silence of utter desolation now reigned supreme. There was a peculiar charm to me in the rich atmospheric tints that hung over this strange land, and the boundless wastes that lay outspread before us; and I drank in with an almost childish delight the delicate and exquisite odors that filled the air, and thought of my early wanderings, years long past, amid the deserts and palms of Araby the Blest.

Yet, strictly speaking, the Colorado is scarcely a desert. Extensive belts of rich soil, that irrigation would render productive, occupy a large portion of the country. In these are seen the evidences of sudden and extraordinary vegetable growth in seasons of abundant rain, or when the Colorado River overflows its banks. A proposition has been entertained by Congress to reclaim this vast tract of country, embracing millions of acres of rich agricultural land, by means of a grand canal from the Colorado, with a connected system of acequias; and proofs are not wanting to show that the Montezumas and early Spaniards thus redeemed extensive ranges of country in Sonora and Arizona that would otherwise have remained valueless. The ruins of ancient cities, many miles in circumference, are found on the Rio Verde, above its junction with the Salado, where the whole country is now barren; and below the junction, on the Salado, the remains of immense acequias, with walls twenty feet high, are still to be seen. At least one hundred thousand acres of land were formerly irrigated by this system of acequias on the Salado. It is now a barren sand-plain, upon which stands in solitary majesty the *Cereus grandeus*—the Sentinel of the Desert.

Dr. O. M. Wozencraft has spent many years in advocating this great measure. The plan of irrigation proposed by him is generally ridiculed as impracticable, and the Doctor enjoys rather a visionary reputation based upon his Grand Colorado Scheme, which has been compared by unthinking men with the Great South Sea Bubble. I don't intend to establish a farm there myself until the canal is completed; but still I can see no great obstacle to success except the porous nature of the sand. By removing the sand from the desert success would be insured at once. An elaborate and exceedingly able report upon this subject has recently been issued by the Commissioner of the General Land Office.

As we advanced into the desert each shifting scene developed its peculiar beauties. The face of the country, for the most part, is well covered with mesquit trees, sage bushes, grease-wood, weeds, and cactus. Mountains are in sight all the way across, and the old stage-houses of the Overland Mail Company still stand by the watering-places. Many indications of the dreadful sufferings of emigrant parties and drovers still mark the road; the wrecks of wagons half covered in the drifting sands, skeletons of horses and mules, and the skulls and bones of many a herd of cattle that perished by thirst on the way, or fell victims to the terrible sand storms that sweep the desert. Only in a few instances, when we struck out upon the arid sand-belts that lie between the alluvial beds of earth, did we encounter any thing resembling the deserts of Arabia, and then only for ten or twelve miles at a time.

The climate in winter is indescribably delightful; in summer the heat is excessive, and travellers and animals suffer much on the journey. It was a perfect luxury to breathe such pure soft air as we enjoyed in the middle of December, when our Atlantic friends were freezing amid the ice and snow-banks of that wretched part of the world. Between the desert of the Colorado and the city of New York there is no comparison in any respect. Give me a pack-mule, a shot-gun, and a sack of pinole, with such a climate as this, and take your brick deserts on Fifth Avenue, and your hot-air furnaces, and brain-racking excitements, and be happy with them! Accept my pity, but leave me, if you please, to chase rabbits and quail where the sun shines, and to lie down of nights and sleep on the warm bosom of my mother earth.

There was a scene on a pleasant morning as we sallied forth on our journey from the Indian Wells never to be forgotten. The eye that looks upon it once must see it as long as mortal vision lasts. An isolated mountain in the distance seemed at the first view to rise abruptly out of a lake of silver, the shores of which were alive with water-fowl of brilliant and beautiful plumage. As we journeyed toward it the lake disappeared and the mountain changed to a frowning fortress, symmetrical in all its parts—a perfect model of architectural beauty. Still nearing it, the ramparts and embattlements melted into a dreamy haze, out of which gradually emerged a magnificent palace with pillars, and cornices, and archways, and a great dome, from which arose a staff, surmounted by a glowing blue ball, encircled by a halo. At the same time another mountain on the right, distant many miles, assumed equally strange and fantastic shapes; and when the ball arose upon our palace, another ball answered the signal from the distant mountain on the right; and then a great railway opened up between them, supported by innumerable piles, stretching many leagues over the desert. So perfect was the illusion that we stopped in breathless wonder, almost expecting to see a train of cars whirl along and vanish in the warm glow of the horizon. This strange and beautiful display of the mirage has been witnessed by many travellers on the Colorado desert, who will attest that, so far from exaggeration, I have but faintly pictured its wonders. Nothing of the kind that I have seen elsewhere can compare with it in the variety and beauty of its illusions.

There was but one drawback to our happiness—the increasing wretchedness of our driver, George, who, by some fatal element in human nature, grew darker in soul as the light and joyousness of the outer world broke upon him with increasing splendor. " No," he muttered to himself in despairing accents, " 'tain't no use; I can't forget her. Oh, golly! golly!" And here, with an audible sob, he started as if from a trance, and swinging his black-snake over his head, yelled at the mules with ungovernable fury, " You git, dodburn you! What d'ye stand flopping yer ears for? Git!" Sic transit!— thus pass away the illusions of this world!

The entire distance from Cariso across the desert to Fort Yuma is 116 miles. Four stations where water can be had intervene on the road—Indian Wells, Alamo Mocho, Gardner's, and Cook's Wells. At all these points the water is tolerably good; and there are other points where brackish water can be had by digging a few feet.

About fifteen miles beyond Cook's Wells, after coursing along the belt of the great sand-desert on the left, we struck into the Colorado bottom. Indications of our approach to water were everywhere perceptible. Thickets of arrow-weed lined the way, and forests of cotton-wood loomed up ahead, over which geese and cranes uttered their wild notes. Soon we passed some deserted rancherias, and in a little while more our eyes were rejoiced with a refreshing view of the great Colorado of the West, as it swept like a mighty serpent over the desert.

At Pilot Knob a delegation of the Yuma Indians, headed by Pasqual the chief, came out to meet us. They had heard of our coming, and were eager to do us honor. Every brave had his package of greasy certificates, derived from the officers who had at various times been stationed at the fort. These they thrust at us with the utmost simplicity, and in full faith that they would result in an immediate recognition of their claims to our distinguished consideration. There were good certificates and bad; complimentary notices of the services rendered by bearer to the American nation, and warnings to be on the lookout for other bearers, who were represented to be incorrigible thieves, addicted to stealing the buttons off travellers' coats and the teeth out of travellers' heads. It was all the same—all strong medicine from the white man; and we so regarded these testimonials, and shook hands with good and bad bearers, and gave them tobacco, and promised them more in a few days. There was a child-like simplicity about the poor creatures that touched our sympathies. Most of them looked gaunt and thin, and it was evident they had based some hopes of relief upon our arrival.

As it was incidentally my business to look after the Indians, in virtue of an honorary commission which I held from the Department of the Interior, I soon ascertained that those who reside in this vicinity were in a very destitute condition, owing to the low stage of the river during the past season and the failure of the customary crops. Heretofore the Yumas have supported themselves without much difficulty, and have only occasionally and at remote intervals received aid from the Government. Under ordinary circumstances, when the an-

nual overflow of the Colorado takes place, they cultivate
the low lands in their rude way, and generally succeed
in raising abundant crops of corn, wheat, pumpkins, and
melons.   These bottom lands along the Colorado are
light, rich, and easily worked, and afford ample means of
subsistence to the tribes bordering on the river.   During the past year there was no overflow, and consequently no crops were raised.   It was a season of unusual
drought—such a drought as the oldest inhabitant did not
remember to have seen before.   Even the mesquit beans,
wild peas, and berries, upon which the Indians had been
accustomed to depend in unfavorable seasons, had entirely failed, so that they were now left destitute.   Their
seed-wheat, which they had stored for planting, had long
since given out; and for some months prior to our arrival they had been subsisting on rats, mice, lizards,
snakes, and such other poor and scanty food of the kind
as they could gather on the deserts and banks of the river.   From their agricultural habits they are unskilled in
procuring this kind of food, and many of them were in
a starving condition.   In some instances children had
died from want of proper nourishment, and disease had
spread among them with greater virulence than usual, as
it always does in seasons of scarcity.

From Pilot Knob we had a pleasant drive through the
mesquit thickets bordering on the river, as far as Mr.
Hamblin's, where we made a halt to refresh ourselves
with a first experience of civilization on the Colorado.
Here, in a good adobe house, with such comforts as this
wild region affords, dwell Mr. Hamblin and his wife, an
excellent and intelligent couple, who received us most
cordially, and generously offered us all the accommodations of their establishment.   Little did I expect to find
in this isolated part of the world a lady of refined literary tastes ; yet I have rarely met with one of more gracefully cultivated mind than Mrs. Hamblin, to whose pleasant conversation we were subsequently indebted for
many delightful hours.

A little beyond we reached head-quarters and rancheria of Don Diego Jaeger—the famous pioneer of Fort
Yuma, without whom that military establishment could
no more have existed up to the present day than without light or air, fire, water, or frijoles. A German by
birth, a frontiersman by instinct, Don Diego abandoned
the haunts of civilization fourteen years ago and settled
here among the savages. Many a hard rub has he had
for his life during the years of trouble with the Yumas.
Industry, energy, and perseverance prevailed over all
difficulties; and in time prosperity rewarded his trials.
Who, for the last dozen years or more, has ferried the
military and the public across the Colorado?—Don Diego. Who has clothed the naked and fed the hungry of
this howling wilderness during all that time?—Don
Diego. Who has kept the military arm of the Government from becoming paralyzed for lack of beef, pork,
frijoles, and forage; supplied the roads with sustenance
for man and beast; kept needy officers and thriftless men
in funds? who but Don Diego? When the burning suns
of the Colorado wilted every other man down to a state
of inanity, who was it that always remained fresh and
vigorous, and brimful of enterprise?—The irrepressible,
the irresistible Don Diego! I say irresistible advised-
ly; for his only fault has been an overruling devotion to
the fair sex, upon whom he has squandered his money
even as the prodigal of old. But he is now the happy
husband of a charming Sonoranian lady, Doña Cloena,
whose fascinations have at length subdued his erratic
heart, and his children are even as the apples of his eyes.
Rich in experience, rich in ranches, rich in silver mines,
rich in family—long live Don Diego!

FORT YUMA.

CHAPTER IV.

IN half an hour more we reached Fort Yuma, where we were received with great kindness and hospitality by Colonel Bennet, the commanding officer, who provided us with excellent quarters. Twelve days had passed since our departure from Los Angeles ; and we were not slow to enjoy the luxury of a bath and a change of raiment. Captain Gorham and his command, a cavalry company of volunteers, had preceded us from Camp Drum, and were encamped near the fort. This command was destined for the protection of Arizona, and would probably soon be stationed at Tucson.

As soon as we had refreshed ourselves with the customary appliances of civilization at frontier posts—lemonade, if you please—we sallied forth to enjoy a view of the fort and surrounding country from the opposite side of the river.

I was not disappointed in my first impressions of Fort Yuma. Weird and barren as the adjacent country is, it is not destitute of compensating beauties. The banks of the river for many miles below are fringed with groves of mesquit and cotton-wood; above the junction of the Gila and the Colorado an extensive alluvial valley, clothed with willow, cotton-wood, mesquit, and arrow-weed, stretches far off to the foot-hills of Castle Dome; and toward the great desert a rugged range of mountains, over which rises in solitary majesty the "Chimney Peak," forms the background. An atmosphere of wonderful richness and brilliancy covers the scene like a gorgeous canopy of prismatic colors, and the vision is lost in the immensity of the distances. The fort stands on an elevated bluff, commanding the adjacent country for many miles around, and presents an exceedingly picturesque view with its neat quarters, store-houses, and winding roads. It was with emotions of national pride that we gazed upon the glorious flag of our Union as it swelled out to the evening breeze from the flag-staff that towered above the bluff; and we felt that, so long as that emblem of our liberty floated, there was hope for the future of Colorado and Arizona.

The climate in winter is finer than that of Italy. It would scarcely be possible to suggest an improvement. I never experienced such exquisite Christmas weather as we enjoyed during our sojourn. Perhaps fastidious people might object to the temperature in summer, when the rays of the sun attain their maximum force, and the hot winds sweep in from the desert. It is said that a wicked soldier died here, and was consigned to the fiery regions below for his manifold sins; but unable to stand the rigors of the climate, sent back for his blankets. I have even heard complaint made that the thermometer failed to show the true heat because the mercury dried up. Every thing dries; wagons dry; men dry; chickens dry; there is no juice left in any thing, living or dead, by the close of summer. Officers and soldiers are supposed to walk about creaking; mules, it is said, can only bray at midnight; and I have heard it hinted that the carcasses of cattle rattle inside their hides, and that snakes find a difficulty in bending their bodies, and horned frogs die of apoplexy. Chickens hatched at this season, as old Fort Yumers say, come out of the shell ready cooked; bacon is eaten with a spoon; and butter must stand an hour in the sun before the flies become dry enough for use. The Indians sit in the river with fresh mud on their heads, and by dint of constant dipping and sprinkling manage to keep from roasting, though they usually come out parboiled. Strangers coming suddenly upon a group squatted in water up to their necks, with their mud-covered heads glistening in the sun, frequently mistake them for seals. Their usual mode of travelling down the river is astride of a log—their heads only being visible. It is enough to make a man stare with amazement to see a group of mud-balls floating on the current of a hot day, laughing and talking to each other as if it were the finest fun in the world. I have never tried this mode of locomotion; have an idea it must be delightful in such a glowing summer climate.

The Colorado was lower than any of the residents at Fort Yuma had ever before known it. It could scarcely fall any lower without going entirely through its own bottom. A more capricious river does not exist. Formerly it ran through the desert to the north-west, but for some reason or other it changed its course, and now it runs about three feet above the level of the desert. As a navigable stream it possesses some advantages during the dry season; boats can seldom sink in it; and for the matter of channels it has an unusual variety. The main channel shifts so often that the most skillful pilot always knows where it is not be found by pursuing the course of his last trip. The little steamer which plies between the fort and the mouth of the river, distant one hundred miles, could not make the round trip in less than two weeks, owing to shoals and shifting bars. Up to La Paz and Fort Mojave the navigation was still worse. Twenty or thirty days up and down was considered a fair trip. The miners in that region were suffering for supplies, although six hundred tons of freight lay at the embarcadera awaiting transportation. I mention this as a hint to the delegate soon to be elected to Congress from Arizona. If he can prevail upon that liberal body to grant half a million of dollars toward plugging up or calking the bottom of the river so that it won't leak, or procuring rain by joint resolution, he will forever after merit the suffrages of his fellow-citizens.

Christmas Day came, and with it some natural longings for home and the familiar faces of the family circle. Yet

C 2

we were not so badly off as one might suppose in this region of drought and desert. Colonel Bennet and his amiable wife got up an excellent dinner at the fort; and in the evening we had a *báile*, or Spanish dance, at which there were several very dusky belles of the Sonoranian race. Unfortunately two Jesuit Padres, attached to the Arizona command, had previously secured the attention of the principal Señoritas in the neighborhood; and what with baptizing and marrying and confessing, it was difficult to get up a quorum at the dance. However, there were plenty of officers, and what the ladies lacked in number they made up in spirit. The fiddlers scraped with an inspiring vim; whisky flowed, and egg-shells, containing dust and gilt-paper, were broken in the true Spanish style upon the heads of handsome gallants.

Not aspiring to distinction in that way, I was quietly seated on a bench, enjoying the dance, and unsuspicious of this peculiar custom, when a lovely belle of the darkest hue whirled by in the giddy waltz, dexterously cracking an egg on the crown of my head as she passed, and leaving me a spectacle of confusion and astonishment before the eyes of the crowd. The mischievous beauty struck me exactly on the spot where Time has already laid his relentless hand; and I was not surprised at the merry shouts of laughter that ensued; for if my head looked like any thing upon earth, it must have borne a close resemblance to a boulder surmounted by croppings of gold and silver.

Next day Superintendent Poston and myself held a grand pow-wow with the Yuma chiefs and their people. From all parts of the neighborhood they came; warriors, squaws, and children; from the mesquit bushes and mudholes of the Colorado; from the sloos and the arroyas of the Gila; the cotton-woods and the deserts and the mountains of Castle Dome. Every village had its delegation of dusky tatterdemalions. Lizards and snakes and mice were hastily cast aside in the wild anticipation of muck-a-muck from the Great Father. Hungry and lean, painted and bedizened with ornaments, they came in to receive the bounty of the mighty Federal chief.

Great were the rejoicings when we opened the boxes and bales of merchandise so liberally furnished by the Government contractors, Cronin, Huxtall, & Sears, of New York. Red, white, green, and gray blankets; military suits, glittering with tinsel; old swords, four feet long; sun-glasses for lighting cigars; and penny whistles for the small fry. It was indeed a wonderful display of the artistic triumphs of civilization, well calculated to impress the savage tribes of the Pacific with awe and admiration. There were axes of the best Collins brand, that flew to pieces like glass against the iron timbers of this anomalous region; and hats made by steam, and flaming red vests stitched by magic, and tobacco-boxes and tin kettles that might be opened, but never upon earth shut again. Surrounded by all the military paraphernalia of Fort Yuma, and with ceremony the most profound and impressive, we delivered our speeches and dry goods to the various chiefs; we gave them damaged hominy and hoes, and spades and shovels, and sashes and military buttons, charms, amulets, tobacco-boxes, and beads; shook them by the hand collectively and in detail, and pow-wowed generally in the approved style.

Pasqual, the doughty head-chief of all the Yumas, long known to fame as the longest of his tribe, predominated over the ceremonies. A grave, cadaverous, leathery old gentleman, with hollow, wrinkled cheeks, and a prodigious nose, through the cartilage of which, between the nostrils, he wears a white bone ornamented with swinging pendants, is Pasqual the doughty. On account of the length of his arms and legs—which, when stretched out altogether, bear a strong similitude to the wind-mill against which Don Quixote ran a tilt—the mighty Pasqual is regarded with much respect and veneration by his tribe. His costume, on the present occasion, consisted of a shabby military coat, doubtless the same worn in ancient times by his friend, Major Heintzelman, the em-

YUMA INDIAN.

broidery of which has long since been fretted out by
wear and tear, and the elbows rubbed off by long collision with the multitudes of office-seekers among his tribe.
Of pantaloons he had but a remnant; and of boots or
shoes he had none at all, save those originally furnished
him by nature.   But chiefly was Pasqual conspicuous for
the ponderous bone and appendages that hung from his
nose.   A slight catarrh afflicted him at the time of our
pow-wow, and it was not without great inconvenience
that he managed the ornamental part of his countenance
—turning repeatedly away to blow it, or adjust the awk-
ward pendants that swung from it, and always re-appear-
ing with tears of anguish in his eyes.   I took pity upon
his sufferings and gave him some snuff, assuring him it

was a sovereign remedy for colds in the head. The result was such a series of explosions, contortions of the facial muscles, and rattling of the ornamental bones, as to alarm me for the sanity of the doughty chief, who seemed quite wild with the accumulation of his agonies. The assembled wisdom of the nation grunted repeatedly in token of amazement; and Pasqual muttered, between the paroxysms of his affliction, "Ugh! muchee pepper! belly strong dust! Burn 'um Injun nose!"

Vincente, the next chief in command, dressed in a blue cotton shirt of the scantiest pattern. It reached only a short distance below his waist, and, for the matter of respect to the prejudices of civilization, might have ended at the collar. I really wish the contractors would furnish longer shirts for the Indians. The Yumas are tall, and I know of no tribe on this coast averaging only fourteen inches from the crown of the head to the soles of the feet. Vincente had probably received a hint that the distribution would be honored by the presence of ladies. What he lacked in costume he made up in paint. Both his eyes were encircled with yellow ochre; blue streaks adorned his cheeks; his nose was of a dazzling vermilion, and his legs were gorgeously striped with mud. His only additional article of costume, visible to the eye, was a dusky cotton diaper, ingeniously tied behind, leaving a long tail to flutter majestically in the breeze.

Tebarro, the next great chief, wrapped himself in an American blanket, and dyed his face a gloomy black. I think he was in mourning. He wore tar on his head, and tar on his cheeks, and tar on his nose and chin, which becoming mingled with the grit and dust of the Colorado desert, gave him a sort of asphaltum look, like the house-tops and pavements of Los Angeles. When he stood in the sun he melted—such was the force of his grief. Black tears ran down from his head and cheeks and chin, and mingled with the wool of his blanket. Literally he wept tar.

Antonio, the fourth great chief, wore a strap round his

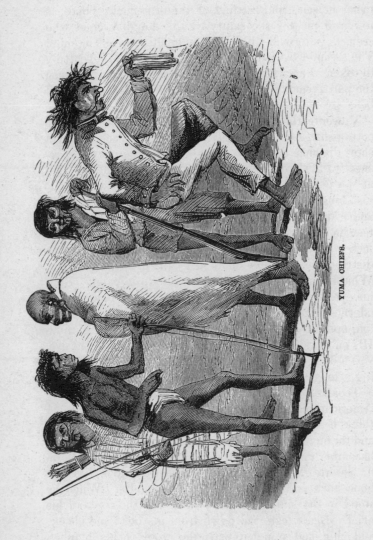

YUMA CHIEFS.

waist, with a rusty old sword tied to it by means of rawhide. He didn't wear any thing else, save the usual girdle of manta upon his loins, that could be considered an
article of costume; but his eyes were gorgeously encircled by a cloud of blue paint fringed with vermilion.
Like his illustrious superior, Pasqual, he wore pendent
ornaments in his nose, of the most inconvenient pattern.
I should judge Antonio carried a quarter of a pound of
native jewelry, consisting of bone and lead, upon the cartilage of his proboscis.

Juan, the fifth and last of noted warriors and head-men,
was redundant in gamoose breeches and cotton rags.
On his head he wore a helmet of Colorado mud, dried
into the roots of his hair by the action of the sun. This
I believe is accounted by the Yumas a sovereign remedy
for vermin. The liveliest skipper is forever deprived
of locomotion by the conglomerate of dried mud. When
the helmet is broken off in segments, like a piece of
baked crockery, it must present a curious spectacle of
embalmed bodies.

These distinguished chiefs and their people received
the presents allotted to them with great dignity and
good-humor. There was no grabbing or stealing, nor
any sign of discontent. Every man received his share
with satisfaction, and with gratitude to the Great Father
in Washington. When they shook hands with us for
the last time, and we were about to part, the scene was
really affecting. I almost shed tears at it myself, un-
used as I am to crying about what can't be helped. In
squads, and couples, and one by one, they affectionately
took their leave, with their hoes and axes, spades and
shovels, gimcracks and charms stuck all over them—in
their sashes, breeches, clouties, blankets, and pinafores.
One went with a necklace of mattocks around his neck
and three Collins axes in his girdle; another with his
head thrust into a glittering pile of tin-ware; while a
third, one of the unbreeched multitude, wore a frying-pan
in front by way of an apron, and a corn-hoe behind, in

AFTER THE DISTRIBUTION.

the usual fashion of a rudder. Old men and young were
tuning their jews'-harps; luxurious squaws were peeping at the redundant beauties reflected by their little zinc
looking-glasses; children were blowing their tin whistles, and small fat papooses were hanging their heads out
of compressed bundles behind their mothers, wondering,
with open mouths and great round eyes, what could be
the cause of all the hubbub. It was an impressive scene
of barbarous happiness not easily forgotten. And so
ended the Grand Pow-wow.

Our unhappy driver, George, who had never smiled
during the whole course of the ceremonies, now turned
away with an expression of the most profound and confirmed melancholy. Not even the warrior with the rudder, nor the chief with the mud roof to his head, could

GEORGE.

dissipate the intensity of his gloom. Nor were the blandishments of the dusky Yuma belles of any greater avail. With his hand pressed upon the pit of his stomach he groaned in agony of spirit as he descended the hill; and I fancied the plaintive words reached my ears, "Oh! Mary Jane, how could you? Think of him that loves you, and he among Injuns and savigges!"

CHAPTER V.

I WAS now on the borders of a region in which the wildest romance was strangely mingled with the most startling reality. Each day of our sojourn at Fort Yuma brought with it some fabulous story of discovery or some tragic narrative of suffering and death. There were vague rumors of silver veins found on the banks of the Colorado of such incredible richness that Washoe was left in the shade; there were hints of a golden region east of the Rio Verde and north of the Gila which Spaniards, Mexicans, and Americans had been trying to reach for over three centuries, now opening up with all its glittering treasures: credulity was taxed with the marvellous stories of mineral wealth in and beyond the San Francisco mountains. No longer was the narrative of the brave old adventurer, Francis Vasquez de Coronado, to be deemed a mere romance, for truly the Indians " had great store of gold." Their precious bullets were already finding their way down to the Pimo villages and Fort Yuma—a fact that I could not doubt, since I saw many of them myself. Nor was it beyond credit that Friar Marco de Niça found in this region, as early as 1540, " a greater use and more abundance of gold and silver than in Peru "—if but half we now heard was true; and who could doubt it with the evidence of his own eyes? The least imaginative and most incredulous reader of the old Spanish chronicles could not dispute the statement of Antonio de Espejo, that he found in his journey to the Zuñi, in 1583, " rich mines of silver, which, according to the judgment of skillful men, were

PIMO INDIAN GIRLS.

very plentiful and rich in metal." But far beyond these
musty records of early Spanish enterprise were the verbal narratives to be heard every day from men who had
explored various portions of the country lying to the
north of the Gila, and along the range of the 35th parallel of latitude. At the store of Messrs. Hooper and

Hinton, in Arizona City, I saw masses of pure gold as large as the palm of my hand brought in by some of these adventurers, who stated that certain Indians had assured them they knew of places in the mountains where the surface of the ground was covered with the same kind of " heavy yellow stones." Neither threats nor presents, nor offers of unlimited reward could induce the wily savages to guide the white men to these fabulous regions of wealth. " Why should we ?" said they—and with good reason—" you are already taking our country from us fast enough ; we will soon have no place of safety left. If we show you where these yellow stones are, you will come there in thousands and drive us away and kill us." It was equally in vain the white men offered to buy the gold from them. Whisky, knives, tobacco, blankets—all the Indians craved had no effect. On that point they were immovable. The excitement produced by the information they had given, and the effect of their obduracy in refusing to disclose the locality of the " yellow stones," alarmed them, and they evaded all further importunities by saying they knew nothing about it themselves; only the old men of their tribes had told them these things, and they thought it was all a lie. If the statements gathered up in this way were not corroborated from so many different sources it would be easy to attribute them to a natural proclivity on the part of mankind toward the marvellous in every thing connected with the discovery of the precious metals. But we have this story in various shapes throughout Arizona, not only from different tribes of Indians, but from wholly different races of men, and all tending toward the region north of the Gila and east of the Rio Verde. Felix Aubrey, the famous explorer (killed a few years ago in an affray at Santa Fe), tells us, in his journal of 1853, that he found gold in such abundance along the banks of the Colorado that in some places " it glistened upon the ground." After crossing a branch of the Gila he met some Indians from whom he obtained over fifteen hundred dollars' worth of gold for a few old articles of clothing; and he further mentions that these Indians use gold bullets of different sizes for their guns, and that he saw one of them put four such bullets in his gun to shoot a rabbit. Next day his mule broke down, and an Indian gave him for it a lump of gold weighing a pound and a half less one ounce.

As an offset to these exciting reports, corroborated to a great extent by the masses of virgin ore brought in from time to time, the stories of escape from the barbarous Apaches that inhabit the country, their sagacity, cruelty, and relentless hostility to white men; the thrilling accounts of suffering from scarcity of food and water, and the various perils of life and limb encountered in the rugged mountains and rock-bound cañons, were well calculated to moderate the enthusiasm with which we looked forward to our tour and its probable results. Still, hope was ever uppermost, and I doubt if there was one in the party who would have taken less than fifty thousand dollars, cash in hand, for his chances of a fortune, unless it was George, our unhappy driver, who, on the occasion of every new proof tending to show the unbounded richness of Arizona, groaned aloud in agony of spirit, as if he thought gold and silver of no consequence whatever compared with the treasures of Mary Jane's affection.

Conspicuous among the mines of which we had glowing accounts was the Moss Lead, near Fort Mojave. This mine was long known to Iretaba, the distinguished Mojave chief, who, in consideration of friendly services rendered him by Mr. Moss, the first American proprietor (whose name it bears), conducted him to it. Iretaba has reaped his reward in his recent visit to San Francisco and the Atlantic States. There was also the "Apache Chief"—a silver mine, said to be quite equal to any thing in Washoe, though it may be long before the dividends satisfy the stockholders on that point. The town of La Paz was growing into importance. Miners and

traders were opening out the placer region to the eastward, and the accounts brought down by stray "pilgrims" were of the most flattering character. Walker's
and Weaver's diggings, and the placers on the Hasiampa,
were represented to be so rich that fortunes could be
made in an incredibly short time, if there was only water enough to "wash the dirt." But lack of water and
abundance of marauding Indians were a constant source
of trouble to the miners, who somehow were always
getting poorer the longer they stayed there. The few
that I saw come down to Fort Yuma were bronzed, battered, ragged, and hungry; they went into Arizona with
an outfit, and were leaving it without any fit at all save
disgust. Yet the general concurrence of testimony was
encouraging. It was beyond question a region rich in
the precious metals. Water was the principal desideratum. The season had been unusually dry. It was not
so always: the time would come when Heaven would
shed some tears of commiseration upon the suffering
miners.

New and rich silver veins had been discovered a short
distance above Fort Yuma on the Colorado, which were
attracting considerable attention. In the vicinity of
Castle Dome, twenty-five miles from the river and thirty-
five from the Fort, the veins prospected were numerous
and extensive, and the ores of a very promising character. I saw some of them myself, and am satisfied they
contain a great abundance of lead. No assays had been
made that I heard of, but gentlemen who owned in
them assured me there was silver in them as well as lead,
whether much or little remained to be seen. The main
trouble about the Castle Dome district is, that if ever it
becomes a valuable mining region, some different arrange-
ment must be made for the supply of water. At present it has to be hauled, or carried on pack animals, a distance of twenty-five miles. The country is one of the
roughest ever trodden by the foot of man. I think it
must originally have been designed for mountain sheep,

which are said to abound in that vicinity. These animals have prodigious horns, upon which they alight when they tumble down the cliffs. How they get up again is difficult to conjecture. My own impression is that they are born there, and are pushed over by other sheep.

Very little work has yet been done in the Castle Dome district, although some hundreds of claims have been prospected, and extensions run upon the most promising.

The Eureka, another district of recent discovery, lies on the banks of the Colorado, about thirty miles above Fort Yuma. Considerable attention has been attracted to the silver veins alleged to exist in this district. I saw quantities of the ore, which certainly present some very fine indications of galena. A gentleman presented me with a specimen from one of his mines, containing a piece of pure silver about the size of a marrowfat pea. Whether it was melted out of the rock or into it I have no means of knowing, though my confidence in the integrity of the donor remains unshaken. I believe there is silver in Eureka, and I believe a very good yield will come out of it as soon as the parties who hold the claims sell out to some other parties. At present the great drawback to mining here is, that the owners of feet have no money to expend in extracting their wealth from the ground; and when people who have money desire to invest, the men of feet demand extraordinary sums, because they think claims that attract capital must be of extraordinary value. Offer one of them fifty dollars a foot, and he will refuse a hundred; but let him alone till his beans give out, and he will sell for fifty cents. For this reason, although claims are numbered by the score, and cities containing from one to three houses are springing up all along the banks of the river, very little work has yet been done in the development of the mines. The Guadaloupe and the Rosario, from which some promising ores have been taken, will probably be in successful operation within a few years. It is not improbable that by a

proper system of smelting the average of the ores found
in the Eureka and Silver district would yield a hundred
dollars to the ton. Abundance of mesquit and cotton-
wood grows in the valleys and bottoms, and there is
water enough in the Colorado River, even at its present
low stage, to run several steam-engines.

Is it a matter of surprise that, under the influence of
these glowing reports, I began to look upon Arizona

CASTLE DOME.

D

with distended eyes; that a conviction possessed me that
I was born under a lucky star, however roughly the
world had used me up to the present date? All the
trials and tribulations of past years; my early experience as a whale-fisher; my public services as an Inspect-
or of Customs, so ungratefully rewarded by a note of
three lines; my claim agency at Washoe, and the bank-
ruptcy that resulted from my investments in the Dead-
Broke and Sorrowful Countenance, were but the prices
paid for that valuable experience which was now about
to culminate in discoveries that would electrify the world,
and result in an effort on my part to liquidate the public debt? When I walked out, on the plea of exercise, I
secretly picked up every conspicuous stone by the way-
side, examined it carefully, and thought it contained indications; I burrowed into gravel and sand banks, and
carried a hammer in my pocket for the purpose of knock-
ing off croppings; I closely investigated the general con-
figuration of the earth; entered into negotiations with
my friend Poston, the original projector and principal
owner of Arizona City, for the purchase of a thousand
water-lots. In fine, I laid all my plans with such fore-
sight and sagacity that the result astonishes me.

CHAPTER VI.

TRAVELLING UP THE GILA.

WE remained a week at Fort Yuma, at the expiration of which, all being ready—damages to our ambulance repaired, stores laid in, an escort provided, letters written home, and orders given to forward the Indian goods designed for the Pimos, Maricopas, and Papagoes, as soon as possible—we bade good-bye to our hospitable friends at the Fort, and set forth on our journey. Before us, as far as the eye could reach, stretched vast deserts dotted with mesquit, sage, and grease-wood, and distant ranges of mountains rugged and barren, but singularly varied in outline. A glowing, hazy, mystic atmosphere hung over the whole country—according well with the visionary enterprises and daring explorations of the old Spanish adventurers, who, three centuries ago, had journeyed along the banks of the Gila—the river of the Swift Waters.

Little was there now to indicate the grandeur of this wild stream of the desert during seasons of flood. A glaring sand-bottom fringed with cotton-wood and arrow-weed, through which in shallow veins the water coursed, leaving here and there patches of sand as a resting-place for numerous aquatic fowl, whose wild cries disturbed the solitude, formed the chief characteristics of the Gila in January, 1864. A few miles beyond Arizona City we struck off to the right, and for the next ten or fifteen miles travelled on the upper stratum of the Gila bottom, which we found well wooded with mesquit. The roads range anywhere within two or three miles of the direct route. Every traveller seems to take a road to suit him-

self, the chief object being to find one that is not cut up
by heavy Government wagons. I had a new experience
here—apparently smooth roads so full of " chuck-holes"
that it was impossible to go a hundred yards without danger of breaking the wheels of our ambulance.

Quail were very abundant as we drew near our first
camping-place on the Gila. I killed about two dozen on
the wing; that is to say, I was on the wing myself when
I shot; but the quail were on the ground. If that does
not amount to the same thing I crave pardon of the
sporting fraternity. Travellers in Arizona can not afford
to waste powder at $2 per pound, and shot at $1, on mere
fancy shots. No man belonging to the party was permitted, on pain of the severe displeasure of our commander-in-chief, to kill less than four quail at a shot. I killed three once, and only succeeded in evading the penalty
that attached to the offense by boldly asserting my belief that there were only three grains of shot in the gun.

We camped at Gila City, a very pretty place, encircled
in the rear by volcanic hills and mountains, and pleasantly overlooking the bend of the river, with its sand-flats,
arrow-weeds, and cotton-woods in front. Gold was found
in the adjacent hills a few years ago, and a grand furor
for the " placers of the Gila" raged throughout the Territory. At one time over a thousand hardy adventurers
were prospecting the gulches and cañons in this vicinity.
The earth was turned inside out. Rumors of extraordinary discoveries flew on the wings of the wind in every
direction. Enterprising men hurried to the spot with
barrels of whisky and billiard-tables; Jews came with
ready-made clothing and fancy wares; traders crowded
in with wagon-loads of pork and beans; and gamblers
came with cards and monte-tables. There was every
thing in Gila City within a few months but a church
and a jail, which were accounted barbarisms by the mass
of the population. When the city was built, bar-rooms
and billiard-saloons opened, monte-tables established, and
all the accommodations necessary for civilized society

placed upon a firm basis, the gold placers gave out. In other words, they had never given in any thing of account. There was "pay-dirt" back in the hills, but it didn't pay to carry it down to the river and wash it out by any ordinary process. Gila City collapsed. In about the space of a week it existed only in the memory of disappointed speculators. At the time of our visit the promising Metropolis of Arizona consisted of three chimneys and a coyote.

The next day we travelled over a series of gravelly deserts, in which we saw for the first time that peculiar

GILA CITY.

and picturesque cactus so characteristic of the country, called by the Indians the *petayah*, but more generally known as the *suaro*, and recognized by botanists as the *Cereus grandeus*. A difference of opinion exists as to whether the petayah is not a distinct species from the suaro; but I never could find any two persons who could agree, after exhausting all their erudition on the subject, upon any point except this—that neither of them knew any thing about it. I am inclined to believe the petayah is the fruit of the suaro, of which the

Indians make a kind of molasses by expressing the juice. They also eat it with great avidity during the season of its maturity; and it is a common thing, in travelling along the road, to see these gigantic sentinels of the desert pierced with arrows. The Indians amuse themselves shooting at the fruit, and when one misses his aim and leaves his arrow sticking in the top of the cactus, it is a source of much laughter to his comrades. The ribs or inward fibre of this singular plant become quite hard when dry, and make excellent lances, being light, straight, and tough. It presents a green, ribbed, and thorny exterior, with branches growing out of it toward the top, resembling in general effect a candelabra. Some of them grow as high as 40 or 50 feet; the average is probably from 20 to 30.

At Mission Camp, 14 miles from Gila City, we had a fine view of the Corunnacion Mountain, distant about 10 miles on the north side of the Gila. Mr. Bartlett compares it to a pagoda, and so styles it in the sketch accompanying the description in his book. I think the Spanish name is more appropriate. The peaks bear a strong resemblance to those of a mitred crown, and, seen in the glow of the setting sun, would readily suggest the idea of that gilded emblem of royalty. I made a sketch of it from our camp, embracing a large scope of country bordering on the Gila.

We had a very pleasant time here. Small game was abundant, and we lived in princely style, or rather, I should say, in such style as no prince or potentate in Europe could afford to live without an extraordinary change of climate. For dinner we had quails, ducks, rabbits, frijoles, and that most gorgeous of camp luxuries, so highly appreciated by our friend Ammi White —good fat pork. We had Chili colorado and onions and eggs, and wound up with preserves and a peach-cobbler. Doctor Jim Berry, our contraband, was in high feather. His face and his top-boots were resplendent with grease and glory. He danced around the fire, stir-

MISSION CAMP—CORUNNACION PEAK.

red the pots, tipped the frying-pans, titillated the gravies, scattered his condiments over the fizzing game, sang snatches of that inspiring ditty, " Oh, Baltimore gals, won't you go home with me ?" and, in fine, was the very perfection of a colored Berry.   Jim was a wit, a songster, a gallant gay Lothario, a traveller, and a gentleman—or, at all events, a gentleman's son.   He belonged to the aristocracy of Maryland, and claimed the head of one of the first families as his distinguished progenitor.   He said he had brothers who used to go to Congress, but now they were secesh and belonged to the Suvern army. Of course we praised his skill as a cook, which elevated him to the seventh heaven.   Flattery was food and raiment to him ; without it he would wither and die.   " I know I'se a good cook ; I know I'se de bess cook in de worl'," he would say, with genuine satisfaction beaming from his eyes ; " I kin make omlit, en fricasee, en punkin pie, en all kinds o' sass—I kin ; en ef I had de conbeniences I'd make corn pone."

The mental afflictions of our driver, George, reached their culminating point at this scene of moral and physical enjoyment.   Unable to stand the general flow of soul, he retired behind the baggage-wagon and held a private conversation with himself, which ended in such a series of pathetic groans that Dr. Berry, in the fullness of his heart, rushed to the spot and offered him a tin plate filled up with peach - cobbler.   " Look - a - here, George," he said, sympathetically, " sighin' and groanin' won't do it any good.   I was wuss in love den dat once, en nuffin but peach-cobbler would set on my stomach.   Eat dis, George, it's wery sooving to de pangs ob unrequited affliction !"   George took the proffered remedy, but I was unable to perceive any diminution of his lamentations during the night.   On the contrary, it was not until I had thrown several clods and both my boots at his head that he ceased to disturb my repose.

The next point of interest on our journey was a volcanic peak, distant fifteen miles from Corunnacion Camp.

Some of the escort who had preceded us had already mounted this singular pile of rocks, and could be distinctly seen prospecting for gold. We found here a station at which hay was supplied for the Government teams. Two soldiers had charge of it. Had I not been told that the loose stack of forage near which we camped was hay I should have called it brush-wood. It grows in bunches, and is cut with a hoe. When dry it makes good fire-wood. The animals seemed to relish it, though I should as soon have thought of feeding them on cord-wood. Our camp at Antelope Peak was as pleasant as the most fastidious traveller could desire. The weather, as usual, was quite delightful—soft, balmy sunshine in the afternoon; clear and frosty at night; and atmospheric tints morning and evening that would enchant an artist, and set a poet to rhyming. Under the inspiration of the occasion I made a sketch, which is at the service of the reader.

Desert mesas and sand-bottoms formed the characteristic features of our journey from this point to Texas Hill and Grinnell's Station. While the Company were encamped at Grinnell's, Poston, White, and myself crossed the Gila, and rode about six miles to the ranch of Martin and Woolsey, situated near the Aqua Calliente. Mr. Woolsey had left, a few days before, with a large quantity of stock for the gold placers. We were hospitably entertained by his partner, Mr. Martin, who is trying the experiment of establishing a farm here by means of irrigation. The soil is excellent, and the prospect is highly encouraging. An abundant supply of water flows from the Aqua Calliente. We had a glorious bath in the springs next morning, which completely set us up after the dust and grit of the journey. They lie near the point of the hill, about a mile and a half from Martin's. I consider them equal to the baths of Damascus, or any other in the world. The water is of an exquisite temperature, and possesses some very remarkable qualities in softening the skin and soothing the nervous system.

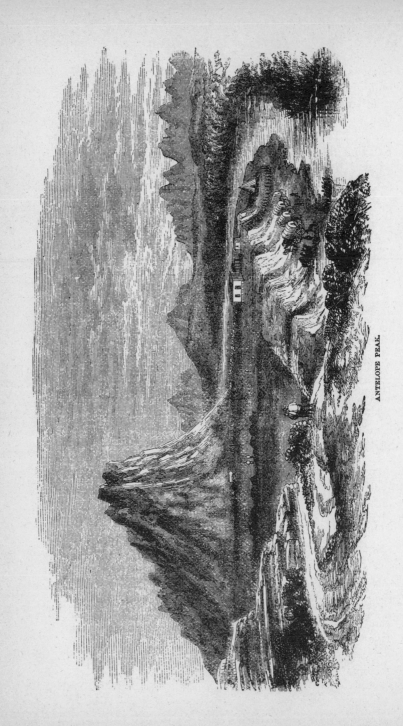

ANTELOPE PEAK.

A Mr. Belcher lived at this place for four years, surrounded by Apaches. Indeed it was not quite safe now ; and I could not but think, as Poston, White, and myself sat bobbing about in the water, what an excellent mark we made for any prowling Tontos that might be in the vicinity. It was here that the Indians who had in captivity the Oatman girls made their first halt after the massacre of the family. The barren mountains in the rear, and the wild and desert appearance of the surrounding country, accorded well with the impressive narrative of that disaster.

It had been arranged that our party should meet us at Oatman Flat, where we were to camp for the night. We rode for about ten or twelve miles over the mesa, following the tracks made by King Woolsey's wagon, and then struck for the river, thinking we were opposite the Flat. Experience has since taught me that there is no safety in diverging from the main road or trail in Arizona, however circuitous it may appear. We soon found ourselves involved in a labyrinth of thickets and arroyas bordering on the river, through which we struggled for three hours before we could get to the water. When we finally made our way down to the sand-bottom, the opposite side of the river presented a perpendicular wall of rocks which forbade any attempt at an exit ; so we had to turn back and struggle through the thickets and arroyas for two hours more, by which time we found ourselves on a mesa covered with round smooth stones, apparently burned and glazed by fire. All round us, as far as sight could reach, the face of the country was a continued sea of dark glazed stones, bounded only in the distance by rugged mountains. Following the road over this dreary waste we at length descended from the mesa, and reached the stretch of sand-bottom opposite Oatman's Flat. In crossing the river, which appeared to be only a few inches deep, our animals sank in a bed of quicksand, and had a fearful struggle before they could gain the opposite bank. As usual, I rode a mule defective in the legs. They were too short by at least twelve inches, and it fell to my lot to be the only member of the party who was thoroughly and effectually ducked. I must say, however, my labors in the quicksand were not wholly lost; for they afforded infinite diversion to my friends Poston and White, who stood on the opposite bank enjoying the picturesque attitudes which I chose to assume while the mule was plunging and struggling to rid himself of his burden. I would take a ducking any time to oblige a couple of disinterested friends, having full faith that they would pull me out at the last extremity.

We found our party encamped in the bottom. Antonio Azul and his interpreter Francisco were in great joy. The Pimo Indians had heard that the white men of San Francisco had put them to death with great ceremony and much rejoicing. Faint rumors had reached the Pimo villages that Antonio and Francisco had been paraded about the city for many weeks, to be tortured by the white squaws; after which, public vengeance being satisfied, their ears were cut off, and their bodies hung up by the heels to a tree, and fires placed under their heads, as a matter of general amusement. Such was the indignation of Antonio's people when they saw his wife and children weeping and wailing for these cruel atrocities—doubtless the invention of some mischievous teamster—that they resolved to take summary vengeance upon some half a dozen Americans who resided at the villages. Mr. White's half-brother, Cyrus Lennan, fortunately received a letter about that time dated at Fort Yuma, stating that Antonio and Francisco were safe, and would be at Oatman's Flat on a certain day. Immediately a delegation of Pimos, headed by Antonio's son, started off to meet them. This was the occasion of the rejoicing. The meeting had just taken place. Antonio and his son had tipped fingers and grunted in token of joy; Francisco had appeared before his astonished friends in the full glory of brass buttons, sashes, feathers, beads, and brilliant yellow cheeks; and now they were all seated around the camp-fire, and the unsophisticated delegation were listening to the wonderful history of the adventures and observations of Antonio Blue-Bottom and his doughty interpreter, Francisco, Knight of the Yellow Cheeks.

A good supper, prepared by the skillful hand of Dr. Jim Berry, amply compensated us for the tribulations of the past two days; and a glorious night's rest on the bosom of our mother earth set us up for any thing that might transpire to tax our energies for some time to come.

CHAPTER VII.

HAVING started our escort and baggage-wagon on the road, a small party of us made a visit to the grave of the Oatman Family, whose sad history had been the theme of much conversation in camp since our arrival in this desolate region. A small inclosure near the road, with a board and inscription, marks the spot. The bones of the unfortunate emigrants were gathered up in 1854 by Mr. Poston, and buried here. He carved the inscription with his penknife on a piece of board from his wagon.

Although a detailed narrative of the massacre of the family and captivity of the Oatman girls, written by the Rev. R. B. Stratton, was published a few years ago, a brief sketch of their eventful career, for which I am indebted in part to Mr. Stratton's narrative and in part to verbal details furnished me by Mr. Henry Grinnell at Fort Yuma, may derive a new interest from the drawings made by myself on the spot. It will show, at least, as well as any thing I can offer, some of the causes which have so long retarded the progress of Arizona.

Early in January, 1851, Mr. Royse Oatman and his family entered that portion of the New Mexican territory now called Arizona, in company with an emigrant party of which he was a member. Originally the party numbered some eighty or ninety persons, but disagreements had divided them during the journey; Mr. Oatman and his friends took the Cook and Kearney route from the Rio Grande, with a train consisting of eight wagons and some twenty persons. After a series of

continued hardships and disasters they reached Tucson
entirely destitute of provisions, their stock broken down
and most of them unable to proceed. At this point the
lands were good, and inducements were offered them to
remain awhile for the purpose of recruiting. The families of Oatman, Wilder, and Kelley resolved to push on,
in the hope of being able soon to reach California, of
which they had heard glowing accounts. They were
very poorly provided for the journey ; but to remain
with their large families, under the discouraging prospect of supplies from crops not yet in the ground, seemed to them almost certain to result in starvation. With
their jaded teams and a slender stock of provisions they
pushed forward across the ninety-mile desert, and arrived about the middle of February at the Pimo villages, where they hoped to procure fresh supplies. It
was a bad season for the Pimos. Their grain had nearly given out, and they had little or none to spare. Wilder and Kelley, however, concluded to remain in consequence of some bad accounts of Indian depredations
on the road to Fort Yuma. Mr. Oatman saw nothing
but utter destitution before him if he tarried among the
Pimos, and he was sorely embarrassed what to do. His
stock had been reduced to two yoke of cows and one of
oxen, and was so jaded after the long journey from the
Rio Grande that it was not probable they would hold
out much longer. Nearly two hundred miles of a desert
country lay between the Pimo villages and Fort Yuma ;
and beyond the Colorado there was still a terrible desert
to pass before they could reach the southern counties of
California. While suffering the tortures of anxiety and
suspense, with the gloomiest prospect if they remained,
a Dr. Lecount, who had extensively explored the Pacific
coast, arrived from Fort Yuma, and reported the route
safe. He had seen no hostile Indians, and had heard of
no recent depredations on the way. Encouraged by
this information, Mr. Oatman determined to push forward at once for California; and accordingly, on the

11th of March, he set out with such slender outfit of provisions as he could procure. Travelling for seven days under great difficulties, his family on the verge of starvation, his cattle scarcely able to drag the wagon, he was overtaken by Dr. Lecount and a Mexican guide at a point below the Big Bend of the Gila. It was evident from the exhaustion of his team that he would be unable to reach Fort Yuma without assistance; Dr. Lecount agreed to hurry on as fast as possible and send back assistance from the Fort, which was still distant about ninety miles. The first night beyond the Oatman camp an attack was made by a band of Indians upon Lecount and his guide, and their animals stolen. Left on foot, without any means of subsistence, they were compelled to hurry on or starve. The Mexican was sent ahead to procure assistance. It was thirty miles back to the camp of the Oatmans. Lecount saw no alternative but to push on after his guide. He left a card, however, conspicuously fastened to a tree, stating what had occurred, and warning the emigrant party behind to be on the lookout for the Apaches. Although the Oatmans camped at the same spot, they failed to see the notice; or, as some suppose, Mr. Oatman saw it and concealed it from his family in order that they might not be uselessly alarmed. On the 18th of March they spent a dreadful night on a little sand island in the Gila River. A terrific storm blew the water up over them; their scanty supply of provisions was damaged, their blankets and clothing were wet through, and the starving animals driven nearly frantic with fear. It was a wild and desolate place, many days' journey from any civilized abode. Hitherto Mr. Oatman, naturally a man of sanguine temperament, had borne every disaster and braved every danger cheerfully and without flinching, but the presentiment of some terrible doom seemed to have fallen upon him at this place, and he was seen by some of the family to shed tears while sitting in the wagon. The next day they proceeded but a short way, over a very

MESA TOWER.

rough mesa, when the jaded animals utterly refused to move. It was impossible to urge them on with the loaded wagon—their strength was spent, and the faithful creatures seemed ready to lie down and die. By unloading the wagon, and pushing the wheels from time to time, the distressed emigrants succeeded at length in getting upon a narrow flat, bordering on the river, where they halted awhile to recruit.

The sketch on the preceding page represents the upper entrance into this little valley. A curious mesa formation, not uncommon in Arizona, is seen on the right. The dark bluff resembling a colossal tower is the termination of the strata forming the mesa. From the summit, upon which stands, like some giant sentinel, a solitary *suaro*, the vertical depth to the valley is about two hundred feet. A mile beyond the tower, the lower extremity of the valley or flat, through which the road runs, is abruptly walled in by nearly a similar embankment of natural fortifications, presenting apparently no place of exit. Upon a close inspection, however, a thin yellowish vein is seen winding up the brow of the precipice. This is the road to Fort Yuma; and the summit of the mesa is the scene of a tragedy which will be ever memorable in the history of Arizona.

Crossing an arroya, or dry bed of a creek, near the bottom of the mesa, and passing through some dense thickets of mesquit and ocochilla, the struggling family found themselves at the foot of a rocky bluff more difficult of ascent than any they had yet attempted. Again they unloaded the wagon, and for hours they toiled to get their packs and wagon up the hill. To one who had passed over the road even in its present improved state it seems marvellous that they ever succeeded in making the ascent, weak and dispirited as they were; but success at length crowned their efforts, and they sat down upon the edge of the precipice to rest after their labors. Mr. Oatman was greatly dejected. It was observed by his family that he looked anxiously down the road over which they had passed, and that he never before seemed so utterly despondent. The sun, which had blazed upon them fiercely all day, was now just setting. They were beset by difficulties. Before them lay a vast desert ; behind and to the right a wilderness of mountains. It was starvation to stay, and almost inevitable disaster to go forward. Mrs. Oatman, the noble wife and mother, always patient, hopeful, and enduring, busied herself in attending to the wants of her children and in uttering words of encouragement to her husband. He, however, seemed utterly overwhelmed with gloomy forebodings, and continued to look back upon the road, till suddenly an expression of indescribable horror was observed in his face, and the next moment a band of Indians was seen leisurely approaching along the road. The children perceiving instinctively that their father—to whom they had always been accustomed to look for protection—was agitated by no ordinary emotions, became alarmed ; but he succeeded by a strong effort in maintaining an appearance of composure, and told them not to be afraid, that the Indians would not hurt them. It was a favorite theory of his that misconduct on the part of the whites was the cause of all trouble with Indians, and that by treating them generously and kindly they would not prove ungrateful. Strange that one who had lived in frontier countries should so fatally misconstrue the character of that race !

When the Indians came up Mr. Oatman spoke to them kindly in Spanish, and motioned to them to sit down. They sat down, and asked for tobacco and pipes ; which he gave them, and they smoked awhile in token of friendship. Then they asked for something to eat. Mr. Oatman told them his family were nearly starving—that they had a long journey before them, and could ill spare any portion of their scanty stock. However, he gave them a little bread, and said he was sorry he could not give them more. After this they stood off a little and talked in a low tone, while Oatman set to work to reload

SCENE OF THE OATMAN MASSACRE.

the wagon. It was observed that the Indians looked anxiously down the road as if expecting some approaching party. Suddenly, with a terrific yell, they jumped in the air, and dashed with uplifted clubs upon the doomed family. Lorenzo, a boy fourteen years of age, was struck on the head and felled to the earth the first blow. Several of the savages rushed upon Oatman, and he was seen for a moment struggling in their midst, but soon fell a mutilated corpse at their feet. Mrs. Oatman pressed her youngest child to her bosom, and struggled with a mother's heroic devotion to save it, shrieking in piercing accents, "Help! help! Oh, for the love of God, will nobody save us!" A few blows of the murderous clubs quickly silenced the poor mother and her babe; and in less than a minute the whole family, save Lorenzo, Olive, and Mary Anne, were lying dead or moaning in their death-struggles upon the ground. Olive, a girl sixteen years of age, and Mary Anne, a frail child of eleven, were dragged aside and held in the iron grasp of two Indians. Lorenzo, the boy, was stunned by the crushing blows which had fallen upon his head, and lay bleeding by the edge of the precipice. In his narrative he states that he soon recovered his consciousness, and distinctly heard the yells of the Apaches, mingled with the shrieks and dying groans of his parents. The savages, seeing him move, rifled his pockets and cast him over the precipice. Upon a careful examination of the spot—as shown to the right of the road in the accompanying sketch—I estimated that he must have fallen twenty feet before he struck the rocky slope of the mesa. That he was not instantly killed or maimed beyond recovery seems miraculous. Strange discordant sounds, he tells us, grated upon his ears, gradually dying away, and then he heard "strains of such sweet music as completely ravished his senses."

Thus he lay till reason became gradually restored, when, with great difficulty, he crept back up the hill. The sight of the dead bodies of his parents, brothers, and sisters, lying scattered about by the broken wagon, mutilated and bloody, was too much for him, and for a while he felt like one laboring under some horrible phantasm. He knew that his sisters Olive and Mary Anne had been taken captive, and the fate to which they were doomed was even more dreadful to him than the sight of the murdered family. Sick at heart, and faint from loss of blood, he turned away and crept toward the river. A burning thirst consumed him. He thought he was dying. With incredible difficulty he reached the river, where he satisfied his thirst and slept a few hours. Thus refreshed, he resolved upon an attempt to reach the Pimo villages, which, though distant a hundred miles, was the nearest place known to him, where he could hope to procure relief. During the next two days he made his way along the road—sometimes walking, sometimes creeping on his hands and knees, resting every few minutes when he could procure the friendly shelter of a bush; at times delirious, and constantly haunted by the horrible dread that he might again fall into the hands of the Indians. He grew weaker every mile from hunger, thirst, and fever; and, worn down at last, lay down to die. A strange noise aroused him from his stupor. Upon opening his eyes he found himself surrounded by wolves, panting and lapping their tongues for his blood. He shouted as loud as he could, and threw stones at them. The nearest he struck with his hand. Rising again, he pushed on, the wolves following closely at his heels. About noon of the second day, as he was passing through a dark cañon, two Pimo Indians, riding on fine American horses, appeared before him, and seeing so strange an object, fixed their arrows and raised their bows to shoot. He addressed them in Spanish, telling them he was an American, and begging them not to kill him; upon which they lowered their bows and manifested signs of interest and sympathy. When they learned what had happened they gave him some ash-baked bread and a gourd of water. Then they told him to await their return, and rode away. He stayed a little while, but fearful of treachery started on again. Wandering along the road till he came out of the cañon and overlooked the plain, he discerned some moving objects in the distance, which he speedily recognized as two white-covered wagons. He knew they must be American. Overcome by emotion, he sank to the ground unconscious of all his sufferings. Within an hour or less he was aroused by the voice of Wilder, saying, " My God, Lorenzo ! what has happened ?" The wagons contained the families of Wilder and Kelley, who had started for Fort Yuma. Next day the unhappy sufferer was safe among the Pimos. The emigrants halted a few days until he gained sufficient strength to join them. He travelled with Wilder and Kelley to Fort Yuma, which they reached after a journey of eight or ten days.

As soon as the Apaches had consummated the massacre of the Oatman family and plundered the wagon of its contents, they fled across the river, taking with them the two captives, Olive and Mary Anne. These unfortunate girls had seen their parents, brothers, and sisters cruelly murdered, and were now dragged away, bare-headed and shoeless, through a rude and desolate wilderness. Ferocious threats and even clubs were used to hurry them along. Their feet were lacerated, and their scanty clothes were torn from their bodies in passing over the rocky mesas and through the dense and thorny thickets. Sometimes the younger sister faltered from sheer lack of strength, but the savage wretches, unmindful of her sufferings, beat her and threatened to dispatch her at once if she lagged behind. She said it was useless to try any more—she might as well die at once. A brutal wretch of the tribe seized her as she sank to the ground, and casting her across his back started off on a trot. Thus they travelled till late in the night, when they halted for a few hours. On the following day they met a rival party of Indians, among whom was one who had lost a brother at the hands of the whites. The strange Indians charged furiously upon the captives, and would have killed them but for the resolute interference of their captors, who were not willing to lose their services. On the third day of their journey, after the most incredible hardships, having travelled over two hundred miles, they came in sight of a cluster of low thatched huts down in a valley. This was the Apache rancheria. The captives were ushered in amid shouts and songs and wild dancing. For many days the savages indulged in their disgusting revels. The two young girls were placed in the centre of a large circle, and compelled to witness sights so brutal and obscene that they were filled with dismay. They prayed that they might die before they should be subjected to the cruel fate that threatened them. The tribe consisted of about three hundred, and lived in the most abject condition of filth and poverty. From this time, for many months, they lived a life of servitude, working from morning till night for their captors, and subject to the most cruel and brutal treatment. The scantiest pittance of food was allowed them, and that they had to gather themselves. Often they were without food for two days at a time, save such roots and insects as they could secretly devour while gathering supplies for the lazy wretches who held them in bondage. The younger sister, Mary Anne, was of a weakly constitution, and gradually declined under the terrible hardships to which she was subjected. There is a touching pathos in the gentleness and fortitude with which she bore her sufferings. She seldom complained; and it was her custom when alone with her sister to sing hymns, and say she thought God would take pity on them some day and deliver them.

In March, 1852, the tribe with whom they lived was visited by a band of Mojaves, who were in the habit of trading with them, and a bargain was made for their purchase. The Mojaves remained a few days carousing with their friends, and then set out with their prisoners for the Colorado. A dreary journey of two hundred miles over a desert and mountainous country, during which they suffered hardships surpassing any thing they had hitherto endured, brought them to the village of the Mojaves, where they were received with dancing, shouting, and jeering. The crops on the Colorado were short, and here again they suffered all the horrors of gradual starvation. Even some of the Indians died from insufficiency of food to sustain life. The gentle child, Mary Anne, worn down by the fatigues of the trip and want of nourishment, wasted away gradually till it was apparent to Olive she was dying. The sisters one evening sat hand in hand. Mary Anne sang one of the favorite hymns she had been taught by her mother. Then gazing with steadfast and loving eyes in her sister's face she said, " I have been a great deal of trouble to you, Olive. You will miss me for awhile, but you will not have to work so hard when I am gone." The Indians gathered around in mysterious wonder. But the dying girl saw them not. A smile of ineffable happiness beamed upon her features. Peacefully she sank to rest in her sister's arms. Olive was left to bear the burden of life alone.

It is the custom of these Indians to burn their dead. Preparations were made for this ceremony in the present case ; but the wife of the chief, pitying the distress of the surviving girl, prevailed upon him by much entreaty to let Olive bury the body according to the custom of her people. A grave was dug in a little patch of ground which had been cultivated by the sisters. They had often worked together in this little garden, and talked of their happy home before misfortune had come upon the family. All that was mortal of the gentle captive-girl was here consigned to the earth. Olive was thenceforth without friend or companion.

During these dreary years the brother, Lorenzo, had vainly striven to procure the rescue of his sisters. No aid was furnished by the military authorities at Fort Yuma. The only person there who took any interest in the matter was Mr. Henry Grinnell, a private citizen,

E

who from 1853 up to the date of their rescue never ceased to exert his energies to that end. And here a singular coincidence occurs. While the Grinnell expeditions, organized through the generosity of a merchant-prince—Mr. Grinnell, of New York—were prosecuting their search at the Arctic Circle for Sir John Franklin, an erratic nephew of the same Grinnell, who from love of adventure had wandered into the wilds of Arizona, was nobly devoting his energies to the rescue of two emigrant girls who had fallen into the hands of the Apaches. If there is nothing in blood, surely great hearts run in families; for here was one, without means, doing as much for the cause of humanity as the other with all the resources of fortune.

Through the services of Francisco, a Yuma Indian, the purchase of Olive from the Mojaves was effected by Mr. Grinnell, in February, 1856. She was brought down to a place on the Colorado at an appointed time. Here Mr. Grinnell met her. She was sitting on the ground, as he described the scene to me, with her face covered by her hands. So completely was she disguised by long exposure to the sun, by paint, tattooing, and costume, that he could not believe she was a white woman. When he spoke to her she made no answer, but cried and kept her face covered. It was not for several days after her arrival at Fort Yuma that she could utter more than a few broken words of English. Subsequently she met her brother, and was taken by him to his residence near Los Angeles. After that they lived awhile in Oregon. I believe they now reside in the State of New York.

CHAPTER VIII.

CRUCIFIED APACHES.

BETWEEN Grinnell's and Oatman Flat is the former
overland mail-station called Burke's, of which nothing remains but a small hacqual on the bank of the river,
occupied at present by two soldiers who have charge of
the Government hay. The route taken by myself and
friends on the opposite side of the Gila compelled us to
leave Burke's considerably to the right, which I greatly
regretted, as I was desirous of seeing an Apache chief
whose body, I was informed, dangled from a tree within
a few miles of the station. Subsequently, in passing down
the Gila, I had an opportunity of gratifying my curiosity.
I was travelling without an escort, in company of Mr. Allen, a trader from Tucson, and having seen what we supposed to be fresh Apache tracks on the main road, it was
deemed prudent to make a short cut through the bottom in order to reach the station as soon as possible.
On the way, near the point of a sand-hill to the left, Mr.
Allen directed my attention to an open space fringed
with brush-wood and mesquit, in which a sharp fight had
taken place two years before between a party of three
Americans, one of whom was King Woolsey, and about
fifteen or twenty Apaches. Mr. Woolsey, who has since
become quite famous in Arizona as an Indian fighter, had
contracted tó supply the Government with hay, and was
returning from the grass range with his loaded wagon
and two hired hands, entirely unsuspicious of danger.
They had but one gun with them, which by good luck
rather than precaution was charged with buck-shot. In

emerging from the bushes, where the road approaches the point of the sand-hill, a terrific yell burst upon them, and in a moment the Apaches sprang up from their ambush and charged upon them like so many devils incarnate. Woolsey said: " Hold the mules, boys, and give me the gun!" which they did with great coolness. The Indians wheeled about and dodged, but kept shooting their arrows with such fearful dexterity that Woolsey thought it advisable to give them a load of buck-shot. The distance was too great, and no damage was done. At this the savages renewed their diabolical yells; closer and closer they crowded, the brave little handful of whites standing coolly by the wagon and mules, ready to sell their lives as dearly as possible. The leader of the Apaches, a warrior of gigantic stature and hideous features, rushed forward brandishing his war-club, and called upon his men to follow. Woolsey waited until the chief had approached within twenty paces, when he discharged the other barrel of his gun. Down tumbled the yelling savage, with a hole through his head. In the panic and confusion that followed, it was deemed advisable, as there was no more ammunition, to cut loose the mules and retire to the station. Here they procured additional force and armed themselves. Returning as soon as possible to the scene of the conflict, they found that the cowardly wretches who had attempted to murder them had fled, not even taking time to destroy the wagon. The chief lay just where he had fallen, stiff and stark, as peaceable an Indian as one could wish to meet of a summer's afternoon. It is a curious fact that the Apaches never remove their dead. A superstition seems to prevail among them on this point; and I have been told that they will not approach a spot upon which one of their comrades has been slain.

Woolsey and his party determined to make a conspicuous mark of the dead chief, from which marauding Indians might take warning. They dragged it to the nearest mesquit-tree and hung it up by the neck, leaving the

APACHE HANGING.

feet to dangle about a yard from the ground. This affair took place something more than two years ago.

On a pleasant sunshiny afternoon in March I stood by the tree and gazed with strange feelings upon the dead Apache. The body was dried and shrunken, and of a parchment color. One of the feet and both hands had been cut off or torn away by the coyotes. The head was thrown back, and the eye-sockets glared in the sun. A horrible grin seemed fixed upon the mouth, and when a slight breeze gave motion to the body I was startled at the ghastly but life-like expression of the face as it slowly turned and stared at the bright blue sky. Arrows were sticking all over the breast and abdomen; doubtless tokens of barbarous hatred left by some passing Pimo or Maricopa.

Six miles beyond Oatman's Flat we reached a pile of rocks, jutting out of the desert plain like an island, which, upon a near approach, we found to be the celebrated Pedras Pintados. We camped awhile to examine the inscriptions, and make some sketches. There seems to be a mystery about these painted rocks which yet remains to be solved. Antonio, our Pimo Chief, said the inscriptions were made a great many centuries ago, in the time of the Montezumas, and this seems to be the general tradition of the Indians. I could not believe, however, upon a close examination, that they were of so ancient a date. The figures are rudely impressed upon the rocks with stone and painted over; some of them being apparently of recent date. Mr. Poston's opinion is—and I am disposed to coincide with him—that these paintings are the records of treaties made at different times between the Indians of the Gila and those of the Colorado.

From this point of our journey till we passed through the cañon above the Big Bend of the Gila nothing of special interest occurred.

At the Maricopa Wells, the scene of a great battle, fought in 1857 in front of the station-house, between the Pimos and Maricopas on one side, and the Yumas on the

APACHE CRUCIFIED.

other, was pointed out to me. Of seventy-five Yumas who had attempted, in connection with the Hualpais and Mojaves, to overthrow the Pimos and Maricopas, but three lived to tell the tale of their disaster. Their allies deserted them in the hour of extremity, and the bones of seventy-two Yuma warriors still moulder on the plain. Mr. R. W. Laine, subsequently an express messenger for Wells, Fargo, and Co., and now an officer in the United States navy, saw the fight and gave me a most thrilling account of it.

A few miles beyond the Maricopa village, on a rocky hill to the right of the road, our attention was attracted by a spectacle at once startling and characteristic of the country through which we were travelling. Looming up on the side of the hill, in bold outline against the sky, stood a rude cross upon which hung the dried body of an Apache, crucified about two years ago by the Maricopas. The legs and arms were fastened with cords, and the head hung forward, showing a few tufts of long hair still swinging about the face. It was a strange and ghastly sight. The Maricopas do not profess the Christian faith, but this much they had learned from the missionaries who had attempted their conversion, that crucifixion was a species of torture practiced by the whites. As it was a novel mode of punishment to them, the probability is they adopted it as a warning to their enemies not to come in that neighborhood again.

CHAPTER IX.

THE PIMO VILLAGES.

AN hour more and we were snugly lodged at the mill and trading establishment of our friend Ammi White near the Casa Blanca. Crowds of Indians from the neighboring villages came in to welcome us; and for several days there was no end to the shaking of hands and complimentary speeches that signalized the arrival of the Superintendent and his party. I vow the labors through which I went on that occasion surpassed all the fatigues of the journey; and if Mr. Dole does not give me full credit for my sufferings in his report to Congress, I shall always consider him deficient in gratitude. As for Poston, he lost ten pounds of flesh; and the only reason I was more fortunate was that I had none to lose, being by this time as dry as a mummy.

In the old Spanish records of the expeditions made to the Gila River, during the sixteenth and seventeenth centuries, special reference is made to the Pimo, or, as the Spaniards called them, Pimas Indians. As far back as 1539 Friar Marco de Niça encountered, during his famous expedition to the north of the Gila, a tribe whom he designated the Pintados, from the fact that they painted their faces. These were probably the Papagoes, who are of the same nation as the Pimos and speak the same language. In the seventeenth century Father Kino explored the country of the Coco-Maricopas south of the Gila, and also gives an account of the Pimos, with whom they now live in juxtaposition. Savedra, an excellent authority respecting the Indian races of Sonora, having spent much time among them, says the Pimos, Marico-

E 2

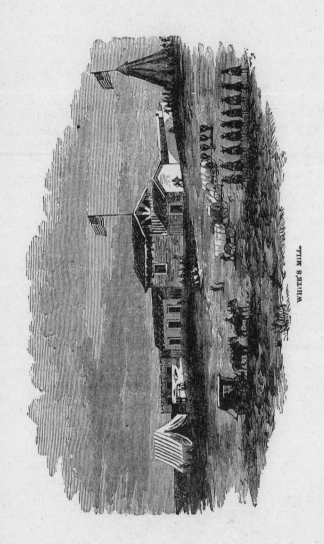

WHITE'S MILL.

pas, Cuchans, and Mojaves are all " Indians of Montezuma:" in proof of which he refers to one custom common to all—that of cropping their hair across their foreheads, leaving the back part to fall its full length behind. This statement is corroborated by the Pimos of the present day, who proudly boast of their descent from the Montezumas. The most interesting fact in the history of these people is, that as far back as the records extend they lived, as they do to this day, by cultivating the earth ; showing a direct affinity with the Pueblo Indians of New Mexico. Alarcon, who visited the great valley of the Colorado in 1540, mentions that it was cultivated to a considerable extent by tribes having a fixed residence and permanent abodes. Unlike the Apaches and the mountain tribes to the north, who live a wandering and predatory life, the Pimos have always manifested a friendly disposition toward the whites, and seem much devoted to the peaceful pursuits of agriculture and stock-raising.

In consideration of their industry and their amicable conduct toward Americans, the Government of the United States, in 1859, caused a reservation to be set apart for them, embracing all the lands which they had in cultivation at the period of the acquisition of Arizona. The survey was made by Colonel A. B. Gray, and embraced 100 square leagues of arable land, most of it susceptible of irrigation. The length of the reservation is about twenty-five miles—breadth, four ; and the River Gila runs through it from one end to the other. Three large acequias take their head near the upper boundary ; one on the south side of the river two miles below Sacatone, and the other on the north side. These, with their various branches, comprise nearly five hundred miles of well-defined acequias, and extend over a tract of land eighteen miles in length. We have authentic history in proof of the fact that for three hundred years the same land has been under cultivation, producing two crops a year without manure or renewal of any kind ; yet it con

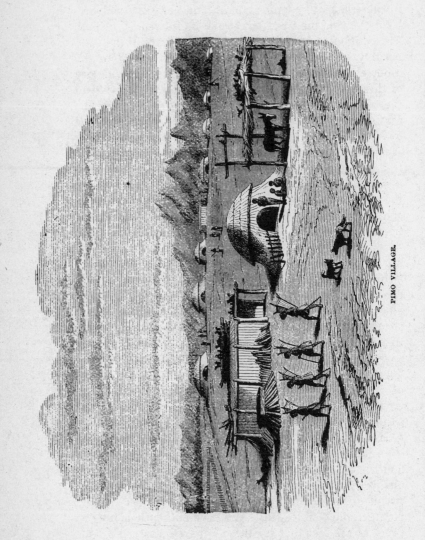

PIMO VILLAGE.

tinues as productive as ever. It is probable the deposits left by the water are of a fertilizing nature. The return in wheat is twenty-five fold. The season of wheat-plant-

PIMO VARSOMA.

ing is December and January. Tobacco and cotton, which flourish with remarkable luxuriance, are planted when the mesquit leaves put forth—generally about the 1st of March. The summer rains commence about the

PIMO HAMPTA.

25th of June, by which time the wheat harvest is over, and corn is then planted in the same ground; also pumpkins, melons, and other vegetable products requiring great heat and moisture. Considering the rude system of agriculture pursued by these people, and the indolence of their young men, who seldom do any thing but ride about and gamble, it is remarkable what crops they have produced on this reservation.

The number of Pimo villages is 10; Maricopas, 2;

PIMO WOMAN GRINDING WHEAT.

separate inclosures, 1000; total population, 6000. In 1858, the first year of the Overland Mail Line, the surplus crop of wheat was 100,000 pounds, which was purchased by the Company; also a large quantity of beans called *taperis,* and a vast quantity of pumpkins, squashes, and melons. In 1859 Mr. St. John was sent among them as a Special Agent with a supply of seeds and some agricultural implements. That year they sold 250,000 pounds of wheat and a large supply of melons, pumpkins, and beans. In 1860 they sold 400,000 pounds of wheat—all the Mail Company would purchase. They had more, and furnished the Government and private teamsters all

that was necessary for transportation from Fort Yuma
to Tucson. Beyond this they had no market, except for
about 40,000 pounds of wheat which Mr. White purchased for the supply of Fort Breckenridge. In 1861
they sold to Mr. White 300,000 pounds of wheat, 50,000
pounds of corn, 20,000 pounds of beans, and a large
amount of dried and fresh pumpkins, which was all intended for the supply of the California column. The
greater part of this crop was destroyed or given back to
the Indians by the Texans under the guerrilla, Hunter,
who arrived at the Pimo villages that year, robbed Mr.
White of his property, and took him prisoner in their
flight to the Rio Grande. The Pimos sold, during the
same year, 600 chickens and a large amount of other
stuff, showing a gradual increase of production under the
encouragement of an increased demand. In 1862 they
sold to the Government over a million pounds of wheat,
included in which was a portion of the previous year's
crop, returned to them by the Texans. They furnished
pinole, chickens, green peas, green corn, pumpkins, and
melons for the entire California column, subsisting nearly a thousand men for many months. In 1863 they furnished the Government with 600,000 pounds of wheat,
and disposed of about 100,000 pounds made into flour
and sold to miners and traders. Their crop was smaller than usual, owing to the breakage of their main acequia at a critical period of the season, and in January,
1864, they were nearly out of wheat, but still had a good
supply of other products.

It will thus be seen that the Pimos are not a race to
be despised. They have always proved themselves good
warriors, and have been uniformly successful in resisting
the incursions of the Apaches. Their villages have afforded the only protection ever given to American citizens in Arizona. If it were not for the Pimos and Maricopas it would now be impossible to travel from Fort
Yuma to Tucson.

Many of the customs which prevail among this inter-

PIMO WIDOW IN MOURNING.

esting people might profitably be introduced into our judiciary system. As administrators upon the estates of deceased members of their tribe they are especially worthy of imitation. No wrangling about wills, no jealousy among relations, no grabbing of effects by avaricious lawyers disturb the exit of the dying man. Peacefully and without worldly concern he shuffles off the mortal coil, satisfied that all will be well when he is buried. His property is fairly and equitably distributed among his people. If he be a chief, and possessed of fields and corn and cattle, his death is a windfall to the community. The villagers are summoned to his burial. Over his grave they hold a grand festival. The women weep and the men howl, and they go into a profound mourning of tar. Soon the cattle are driven up and slaughtered, and every body, heavily-laden with sorrow, loads his squaw with beef, and feasts for many days. All the effects of the deceased become common property: his grain is distributed; his fields shared out to those who need land; his chickens and dogs divided up among the tribe; and his widow is offered by public proclamation to any man who desires a wife. If she be an able-bodied woman, capable of doing much work, she is generally consoled within a few days by another husband, though custom allows her to howl for the last until the conventional demands of grief are satisfied. Marrying a wife with a tar-covered face having its inconveniences, the new husband is also permitted to wear tar, which doubtless has a tendency to cement the union. The bow and arrows, blankets, beads, paints, jews'-harps, and other personal effects of the deceased are buried with him. The body is placed in a sitting posture, with the face toward the sun; over the grave sticks and stones are placed; and thus he sleeps the sleep that knows no waking till the day of resurrection.

CHAPTER X.

THE CASAS GRANDES.

AT the Pimo villages Mr. Poston and myself organized a party consisting of Captain Gorham, Lieutenant Arnold, and thirty of the California Volunteers, with ourselves, under the guidance of Mr. Cyrus Lennan, a resident trader, to visit the Casas Grandes, situated about twenty miles above, near the Gila. The first night we spent at the Sacatone Station, from which the Tucson road diverges across the ninety-mile desert. Following the banks of the river next morning through dense groves of mesquit, keeping in view, a little to the left, a peculiar conical peak, which forms a prominent landmark, we travelled some eight or ten miles, till we struck the remains of an ancient acequia, very large and clearly defined. This was evidently the main artery of a series of acequias, by which a large tract of river-bottom was irrigated in ancient times. That villages and farms extended over a vast area of valley land in this vicinity was evident from the quantity of broken pottery and indications of cultivation we found on all sides. Mesquit-trees, apparently falling into decay from age, now stand in the bed of the main acequia. Diverging to the right when within a few miles of White's ranch, we struck out through the mesquit groves, and in about half an hour's ride from the river reached the famous Casas Grandes of the Gila. Mr. Bartlett has given so correct and elaborate a description of these wonderful ruins that I shall merely, for the information of the general reader, refer to a few points of prominent interest.

The remains of three large edifices are distinctly visi-

CASAS GRANDES.

ble, one of which is in a remarkable state of preservation, considering its great antiquity and the material of which its walls are composed.   This grand old relic of an age and people of which we have no other than traditionary accounts looms up over the desert in bold relief as the traveller approaches, filling the mind with a strange perplexity as to the past.   What race dwelt here ? by what people were these crumbling walls put together ? how did they live ? and where are they gone ? were questions that we were reluctant to believe must forever remain unanswered ; and yet modern research has not to this day approached a solution of the mystery.   The earliest account we have of the Casas Grandes of the Gila is that of Mangi, who visited them in company with Father Kino in 1694.   He speaks of the main ruin as a great edifice, with the principal room in the middle four stories high, and the walls two yards thick, and composed of strong mortar and clay ; and also mentions the existence of twelve other ruins in the vicinity.   Only three of these are now seen above the surface of the ground, although there are evidences of many more in detached mounds which abound in the neighborhood.   The probability is that the main building, which at present forms the most prominent object in view, was the nucleus of an extensive city.   From the account given by Father Pedro Font of his visit to this region during his journey from Orcasitas, in Sonora, to Monterey, California, in 1775, '6, and '7, it appears that he found the Casas Grandes very much in their present condition.   The Indians, he states, had a tradition among them that these Great Houses were built five hundred years ago.

Each group of ruins stands upon a slight eminence distant from the other a few hundred feet.   The tower or central part of the principal building is about forty feet high, and there were originally four stories in the main body of the building, as well as we could judge by the holes in the walls, in which are still seen the ends of the round poles, or rafters, which supported the floors.

THE PAINTED ROCKS ON THE GILA.

Several of these that we took out are some five or six inches in diameter, and seem to be composed of a species of cedar. The ends show very plainly marks of the blunt instrument with which they were cut—probably a stone hatchet. It is evident the use of iron was unknown to the people who originally dwelt here. Mr. Lennan informed us that during a previous visit he had made some slight excavations in the ground, and found a number of bone awls; and other instruments of flint, stone, and bone have also been discovered, of which we had accounts from Mr. White.

The walls of the Casa Granda are composed of a concrete of mud and gravel, very hard, and capable of long enduring the wear and tear of the seasons in this equable climate. The upper portion has been somewhat washed and furrowed by the rains, and the base is worn away to such a depth as to threaten the permanency of the whole fabric, from which one may judge of its antiquity. This concrete, or adobe, was cast in large blocks, several feet square, presenting originally, no doubt, a smooth flat surface; but the outside has been affected by the changes of the seasons. The inner surface is as smooth and hard as the finest plastered room. At the time of Mr. Bartlett's visit there were traces of rude paintings and hieroglyphics to be seen on the interior walls; but these have been either so defaced as not now to be perceptible, or washed away by heavy rains. I saw no hieroglyphics in the building except the names of some Texan adventurers and California Volunteers, scribbled with a piece of charcoal. Rude sketches of Jeff Davis hung by the neck and President Lincoln fleeing from the vengeance of the Chivalry indicated rather forcibly that we were not beyond the reach of sectional prejudices. One name was especially worthy of note—that of Paul Weaver, 1833, a famous trapper and pioneer, whose history is closely identified with that of Arizona.

The outer dimensions are fifty feet north and south,

and forty feet east and west; the thickness of the walls at the base four feet. I made a sketch and ground plan of the buildings, both of which differ from any that I have seen published.

We spent half a day very pleasantly in exploring these interesting ruins, and took our departure for the camp on the Gila late in the evening, well laden with curiosities. Every member of the party had his fragment of pottery and specimen of adobe and plaster.

The next day we returned to the Sacatone and prepared for our journey across the desert. Little did I think, in parting from our kind friend Mr. Lennan, who had interested himself to make our visit to the Casa Granda both agreeable and profitable, that we were destined never more to meet in this world. A brief narrative of his subsequent adventures and death will afford the reader a better idea of the present condition of Arizona than any thing I can say in the way of description.

About the middle of January twenty-eight head of stock were stolen from the corral of Messrs. Peoples and Dye, on the Antelope ranch, twelve miles north of Weaversville; at Granite Creek sixteen head were taken; and King Woolsey lost thirty-three head of cattle from the Aqua Frio ranch, thirty miles south-east of Fort Whipple. The miners in the vicinity had also lost many animals, and were almost destitute of transportation. A company was organized under the command of King Woolsey to follow the trail of the missing stock, and, if possible, punish the depredators, who were supposed to be Pinal Apaches. Twenty-eight men, well-armed and equipped, set out on this expedition. Following the trail from the Hasiampa to the Aqua Frio, they crossed twelve miles above the Frog Tanks, thence to the mouth of Black Cañon, which they followed down to the San Francisco River, striking it at the head of the lower valley. All this time they were on the trail of the stolen stock, but had not as yet seen any Indians. When out sixteen days from the Hasiampa they fell short of provisions, so that it became necessary to divide the company and send a small party down to the Pimo villages for fresh supplies. On the return of this party they all started up the Salinas from its junction with the Rio Verde or San Francisco. At that point they were joined by a party of fourteen Maricopas, under the chief Juan Chivaria, headed by our friend Cyrus Lennan, who had volunteered to join the expedition. Stock had been stolen at the Maricopa Wells from Mr. Rogers, who was hauling up the Indian goods; also from the Maricopas. Lennan had generously offered his aid to recover the animals. As it subsequently appeared, this stock was stolen by Mr. Rogers's vaquero. I saw two of the mules myself in Tucson. The Indians, however, were killed on general principles, and the recovery of the stolen animals did them no good in this world or the next. Another American named Fisher accompanied the expedition. All joined and travelled a day and night through Endless Cañon; scaled it, and travelled for thirty-five miles on the ridge, when they descended into a small valley surrounded by mountains. There was no outlet to the valley, and no way of getting into it other than the way the company entered. They were still on the trail of the missing animals; stopped at what is now called Bloody Tanks, and having travelled all night without eating, they built up a fire for the first time in day-light and set about cooking their morning repast. As soon as the fire blazed up some Indians answered it by building another on the top of a high mountain to the east. Not long after, the Indians discovered themselves, and advancing toward the camp began waving their guns, yelling, and making other hostile demonstrations as if bantering the white men to come up and fight them. King Woolsey sent up Tonto Jack, an interpreter, to learn what they had to say, and at the same time to tell them it was not the wish of his party to fight them; that he wanted them to come down and he would give them some pinole. As a reason for this invitation it is alleged that nobody

F

could tell whether the Indians were friends or enemies. Mr. Dye states that when they came close enough to talk they were very bold in their manner, and said, tauntingly: "We are your enemies; we have stolen your horses and cattle; we have killed you whenever we could; and will continue to kill you whenever we meet you. If you are not squaws, come on and fight us." After a long talk, and the profession of peaceful intentions on the part of Woolsey and his command, the Indians were finally persuaded to come into camp. Most of them laid down their arms outside as directed; a few secreted their bows and arrows under their serapas; and while they were talking, others, coming in one by one, brought the remaining arms along with them, till some thirty or thirty-five were gathered in camp. Woolsey told them, after some talk, that he would give them a passport, informing all Americans that they were good people, and requesting that they should be treated as friends, with which, he said, they would be all right hereafter; nobody would molest them. Par-a-muck-a, the chief, came up, and waving his hand with a haughty air, ordered Woolsey to smooth a place on the sand for him to sit upon; that he was a great chief, and didn't choose to sit on the rocks while talking. Woolsey, suppressing his indignation, calmly folded up a red blanket and offered it to the chief. Par-a-muck-a sullenly accepted the gift, and spreading it upon the ground sat down. These were the preliminaries of an Arizonian "treaty." Then Woolsey called up eight of the Maricopas and stationed them on his left, informing them that they should assist in signing the document. The white men were drawn up on the right, and were instructed to be " on hand." These movements created a good deal of suspicion. The strange Indians were evidently uneasy. For a moment there was a death-like silence. Suddenly Woolsey drew his pistol, levelled it, and shot Par-a-muck-a dead on the spot. This was the signal for the signing of the treaty. Simultaneously the whole party commenced fir-

ing upon the Indians, slaughtering them right and left.
Lennan stood in advance of the Maricopas, and was
warned by Woolsey to make sure of a lame Indian with
a lance, who was eying him suspiciously. " I'll look out
for him," was Lennan's reply; and the slaughter became
general. Those of the Indians who were not shot down
instantly fought with desperation, retreating a little way
and then turning back. Some of them kept running,
and shot their arrows as they ran. The fight, if such it
could be called, lasted seven or eight minutes. Lennan
had incautiously closed upon and shot an Indian near
him, forgetting the lame one against whom he had been
cautioned, who the next moment ran him through the
body with his lance. Dye coming up killed this Indian.
Lennan fell back on the ground, exclaiming, " I am killed !" He lived only a few minutes. The lance passed
directly through his breast, cutting a portion of his heart.
The only other person wounded was Tonto Jack, who
was shot in the neck with an arrow. Juan Chivaria, the
Maricopa chief, fought with great courage, and did good
service. These were found to be Tonto and Pinal Apaches. Four of them were recognized as Pinals, belonging to the tribe of Mangus Colorado. Twenty Tontos
and four Pinals lay dead upon the ground. Others were
seen running off with the blood streaming from their
wounds, and it is supposed some of them died. Of the
whole number that came into the council it is estimated
that not over five or six escaped. During the fight
there were more Indians seen on the hills; but they
were afraid to come down. The scene of this massacre
has been appropriately named the " Bloody Tanks."

Mr. Lennan's body was wrapped up in a blanket and
packed on his own saddle-mule as far down as the junction of the Salinas and Rio Verde. It was found impossible to carry it any further, and his companions dug
a grave and buried it near a cotton-wood tree, upon
which they cut his name and the day of the month. A
brush-fire was made over the grave to destroy the traces

and keep the Indians from finding the body. The Maricopas then left, and those of the party who belonged north returned to the Hasiampa.

Mr. Lennan was a young man of kindly and genial manners, much beloved by all who knew him. His death derived a sad interest to me from the fact that he had shown great hospitality to us during our sojourn at the Pimo villages, and subsequently had been our guide and companion to the Casas Grandes. I was most favorably impressed by his good-nature and friendly interest in the objects of our tour, and felt that we, as well as our fellow-traveller Ammi White, had suffered a personal loss.

CHAPTER XI.

SKETCHING in Arizona is rather a ticklish pursuit. I shall not readily forget my experience of the cañons and thickets, and the queer feeling produced by the slightest sound that fell upon my ears as I hurriedly committed the outlines to paper. It has been my fortune to furnish the world with sketches of Madagascar, Zanzibar, Palestine, the Continent of Europe, Iceland, and some few other points, many of which were achieved under circumstances of peculiar difficulty; but I never before travelled through a country in which I was compelled to pursue the fine arts with a revolver strapped around my body, a double-barreled shot-gun lying across my knees, and half a dozen soldiers armed with Sharpe's carbines keeping guard in the distance. Even with all the safeguards of pistols and soldiers I am free to admit that on occasions of this kind I frequently looked behind to see how the country appeared in its rear aspect. An artist with an arrow in his back may be a very picturesque object to contemplate at one's leisure; but I would rather draw him on paper than sit for the portrait myself. All the way up from Fort Yuma I was beset by these difficulties; and if any man of genius and enterprise thinks he could do better under the circumstances he is welcome to try.

At Sacatone we had a grand pow-wow with the Pimo chiefs. Antonio Azul and his interpreter, Francisco, had apprised the nation of the munificent presents that we had for distribution. Great was the sensation throughout the Pimeria. Scarcely had the sun risen

above the scraggy brush of the desert when the dusky
chiefs, head-men and people came pouring in. They
came from the river-bottom, from the villages, from the
weeds, from the grass, and possibly from the holes in the
ground.   On horseback and on foot they came; by twos
and by threes, and by sixes and by dozens. Paint and

THE FINE ARTS IN ARIZONA.

red blankets, beads and brass buttons, shone with resplendent brilliancy around our encampment. By noon it presented a busy scene of savage enjoyment. The Pimo belles were in their glory. Plump and good-natured; their pretty eyes fringed around with black paint; their teeth shining in pearly whiteness; their bosoms bare; their forms of almost Grecian symmetry and delicacy. Poston, with his enthusiastic appreciation of beauty, would have lost his balance completely had I not warned him of the dangers that surrounded him ; so that when severely pressed by a bevy of Pimo maidens for beads, calicoes, and the like, he usually closed both his eyes and handed out the presents at random. In this way I observed that he frequently gave a sash, or shawl, or string of beads to some stalwart buck, and a shovel or pickaxe to some tender maid. When the looking-glasses and tin jewelry were distributed, never was there such a sensation in Pimeria; and as for the fancy calicoes, the excitement produced by the sight of them can not but descend to the Pimo posterity, and the name of Mr. Commissioner Dole be blessed unto the last generation of these good people. I have no doubt many of them will name their children Dole. I conscientiously believe that historians in future ages will find the name of Dole common among the Pimos. My friend Poston made a speech to Antonio Azul that in point of metaphor and eloquence has never, I venture to assert, been surpassed in this region of country.

Availing ourselves of the friendly professions made by the chiefs and people, we signified that two pumpkins for our journey across the desert would be a most acceptable return for the laborious services we had rendered the great cause of civilization ; whereupon over a dozen pumpkins were immediately dragged forth from the loose and somewhat discolored drapery that hung around the squaws. We gracefully thanked them and proceeded to pick up our vegetables. " *Dos reáls,*" said the Indians. We gave them two bits. " *Quatro reáls,*" they observed. We offered them four bits. They gravely wrapped up their pumpkins. We offered a dollar for two. They coolly demanded two dollars. We indignantly showed them the way out of camp. Antonio and Francisco had long since disappeared before the impending storm. Not so their followers, who, in this case, were no followers at all. Firmly as rocks of adamant they sat gossiping upon the ground, regardless of our displeasure. Some of them considered it in the light of a friendly invitation to supper, and hung about the fire snuffing the odorous fumes of the pots and frying-pans. Toward the shades of evening the pumpkin-venders had sufficiently warmed their backs and were about to depart. Our cook, Dr. Berry, was in favor of seizing a choice pair of pumpkins as a military necessity, but that proposition was overruled as beneath the dignity of our official position. Have them, however, we must. They were indispensable to our health. I left it all to Poston, whom I knew to possess a high order of genius for trade. He traded for two hours; he was calm and violent by turns; he reasoned and raved alternately. I fell asleep. When I awoke, triumph sat perched upon his brow. The Indians were gone. Success had crowned his efforts. Two pumpkins, the spoils of victory, lay at his feet. "What did they cost?" was my natural inquiry. He looked a little confused, but quickly rallied, and replied, "Oh, not much—for this country! Let me see—five, ten, eighteen, twenty-two. Only about TWENTY-TWO dollars in trade."

It was gratifying at all events to know that the Pimos were rapidly becoming a civilized people. Under these circumstances we thought it advisable to pursue our journey without further waste of time.

Travelling all day from Sacatone we reached the Blue-Water Wells early in the evening, where we camped till dark. A few hours of night-travel brought us to the Pecacho, a little beyond which we made a dry camp till morning. The country between the Gila River and

EL PEDACHO.

Tucson is a hard, gravelly desert, partially covered with
a scrubby growth of mesquit and cactus, and at this
season destitute of water except at two or three points,
where the wells dug by the Overland Mail Company still
remain.   In former years emigrant parties suffered
much in crossing this inhospitable desert.   At certain
seasons of the year some pools of water near the Pecacho afford relief to the trains, and enable the emigrants to reach the Gila ; but these are a very uncertain
dependence.

The Pecacho lies forty-five miles from the Gila, and
is about the same distance from Tucson.   It presents a
prominent and picturesque landmark from both points,
and is seen at a great distance from the Papagoria.   The
name is Spanish, and signifies " point," or " peak."
Some travellers have discovered in this curious formation of rocks some resemblance to an axe-head.   There
are many Pecachos throughout Arizona.   I have been
unable to see in any of them the most remote resemblance to an axe-head.   Generally they consist of two
sharp-pointed rocks, one of a triangular and the other
of a rectangular shape, growing out of the top of some
isolated mountain, and serve to indicate the routes across
the desert, which would otherwise be difficult to find.

CHAPTER XII.

TUCSON.

I HAD no idea before my visit to Arizona that there existed within the territorial limits of the United States a city more remarkable in many respects than Jericho—the walls of which were blown down by horns; for, in this case, the walls were chiefly built up by horns—a city realizing, to some extent, my impressions of what Sodom and Gomorrah must have been before they were destroyed by the vengeance of the Lord. It is gratifying to find that travel in many lands has not yet fatally impaired my capacity for receiving new sensations. Virginia City came near it; but it was reserved for the city of Tucson to prove that the world is not yet exhausted of its wonders.

A journey across the Ninety-mile Desert prepares the jaded and dust-covered traveller to enjoy all the luxuries of civilization which an ardent imagination may lead him to expect in the metropolis of Arizona. Passing the Point of the Mountain, eighteen miles below, he is refreshed during the remainder of the way by scraggy thickets of mesquit, bunches of sage and grease-wood, beds of sand and thorny cactus; from which he emerges to find himself on the verge of the most wonderful scatteration of human habitations his eye ever beheld—a city of mud-boxes, dingy and dilapidated, cracked and baked into a composite of dust and filth; littered about with broken corrals, sheds, bake-ovens, carcasses of dead animals, and broken pottery; barren of verdure, parched, naked, and grimly desolate in the glare of a southern sun. Adobe walls without whitewash inside or out,

TUCSON.

hard earth-floors, baked and dried Mexicans, sore-back-
ed burros, coyote dogs, and terra-cotta children; soldiers, teamsters, and honest miners lounging about the
mescal-shops, soaked with the fiery poison ; a noisy band
of Sonoranian buffoons, dressed in theatrical costume,
cutting their antics in the public places to the most diabolical din of fiddles and guitars ever heard; a long train
of Government wagons preparing to start for Fort Yuma
or the Rio Grande—these are what the traveller sees,
and a great many things more, but in vain he looks for
a hotel or lodging-house. The best accommodations he
can possibly expect are the dried mud walls of some un-
occupied outhouse, with a mud floor for his bed; his
own food to eat, and his own cook to prepare it; and
lucky is he to possess such luxuries as these. I heard
of a blacksmith, named Burke, who invited a friend to
stop awhile with him at Tucson. Both parties drank
whisky all day for occupation and pleasure. When bed-
time came, Burke said, " Let's go home and turn in."
He led the way up to the Plaza, and began to hand off
his clothes. "What are you doing?" inquired his guest.
" Going to bed," said Burke—" this is where I gen'rally
sleep." And they both turned in on the Plaza, which if
hard was at least well-aired and roomy. The stranger
started for the Rio Grande the next day.

For various reasons Tucson has long enjoyed an extensive reputation. Before the acquisition of Arizona by
the United States the Mexicans had a military post at
this place, with a small command for the protection of
the missions and adjoining grain fields against the Apaches. It then numbered some four or five hundred souls.
Since 1854 it has been the principal town in the Territory, and has been occupied successively by the Federal
and rebel troops.

As the centre of trade with the neighboring State
of Sonora, and lying on the high-road from the Rio
Grande to Fort Yuma, it became during the few years
preceding the " break-up" quite a place of resort for

traders, speculators, gamblers, horse-thieves, murderers, and vagrant politicians.   Men who were no longer permitted to live in California found the climate of Tucson congenial to their health.   If the world were searched over I suppose there could not be found so degraded a set of villains as then formed the principal society of Tucson.   Every man went armed to the teeth, and street-fights and bloody affrays were of daily occurrence.   Since the coming of the California Volunteers, two years ago, the state of things in this delightful metropolis has materially changed.   The citizens who are permitted to live here at all still live very much in the Greaser style— the tenantable houses having been taken away from them for the use of the officers and soldiers who are protecting their property from the Apaches.   But then, they have claims for rent, which they can probably sell for something when any body comes along disposed to deal in that sort of paper.   Formerly they were troubled a good deal about the care of their cattle and sheep: now they have no trouble at all; the cattle and sheep have fallen into the hands of Apaches, who have become unusually bold in their depredations; and the pigs which formerly roamed unmolested about the streets during the day, and were deemed secure in the back-yards of nights, have become a military necessity.   Eggs are scarce, because the hens that used to lay them cackle no more in the hen form.   Drunkenness has been effectually prohibited by a written order limiting the sale of spirituous liquors to three specific establishments, the owners of which pay a license for hospital purposes, the fund whereof goes to the benefit of the sick and disabled who have fallen a sacrifice to their zeal in the pursuit of hostile Indians.   Gambling is also much discountenanced; and nobody gambles when he is out of money, or can't borrow from any other sources.   The public regulations are excellent.   Volunteer soldiers are stationed all over the town— at the mescal-shops, the monte-tables, and houses of ill-fame—for the preservation of public order, or go there of their own accord for that purpose, which amounts to the same thing. Public property is eminently secure. The Commissary's store-house is secured by a padlock on the door and a guard in front with a musket on his shoulder; so that nobody can go in at any time of the day or night and steal one hundred pounds of coffee and one hundred pounds of sugar, deposited there by private parties for safe-keeping, without killing the guard and breaking open the padlock, or cutting a hole through the adobe wall. If such a thing did occur it would be considered a reflection upon the entire post, and the loss would at once be reimbursed either from public or private sources. Otherwise people would naturally think very strange of such an occurrence.

Although there are two companies of able-bodied men well-armed and equipped at Tucson, and although the Apaches range within three miles of the place, there is no apprehension felt for the public safety. Citizens in small parties of five or six go out whenever occasion requires, and afford aid and comfort to unfortunate travellers who happen to be waylaid in pursuit of their legitimate business; and the Papago Indians also do good service by following up and killing the hostile savages who infest the country. It is confidently believed, therefore, that as long as the troops are kept within the precincts of the ancient Pueblo of Tucson, they will not be molested by any enemy of a more deadly character than mescal, against which the regulations provide a remedy, and if they don't the physician of the post is prepared to do so free of compensation for eighteen months. Neither can the pangs of starvation assail this important stronghold, unless the climate should unfit them for the heavy labor of lifting the food to their mouths; for, unlike the poor wretches of miners and traders who are prowling around the country in search of a living, the troops here stationed receive their regular salary and rations, and the Government liberally provides them with clothing, medicines, and all they require, and vast numbers of wagons and mules to haul the same from distant points. Besides, there are private traders always ready to furnish them with food from Sonora at a reduction upon the present cost to Government; and even if none of these sources could be relied upon, there are abundant tracts of rich arable lands lying within a few miles, upon which it would be mere pastime for the men to raise fifty or sixty bushels of wheat or corn to the acre at an extra compensation of fifty cents per day—convenient places where the Papagoes would be willing to protect them from the Apaches for the trifling consideration of a few strings of beads or yards of manta. I say, therefore, there is no reason to apprehend that the command at Tucson will ever be reduced to the humiliating necessity of depending upon the Pimo Indians who live on the Gila River for wheat upon which to feed their mules, to the exclusion of miners, traders, and other human beings engaged in developing the resources of the country, whose appetites may crave the same sort of sustenance, and who, under the ordinary rules of trade, may come in competition with them, or offer more to the Indians for the products of their la or. Such a degradation could never befall California Volunteers. Far rather would they go to work and raise wheat for their mules, or let the mules die, than squabble over a miserable pittance of wheat raised by the industry of a degenerate race, whom they are expected to elevate by their example to the standard of civilization; nor would they undertake to evade the imputation that would rest upon them for such an act by placing it on the ground of military necessity, when such necessity, if it existed at all, could only have arisen from negligence, incompetency, or dishonesty in their own departments, and which, at all events, would be a very dangerous plea to establish in a Territory remote from the seat of rebellion, and under the acknowledged protection of civil law. By proclamation of the Governor, and by orders of the commanding officer of the department, declaring that martial law no longer pre-

REAR VIEW OF TUCSON.

vailed, and that the military should afford all the aid in their power in carrying the civil law into effect, such a mortifying state of things is expressly provided against.

News reached us at this place of the massacre by the Apaches of two gentlemen well known to the members of our party—Mr. J. B. Mills, Superintendent of the Patagonia Mines, and Mr. Edwin Stevens, who had just come down by the way of Guyamas to take his place; also of an attack by the same band of Indians upon Mr. S. F. Butterworth, President of the Arizona Mining Company. The statements were conflicting, and there were still some members of Mr. Butterworth's party for whose safety great anxiety was felt. As our route lay in part through the same region of country in which these startling events had taken place, we made immediate application for an escort from the detachment who had accompanied us from Fort Yuma, in the hope of being enabled to render some assistance to our friends.

A sojourn of two or three days quite satisfied us with the metropolis of Arizona. It is a very delightful place for persons of elegant leisure; but as we belonged to the class who are compelled to labor for a living, there was no excuse for our staying beyond the time necessary to complete arrangements for our tour through the silver regions of the South.

From which it will at once be seen that Tucson has greatly improved within the past two years, and offers at the present time rare attractions for visitors from all parts of the world, including artists, who can always find in it subjects worthy of their genius. The views of life, the varied attitudes of humanity that I, a mere sketcher, found in the purlieus of the town as well as in public places, will be valuable to posterity; but, as Dr. Johnson said when looking from an eminence over the road that led out of Scotland into England, it was the finest view he had seen in the country, so I must be permitted to say the best view of Tucson is the rear view on the road to Fort Yuma.

On the 19th of January we set forth on our journey
with an escort of thirty men belonging to Company G,
California Volunteers, under command of Lieutenant
Arnold. I may here be allowed to say that a better set
of men I never travelled with. They were good-humor-
ed, obliging, and sober, and not one of them stole a pig
or a chicken during the entire trip.

CHAPTER XIII.

SAN XAVIER DEL BAC.

NINE miles from Tucson we came to the fine old mission of San Xavier del Bac, built by the Jesuits in 1668. This is one of the most beautiful and pictur-esque edifices of the kind to be found on the North American continent. I was surprised to see such a splen-did monument of civilization in the wilds of Arizona. The front is richly ornamented with fanciful decorations in masonry; a lofty bell-tower rises at each corner, one of which is capped by a dome; the other still remains in an unfinished condition. Over the main chapel in the rear is also a large dome; and the walls are surmounted by massive cornices and ornaments appropriately design-ed. The material is principally brick, made, no doubt, on the spot. The style of architecture is Saracenic. The entire edifice is perfect in the harmony of its pro-portions. In every point of view the eye is satisfied. Mr. Mowry well observes, in his pamphlet on Arizona, that, " incredible as it may seem, the church of San Xa-vier, with its elaborate façade, its dome and spires, would to-day be an ornament to the architecture of New York."

A village of Papago Indians, numbering some two or three hundred souls, partially surrounds the mission. There are also a few Mexicans living among the Indians; but they are regarded with distrust, and complaint is made that they have intruded themselves against the wish of the tribe. Mr. Poston, upon investigation of the matter, ordered the Mexicans to leave.

As far back as our knowledge of the Papagoes extends they have been a peaceable, industrious, and friendly

race. They live here, as they lived two centuries ago, by
cultivating the low grounds in the vicinity, which they
make wonderfully productive by a system of irrigation.
Wheat, corn, pumpkins, and pomegranates are the principal articles of subsistence raised by these Indians;
and they seem to enjoy an abundance of every thing
necessary for health and comfort. They profess the
Catholic faith, and are apparently sincere converts. The
Jesuit missionaries taught them those simple forms
which they retain to this day, though of late years they
have been utterly neglected. The women sing in the
church with a degree of sweetness and harmony that
quite surprised me. At the time of our visit two Padres
from Santa Clara, California, who had come as far as

CAPTAIN JOSE, PAPAGO CHIEF.

Tucson with the command, had just taken up their quarters in the mission. From my acquaintance with them on the road, I judge them to be very sincere and estimable as well as intelligent men. We furnished them with a Pimo grammar, published by Mr. Buckingham Smith, late American Secretary of Legation to Spain; and they are now studying that language with a view of holding more advantageous intercourse with the Papagoes, who are originally a branch of the Pimos, and speak the same language. The reverend fathers entertained us during our sojourn with an enthusiastic account of their plans for the restoration of the mission and the instruction and advancement of the Indian tribes, with whom they were destined to be associated for some years to come.

Subject as the Papagoes are to frequent encroachments from the Apaches, they are compelled to keep their cattle closely watched. At present they possess scarcely sufficient stock for the ordinary purposes of agriculture. Not more than five or six months ago a small band of Apaches made a foray within a mile of the village, and carried away with them at a single swoop most of the stock then grazing in the pastures. Though naturally disposed to peaceful pursuits, the Papagoes are not deficient in courage. On one occasion, when the principal chiefs and braves were away gathering *patayah* in the desert, the old men and boys of the tribe kept at bay, and finally beat off, a band of over two hundred Apaches who made a descent upon the village. Frequently they pursue their hereditary enemies to the mountains, and in almost every engagement inflict upon them a severe chastisement.

Leaving San Xavier, we followed the course of the Santa Cruz Valley for two days, making only one camp at Rhodes's ranch. I had supposed, previous to our entrance into this region, that Arizona was nearly a continuous desert, as indeed it is from Fort Yuma to Tucson; but nothing can be a greater mistake than to form a general opinion of the country from a journey up the

SAN XAVIER DEL BAC.

Gila. The valley of the Santa Cruz is one of the richest and most beautiful grazing and agricultural regions I have ever seen. Occasionally the river sinks, but even at these points the grass is abundant and luxuriant. We travelled, league after league, through waving fields of grass, from two to four feet high, and this at a season when cattle were dying of starvation all over the middle and southern parts of California. Mesquit and cotton-wood are abundant, and there is no lack of water most of the way to Santa Cruz.

Three years ago this beautiful valley was well settled by an enterprising set of frontiersmen as far up as the Calabasas ranch, fifteen miles beyond Tubac. At the breaking out of the rebellion, when the Overland Stage Line was withdrawn, the whole Territory, as stated in a previous chapter, went to ruin with a rapidity almost unparalleled. The Apaches, supposing they had created a panic among the whites, became more bold and vigorous in their forays than ever. Ranch after ranch was desolated by fire, robbery, and murder. No white man's life was secure beyond Tucson; and even there the few inhabitants lived in a state of terror.

I saw on the road between San Xavier and Tubac, a distance of forty miles, almost as many graves of the white men murdered by the Apaches within the past few years. Literally the road-side was marked with the burial-places of these unfortunate settlers. There is not now a single living soul to enliven the solitude. All is silent and death-like; yet strangely calm and beautiful in its desolation. Here were fields with torn-down fences; houses burned or racked to pieces by violence, the walls cast about in heaps over the once-pleasant homes; everywhere ruin, grim and ghastly with associations of sudden death. I have rarely travelled through a country more richly favored, yet more depressing in its associations with the past. Day and night the common subject of conversation was murder; and wherever our attention was attracted by the beauty of the scenery

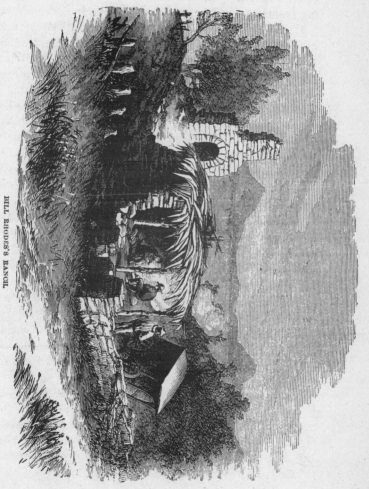

BILL RHODES'S RANCH.

or the richness of the soil a stone-covered grave marked
the foreground.

The history of Bill Rhodes, at whose ranch we camped, was an example. In the full tide of success this daring frontiersman returned to his house one evening, and
found his comrades murdered and himself surrounded
by a large band of Apaches. By some means he managed to break through their lines; but his horse being
jaded it soon became apparent that escape was impossible. Just as the pursuing Indians were upon him he
flung himself into a willow thicket and there made battle. A circle was formed around him by the blood-
stained and yelling devils, who numbered at least thirty;
but he was too cool a man to be intimidated by their infernal demonstrations. For three hours he kept them
at bay with his revolver; although they poured into the
thicket an almost continuous volley of rifle-shots and
arrows. A ball struck him in the left arm, near the elbow, and nearly disabled him from loss of blood. He
buried the wounded part in the sand and continued the
fight till the Indians, exasperated at his stubborn resistance, rushed up in a body, determined to put an end to
him at once. He had but two shots left. With one of
these he killed the first Indian that approached, when
the rest whirled about and stood off. They then addressed him in Spanish, calling him by name, and telling him he was a brave man, and if he would come out
they would spare his life. " No," said he, " d—n you !
I'll kill the last one of you before you shall take me !"
He had given such good evidence of his ability in that
way that they held a parley and concluded he was about
right; so they retired and left him master of the field.
Bill Rhodes's Apache fight is now one of the standard
incidents in the history of Arizona.

CHAPTER XIV.

ON reaching the old Peublo of Tubac we found that we were the only inhabitants. There was not a living soul to be seen as we approached. The old Plaza was knee-deep with weeds and grass. All around were adobe houses, with the roofs fallen in and the walls crumbling to ruin. Door and windows were all gone, having been carried away by the Mexicans three years ago. Old pieces of machinery belonging to the neighboring mines lay scattered about the main building, formerly the head-quarters of the Arizona Mining Company. Many of these are still valuable. At the time of the abandonment of the country in 1861, the Arizona Company had upward of $60,000 worth of machinery stored in the building attached to the old tower, every pound of which was hauled in wagons at great expense from Lavaca in Texas, a distance of twelve hundred miles. Two boilers, weighing 6000 pounds each, were hauled in the same way, one of which was taken by the Patagonia Mining Company. The other, at the time of our journey, lay on the Sonora road a little beyond the Calabasas. Some Mexicans were hauling it away when they were attacked by a band of Apaches, who killed two of the party, took the teams, burned the wagon, and left the boiler on the road-side, where it lay when we passed.

Tubac was first settled by the Americans in 1856, when my friend Poston, the Arizona pioneer and late superintending agent of the silver mines in this vicinity, established it as his head-quarters. It lies on a pleasant slope in one of the most beautiful parts of the valley of the San-

TUBAC.

ta Cruz, within twelve miles of the Santa Rita silver mines, and about twenty-two from the Hcintzclman or Cerro Colorado, two of the richest mining districts within the limits of the Territory. Under the direction of Mr. Poston, Tubac was soon partially rebuilt. Good houses and store-rooms were erected, old buildings were repaired; a farm was fenced in and put under cultivation; a fine garden was started and irrigated by acequias in the Mexican style; and it may literally be said " the wilderness blossomed as the rose." In 1858, '59, and '60, during which the mines were in progress of development, Tubac might well be regarded as the head-quarters of civilization in the Territory. Men of refinement and education connected with the mines were here occasionally assembled, and even the fair sex was well represented. The gardens afforded a pleasant place of retreat in summer, with their shady groves of acacias and peach-trees; and deep pools in the river, overhung by willows, were cleared out and made into bathing-places, in which all who pleased might refresh themselves with a luxurious bath. Poston used to sit in the water, like the Englishman in Hyperion, and read the newspapers, by which means he kept his temper cool amid the various disturbing influences that surrounded him.

Tubac is now a city of ruins—ruin and desolation wherever the eye rests. Yet I can not but believe that the spirit of American enterprise will revisit this delightful region, and re-establish, on a more permanent footing, all that has been lost, and as much more as its enterprising American founder conceived in his most sanguine anticipations. The mines are proverbially rich; and rich mines will sooner or later secure the necessary protection for working them. A view of the Plaza, and especially the old tower upon which, amid the cheers of our escort, we planted the glorious flag of our Union, will convey some idea of the general character of the town.

As a matter of historical interest, characteristic of the vicissitudes suffered by these border towns of Arizona, a few incidents connected with the depopulation of Tubac will not be deemed out of place. In 1840, according to Valesquez, the post was garrisoned by thirty men, and the town contained a population of four hundred. After the boundary-line was established and the Mexican troops were withdrawn, the entire population retired to Santa Cruz, Imuriz, Magdalena, and other points within the Sonora line. Subsequently, when it became the head-quarters of the Arizona Mining Company, it contained a mixed population of four or five hundred, consisting of Americans, Germans, Mexican peons, and Indians. When the Federal troops were withdrawn to the Rio Grande, Tubac was again partially abandoned, only twenty-five or thirty souls remaining. At this period (1861) the Apaches came down from the mountains in large force, and surrounded the town with a view of plundering it; but the few Americans left made a bold defense, and kept them at bay for several days, although it is estimated they numbered over two hundred. The beleaguered residents, finding they would ultimately be overwhelmed or starved out, sent an express to Tucson during the night, stating their condition and asking for assistance. A brave and generous American, Mr. Grant Ourey, got up a party of twenty-five men, and by rapid and skillful movements came suddenly upon the Apaches, whom they attacked with such spirit that the whole band fled in a panic to the Santa Rita mountains. At the time of Mr. Ourey's arrival a party of seventy-five Mexicans, who had heard that the Government of the United States was broken up, came in from Sonora with the same purpose of plunder which the Apaches had just attempted to carry into effect. Seeing the preparations for defense they fell back upon Tumacacari, three miles distant, where an old American lived, whom even the Apaches had spared, killed him in cold blood, robbed the place of all it contained worth carrying away, and retired to Sonora. Thus harassed on both sides by Apaches and Mexicans, and without hope of future protection, the inhabitants of Tubac for the last time abandoned the town; and thus it has remained ever since, a melancholy spectacle of ruin and desolation.

We were exceedingly anxious to discover some trace of our American friends who had recently suffered such a disastrous attack from the Indians — especially of Messrs. Küstel, Janin, and Higgins, who had crossed over from the Patagonia mines, and of whose safety we had no intelligence. There was abundant reason to suppose they had fallen into the hands of the same band of Apaches who had killed Mr. Mills and Mr. Stevens and robbed Mr. Butterworth. Our vaquero discovered fresh traces of a wagon on the Santa Rita road, which somewhat re-assured us of their safety; but we were not yet satisfied. It was deemed advisable under the circumstances to send the vaquero with a detachment of five men over to the Santa Rita hacienda, with instructions to make a careful examination of the premises, and join us the next day at Calabasas. As an instance of the wonderful sagacity of the Mexicans in determining the number and movements of parties entirely unknown to them, from signs which to us would be quite unintelligible, the vaquero reported next day that he had found traces of our American friends. He stated the number exactly; gave many curious particulars in regard to their movements, and said we had missed them by eight days. Nor was there any mere conjecture about this information. It was all demonstrated by the closest reasoning upon isolated and trifling yet incontrovertible signs; and what is most remarkable, his statement was subsequently corroborated by the facts in every particular.

We killed several deer in the vicinity of Tubac, which contributed materially to our scanty stock of provisions. Wild turkeys were also abundant, but our hunters failed to get a shot at them, although their tracks were to be seen within a stone's-throw of the Plaza.

Leaving a written notice upon the wall of the old fort,

informing all persons who might pass this way of our arrival and departure, we proceeded without loss of time on our journey.

Three miles beyond Tubac we made a halt to visit the old mission of San Jose de Tumacacari, another of those interesting relics of Jesuit enterprise which abound in this country. The mission lies a little to the right of the road, and is pleasantly situated on a slope, within a few hundred yards of the Santa Cruz River. A luxuriant growth of cotton-wood, mesquit, and shrubbery of various kinds, fringes the bed of the river and forms a delightful shade from the heat of the sun, which even in midwinter has something of a summer glow about it. Like San Xavier and other missions built by the Jesuits, Tumacacari is admirably situated for agricultural purposes. The remains of acequias show that the surrounding valley-lands must have been at one time in a high state of cultivation. Broken fences, ruined out-buildings, bake-houses, corrals, etc., afford ample evidence that the old Jesuits were not deficient in industry. The mission itself is in a tolerable state of preservation, though by no means so perfect as San Xavier del Bac. The dome, bell-towers, and adjacent outhouses are considerably defaced by the lapse of time, or more probably by the Vandalism of renegade Americans. A strong adobe corral adjoining the back part of the main edifice, with a massive gate-way and with loop-holes for purposes of defense, show the insecurity under which the worthy fathers carried on their agricultural pursuits. Valesquez writes in strong terms of the richness and beauty of this part of the valley. I spent some hours making sketches of the ruins, and succeeded, I flatter myself, in getting some tolerably good views, one of which appears on the following page.

Proceeding on our journey, we reached at an early hour in the afternoon the fine old ranch of the Calabasas or " pumpkins." This splendid tract of country belongs, I believe, to Señor Gandara, formerly Governor of Sonora.

MISSION OF SAN JOSE DE TUMACACARI.

As an instance of the vicissitudes of life in Sonora, I may mention that we met Señor Gandara just before crossing the Colorado Desert, making his way into California, with a few broken-down retainers, mounted on mules and burros. All he possessed in the world was a rickety ambulance, his animals, and a few pounds of corn. He was a sad spectacle of a used-up Governor; was old and poor, and had no hope in the future save to die at peace away from the country that gave him birth. The " Calabasas " will never profit him more. An ex-Governor is an outlaw in Sonora. And yet this ranch is one of the finest in the country. It consists of rich bottom lands and rolling hills, extending six leagues up and down the Santa Cruz River by one league in width, embracing excellent pasturage and rich arable lands on both sides. Situated as it is at the junction of the two main roads from Sonora, the Santa Cruz and Magdalena, it might be made a very valuable piece of property in the hands of some enterprising American. A ready market for its productions could always be had at the neighboring silver mines and also at Tucson. At present, however, and until there is military protection in the country, it is utterly worthless, owing to the incursions of the Apaches.

For the past two or three years a stout-hearted frontiersman by the name of Pennington lived at this place, with a family ranging from ten to a dozen daughters, and raised fine crops of corn, besides furnishing the troops at Tucson with a large amount of hay.

" Old Pennington," as he is familiarly called, is one of those strange characters not unfrequently to be met with in the wilds of Arizona. During the whole time of the abandonment of the country by the Americans he occupied with his family a small cabin three miles above the Calabasas, surrounded by roving bands of hostile Indians. He stubbornly refused to leave the country—said he had as much right to it as the infernal Indians, and would live there in spite of all the devils out of the lower regions. His cattle were stolen, his corrals burned down, his fields devastated; yet he bravely stood it out to the last. When hard pressed for food he was compelled to go out in the hills after deer, which he packed in on his back, always at the risk of his life. At times he was several days absent; and I am told his daughters frequently had to stand guard with guns in their hands to keep off the Indians who besieged the premises. One of them, a Mrs. Paige, was on one occasion travelling with her husband, when the Indians attacked the party, killed all the men, beat her on the head with a club, and cast her over a precipice, where they left her for dead. Maimed and bleeding, she crept away during the night, and for sixteen days endured the most dreadful tortures of hunger and thirst, subsisting on roots and berries, and suffering indescribable agony from her wounds. When rescued by a party of whites, she was nothing more than a living skeleton. She now lives with her father, and is an active, hearty woman. Three months ago the family moved down to the neighborhood of Tucson, where I had the pleasure of an introduction to the eccentric "Old Pennington." He is a man of excellent sense, strange as it may seem. Large and tall, with a fine face and athletic frame, he presents as good a specimen of the American frontiersman as I have ever seen. The history of his residence in the midst of the Apaches, with his family of buxom daughters, would fill a volume.

While camped at the Calabasas, some of us slept in the old building, as the nights were rather cool. The escort remained by the bank of the river, which is the best place for pasturage. Calabasas presents something the appearance of a Mexican military post, which I believe it was in former years. The houses are built of stone and adobe, and are still in a good state of preservation, except some of the roofs and a portion of the tower. Major Stein had his head-quarters here in 1856–'57. It was occupied for nearly a year by the First Regiment of Dragoons under his command. It was also temporarily occupied by Colonel Ewell, late of the rebel service. A characteristic anecdote of Ewell was related to me during the evening. He wished to procure a supply of water from a spring in one of the neighboring hills, and went out one day with four or five of his men to survey the ground. Having no apprehension of an enemy in such close proximity to his command, he had omitted to take any arms with him, and his men were only provided with axes and spades. About half a mile from the house they were suddenly surprised by a band of Apaches, who commenced shooting at them with their arrows from every bush. The men started to run for the fort, so that they might obtain their arms and make something of a decent fight. " Halt!" shouted Ewell, in stentorian tones, while the arrows fell around him in a perfect shower. " Halt, boys! *let us retreat in good order!*" And, as the story goes, he formed his men in line, and deliberately marched down the hill to an imaginary quickstep, stopping every now and then as the arrows pricked their skins or pierced their clothing to deliver a broadside of imprecations at the cowardly devils who had taken such a dirty advantage of them. It was said of old Ewell that he could swear the scalp off an Apache any time ; and one can readily imagine that he did some tall swearing on this occasion.

During the night we were visited by a detachment of the common enemy, evidently on a tour of observation. Next morning their tracks were visible in the road near the river, showing how they had come down and where they halted to inspect the camp, as also their return. Their purpose evidently was to steal our horses ; but they must have seen the sentinels and concluded it would not be a safe investment of time or labor. Had the command been less vigilant we would doubtless have made the remainder of our tour on foot, as many a command has already done in this country. Pleasant prospect, is it not ? where one stands an even chance of being shot with a rifle-ball or an arrow as he sleeps, and does not know when he wakes up but he may have to cross deserts and mountains on foot before he reaches any point inhabited by white people. But I suppose in war-times, when men are slain every day by thousands, such incidents must appear very tame and commonplace. A few years ago I would have regarded my tour through Arizona as something of an achievement. Now I write the details with a humiliating consciousness that they are scarcely worthy of record, except as pictures of every-day life in a country but little known.

As the main object of our journey down in this direction was to ascertain the fate of our American friends who had been waylaid, we posted up notices advising them of our movements in case they should pass along the same road; and determined after some consultation to proceed to Magdalena, Sonora, so as to intercept them in case they had started to return by the way of Guyamas. A few miles beyond Calabasas we encountered a party of Mexicans and Yaqui Indians, on their way up to the placers on the Colorado River, from whom we learned that Mr. Butterworth and his party had passed through Magdalena eight days before. The Mexicans said they met them on the road between Magdalena and Hermosillo, and that they were in an ambulance with a white cover to it, and were travelling " muy racio," with their rifles in their hands. The cover to the ambulance, and some other details, showing the manner in which the Apaches had cut away the leather, identified our friends, and we were satisfied it would be impossible for us to overtake them. It was necessary, however, that we should continue our journey to Magdalena in order to procure a fresh supply of provisions, as we were nearly out, and there was but little prospect of procuring any thing at Santa Cruz.

This day's journey through the valley of Nogales, or the " walnut-trees," was one of the most pleasant of our trip. Every mile we travelled the country improved in beauty and fertility. Grass up to our horses' shoulders

BOUNDARY MONUMENT.

covered the valley, and the hills were clothed with luxuriant groves of oak. Much of the country reminded me of the coast range in California.

We stopped awhile at the boundary-line to examine the monument erected by Colonel Emory in 1855. Very little of it now remains save an unshapely pile of stones. Wandering bands of Sonoranians, in their hatred of every thing American, had doubtless mutilated it as an expression of national antipathy. These people say they never consented to the sale of any portion of Sonora, and still regard Arizona as legitimately a part of their territory.

I could not help regretting, as I looked beyond the boundary of our territorial possessions, that we had not secured, by purchase or negotiation, a line sufficiently far south to afford us a port on the Gulf of California. Without such a port Arizona will always be difficult of access. Major Fergusson, in his report of a reconnoissance from Port Lobos to Tucson, *via* Caborca and Arivaca, demonstrates clearly the vast importance of this strip of territory, not only to Arizona but to Mesilla and a large portion of New Mexico. He shows also the urgent desire of the people of the South to secure it, together with Arizona, and the advantages it would give them as a port for their Pacific commerce, in the event of a permanent division of the Union. General Carleton, in transmitting this report to Washington, urges the importance of securing this strip of territory from Mexico before it becomes a possession of France. I do not believe our Government, in the multiplicity of its present labors, is quite aware of the importance of the proposed purchase. It would give to Arizona and its rich mineral regions an easy and direct communication with the Pacific Ocean. It would encourage the settlement of the country, by affording facilities for the transportation of mining and agricultural implements and supplies of all kinds, which can now be had only at enormous expense. It would open a route for a railway to the ocean from the valley of the Mesilla.   The country is for the most part nearly a level plain, and a very small expenditure of money would make one of the finest wagon-roads in the world from La Libertad to Tucson.   The total distance, as measured by Major Fergusson, is 211 miles.   It is to be hoped our Government will take this matter into consideration at as early a period as practicable.

CHAPTER XV.

COCOSPERA CAÑON.

PASSING into Sonora we continued our journey through the valley and cañon of San Ignatio, another of those beautiful regions highly favored by nature, but at present utterly desolated by the Apaches. From time immemorial the San Ignatio cañon has been a famous place for bloody battles, ambushes, and robberies. Nature never designed a fitter locality for the destruction of unwary travellers. Every rock is a natural fortification, and every thicket affords a hiding-place for the enemy. Ruined houses, broken fences, and deserted pastures are the prominent marks of their ravages. Where vast herds of cattle once grazed is now a rank growth of mesquit, grass, and weeds, inhabited only by deer, rabbits, and wild turkeys.

Our present driver, who had taken the place of George (the love-sick swain from the Monte), was a discreet Irishman, who had served for some years as a soldier in Oregon. He was a lively, intelligent man, a clever whip, and an experienced Indian fighter; but, like all Irishmen, his judgment was very precarious. A favorite crotchet of his was that all this talk about Apaches was "blatherskite," and that there "wasn't a divil of 'em widin a thousand miles." In proof of which he was willing to risk his life in any part of the country without "a livin' sowl besides himself." Upon entering the San Ignatio cañon, where we all considered an attack by no means unlikely, this sagacious Irishman put whip to the mules, and, despite my most earnest remonstrances, continued to keep about two miles ahead of the escort dur-

COCOSPERA CAÑON.

ing the entire passage through.   Poston, with equal sagacity, was scouting the cañon in search of a deer, and
Paddy and I took the lead—he yelling like a devil at the
mules, and I begging him not to run into a hornet's nest
of red-skins.   " Sure," said he, " they'd scalp me the first
anyhow."   " Why so ?" said I.   Paddy smiled and rub-

bed the top of his head, which was covered with a luxuriant growth of hair—"Becase," he quickly answered, "I don't *think* so much as other gintlemen that's always writin'."

We had a number of experienced hunters in our company, who were famous for slaughtering game in California; but owing either to some derangement of the
nerves in creeping around the bushes or through the tall
grass at a distance from camp, they could not generally
hit a deer at twenty paces in Sonora. We were fortunate enough, however, to kill a couple just as we
emerged from the San Ignatio cañon. I shot at a great
many myself, and struck but one, which ran faster after
I struck him than he did before. I believe he thought
it was lightning struck him, for he made a thundering
noise jumping through the bushes.

I shall long remember our journey through this beautiful and picturesque part of Sonora. If there is any
thing finer than the winter climate, I do not know where
it is to be found. Every afternoon we camped in a luxuriant bed of grass, under some wide-spreading oak or
walnut-tree; and it was a great pleasure to bathe in the
clear, sparkling stream that coursed through the valley.
Hunting, bathing, eating, drinking, and sleeping formed
the routine of our camp life. For the first time in my
life I grew fat, but like a hare lost it all again in about
three days. Wood is abundant in the valleys. It was
a cheery sight to see our little command of soldiers seated around the glowing camp-fires, their horses picketed
close by, the fumes of many a savory mess regaling the
senses, while song and joke passed merrily around. I
did not wonder that men should volunteer for such service as this. It was all easy, holiday life, with just adventure and danger enough to give it zest. I had some notion of giving up civilization altogether myself, and devoting the remainder of my days to hunting Indians in
Arizona.

All along the road, wherever we entered a town or

village, our excellent lieutenant drew up his cavalry in imposing style, gave the natives a blast on the horn, and performed the most skillful and effective military evolutions with both horses and fire-arms. The "blanketed thieves," as Mr. Calhoun once called these mongrel Mexicans, peeped from behind the corners of their wretched adobe huts, and looked for all the world like pickled cucumbers shivering in their skins. Since the Crabbe massacre they entertain a natural dread of retribution. Couriers were sent ahead of us, from village to village, informing the inhabitants of our approach; and it was evident there was a lurking suspicion in the minds of the people, notwithstanding our peaceful professions, that we had entered the country on some mission of vengeance. Our thirty volunteers, with their devil-may-care bearing and style of costume, looked very much like a band of invaders.

At Imuriz, the first town of any consequence on the way, some little excitement was occasioned by an incident that occurred during the night. Our horses were closely picketed in the milpas, or corn-fields, down by the river. Some time after dark the sentinels perceived two men stealthily approaching on horseback through the bushes. It was thought they designed stealing some of the animals. As usual, they were hailed, but instead of answering they attempted to run, when one of the sentinels fired. The Mexicans shouted, "*Mas ariba! Mas ariba!*" and still continued to run. In a few minutes the whole command was scouring the bushes in search of loose "Greasers." Nothing further transpired till morning, when a suspicious-looking vagabond called upon the lieutenant and complained that, while hunting cattle, some of the men had fired upon him and made a hole through his hat. The hat, which he dolefully exhibited, certainly had a hole through it a little above the range of the scalp, but whether made by a Minié ball or gouged out with a knife for purposes of indemnity could not be determined. If the damage was done by force of pow-

IMU'IZ.

der and ball, it was a very appropriate cry uttered by the Mexican—*Mas ariba*—(higher) ! Almost any body whose scalp had been so closely grazed would like to be shot at a little higher up.

Another of these miserable vagabonds made a great fuss because the soldiers had burned a couple of worthless logs which they found on the road. He claimed damages to the amount of "cinco pesos." Upon examination it turned out that he was one of a party who had committed a robbery, and attempted to assassinate Mr. Pierce (a nephew of ex-President Pierce), at the Heintzelman Mine, a year ago last summer. Mr. Pierce had joined us at Tucson, and was now of our party. He speedily identified the man, and informed the lieutenant of the fact. Not wishing to have any trouble, the lieutenant quietly advised the professed owner of the logs to make himself as scarce as possible within the period of five minutes, or he would be tolerably certain to receive his "cinco pesos" in lead, skillfully inserted in his ear. No more was heard of the "cinco pesos" after that, except that the logs belonged to another party, who attached no value to them.

We stopped awhile at the village and mission of San Ignatio, to examine the ruins and witness a horse-race which came off during the day. There was but little to interest us in the race. The horses were wretchedly poor, and looked much more disposed to die than to run races for a wager. In truth, horse-flesh is in rather a low condition just now in Sonora. The best horses are all in possession of the Apaches. Kuchies, the famous chief and warrior of the Pinals, rides the finest horse in the country. These vagabond Indians have a saying, no less sarcastic than true, that the Mexicans are their vaqueros, upon whom they depend for their horses and cattle; and that the Americans are their teamsters and mechanics, who haul goods for them and supply them with arms. I did not see one horse in Arizona or Sonora that would bring eighty dollars in California.

A little beyond San Ignatio, as we were peacefully pursuing our way, we were overtaken by the Prefect of Magdalena, a fat gentleman of imposing dignity, who touched his hat with official courtesy, and made us a diplomatic speech on the propriety of observing the obligations of international law. Although we had been but two days within the inhabited limits of the country, news of our arrival had been dispatched by a courier to the Governor, Pesquiera, then on a visit to his silver mines, sixty miles from Imuriz, and a letter received from him by the Prefect of Magdalena directing a strict inquiry to be made into the object of our visit, and a suitable explanation to be obtained of our entrance into a friendly State with an armed party of thirty men in military costume. We assured his excellency the Prefect that our intentions were entirely pacific ; and, so far as international law was concerned, that we had no idea whatever of violating it (though, between ourselves, reader, it *was* a little irregular to enter a foreign State with thirty soldiers, who would have been delighted to sack, burn, and destroy any town within the range of our travels—especially Fronteras, the trading-post of the Apaches). The Prefect professed himself satisfied with our explanation, and informed us that he would see us at Magdalena on the following day. As an excuse for our escort we stated, and with truth, that the condition of the country rendered it necessary for our personal safety. A party of Americans, of whom we were in search, had been waylaid and robbed by the Indians, and two of our countrymen had just been murdered. It was for this reason we travelled with such an imposing escort.

On the way down to Magdalena we passed through several small villages and rancherias watered by the Cocospera and San Ignatio rivers. In referring to rivers it does not necessarily follow that they contain water in this part of the world. Most of the rivers I have seen in Arizona and Sonora contain nothing but dry sand. A traveller might perish from thirst if he depended for water upon the various rivers and their tributaries as laid down on the maps. The Cocospera and San Ignatio combined would scarcely turn the wheel of a small grist-mill. The mills on these streams are driven by horse-power. It should be observed, however, that this was a very dry season. So long a drought had not been known for many years.

The inhabitants of Imuriz, Terrenati, San Ignatio, and the smaller villages or rancherias are miserably poor and lazy. Their cattle have nearly all disappeared, in consequence of the frequent raids of the Apaches; and their milpas, or fields, formerly cultivated with considerable success, have gone to ruin. Scarcely sufficient food to sustain life is now produced. The ground is rich and the climate unsurpassed, and with the rudest cultivation abundant crops of wheat, maize, pomegranates, and oranges might be produced; but all hope for the future seems to have been crushed out of these miserable people. All day long they sit by the doors of their filthy little adobe huts, smoking cigarritos and playing cards. I fancy they like it better than working. At least they live by idleness. Industry would kill them. When these mixed races are compelled to work they sicken and die.

CHAPTER XVI.

MAGDALENA.

WE arrived at Magdalena without a fight, funeral, wedding, or casualty of any kind, and were hospitably received by Don Francisco Gonzales Torraño, an intelligent merchant from old Spain, for some years past a prominent citizen of Sonora. Don Francisco lives in rather comfortable style, considering the wretched character of the place and its surroundings. A good room with a bedstead, and the still rarer luxury of a wash-basin, was kindly allotted to the principals of the party. I had not seen my face in a looking-glass for over two weeks, and was astonished to recognize in the rough, sunburnt, and dilapidated individual before me the little that remained of my former self. Some scented soap and a bottle of rose-water, also furnished by our generous host, brought on a spell of sentiment that threatened for a time to unfit me for the ordinary duties of life; and when Don Francisco produced his best Champagne and exchanged sundry compliments with us, I think an ode to the fair sex would have been within the limits of my resources in a poetical point of view.

Magdalena is next to Hermosillo and Ures in population. From its geographical position it has assumed considerable importance since the acquisition of Arizona by the United States. It is now the chief dépôt of supplies for the mining regions of Northern Sonora and the adjacent part of Arizona. There are three or four stores in the place, one of them kept by a Mr. Kitchen, an American, and another by a German. The population is about 1500. The town is like all I have seen in Sonora,

H

THE PREFECT OF MAGDALENA.

a parched-up confusion of adobe huts, scattered over the slope of a barren hill like so many mud boxes. A notable feature is the old church, of which I made a sketch for Don Francisco. He prizes this token of regard and artistic skill so highly that he has since had it photographed, and I am thus enabled to present the reader with a copy.

The earth and houses are pretty much of the same general material and color. Mesquit and petayah are the chief surrounding objects of interest and ornament in the way of vegetable life; and a few Yaqui women, with ojas or earthen pitchers on their heads, give grace and animation to the watering-places—like Rebecca at the well in the days of yore. A moving pile of mesquit wood, with the legs of a small burro or donkey underneath, is now and then seen passing along the principal street; but otherwise a delusion seems to prevail among the inhabitants that every day is Sunday, and must be respected by total abstinence from labor. I saw but few people in the place, and they were propping up the houses in a manner customary with natives of the country—by leaning or sitting with their backs against them.

The only production against which there seems to be no limit, and certainly no effective law, is that of children. Owing to the climate, perhaps, and idleness, which is the father of all mischief and many mixed breeds of babies, these mongrel little humans abound to an amazing extent in the small towns of Sonora. Nearly all of them have Indian blood in them, and many denote a growing proclivity toward the American race. Hence you often see in one family a remarkable variety of races. A mother with white-headed and blue-eyed children, and black-headed and black-eyed children, and children with straight hair, and curly hair, and thin lips, and thick lips, and noses long, and noses short, all bearing a strong family resemblance, is a very common kind of mother in this latitude. Occasionally some beneficent Padre goes through the country doing up a long arrearage of mar-

riages, putting together in the holy bonds of wedlock all
who desire to secure by the rites of the Church the part-
ners with whom they chance at the time to be on terms
of domestic intimacy. For this reason I think Sonora
can beat the world in the production of villainous races.
Miscegenation has prevailed in this country for three
centuries. Every generation the population grows
worse; and the Sonoranians may now be ranked with
their natural compadres—Indians, burros, and coyotes.
The worst of the whole combination of races is that
which has the infusion of rascality in it from American
sources. Mexican, Indian, and American blood concentrated in one individual makes the very finest specimen
of a murderer, thief, or gambler ever seen on the face of
the earth. Nothing in human form so utterly depraved
can be found elsewhere. I know of no exception, and do
not believe a good citizen of sound morals ever resulted
from such an abominable admixture. Of such material
as this is the town of Magdalena composed. It is said
to be a very quiet and orderly place compared with Hermosillo, and I can well believe the statement; for while
Magdalena has not been much favored with the presence
of renegade Americans within the past few years, Hermosillo has long been their favorite place of resort, chiefly because it affords a more extensive field for the exercise of all the depraved passions of human nature.

We remained about two days in Magdalena, during
which we greatly enjoyed the hospitality of our friend
Gonzales Torraño. It is due to this gentleman to say,
that he has done more for the accommodation of American
travellers on their way through Sonora, and afforded
them more assistance in procuring supplies of implements and provisions for their mining operations than any
man in the country. He has done this without profit or
reward, chiefly from the natural promptings of his heart,
and incidentally from a liberal and intelligent desire to
see the resources of this vast mineral region properly developed.

CHURCH AT MAGDALENA.

It is evident to any one passing through Sonora, even as far north as we did, that a great change is going on throughout the State. Every steamer from San Francisco lands at Mazatlan and Guyamas from 100 to 200 passengers, many of whom, disappointed in more northern regions, desire to establish themselves in the rich mineral fields of the south. Political disaffection toward their own Government may have something to do with this influx of Americans within the borders of Sinaloa and Sonora; but I would not like to say any thing vindictive on that point—especially as most of these enterprising adventurers are at present without money, and not a few of them dependent upon the charity of the Mexicans, who complain that they are obliged to support them. Quite a number of the more energetic, however, are making an honest living by driving teams, blacksmithing, or doing rough jobs of painting and housework. As yet but few have derived any income from the silver mines, though all are pretty rich in claims.

In respect to mines, owning silver lodes in Mexico is a pretty precarious business at present. In Sonora, at least, there is too much mescal and too little law. The central Government is no more recognized than the Government of Spain.   Mines may be held by interest or force, but it is very questionable if they can be held by law.   So long as it is beneficial to have the Americans come in, put up machinery, and develop the mines, so long, perhaps, will their rights be respected.   But the Sonoranians are a treacherous and uncertain people, and can never be relied upon.   Nor was there at the time of our visit any guaranty that the rights of Americans, whom they hate in their hearts, would, even if uncontested by the Sonoranians, be respected by the French, who were then, as we heard, about to occupy the port of Guyamas and assume possession of the State.   Their promise of a liberal policy might just be taken for what it was worth —which, in my opinion, was less than this sheet of paper.

These are suggestions worthy of serious consideration on the part of our fellow-citizens of California who are moving in this direction.   There can be nothing urged in favor of Sonora as a field of enterprise for our miners and capitalists which will not apply with equal force to Arizona, a Territory within our own borders, abounding in mines as rich as any discovered by the Spaniards in Sonora, and where investments of labor and money are in no apparent danger of being lost from extraneous circumstances.

WAITING FOR SOMETHING TO TURN UP.

CHAPTER XVII.

DOÑA INEZ.

ON leaving Magdalena we returned by the San Ignatio road as far as Imuriz, from which we diverged to the right, taking the road through the cañon of Cocospera for Santa Cruz. We were accompanied by Don Francisco Gonzales as far as the ranch of Babesaqui, near which he owns a silver lead which he wished us to visit. Six or seven of us rode up a small cañon to the left, extending into the mountains about three miles, and took an observation of the mine. As yet it is but little developed. The ore is apparently rich in copper and galena. Our friend thinks it is rich in silver also, and is apparently rather enamored of his vein, which he floridly calls "El Primo del Mai." It is not very convenient to water, but what it lacks in that respect it makes up in proximity to Apaches, a band of whom attacked Don Francisco in the adjacent cañon of Cocospera a year or two ago, killed two of his men, took possession of his animals, burned his ambulance, and pursued himself and the remainder of his escort, who had taken to their heels, for about three miles. Don Francisco says that, although forty-eight summers have passed over his head, he can, when occasion requires it, run as fast as he ever did. It is due to him to add that a braver man, or one who has more generously risked his life for others, does not exist in Sonora. In cases of this kind prudence is the better part of valor.

The Cocospera Cañon, through which we passed leaving the ranch of Babesaqui, is a line of natural fortifications and masked batteries for a distance of about nine

miles. Dense thickets of willow, mesquit and cotton-
wood cover the narrow bottom through which the river
runs; and the sides of the cañon are precipitous and
rock-bound, rising in many places into a massive range
of fortifications, almost as regularly formed for purposes
of assault and defense as if constructed by a military
engineer.

Behind these solid ramparts of stone a few determined men, well armed, could keep at bay and slaughter
ten times their number, with comparative safety to themselves and an easy way of exit over the mountains in the
rear. It is for this reason marauding bands of Indians
have chosen the Cocospera Pass for many of their most
daring assaults upon the Mexican soldiery, and upon
travellers attempting to make their way up north. The
bones of the unfortunate men and families killed here
would, it is said, pave the road from one end of the cañon
to the other.

I was interested in taking some views of the scenery
in the Cocospera by Mr. Bartlett's romantic narrative of
the captivity and sufferings of Doña Inez, a young Mexican girl, whose family were murdered in this cañon
about twelve years ago, and herself captured and held in
bondage by the Apaches for fifteen months, subject to
the most cruel treatment. News of her captivity having
reached Mr. Bartlett during his service as Boundary
Commissioner, he made a demand upon Mangus Colorado, the Apache chief, for her release. The answer was
insolent and characteristic—that it was none of his business; this was a matter between the Apaches and the
Mexicans. Mr. Bartlett explained that under the treaty
between his Government and Mexico the officers of the
United States were bound to aid the authorities of Sonora in suppressing Indian hostilities; that this was a
very flagrant case, and if the girl was not at once delivered up he would proceed to take her by force. Having
a strong party to back up his demand, it was deemed
prudent by the cunning Apache to comply with it, and

H 2

Doña Inez was reluctantly delivered to the Commissioner, who turned her over to Captain Gomez, of the Mexican army, then commandant at Tubac. It was admitted by all that Mr. Bartlett had manifested a most praiseworthy and chivalrous interest in the misfortunes of this young woman. At the tender age of fifteen she had seen her relatives murdered before her eyes; had been dragged over mountains and deserts by ruthless savages; had suffered the most cruel barbarities at their hands; and was now once more, by the exertions of this humane American, restored to her friends and to civilization.

DOÑA INEZ.

The delicate and chivalrous conduct of Mr. Bartlett toward the fair captive can not be too highly estimated, considering her beauty and the peculiar circumstances of her career. Far different was the course of Captain Gomez, who, upon finding a beautiful young woman placed in his charge—of his own country too—fell desperately in love with her, and, contrary to all the rules of propriety, took her to lodge in his own quarters. When Mr. Bartlett next heard of her she was the idol and the ornament of the house of Gomez, who loved her not wisely but too well to marry her, having already a wife in the city of Mexico. This breach of duty and implied faith aroused the indignation of our Commissioner, who had so nobly rescued and delicately cherished the divine Inez; and it is currently stated in Arizona that he made it a subject of official protest to the Governor of Sonora and a letter of serious complaint to the Bishop. The Governor and Bishop, as I am told, were greatly mortified at the conduct of Gomez; but upon receiving his explanation, which was to the effect that his wife was still living, and would be very unhappy if he married another woman, they acquitted him of all blame in the matter, and Doña Inez continued to enjoy the hospitality of his mansion.

The sequel of the romance I find recorded in my own note-book. Doña Inez is married and settled at Santa Cruz. Her husband is not Captain Gomez. I called at her house in company with Mr. Poston, and had an interview with her on the subject of her captivity among the Apaches. She had heard of the narrative of her adventures written by Mr. Bartlett, but had never seen his book. She spoke kindly and gratefully of her deliverer. On the subject of her treatment by the Apaches she was somewhat reserved. Her husband was much more communicative.

Doña Inez is now about twenty-seven years of age, though she looks older. Her features are thin, sharp, and care-worn, owing to ill-health. Possibly she may have been pretty in her youth. Mr. Bartlett thought so, and he ought to be a judge. He saw a great deal of beauty unadorned in his tour of exploration.

CHAPTER XVIII.

THIS pleasant little history of captivity, suffering, and love, so impressively associated with the wild region through which we were passing, will be appropriately followed by the romance of an unprotected American female whom we found at the old Mission of Cocospera. All along the road we heard vague rumors of the adventures and exploits of this remarkable woman, who seemed to be ubiquitous, and to possess at least a dozen different names. Even the Mexicans, when they spoke of her, did so with a smile and a shrug of the shoulders, as much as to say she was " some" even in that country. A party of Americans whom we met at Imuriz, on their way from Hermosillo, prepared us to expect at Cocospera a valuable addition to our transport. They hinted at " a whole team" that was awaiting our arrival there, but warned us to be careful how we undertook to harness *that* team, as it was rather disposed to kick and bite. I must confess it was with considerable trepidation that I set out from our camp in the valley to make a sketch of the old Mission.

A more desolate-looking place than Cocospera does not perhaps exist in Sonora. A few Mexican and Indian huts, huddled around a ruinous old church, with a ghostly population of Greasers, Yaqui Indians, skeleton dogs, and seedy sheep, is all that attracts the eye of a stranger under the best circumstances. Yet here lives the father-in-law of Pesquiera, Governor of Sonora—a poor old man, with a half-Indian family of children, of whom Pesquiera's wife is one. At the date of our visit the Apa-

MISSION OF COCOSPERA.

ches had just cleaned out the community of nearly all the
cattle and sheep it possessed, killed one man, and filled
the souls of the remainder with fear and tribulation, so
that the place presented a very depressed appearance.
To this there was but one exception—that of our hero-
ine, the unprotected American female. I found her sitting upon a pile of adobes outside a dilapidated Mexican
hovel, humming over in a lively strain some popular ditty of the times. Poston seemed disposed to evade the
responsibility of his position as commander-in-chief of
the party by introducing me to her as a gentleman of a
literary turn, who had taken a lively interest in her history. She immediately arose and grasped me by the
hand; I was just the man she was looking for. By-the-
way, hadn't she seen me in Frisco? My countenance was
familiar. Didn't I keep bar on Dupont Street? No?
Well, by jingo! that was funny. She was very glad we
had come, anyhow; shook us by the hand again very
cordially; had been expecting us for several days; wanted to make tracks from Cocospera as soon as possible;
was getting tired of the society; good enough people in
their way, but had no snap about them. So liked people with snap. These Mexicans were dead-alive sort of
cusses. The men had no grit and the women no jingle.
Thought, upon the whole, Cocospera was played out, and
would prefer going to Santa Cruz. She claimed to be a
native of Georgia, and was strong on Southern rights.
Said she had prospected awhile in Australia, and bobbed
around Frisco for the last few years. Got tired of civilization, and came down in the steamer to Guyamas last
July in company with "a friend," who left her at Magdalena. Another "friend" brought her up here and went
"a prospecting." She had claims, and expected they
would turn out rich; but, hang it all, she didn't care a
cuss about the mines. The excitement pleased her; it
was so jolly to be knockin' around among the Apaches!
Wouldn't she like to skelp some of 'em; you bet she'd
make jerked meat of their ears if she once got a show at

'em! She didn't speak Spanish; had been eight days at
this infernal place among a set of scallywags who didn't
understand her lingo. Was about ready to change her
location; didn't care a flip where it was, so there was fiddles around the premises. Was a photographer by profession; that was played out; dull work; didn't pay.

THE FAST WOMAN.

Hadn't any instruments at present, and wouldn't photo-graph scallywags anyhow.   Heigh-ho!   Rickety Jo! Great country this!

Such was the style of address of this astounding female. She was sharp, thin, and energetic, not very old, and comparatively good-looking. After she had shown us around the town, making various sparkling comments upon the natives and their style of living, she ushered us into the church, smiling contemptuously at the sacred daubs on the walls.

"Look-a-here!" said she, mounting a pile of rubbish and hauling out a couple of grinning skulls from an al-cove; "that's what we're all coming to.   Them's monks. Don't they look jolly?"

I must confess I was a little shocked at her levity, and mumbled over something about the dust of the dead.

"Bosh!" cried the lively female; "what's the odds, so long as we're happy!   Your skull and mine, and the skulls of a dozen more of us, may be foot-balls for the Apaches before a week."

I turned away and signalized Poston that we had bet-ter retire to camp.   In the evening we had the honor of a visit from our fast friend.   She stepped with a grand swagger into camp, nodded familiarly to the soldiers, and said, "Them's the boys I like to see."

Poston's buffalo-robe was spread on the ground close by our ambulance.   Without the least hesitation she took possession of it, merely observing, "I like this.   It suits me.   A fellow can sleep like a top in such a bed as this!"

From time to time, as she gave us the benefit of her ideas touching the world and things generally, she laugh-ed heartily at the figure she would cut in society, sun-burnt, freckled, and dressed as she was; and varied the interest of the occasion by singing a few popular songs, and reading choice selections of poetry from a book which she pulled out of a satchel belonging to one of the party.

Having thus cast a glow of inspiration over the younger members of our command, she suddenly jumped up exclaiming, "Hurrah, boys! Let's stir up the town! Who's got a fiddle? By jingo, we'll have a fandango!"

Nobody had a fiddle, but there was a guitar in camp, and it was not long before the fandango was under a full head of steam. Greasers, Yaqui Indians, soldiers, and señoritas were at it full tilt, amid all the noise and din and horrible confusion of a genuine Spanish *baile*. The fast woman jumped and capered and pirouetted in a style that brought down the house; and it was long after midnight when our part of the company began to straggle into camp.

As there was no room in the ambulance even for so entertaining a companion, the proposition to transport her to some point of greater security on American soil was submitted to our gallant young Lieutenant, commander of the escort. The question was debated in camp, Was an American woman to be left by an American party in the midst of an Apache country? Had her character any thing to do with the question of humanity or the duty of placing her at some point where her life would be secure? Of course not. Go she must and go she did, in the baggage-wagon. All along the road, in the wildest and most dangerous places, she popped her head out at intervals to see how things in general were flourishing; twitted the "boys" on their style of riding; sang snatches of Opera, and was especially great on ballads for the multitude.

"'When this cruel was is over,'"

she would scream at the top of her voice, "You bet I'll go to Frisco, a kiting, a kiting,

"'As the swallows homeward fly.'"

Thus she entertained us, and thus she clung to us; taking a grip upon our unfortunate Lieutenant that seemed likely to obliterate him from the face of the earth. She jolted and jogged along in the baggage-wagon to Santa Cruz, and didn't like the place; she rattled on to the San

Antonio ranch, and didn't yearn to stay there; she jingled away to Tubac, and considered it too infernally dull for a coyote or a wild-cat. In fact, she rather enjoyed sloshing around, and manifested a desire to accompany our expedition throughout the entire range of our travels. It was abundantly evident to us all that she was inspired with a romantic attachment for our gallant Lieutenant. The shafts of Cupid began to shoot from her glittering eyes, and their fatal influence became fearfully perceptible. He grew pale and weary; was fretful and impatient; and seemed like a man burdened with heavy cares. After a week or so it became necessary to send the wagon down to Tucson for a fresh supply of provisions. The Lieutenant brightened up; a happy thought struck him; he would shuffle off this incubus that hung upon him like a millstone. What excuse he made I never could learn, but he packed up our enterprising female, addressed a note to the officer in command at Tucson, stating the causes which had induced him to give her transportation, and sent her to that tropical region, which he thought would be congenial to her tastes. The last I heard of her she was enjoying the hospitality of our vaquero.

The country through which we passed after leaving the old mission of Cocospera, consists of a series of broad cañons and open valleys, abounding in rich pastures of gaeta-grass, patches of mesquit, and cactus of various kinds. For the most part it is well watered. A few abandoned ranch-houses and corrals on the wayside indicated that is was once a grazing region for herds of cattle and sheep; but now it is a dreary waste, so far as animal life is concerned. The soil is rich, and the remains of acequias for irrigation show that it was once subject to cultivation. In such a region as this, favored by the finest climate I have ever enjoyed, it is impossible to estimate the variety and value of the crops which it is capable of producing. All the vegetation of the temperate zones, and most of the plants known in the tropics, will

SAN LAZARO.

flourish with wonderful luxuriance.   Millions of acres of
the finest lands thus lie idle in the northern part of Sonora.   Probably these lands, owing to the long droughts
which prevail every few years, will never be in much demand for farming purposes, but as ranges for cattle and
sheep they are unsurpassed.   The grass consists of three
principal varieties ; the sacatone, a coarse, thick, and
strong variety, growing in bunches ; the mesquit, which
covers most of the lands lying within the range of the
mesquit timber ; and the grama, or fine meadow-grass,
occupying the open valleys and hill-sides.

The rainy season commences in June and lasts generally till September.   During the winter there is but little
rain ; but upon the opening of spring there are showers
which start the vegetation.   Immediately after the first
heavy rain the earth becomes clothed in the richest verdure.   The trees burst forth into leaf, and the valleys
and hills are decorated with flowers ; the corn in the
milpas springs into life ; the streams rush down from
every mountain cañon, and the thirsty earth rejoices in
the refreshing deluge.   June is the season of greatest
vegetable growth.   So warm and porous is the ground
that it quickly absorbs the moisture, and in a few days
after the heaviest rain one would scarcely believe such a
blessing was ever enjoyed.   Roaring torrents have become dry arroyas ; floods that covered the low lands
have disappeared, and the dry, cracked earth seems gasping for more water ; vegetation begins to look parched ;
the grass is scorched by the burning rays of the sun ;
and thus it continues till another torrent re-inspires the
earth with new life and vigor.

Our next camping-place was at the ruins of San Lazaro, an old missionary establishment long since gone to
decay.   The ranch of San Lazaro is watered by the Santa Cruz River, and is one of the finest grazing regions in
the State.   As usual, it is now uninhabited.   Lying immediately on one of the Apache trails, it has been robbed of its cattle, till nothing is left save the ruined adobe

walls of the ranch-houses and mission, and the broken fences of the corrals and milpas. At the time the mission was occupied by the Jesuit priests, San Lazaro must have been in a high state of cultivation. The walls of the main building, within which we camped, show evidences of considerable architectural style. Guard-houses and watch-towers are still to be seen; also the remains of an orchard, with acequias for irrigation, and two large tanks for tanning hides. It was evident the good fathers were not deficient in industry.

SANTA CRUZ.

CHAPTER XIX.

THE TOWN OF SANTA CRUZ.

PASSING through the picturesque little cañon of San Lazaro, which extends some three miles from the mission, we soon entered upon the pastures and milpas of Santa Cruz. Wild ducks were abundant here, and we killed enough to last us for several days.

The town of Santa Cruz stands on a barren and elevated plateau, overlooking the grain-fields, and consists of a dilapidated church and about eighty or a hundred adobe huts, inhabited by the usual population of Mexicans, Indians, burros, and dogs. It is the most northern town in Sonora, and derives its support chiefly from the corn-crops and a small trade with the Mowry or Patagonia mine. The total population is about four or five hundred.

Owing to its elevation and the position of the surrounding mountains, Santa Cruz is, perhaps, the only inhabited spot in the State of Sonora which is cool all the year round. The water froze in our buckets while we camped in that vicinity ; and although the sky was clear the air was raw and penetrating. The valley is well irrigated, but the people are too idle and thriftless to do more than derive a bare subsistence from the earth. Stealing and gambling are pursuits much more congenial to their tastes. Exposed to constant encroachments from the Apaches, and robbed of nearly all their stock, they seem to have no hope of bettering their condition. If it were not for the opening of the Mowry and San Antonio mines it is probable Santa Cruz would be at this time entirely deserted. There are no stores in the

SANTA CRUZ GREASERS.

place. A German Jew, named Apfel, keeps mescal and a few dry goods and trinkets. Supplies of goods and provisions to any great extent can only be had by sending to Magdalena. Flour, corn, and pinole may be had occasionally, but the supply is scanty and uncertain.

I thought I had seen the concentration of filth, laziness, and inanity, and the perfection of vicious mixtures of races at Imuriz and Magdalena; but Santa Cruz caps the climax. The more southern towns possess at least the advantage of a genial temperature, and it is not unpleasant to see people enjoy the *dolce far niente*, even if they indulge in it to excess. The chilling climate of Santa Cruz sweeps away all the dreamy illusions of indolence, and reduces the inhabitants to a condition of torpor depressing to witness. Too inert to stir about and gather sufficient wood for a comfortable fire, a genuine native of this region sits shivering all day long over three twigs of mesquit, his dirty serape drawn up over his shoulders, his skin a bilious black yellow, the inevitable cigarrito in his mouth; a score of starved coyote curs snapping around his heels; no gleam of hope in his eye, no spark of ambition in his nature—a dreary spectacle of wretchedness and inanity.

Ask him the simplest question, and the extent of his knowledge is *quien sabe?* His whole life is a *quien sabe* business, signifying nothing. The world can not afford a more depressing specimen of degraded humanity.

An incident that occurred during our stay will show the shifts to which these wretched beings resort to procure the means of subsistence. In passing through the cañon of San Lazaro, one of the escort picked up a few sticks of wood which he found lying by the side of a broken-down fence, and threw them in the box of the forage-wagon, as was customary before entering camp, for convenience in starting a fire. No sooner had we halted on the Plaza than a miserable-looking wretch, shrinking into the folds of his serape, made a formal

I

call upon our Lieutenant in company with the Alcalde, and demanded " cinco pesos " for the wood, alleging that it was gathered on his ground, and formed a part of his fences.   There had not been a fence in use at the place in question for over three years, and the professed owner of the wood no more dared to venture that far from Santa Cruz than to enter an Apache stronghold. The Lieutenant offered him fifty cents for the wood, preferring not to have any dispute about it; but he indignantly rejected the offer, and insisted upon the amount originally demanded.   The Lieutenant then proposed to return him the wood (about an armful), which was also rejected.   To avoid the unpleasant results of a storm that was gathering in the faces of our indignant volunteers, who were spoiling for a chance to raze the town, we repacked the wagons, and proceeded on our journey.   That evening we camped seven miles from Santa Cruz, at the hacienda of the San Antonio Mines, where we learned all the particulars in relation to the unhappy fate of Mills and Stevens, whose tragic death occurred in an adjacent cañon.

CHAPTER XX.

A PLEASANT drive of two hours through the beautiful valley of the Santa Cruz brought us to the hacienda of the San Antonio Mining Company, now in charge of Mr. Yerkes, an intelligent American, who received us with great kindness and hospitality. The buildings of the hacienda do not at present admit of very sumptuous accommodations; but here, at least, we found, for the first time since leaving Tucson, a living nucleus of American civilization—houses with fire-places and fires in them, rude attempts at beds and tables, and a people who furnished us with wood free of charge, and offered us from their scanty store of provisions whatever we needed. A mill, with smelting furnaces and a small engine, had just been erected for reducing the ores, and would be put in operation as soon as the necessary facilities for working the mine could be obtained.

The San Antonio Mine is situated about six miles from the reduction works, in a spur of the Santa Cruz Mountains. The ore is rich in argentiferous galena and lead, easily managed, and will doubtless yield profitable results. It is questionable if the silver lodes in this vicinity will produce so large a proportion of rich ores to the ton as those of the Santa Rita and Cerro Colorado Mountains, but it has been well demonstrated that they are deep, boldly-defined, and reliable, and will, if properly worked, amply recompense the labor and capital invested in them. The magnificent grazing lands of the valleys into which the spurs of the mountains run; the abundant supply of fine oak timber on the foot-hills;

the facilities for procuring provisions from Sonora, and easy access by good roads to the ports of the Gulf, afford them peculiar advantages, which would be greatly enhanced if we possessed the small strip of territory extending as far south as Libertad. No traveller passing through this region can fail to be struck with the sagacity of the Mexican Commissioners in running the boundary-line.

Mr. Yerkes gave us the only detailed and reliable account we had yet received of the assassination by the Apaches of Mr. J. B. Mills and Mr. Edwin Stevens, which had recently taken place in a cañon about three miles from the hacienda, on the trail to the Patagonia or Mowry Mine.

At an early hour on the morning of the 29th of December, while Mr. Yerkes was preparing breakfast in his cabin, Mr. Mills and Mr. Stevens rode up and stopped on their way from Santa Cruz to the Mowry Mine. Mills was in the employ of Sylvester Mowry, Esq., the proprietor of the mine, and was about to turn over the management to Stevens, who had just arrived from Guyamas in company with Mr. Samuel F. Butterworth, President of the Arizona Mining Company. The distance from Santa Cruz to the Patagonia (as it is commonly called by the Mexicans) is about fifteen miles, the hacienda of San Antonio being a little less than half-way.

Some conversation ensued when they rode up, Yerkes pressing them to stop awhile and take some breakfast before riding any further. They said they were anxious to get on; but finally concluded to take breakfast. Both were in excellent spirits, and full of life and hope. After staying about an hour they mounted their horses and rode off toward the cañon. This was the last Mr. Yerkes ever saw of them alive. A short time after two Mexican boys came running in, breathless and panic-stricken, stating that while on the way over to the mine, a little beyond the entrance into the cañon, they saw on

HACIENDA OF SAN ANTONIO.

the top of the ridge, which they had taken for safety, a large number of fresh Apache tracks, forming a trail into the cañon. They immediately turned back, but had not proceeded far when they saw two Americans on horseback rapidly enter the cañon. Suspecting that an ambush was prepared in advance, they shouted, " Apaches ! Los Apaches !" but owing to the distance, or noise of the horses' hoofs, failed to make themselves heard. They then waited awhile till they heard the firing of many guns in rapid succession, by which they knew that the Indians had attacked the two horsemen. Mr. Yerkes and three American employés at his house immediately seized their arms and rode out to the cañon. It was quite silent. The dead bodies of the two young men lay by the road-side, naked and disfigured with wounds. Arrows were scattered around them, and many were found sticking in their bodies. Stevens was doubtless killed at the first fire. He lay close to a little arroya that intersects the trail, and seemed to have fallen directly from his horse at the point of attack. The body of Mills was found thirty yards to the left, on the slope of the cañon, close by a tree behind which he had evidently made a stand and fought for some time. Marks of a desperate struggle were seen all over the ground. Both bodies were entirely stripped, with the exception of a portion of the boots, which the savages in their hurry could not pull off. Stevens's body was lanced in several places, but he had evidently received his death-wound from a rifle-ball at the first fire. That of Mills was pierced with balls, arrows, and lances, showing seventeen distinct wounds, most of them mortal.

A month had just elapsed when we visited the spot. Mr. Yerkes accompanied us, and pointed out each scene of the disaster. Abundant signs of the struggle were still visible. We picked up several broken arrows which had been pulled out of the bodies, some of them still bearing the marks of blood.

The place was peculiarly adapted to an ambush of

SCENE OF THE ATTACK UPON MILLS AND STEVENS.

this kind.   A thick growth of bunch-grass and oak timber, with patches of brush-wood, covers the sides of the
cañon, which are rocky and precipitous.   The road winds
through the bottom, coming suddenly upon a small arroya about four feet deep, fringed with sacatone, and
crosses nearly at right angles.   In this arroya, shielded
from observation by the banks and grassy tufts, the
Apaches lay concealed, so that upon the approach of
their victims the muzzles of their guns could not have
been more than a few paces from the bodies of the unsus-
pecting horsemen.

APACHE BOOTS, HEAD-DRESS, SADDLE, ETC.

It is characteristic of life in Arizona that both of these
young men were well acquainted with the dangers of
the country.   Stevens had served on the Overland Mail
route, and was universally esteemed as a brave, sagacious, and intelligent man.   Mills had lived and travelled
in Arizona for several years, and had seen many tragic
examples of the cunning and cruelty of these Indians;
but like all who have lost their lives in a similar manner,
had become accustomed to such scenes.   Men of this
kind are too apt to rely upon their courage and fire-

arms; when it is a noted fact that in most cases they are murdered without a chance of defense. It was still more characteristic of the country, as showing the reck-lessness acquired by habit, that scarcely two years had elapsed since Dr. Titus, of the Mowry Mine, lost his life in a similar manner, at this very place. He was passing through the cañon with a Delaware Indian, when they were waylaid and fired upon by the Apaches. The Del-aware was killed at the first fire. Titus dismounted from his horse, and fought his way on foot about two hundred yards up the cañon. He would doubtless have effected his escape had not one of the Indians crept upon him from the rear and shot him through the hip. Although the wound was not mortal, he was satisfied that he could not get away, surrounded as he was by savages who were shooting their arrows at him from every bush. To avoid the tortures which they usually inflict upon their prisoners he ended his own life by shooting himself in the head. The Apaches afterward, in describing the fight at Fronteras, said they were about to give it up when Titus received the wound in the hip. They knew they had him then. The Chief said he was a brave man, and would not permit his body to be mu-tilated. When it is considered that the common prac-tice of these wretches is to hang their victims by the heels to a tree and put a slow fire under their heads, few men of generous feelings will be disposed to pronounce judgment upon the manner in which Dr. Titus ended his life. Under all circumstances, I believe it is best that we should live as long as we can, for while there is life there is hope; but no man really knows what he would do in such a case as this.

I visited the burial-place of these young men at the Mowry Mines. On the rise of a hill, overlooking the valley of the Hacienda, surrounded by mountains clothed with the verdure of oak groves, with an almost perpet-ual summer sky overhead, far isolated from the busy haunts of the civilized world, lie the remains of seventeen

I 2

white men.   Fifteen of the number are the victims of
violence.   Only two of them died from ordinary causes.
Three graves, close in a row, prominently mark the
ground—one the grave of Dr. Titus; the last two, covered with freshly-spaded earth, with a board at the head
of each, bearing respectively the simple inscriptions:

J. B. MILLS, Jr.
December 29th, 1863.

E. C. STEVENS.
December 29th, 1863.

CHAPTER XXI.

THE MOWRY MINE.

A FEW miles beyond the cañon we came to a series of hills covered with a fine growth of oak timber. Here we found the first indications we had enjoyed for some weeks of life and industry. Cords of wood lay piled up on the wayside; the sound of the axe reverberated from hill to hill; the smoke of many charcoal pits filled the air, and teamsters, with heavily-laden wagons, were working their way over the rugged trails and by-paths. Gradually the road became better defined, and the clearings more extensive, till we came to the brow of a hill overlooking the hacienda.

A more picturesque or cheering view I had rarely seen. Down in a beautiful little valley of several hundred acres, almost embosomed in trees, stand the reduction works, store-houses, and peon quarters of the Mowry Silver Mines. Smoke rose in curling clouds from the main chimney, which stands like an obelisk in the centre of the mill, and sulphurous vapors whirled up from the long row of smelting furnaces in the rear. The busy hum of the steam-engine and fly-wheels fell with a lively effect upon the ear; the broad, smooth plaza in front of the works was dotted with wagons and teams, discharging their freight of wood and ore; and under the shade of the surrounding trees, amid the picturesque little huts of the peons, groups of women and children, clothed in the loose, variegated costume of the country, gave a pleasing, domestic interest to the scene. It was the last of the month, and consequently pay-day—a very welcome and important day all over the world, but especially in

HACIENDA OF THE MOWRY MINE.

this isolated region, where pay-days are scarce. Such an event, within fifteen miles of Santa Cruz, rises to the dignity of a grand public institution. The citizens of Santa Cruz, who, as already stated, are not proverbial for energy, seem to be inspired with new life on occasions of this kind, and never fail to visit the mines in large numbers for the purpose of participating in the general rejoicing. For two or three days the whole hacienda presents a lively and characteristic scene. Work is out of the question, so far as the peons are concerned. Under the shade of every tree sits a group of thriftless vagabonds, conspicuous for their dirty skins and many-colored serapas, shuffling the inevitable pack of cards, or casting their fortune of greasy "holies" upon the capricious hazards of monte. The earnings of a month are soon disposed of; the women and children are left dependent upon new advances from the store-houses; the workmen are stupefied with mescal and many nights of debauch; and when all is over — the fandango at an end — the monte-tables packed up, every miner bankrupt, and no more goods or money to be had, the posse of sharpers from the border-line of Sonora take their leave; and thus it goes from month to month. Although these poor wretches live from hand to mouth, they are generally cheerful and happy. If they could see their way a few months ahead they would probably die.

This brings me to the reflection that, under the existing system of labor in Southern Arizona, the silver mines can never be developed to their full capacity or profitably worked. The Santa Rita, Cerro Colorado, and Cahuabia mines have been tried in this way, and the result has been invariably unfortunate. Many valuable lives have been sacrificed, and vast amounts of property lost by the treachery, dishonesty, and incapacity of this class of workmen.

It may justly be contended that no other class has been available hitherto; that this is the cheapest and

THE MOWRY MINE.

most convenient labor that could be obtained—indeed the only labor; but the result, I think, sufficiently demonstrates that it can not be relied upon. It is true, fifteen dollars a month, payable mostly in goods at high prices, for men who have had more or less experience in the working of mines, can not be considered an extravagant rate of wages. But that must be determined by the result. Expenses have never yet been paid in any of the mines opened in Arizona by American capitalists. There will be no difficulty in procuring reliable white labor as soon as there is any security for life and property. The climate of Arizona is far more genial than that of Nevada, where white labor is abundant. Men can be found to work wherever they receive an adequate compensation for their services. I do not believe it would be practicable wholly or at once to dispense with Mexican labor. It can always to some extent be made available for the lower grades of mining operations. Under the preponderance of a higher and more intelligent class of labor it may become both convenient and profitable.

During the afternoon we paid a visit to the mine, which is situated in the side of a hill about a quarter of a mile from the offices and head-quarters.

A number of Mexicans were at work getting out the ore, and the scene upon our arrival was both picturesque and lively. I took a seat a little on one side of the " dump," and made a sketch which will convey a better idea of the general appearance of a silver mine in Arizona than any written description.

The Patagonia, now called the Mowry Mine, was probably known to the Mexicans, and worked by them many years ago. The Americans first discovered it in 1858. In 1860 it became the property of Sylvester Mowry, Esq. It is situated within ten miles of the boundary-line between Sonora and Arizona; is 6160 feet above the level of the sea, and is distant 280 miles from Guyamas on the Gulf of California.

It is not my purpose in these casual sketches to write a report on the condition and prospects of each silver or gold mine in the Territory of Arizona, even if I possessed the requisite knowledge of mining operations.   I can only say, therefore, in reference to the Mowry Mine, that the lode appears to be large, bold, and well defined, and the ore of fair average richness.   It is composed of argentiferous galena, impregnated with arsenic, and is easily reduced by smelting.   Three distinct veins are perceptible, which cross each other in the principal lode. The ore which was in process of reduction at the time of my visit yielded, as I was informed, about thirty-five dollars to the ton.   It was not the richest, nor could it be considered a fair average.   Mr. Küstel, the distinguished metallurgist, author of the " Processes of Silver and Gold Extraction," etc., visited the mine about a month prior to my arrival, and made a thorough examination of its ores and resources.   From a report made by him it would appear that some of the ores average $350 to the ton.   If the mines were properly worked he estimates that a general average of $50 to $70 to the ton might be obtained ; and he mentions among the advantages in fluxing the presence of iron ore, manganese, and lime. The result of one day's working he found to be as follows : Produce of twenty tons in silver, $1200 ; in lead, $480—total, $1680 ; expenses of reduction, mining, etc, $400—profit, $1280.   This result is highly encouraging ; but the probability is, a more perfect and extensive system of operations would greatly enhance the net proceeds of the mine.

At the time of our visit this property was in the hands of the Deputy-Marshal of New Mexico, who held it on behalf of the United States.   Mr. Mowry, it appears, had been arrested and imprisoned by order of General J. H. Carleton, and the mine seized under the Confiscation Act.   Of the merits of the difficulty I have no knowledge.   It appears, however, that Mr. Mowry was discharged by the court which tried his case.   His prop-

SYLVESTER MOWRY.

erty, I believe, has since been restored to him by order of the Government.

This gentleman's career in Arizona has been singularly adventurous and varied. In 1855 he was an officer of the Federal army at Fort Yuma. An expedition which he made into the wilds of Arizona inspired him with a high opinion of its great mineral resources, and a most enthusiastic estimate of its future destiny. He resigned his position in the army, and spent several years in exploring the country and attempting to procure a recognition of its claims by Government. At one period he was elected a delegate to Congress, and visited Washington for the purpose of procuring a Territorial organization; but his object was defeated by sectional dissensions in that body. Mr. Mowry is well known through-

out the United States. His name is inseparably connected with that of Arizona. It is a part of himself.
He once declared, in a moment of passion, when his
term of residence was questioned, that " he was *born*
there !" Certainly no man has done more to give no-
toriety to the new Territory than he, and no man loves
it better.

We spent the day very pleasantly, visiting the principal objects of interest at the Patagonia. After enjoying a luxurious dinner at head-quarters, and various
hospitable " smiles," we rode back by the valley road to
the hacienda of the San Antonio. The climate of the
Patagonia is unsurpassed—I might almost say unequal-
ed. How such a paradise ever came to be christened
after the chilly, fog-smitten land where " giants grow
and storms do blow," I am unable to conjecture. No
wonder Mr. Mowry prefers his own name, which, if not
so euphonious, is at least less suggestive of howling
winds and fishy natives.

HEAD-QUARTERS AND OFFICES OF THE MOWRY SILVER MINE.

CHAPTER XXII.

ATTACK ON MR. BUTTERWORTH.

AN early start from the hacienda of San Antonio enabled us to make an unusually good day's journey. We reached Santa Cruz just as the sun was peeping over the mountains, but were delayed some time in procuring corn for our animals. For the benefit of travellers in this region it may be well to mention that forage and provisions are exceedingly scarce, and can only be procured at a few of the principal points. From Tucson to the border-line nothing whatever is to be had. There are no white inhabitants, and consequently nothing is produced except the small pittance of food raised by the Papago Indians. It will be easily understood, therefore, how difficult and inconvenient it is to travel in this country. With wagons a considerable number of animals are required, and these must haul their own forage, besides provisions for a party large enough to protect the train from Indian hostilities. The grazing, it is true, is excellent in the southern range, but for heavy work the draught teams require more substantial nourishment than grass.

Our journey down the valley of the Santa Cruz was one of the most agreeable in our entire tour. We were accompanied by Señor Commodoran, an intelligent Mexican, whose friendship toward Americans travelling through the country has long been proverbial. It was he who, upon receiving news of the attack upon Mr. Butterworth, got up a party and went out to his relief.

After passing through the cañon of the San Lazaro we entered a valley which opens out into a magnificent

grazing range, extending nearly 20 miles to the foot-hills
of the Pinitos Mountains. Groves of cotton-wood of
gigantic size fringe the stream at intervals of every few
miles; the grass is wonderfully luxuriant, covering the
valley and hill-sides as far as the eye can reach with a
rich gold-colored carpeting; the slopes of the hills and
mountains are beautifully adorned with groves of oak,
ash, hackberry, and various kinds of shrubbery, through
the foliage of which the bright yellow grass glistens like
a patchwork of gold; and far in the distance this glowing combination of colors is outlined by the purple peaks
of innumerable Sierras, shivered by some tremendous
convulsion of the earth into the wildest and most fantastic forms. Such sunrises and sunsets, such marvellous richness of coloring, such magic lights and shades, I
have never seen equalled in Europe, not even in Italy or
the islands of the Grecian Archipelago.

Our camp for the night was under a fine grove of
cotton-wood, where the grass, shaded from the crisping
rays of the sun, grew up in luxuriant masses high over
our heads. Here we cut and slashed at the tufts, and
burned out broad spaces for our fires, of which there
was constant danger, till our camp was secure from
conflagration; and then the venison and wild-ducks were
quickly placed in the frying-pans, and their savory odors
mingled with the pleasant fumes of the coffee-pot, and
the creature-comforts of earth were ours in perfection.
No prince or potentate in the plenitude of his power, no
rich man counting his hoards, was ever half so happy as
we, the way-worn, dust-covered, sun-burnt travellers in
Arizona. Prominent in the distance stood the chimney-
like peak of the Pinitos, and around us, for a circle of
30 or 40 miles, arose the rugged ranges of the Santa
Cruz, Arizuma, and Santa Rita mountains. At sunset the
scene was magnificent beyond description. No human
art is adequate to catch the infinite variety of outline
and the incomparable richness of the atmospheric tints
in this enchanting region. Even our volunteer soldiers,

CAMP AT THE PINITOS MOUNTAINS.

rough as most of them were, enjoyed it, and constantly burst forth into extravagant praises of the country.

We were now in a very dangerous pass of the Apaches, and it became necessary to keep a sharp lookout for our animals. Strict injunctions were given to the guard to keep up a vigilant watch. Most of us, as we lay down in the grass, had some serious thoughts, yet all manifested a strong desire to have a brush with the enemy. The night was calm and beautiful, the whole canopy of heaven literally glowing with stars. It must have been a little beyond midnight, during a period of the most profound silence, that our ears were saluted by the sharp, quick report of a rifle, and some unaccountable commotion among the men, who at once rushed from their resting-places, carbines in hand, in search of the supposed Apaches. It was some time before the cause of the alarm could be ascertained. A foolish sailor, who had turned soldier, happening to be on guard, discovered, as he supposed, an Apache creeping toward him, and, without waiting to challenge the object, fired his gun. The object disappeared for a time in the grass. Search was made, and at length the dead body of our own faithful watch-dog, which had accompanied us during the whole journey, was discovered. Poor Bull had become a general favorite. The man who killed him at once fell into disgrace, and never again had any peace of body or mind. He was sent back to the garrison at Tucson by the first opportunity. Before our departure from the scene of this canine tragedy, which produced a gloom all over camp, the soldiers gave the body of Bull a decent burial in military form, and fired a salute of four guns over his grave.

Señor Commodoran was accompanied by an old Mexican—one of the escort by whom Mr. Butterworth had been deserted during his recent fray with the Apaches. About 15 miles beyond San Lazaro we reached the scene of the attack, of which I made a sketch.

As an illustration of the hazards of life in Arizona,

tending to show the causes which have hitherto retarded the development of the mines in that region, a brief narrative of Mr. Butterworth's adventure will not be uninteresting. The positions of honor and trust occupied by this gentleman as United States District Attorney of Mississippi, and more recently as Assistant Treasurer of the United States at New York, together with his recognized financial abilities, and his eminent services in the adjustment of the great Almaden difficulty, have rendered his name familiar to the public throughout the United States. Upon the completion of his business as President of the New Almaden Quicksilver Mines, he received, before his departure from the Pa-

THE SENTINEL.

SAM. F. BUTTERWORTH.

cific coast, an urgent request from some prominent capitalists in New York to visit the silver regions of Arizona, and report upon their condition and prospects.
At the same time he was appointed President of the
Arizona Mining Company, and every facility was ten-
dered him for the prosecution of his inquiries in the
new Territory. A spirit of adventure and a desire to
see something of a country which was beginning to attract so much attention, with a laudable ambition to aid
in its development, induced Mr. Butterworth to accept
these flattering propositions; and on or about the 1st of
December he left San Francisco by steamer for Guyamas. His party consisted of Mr. Küstel, metallurgist,
and Mr. Higgins and Mr. Janin, two young gentlemen
of scientific attainments.

Nothing of particular interest occurred between Guyamas and Santa Cruz. On their arrival there Mr. Küstel
and Mr. Higgins proceeded to the Patagonia mines with
instructions to cross over by the way of Santa Rita, and
meet Mr. Butterworth and Mr. Janin at Tubac.

K

On the same day of the massacre of Mills and Stevens
(December 29), about five or six hours later, Mr. Butterworth's party, which consisted of Mr. Janin, five
Mexicans, an American driver, and himself, were proceeding along the road a little beyond the deserted
ranch of Santa Barbara, when a band of Apaches, numbering some twenty-five or thirty, made an attack upon
them from the brush-wood fringing the bed of the Santa
Cruz River. As soon as the Indians appeared they commenced yelling like devils, and firing their guns and
bows and arrows, evidently with a view of producing
confusion at the first shock of the attack. Mr. Butterworth called upon his men to stand by the wagons, and
expressed his belief that they could easily whip the Apaches. The ambulance and baggage-wagons were driven
up to a mesquit-tree a little to the right of the road,
where the animals could be secured. Meantime the Indians had come out of their ambush and set fire to the
grass, which was tall and dry. The flames swept down
upon the wagons so rapidly that it was found necessary
to abandon the shelter of the tree, and make for a rise
of ground about two hundred yards distant, where the
position would be advantageous for a fight. Just as
they reached this point, the Indians shouting and yelling
all around them, the grass was again fired to windward,
and the flames swept down toward them with fearful
rapidity. Mr. Butterworth stood by the ambulance,
armed with a double-barrelled shot-gun, with which he
kept the Indians at bay for some time. Young Janin
had one of Henry's rifles, and fired five or six shots at
them, with what effect it was impossible to tell. While
these two were making vigorous battle the five Mexicans
were making tracks over the hills, so that when Butterworth undertook to muster his men he was unable to
see any of them. The last he saw of his American
driver, who up to this period was a great Indian fighter,
that valiant individual had unhitched one of the mules,
and was riding full tilt after the Mexicans—doubtless

ATTACK ON MR. BUTTERWORTH.

with a firm determination to bring them back if ever he overtook them. But neither he nor they appeared on the battle-ground again. The Indians perceiving their advantage, began to press in rather forcibly. Young Janin behaved with great coolness. Turning to Butterworth, who had reserved his fire for the last desperate struggle, he said, " Colonel, I can't see them very well— lend me your specs !" But the Colonel saw no speculation in that, and merely observed—" No; you had better save yourself, Janin." " I won't desert you," said Janin; " but they're getting rather too many for us, Colonel, and I think we had both better leave." By this time there were between twenty and thirty of the red devils yelling and shooting at rather close quarters. Under cover of the smoke they retired a short distance from the wagons, where they became separated. Janin made his escape into a ravine, where he lay concealed for some time; and Butterworth took his stand behind a mesquit-tree about a couple of hundred yards from the wagons, where he resolved to make as good a fight as possible.

The Indians set fire to the grass again, and the flames swept toward him with fearful rapidity, compelling him to climb the tree for security, and even then burning part of the legs off his pantaloons. Two bullet-holes which we found in the tree indicated that his position was by no means a pleasant one. Upon further examination of the spot where the wagons stood, we found various fragments of the plunder scattered around, such as sardine boxes, broken candle boxes, cartridges, patent medicines, and a bottle inscribed PHILIP ROACH, San Francisco. This was one of a number bearing a similar brand, containing some brandy reputed to be fifty years old. Mr. Butterworth, I have been informed, said it went harder with them to see these brutal wretches drink up his choice brandy than all the rest of the disaster put together. Plunder was evidently their chief object; for as soon as they had gutted the wagons of their contents they retired across the Santa Cruz River, where they held a grand carousal over their booty. They had succeeded in getting $1700 in gold coin and other property, amounting in the aggregate to about $3000. It is gratifying to know that this band of Apaches has since met with summary vengeance at the hands of the California Volunteers. Most if not all of them have been killed, and $700 of the money taken from their dead bodies. Had there been two resolute men with our unlucky friend when he heard them carousing across the river during the night, he could have had a more prompt and satisfactory settlement. These were the same Indians who had killed Mills and Stevens a few hours before. They had crossed over with the rifles of these unfortunate men from the Patagonia Cañon by the San Antonio Pass; and flushed with success, and seeing a small party approaching along the road, again lay in ambush, and made this new attack. It is supposed by some that there were Mexicans among them from Santa Cruz, and that they were in collusion with the escort; but of this I could find no proof, nor is it sustained by subsequent developments. The same band of Indians next day attacked a party of Mexicans on the Tubatama road, and killed four of the number, putting the rest to flight.

Butterworth was entirely unacquainted with the country, and in attempting to reach Santa Cruz lost his way. Janin and a small Yaqui boy, who had escaped during the fight, reached Santa Cruz without difficulty. Here a relief party was immediately gotten up by Señor Commodoran. Janin was apprehensive that his comrade might have been killed, but still had hopes of his safety, and sent a note by Commodoran announcing his own safe arrival.

Not very far above the Calabasas Ranch we reached the spot where Mr. Butterworth had camped after two days and nights of exposure and extreme suffering from cold, and where he was first seen by Commodoran. The

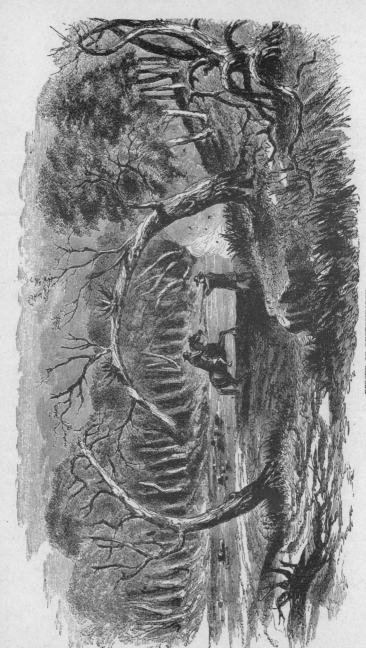

RESCUE OF BUTTERWORTH.

nights were intensely sharp. He had no blankets, and deemed it imprudent to light a fire, until he found it impossible to bear with the cold any longer. What his sufferings were in this wild region, surrounded by lurking foes, without food, without blankets, and beyond the reach, as he supposed, of all human aid, no man who has not travelled in Arizona can conceive. Two days and nights of such suffering as would have caused most men to despair had left their marks upon him. His throat was wrapped with straw, and he was evidently in a very bad condition. Up to this time he could not have wandered much less than fifty miles up and down the valley of the Santa Cruz. On the approach of Commodoran, supposing him to be a Sonoranian marauder, he raised his gun, and was about to kill him, when the frightened Mexican cried out, " *No tira! no tira! Yo Amigo! Amigo!*" Still Butterworth kept his gun pointed at him. " *Vamos!*" was all he could say in Spanish. Commodoran, with great sagacity, jerked up his horse's head, so as to keep it between him and the muzzle of the gun, and slowly approaching, held out Janin's note, shouting, " *No tira! Yo Amigo! Patagonia! Patagonia!*" The last was a lucky hit. The word " Patagonia " was familiar, and partially solved the mystery. Janin's note did the rest, and the most cordial greeting followed this inhospitable reception.

The return of Mr. Butterworth to Santa Cruz, where he procured a new outfit; the recovery of his ambulance and wagon; meeting with his friends Küstel and Higgins at Tubac; visit to the Cerro Colorado, and subsequent adventures on the road to Guyamas ; safe arrival at San Francisco ; return to New York ; continuance in the presidency, with entire control as resident manager, of the New Almaden Quicksilver Mines, as well as of the Arizona Silver Mines at Cerro Colorado, would furnish in detail an interesting sequel to his adventure with the Apaches.

Continuing our journey, we reached by noon the ranch

of the Calabasas, from which point we had diverged three weeks before on our route down into Sonora. All along the Santa Cruz River we passed through the richest ranges of pasture and farming land we had yet seen. Abundance of mesquit, cotton-wood, willow, and walnut is found in the river-bottoms, and the grass is so luxuriant that in many places it is difficult to travel out of the beaten track. We saw great quantities of deer and a few flocks of wild turkeys; but they are unaccountably wild—much more so than in populated countries. We supposed they were not accustomed to the presence of white men.

At an early hour in the afternoon we reached our former head-quarters at Tubac. It was a glorious sight to see the flag of our Union still floating from the old tower upon which we had raised it on the day of our departure for Sonora.

We were now almost entirely out of provisions and forage. A few days' rations only remained. It was necessary, therefore, to send down to Tucson for fresh supplies, and the freight-wagon, with an escort of ten men, was dispatched for that purpose. In the mean time I devoted a couple of days to writing up these rough notes of our adventures, and completing some sketches of the scenery on the way.

CHAPTER XXIII.

SANTA RITA.

A S five or six days would elapse before the return of our wagon from Tucson, a small party, consisting of Mr. Poston, Lieutenant Arnold, and myself, accompanied by ten men belonging to the escort, took advantage of the opportunity to visit the mines of the Santa Rita district. For this expedition we provided ourselves with a pack-mule for our provisions and carried our own blankets on horseback. Crossing the Santa Cruz at the foot of the milpas, opposite the town of Tubac, we followed an arroya for about four miles, when we ascended the right bank and entered a dry elevated plain, called in this country a mesa, or table, stretching almost as far as we could see north and south, and bounded on the east by the mountains of Santa Rita, and on the west by the Santa Cruz Valley and the mountains of Atacosa. It was a matter of surprise to most of us how luxuriant the grass was on this mesa, and what an inexhaustible support it affords for innumerable herds of cattle. No water, however, is to be found nearer than the Santa Cruz River and the cañons of the Santa Rita Mountains. The Pecacho on the left forms a bold and striking feature in the scene, rising like a massive fortress directly on the edge of the plain, and backed by the rugged ribs of the Santa Ritas, the two main peaks of which, called " the teats," form a prominent landmark to travellers for a circuit of over two hundred miles. Our trail over the mesa, otherwise monotonous, was pleasantly diversified by groves of palo-verde and bunches of cactus ; but apart from the peculiarity of the vegetation, it was a luxury to breathe the air. Nothing more pure or invigorating could exist upon earth. The unclouded sky and glowing tints of the mountains; the unbounded opulence of sunshine, which seemed to sparkle in atmospheric scintillations, inspired us with a perfect overflow of health and spirits; and it was no wonder we built many castles in the air, and revelled in dreamy regions of enchantment in which the glittering silver mines of Arizona played a prominent part.

At the first break of the mesa we struck an arroya, or rather rocky ravine, in which I noticed some very remarkable geological formations. A large area of the earth was covered by immense columns of sandstone, standing like the ruined colonnade of some grand old castle, many of them capped by prodigious boulders of rock, which no human power could have elevated to their present resting-places. How they came there, or how long they have thus stood battling with the elements, was beyond our ability to decide. Lieutenant Ives, in his admirable report on the Colorado, refers to similar geological phenomena in the region of the Great Cañon. I believe the theory of geologists is, that the earth has been washed away from these columns, leaving them standing in the open air as they stood in their natural strata underground.

Not far beyond the mesa we entered upon a rugged region, abounding in breaks and arroyas very rocky and difficult for our horses. In one of these desolate places we visited the spot where Mr. H. C. Grosvener, the last manager of the Santa Rita Mines, and the last of three managers whose fate was similar, was killed by the Apaches about two years ago. It appears that a wagon containing supplies had been sent out from Tubac and was on its way to the hacienda, when the men who accompanied it were attacked and killed. Mr. Grosvener and Mr. Pumpelly had passed the wagon and teamsters a few minutes before and proceeded to the hacienda. As the freight-party did not arrive within a reasonable time,

HACIENDA OF THE SANTA RITA MINING COMPANY.

Grosvener walked out alone to see what was the cause of the delay. The Apaches had meantime made their murderous attack on the teamsters and plundered the wagon; and were moving up the cañon, when they saw Grosvener coming, and immediately formed an ambush behind the rocks and shot him dead as he approached. His grave lies a few hundred yards from the head-quarters of the hacienda. A marble head-stone, upon which his name is inscribed, with the additional words, not uncommon in Arizona, "Killed by the Apaches," marks the spot. By the side of this grave is another head-stone, bearing the name of Mr. Slack, his predecessor, who lost his life by the same ruthless tribe of Indians. Another of the managers, also killed by the Apaches, lies buried at Tubac.

Early in the afternoon we reached the beautiful hacienda of the Santa Rita Company, now solitary and desolate. The houses have gone to ruin, and only a few adobe walls, furnaces, and the frame-work of the mill remain to mark the spot formerly so full of life and enterprise. It was sad to stand among these ruins and think how hard a fate had been the reward of nearly all the enterprising men who had built up this little community. A few years ago these houses, now empty and crumbling down in dusty fragments, were replete with busy life; the reduction works were in full blast, and every heart throbbed with the brightest anticipations of the future.

Mr. Poston, who had done more perhaps than any other man to develop the resources of this vast mineral region, had some depressing reflections as he gazed upon this scene of ruin. He had suffered too much, however, in Arizona, and seen too many reverses of fortune, to waste much time in retrospection. The future was still bright and promising. It would not be long before these tenements would be again inhabited, and the sounds of life and industry again enliven the place. With the necessary protection now promised, the Com-

SANDSTONE COLUMNS.

pany is prepared to re-establish the works; an experienced manager, Mr. Wrighteon,* who has had long experience in this region, is now on the way out, and probably not more than a few months will elapse before the mines and hacienda will be occupied by a large working force.

At the distance of a few hundred yards from the hacienda is a silver lead, situated strangely enough in the valley, close by the bed of the creek, upon which some explorations have been made. An assay of the ore, made in 1861, yielded $400 to the ton. Water is furnished by the mine itself, which is not considered a disadvantage in this country, where that element is the great desideratum.

A mile beyond we reached the foot of the Salero Mountain, near which, in a pleasant little valley, stand the ruins of the peon houses, once occupied by the operatives on the Salero Mine. The surrounding hills are clothed with a rich growth of grass, and there is an abundance of oak timber scattered over these hills and the adjacent mountains to supply the requisite fuel for the reduction works for many years. Water is found in an adjacent cañon a few hundred yards from the quarters, but not in sufficient quantities for stock. There would be no difficulty, however, in increasing the quantity by digging.

The Salero, which is the principal mine in this region, is situated in the side of a conical mountain of the same name, rising immediately from this little valley, and presenting some very striking mineral phenomena. The shaft is seen about a third of the way up its face, and is approached by a wagon road, which cuts and leaves exposed a number of veins running into the mountain in nearly the same direction, and all bearing more or less indications of silver.

This mine has long been known to the Mexicans, and

* This estimable gentleman has since been killed by the Apaches, not far from this very spot.

was worked more than a century ago under the direction
of the Jesuits at Tumacacori. A legend is told of the
derivation of the name, SALERO or Salt-cellar, which may
be worthy of record. On the occasion of a visit from the
Bishop of Sonora to Tumacacori, the good father in
charge of that establishment furnished, as in duty bound,
the best entertainment for his superior that his limited
resources would allow. The Bishop was delighted with
the sumptuous feast laid before him; the chickens, the
fruits, the wines were all excellent ; there was only one
thing lacking to complete his temporal happiness—a salt-
cellar ! The poor Padre was deeply mortified ; he had
forgotten all about the salt-cellar; in fact, had long
since forgotten the use of such luxuries. Salt-cellars
were as scarce in Arizona then as they are now. " Never mind !" said he, as a happy thought struck him,
" your Excellency shall have a salt-cellar to-morrow."
A few trusty men were dispatched to the Santa Rita
mountains, with orders to dig and smelt some silver ore
and make a salt-cellar, and sure enough, by dinner-time
the next day a massive salt-cellar was presented to the
Bishop, and from that day forth the mine out of which
the ore was dug was called the Salero. History does
not record, but there can be little doubt that the worthy
Bishop of Sonora enjoyed his dinner at Tumacacori.

During the afternoon, and on the following day, we
visited at least fifteen or twenty distinct mines, all partially opened and well tested, forming what might be
termed a perfect net - work of silver - bearing ledges.
Among these were the Salero, Bustillo, Crystal, Encarna-
tion, Cazador, and Fuller, each one of which has yielded,
under a very imperfect system of working, at the rate of
four to fourteen hundred dollars to the ton. This of
course was from selected ores. The average would
probably not fall short of two hundred dollars, though
sufficient work has not yet been done upon which to
base a reliable calculation. The assays and experiments
of such men as Küstel, Pumpelly, Booth, Garnett, Main-

THE SALERO MINE.

zer, Blake, Dr. Jackson of Boston, and others, demonstrate at least that there is a great abundance of rich ores in the Santa Rita district.

As a grazing country for cattle and sheep the valleys and foot-hills of the Santa Rita can not be surpassed. Grass of every variety known in Arizona covers the ground all the year, and there is practically no winter for live-stock. The climate is so mild, even in the months of January and February, that it is a positive luxury to sleep in the open air. Wood can be obtained in limited quantities in the neighborhood, and when that

A GRAVE ON THE SANTA CRUZ ROAD.

is exhausted the Valley of the Santa Cruz, only twelve miles distant, furnishes an inexhaustible supply. The mines abound in ores easy of reduction by smelting, and they are so situated that access to all of them by good roads can be had at a small expense. The transit to Tucson and Guyamas is over the best natural roads in the world, but will require military protection for some time to come.

Within the distance of eight miles lies the beautiful Valley of the Sonoita, which is watered by the river of the same name, and abounds in very promising gold and silver ledges. Some of the finest farming lands in the Territory lie along the borders of this stream. When Fort Buchanan was occupied, several families from Texas and the borders of Missouri lived in this valley; and I have been told the wheat and corn crops raised by them were absolutely wonderful. There can be no doubt that, with the protection afforded by the mines when in operation, the Sonoita Valley will be settled once more, and the soil again cultivated.

We took a ride over the intervening hills to see a gold ledge, called the " Tenaja," or " Tank," of which I made a sketch. The croppings are very fine; but I could not see any gold in them by the naked eye.

Late in the afternoon of the second day, having completed our tour among the mountains of the Santa Rita, we returned to Tubac, greatly pleased with our ramble, though somewhat tired and hungry. A bath in the Santa Cruz River refreshed us after our rough experience of the past few days; and it was not unpleasant to be once more within hail of a public highway, even though it brought us no news either from above or below. We were all anxious to hear from home. Nothing had reached us from " the States " for over two months. It might be that the war had come to an end, so little did we know or hear of the turmoil of strife or the excitement of speculation. Isolated as we were in a country fraught with dangers, it seemed strange how calm and peaceful the solitude around us looked. Not a stir, not a sound beyond the limits of our own encampment disturbed the intense quietude that reigned over the slumbering earth. Yet every thicket and ravine had its story of bloodshed and death, and around us lay the graves of murdered men!

CHAPTER XXIV.

POSTON'S NARRATIVE.

OUR sojourn at Tubac was pleasant enough, though rather monotonous. Hunting, fishing, and bathing occupied most of our time. It was a lazy, vagabond sort of life, very conducive to health, but not calculated to expand the intellectual faculties. The novelty of eating three good meals a day, and sleeping twelve hours every night, had partially worn away, and I sometimes began to think there was a torpor growing over my brain. I felt an intuitive disrelish for any kind of mental labor. In this extremity, destitute of amusing books, or indeed books of any kind, I appealed to my friend Poston—who, like Peter Schlemil, was ready at any moment to produce any thing in the range of human luxury—to furnish me with something in the way of light reading : a narrative of shipwreck, the murder of a ship's crew, the starvation of an exploring party—any thing, in short, of an amusing character, except statistics of the mineral products of Arizona.

A grim smile came over the expressive features of my friend at the tremendous absurdity of my request. Never at fault, however, he plunged his hand into his knapsack, and drew therefrom a curious medley of what he termed the necessaries of life : viz., a tobacco-pouch ; a tooth-brush ; two hair-brushes for his back hair ; a roll of assorted needles and buttons ; a dozen boxes of matches ; two old flannel shirts, a pair of socks, and a bottle of whisky, with many other strange and incongruous articles too numerous to mention. Finally, upon reaching the bottom, he drew forth a greasy, tattered old journal, containing, as he informed me with an air of triumph, the very kind of reading I wanted. It was a complete history of his first expedition to Arizona, and might be relied upon as strictly true, inasmuch as it was written by himself. I must confess, when Poston handed me his journal, I cast a despairing look at the confused mass of manuscript of which I had thus become the innocent recipient.

"Perhaps," said my friend, consolingly, "if you try a little whisky first, it will go easier."

"No," I answered, resolutely, "you have read some of my articles—I will be generous and make an earnest effort to worry through yours."

And now, should the gentle reader elect to share this hardship with me, as he has kindly shared others incident to Arizona life, he will find what I read in the following transcript from Poston's journal:

The ratification of a treaty with Mexico, in the year 1853, by which the United States acquired a part of Sonora, and settled the vexed questions of a former boundary and the liability of the United States for Indian depredations in Mexican territory under the eleventh article of the Treaty of "Guadaloupe Hidalgo," cost the Government the sum of ten millions of dollars in gold. It was not supposed at the time that this large sum had been expended for nothing. Politicians said the Territory had been acquired because it contained the only practicable pass for a railroad from the Atlantic to the Pacific; miners contended that the northern part of Sonora was the richest mineral country reached by the Spaniards; and all agreed that the new purchase enjoyed the finest climate on the continent, furnished perennial grazing, and abounded in wild game. The spirit of enterprise had been stimulated by the successful occupation of California, and the purchase of a new El Dorado by the Government of the United States enlisted a lively interest on the Pacific coast.

CHARLES D. POSTON.

The French had recently made an effort to get a lodg-ment in the new Territory under the leadership of a brave and adventurous young French Count—Raousset de Boulbon—who was afterward shot by the Mexicans at Guyamas.

On the 20th day of February, 1854, the British bark *Zoraida* sailed from the port of San Francisco for the port of Guyamas, in Sonora, with a party on board des-tined for the newly-acquired Territory. Among them were two men whose names afterward became identi-fied with its history—they were Charles D. Poston and Herman Ehrenberg, the one a native of Kentucky and the other a German.

Herman Ehrenberg was no ordinary man. He had migrated from his native Germany at a tender age, and landing in the metropolis of the western world had work-ed his way to New Orleans, where he was located when the Texas war of independence summoned the youth of America to that field of honor. He enlisted in the "New Orleans Grays" and was present at the battle of Goliad and Fanning's defeat, and was one of the few who survived the barbarous massacre of prisoners who surrendered to the Mexican authorities. At the close of the Texan struggle he returned to Germany and wrote an account in his native language of that interesting period, giving much information of the new country, which has induced a large emigration of Germans to Texas. He afterward returned to the United States, and in 1840, at St. Louis, joined a party which crossed the continent to Oregon. Thence he went to the Sandwich Islands, and after wandering in Polynesia for a few years returned to California in time to join Colonel Fremont in the effort to free California from Mexican rule. He remained in California until the new purchase from Mexico attracted his restless nature, and after a long and arduous service in Arizona, fell a victim to the treachery of the aboriginal race at Palm Springs, in the southern part of California, where he is buried.

The *Zoraida* was ill prepared for sea, and had a slow passage. On the thirty-second day, in trying to enter the port of Navachista in the Gulf of California, she stranded. The consternation of the passengers was great, and as the keen-scented sharks gathered around the doomed ship by hundreds, the passengers looked over the sides with some forebodings that they would soon be food for the monsters of the deep. The difficulty increased until the mainmast was sprung and the ship began to leak. So considering that even rats, which are not supposed to be endowed with reason, leave a sinking ship, it was deemed advisable to find a firmer footing than the few planks which divided us from hungry sharks. A few boats were manned, and with some personal baggage, arms, and a small supply of ship-biscuits, the passengers started for the sandy beach some few miles distant. The boats were run upon the comb of the tide and landed high and dry upon the beach, so that the passengers had time to get beyond the reflux wave of the tide in time to save their lives. It was nearly sundown when we found ourselves upon a lonely barren island, and the roaring of the waves and the breaking up of the ship

THE WRECK.

A BAD INVESTMENT.

did not add any thing to the cheerfulness of our land-ing.

An old Spaniard, named Don Manuel Rubio, immedi-ately set about prospecting the island for signs of the means of existence. He had not gone far before he fell on his knees, and holding his hands up to Heaven in thankfulness, fervently kissing the dry excrement of some wild cattle, rendered thanks to God that we had not been cast away upon an uninhabited island. Fol-lowing up the tracks so auspiciously found, we soon came upon a herd of wild cattle, and before midnight had the choice parts of one of them roasting before a blazing camp-fire.

This proved to be the Island of Navachista, near the eastern shore of the Gulf of California, about seven miles long by two miles and a half wide, and a distance of five or six miles from the main-land. We remained on this island about a week, preparing the means of transporting ourselves and our portable property to the mainland, and in the mean time lived on our sea-bread, roast beef, and the honey and wild fruits of the island. The island contained springs of sweet water, and we saw fine bolls of cotton growing wild in this uninhabited region. In passing up the estuary which led to the mainland we noticed that the oysters, which are abundant and very good here, had attached themselves to the shrubbery which composed a jungle, so that it was only necessary to go alongside with a boat and a long knife, or machete, and at low tide cut these shrubs loose from the root and haul into the boat a tree full of delicious oysters. This is the only place where oysters are known to grow upon trees.

At the landing-place we found a ranche occupied by a Mexican whose father had come there from the Philippine Islands in old Spanish times, and who was called a Manilla man. They were not at all surprised at our appearance, as they had evidently been accustomed to entertaining large parties of persons more suspicious than we appeared to be.

After resting here a few days, we put the whole country under contribution for animals to transport our party and their baggage to the nearest Mexican town, the city of Alamos. On the way to Alamos we stopped at "Mesquite," the estate of General La Vega in Sinaloa, and were treated with hospitality and kindness. The Fuerta River, which we crossed here, is a clear beautiful stream with a bottom of pebbles, a rare thing to see in Mexico. We next came to the Mayo River, inhabited by the Mayo Indians, a stalwart manly race who have often proved their prowess in a contest with the Mexicans. They inhabit a prolific and very delightful country, teeming with a luxuriant vegetation, and enjoy one of the finest climates in the world.

In about a week from the time of leaving the sea-coast we reached the old city of Alamos, famous in Spanish

L

times for its wealth and commercial enterprise.   The
Cathedral is very fine, and yet bears the Royal Arms of
Spain over the grand entrance.   The merchants of Alamos used to import directly from China, and had a large
trade with the smaller towns of Sinaloa and Sonora, but
its principal source of wealth was the rich silver mines
in the spurs of the Sierra Madre, which were worked
with great profit when cheap labor could be obtained
from the native Indians under the system of peonage
adopted and enforced by the Spanish Government.

We arrived in Alamos on Sunday, and caused some
excitement in this quiet old town, as so large a party of

CABALLERO AND SÉNORITA.

Americans had never ventured so far interior before. It presented the appearance of a primitive Mexican city, with all the customs and costumes of a people who have little or no intercourse with the outside world. We obtained comfortable quarters, and soon enjoyed the indescribable luxury of a bath. The baths are tanks in the gardens supplied with water by the acequias, or canals, which are used for irrigation; and to add to the luxury, and give them an Oriental appearance, they are generally shaded by orange-trees, which at this season drooped with the luscious fruit into our very mouths as we enjoyed the luxury of the cool water and the balmy air.

A little after night-fall, as we were sitting in front of our quarters congratulating ourselves upon our escapes by sea and land, the ominous tread of a file of soldiers was heard marching in our direction, and they soon grounded arms in front of our door, when the commanding officer stepped forward and politely summoned us to appear forthwith before the Alcalde and give an account of our sudden and unceremonious appearance in this peaceful and loyal part of the Mexican Republic. Fortunately for us the Alcalde was a gentleman of wealth, intelligence, and liberality — old José Almada, the owner of the rich silver mines of Alamos. We had American passports, and my friend Rubio, who had offered his devotions over the first sign of life on the Island of Navachista, had given me a letter saying that we were not filibusters, but emigrants to the new Territory who had been stranded with him on the island, and asking for us the hospitality and protection of the officers of the Mexican Government. We were treated with great courtesy and furnished with letters of security to protect us from future interruption.

After resting a few days in Alamos we started for Guyamas by the road leading through the Yaqui country, or lands of the Yaqui Indians, a large tribe of semi-civilized Indians inhabiting the most fertile lands of

Sonora and living in comfort and abundance. They are patriarchal in habits and yet preserve the hospitality of a primitive people. They cultivate the soil, raise sugar-cane, make sugar, raise cotton, and weave a strong common cotton-cloth; wheat, corn, and vegetables grow with very little cultivation. They have large flocks of sheep, and weave the wool into serapes or rude blankets; have horses, mares, mules, cattle, hogs, goats, and poultry in abundance, and seem as happy as Diogenes in his tub. The relic of a religion introduced by the Jesuits remains among them, and churches in every village attest the zeal and industry of these pioneers of Christianity. The Yaquis have never been subdued by either the Spanish or Mexican Governments, and yet preserve a quasi independence. The wars with the Yaquis have been some of the fiercest which the Mexicans of Sonora and Sinaloa have been engaged in, and some of the most valiant acts have been performed by these unknown aborigines of this remote region of the western world.

In about ten days after leaving Alamos we arrived at the city of Guyamas, a miserable Mexican sea-port town, containing at that time about 3500 inhabitants. Guyamas is shut in from the Gulf, as well as from the winds, by high rugged hills of black trap-rock, entirely destitute of vegetation, and reflecting the intense rays of the sun until the place seems like a huge bake-oven. The usual sea-breeze comes in from the Gulf in the evening, but unless this is from the quarter directly up the channel, and avoids the hills, it is suffocating, and raises clouds of dust, which drive the inhabitants to the interior of the houses at the very time in the evening when they wish exercise and fresh air. The harbor of Guyamas is good and entirely safe; very much the shape of the harbor of Acapulco and about one-third its size. The soundings around the mole are two to three fathoms, and increase in the middle of the bay to five, six, and seven; but the area of deep water is very small and distant from the shore. The country around Guyamas for a semi-circle of one hundred miles is a blasted, barren desert, entirely destitute of wood, water, or grass, producing only cacti and a stunted growth of mesquit. The water at Guyamas is all procured from wells, and has a brackish unpleasant taste, and generally causes temporary disease with those unaccustomed to its use. From Guyamas we passed over this hard barren country to Hermosillo, the principal town of Sonora and one of the most beautiful cities in the northern part of Mexico, if not on the whole continent of America. The distance is a fraction over one hundred miles, through a plain bounded by wild, desolate, and rugged mountains, destitute of wood, grass, or running water.

The city of Hermosillo is situated on the Sonora River, in the valley of Horcasitas, about sixty miles from the Gulf of California. This valley is about four miles wide at this place and continues a south-western course to the Gulf. The soil is very productive, and near the city is highly cultivated. The principal crop is wheat, of which the valley produces about eighty thousand bushels per annum. There is a great abundance of fruits—grapes, melons, oranges, figs, limes, lemons, citrons, peaches, pomegranates, bananas, and dates. The vineyards are extensive and beautiful, producing about twenty-five hundred barrels of brandy, and a corresponding quantity of wine. Cotton and sugar have also been cultivated here to a considerable extent. The fertility of the bottom-land is extraordinary; in fact, in this salubrious climate and rich soil any kind of produce can be raised with very little labor, the fine flowing river affording always abundant water for irrigation. The city of Hermosillo contains many large and costly houses, built of stone, brick, or adobes, and finished and furnished in the interior in the best European style. It has a large trade with the northern portion of the State, and is the principal distributing point as well as dépôt for the mineral and agricultural products of the country. The forwarding and shipping business is done from Guyamas.   The population in 1845 was estimated by the Secretary of State at nearly 18,000, but has decreased since that time by emigration to California and other deteriorating causes. The climate is dry and warm, the thermometer ranging from 80° to 100°, but the place is considered very healthy and free from all epidemics.   There is always an evening breeze from the Gulf, which, coming over the valley covered with verdure, is refreshing and delightful.   There is a dam across the river above the city for the purpose of turning off the water into numerous acequias (canals) for the purpose of irrigating, cleansing, and cooling the city.   These are trained through the streets, gardens, and yards of the city, affording an abundant supply of water for all the purposes of life, and adding very much to the beauty, cleanliness, and health of the city.   There is a beautiful Alameda at the northern end of the city, and a large Plaza surrounded with shade-trees and amply provided with rows of stuccoed stone settees.

A beautiful view of the city of Hermosillo and the surrounding country may be obtained from a large granite mountain on its northern side, or the domes of its magnificent churches which rise high above the spacious mansions of the inhabitants.   The city lies spread at your feet, with its vineyards and orange gardens, surrounded by wheat-fields and orchards, while the beautiful valley stretches off to the west, covered with verdure, ornamented with villas, and blooming in beauty with its delicate productions.   The river flows through this valley, lending its refreshing waters for the irrigation of the surrounding country; in fact, its body and force are so diminished by this absorption, that in summer-time the remainder never finds its way to the Gulf, but forms a lake, or cienaga, about half-way between the city and the Gulf; but in the rainy season the river forms a bold strong body of water, scarcely fordable at Hermosillo, and emptying into the Gulf of California opposite the Island of

Tiburon. This island forms the western protection of the Bay of San Juan Bautista.

The entrance to this harbor is formed by the northern end of the Island of Tiburon and a point of the main-land, called Sergeante Point, making out south, leaving a channel of one mile or a mile and a half wide. The bay then makes around this point northwardly about one mile and a half, being skirted by a ridge from the aforesaid point of land, protecting it from the ocean. There is also a growth of mesquit along the western side of the ridge, or spur, which afford an agreeable shade. The bay meanders around eastwardly, when a smaller bay, or estuary, makes in to the northeast, of sufficient size for small boats, called Cockle Harbor. The bay is here about four miles wide, has the appearance of being deep water, and is well protected and sheltered on all sides. It continues south-west the whole length of the Island of Tiburon, forming a kind of sound, and meets the Gulf again at the lower end of the island, being there only about two miles wide and quite shallow.

It would be practicable to connect the island with the main-land at this place by a pier or breakwater, which would tend to increase the depth of water in the bay, and add to its security in storms, but would not, in my opinion, result in any benefit except as a means of defense, as the island seems placed there by nature to protect and defend the main-land from the winds and waves, and may be as well prepared for artificial defense against elements of the same character. Its usefulness or adaptability to commercial purposes does not occur to me, but its necessity as a natural or artificial fortification for the protection of the main-land is striking and apparent.

The Bay of San Juan Bautista remains in precisely the same condition which it occupied before the discovery of the continent or the conquest of the country by the Spaniards. The country adjacent was occupied by the most fierce, warlike, and sanguinary tribe of Indians ever known. These are called Ceris, and are supposed to be of Asiatic origin; the Mexicans believe they are descendants of Tartars, and their idiom is said to resemble that language. They have always used poisoned arrows, which are said to produce death. This tribe has now, however, by continual warfare and the many expeditions made against them by the Mexicans, been reduced to the number of fifty or sixty warriors. These with their families reside in a village on the main-land opposite the southern end of the island, and live principally by fishing and hunting; but in case of difficulty with the Mexicans, they take to the islands adjacent in the Gulf. They are deadly in their hostility against Mexicans, but disposed to be friendly with the Americans. In a late expedition the Mexicans captured the Chief's wife and sent her to Mazatlan, at whose loss they seemed very much grieved, and offered any service or reward for her recovery. They are very miserable, and offer fish, oysters, etc., for shirts and whisky. They do not understand the use of fire-arms, but their poison-dipped arrows are sufficiently destructive. These arrows are made of cane, tipped with feathers, and pointed with bone. The point is reversed in the cane, for protection, until ready for use. The points are poisoned by dipping them in the liver of some animal which has been saturated with the venom of rattlesnakes, scorpions, and tarantulas, which abound on the island.

A more lengthy and accurate description of the island will be found in the Report of Señor Don Tomas Spence, now a Captain in the Mexican Navy, which is entitled to full credit, as he is a very intelligent gentleman.

The Bay of San Juan Bautista has never been surveyed by the Spanish or Mexican Governments, consequently nò accurate information can be given of its capacity or surroundings. It was discovered by a Spanish navigator named Bruja, and sometimes bears his

name.   Lieutenant Hardy, of the British Navy, visited
this harbor during a cruise in the Gulf of California in
1825.   Captain Stanley, of the American sloop of war
St. Mary's, anchored in this harbor during the war
with Mexico in 1847, and found abundant anchorage
for his vessel, and plenty of fresh water on shore for re-
plenishing his casks.   He made an able report to the
Secretary of the Navy at that time upon the advantages
of the harbor and island, accompanied by maps, which
information was favorably acknowledged by the Department, and instructions issued that they should be
taken possession of, which, however, was prevented by
the Treaty of Peace.

I am informed by merchants of Sonora that this harbor has been always used for landing contraband goods,
and that large vessels from England had landed whole
cargoes of goods there, which were then packed or
hauled into Hermosillo, and to other towns in the northern part of Sonora, as there is no port of entry north of
Guyamas.   I was also informed by a very intelligent and
once wealthy merchant of Sonora that it was a better
harbor than Guyamas, and that many cargoes of goods
from Europe, as well as from China and South America,
had been landed there and hauled through the country,
and that a great deal of silver had been exported from
the country through the same channel to save the ex-
port duty.   The harbor abounds in oysters, fish, and
game, and the main-land is a rich sandy loam, well
sprinkled with the ever-green mesquit.

It is protected to the south-west by the island, as
heretofore mentioned, and to the north-west by the termination of a chain of mountains of which the spur
runs down to a point on the water opposite the northern end of the island, protecting the harbor entirely
from north-westers or south-westers, the only destructive winds which prevail in this latitude.

There is sufficient timber, stone, and water in the immediate vicinity, and if necessary the Sonora River could

be brought in a canal to any given point on the bay. The back country is the rich and prolific valley bounding the Sonora River to its head-waters, along which the principal estates of the country are located, and a large majority of the towns and villages, including Hermosillo and the capital of the State (Ures). The population along this river from its head to its mouth exceeds fifty thousand souls.

After returning to Hermosillo I remained at the hacienda of Señor Artiasarana two weeks. I then made an excursion, occupying a month, through the silver mines in the north-western portion of the State. Many of them are undoubtedly very rich, and will some day be worked with good machinery and yield a handsome and permanent income on investments. Interests of one-half were frequently offered, in consideration of furnishing machinery and means, from twenty-five hundred to five thousand dollars. Many excellent arrangements of this kind could be made now. These mines are intrinsically of immense value, and much more permanent and regular in the yield than the mines of California. I returned to Hermosillo the 1st of June, having now been in the country three months without having any definite news of the progress of the treaty then under consideration. The country was in a very unhappy condition, and nothing further could be done to facilitate my views at that time.

I learned at this time that Colonel Gray, the surveyor of the "Texas Railroad Company," had come down as low as Altar in Sonora, and was exploring for a port on the Gulf of California. I immediately made up a company of Mexicans and Americans for the purpose of exploring the Gulf of California above the line of 31° north latitude, where it was then proposed our purchase should strike the Gulf of California. I started from Hermosillo with a company of fifteen men and twenty-two animals, well armed and provisioned for the journey. On arriving at Altar (latitude 30° 45') we

learned that Gray had been there and made observations. There is a port on the Gulf, about sixty miles
south-west of Altar, called the Ensenada de Lobas, in latitude 30° 15′ 25″ — longitude 112° 30′. This is little
better than an open roadstead, protected slightly on the
north-west by a sand-spit making out into the Gulf. It
is approached over a desert sand-beach, and can never
become a place of any importance. A reconnaissance of
the place for its capacities as a port has been made by
Captain Tomas Spence, and an accurate report made to
the Government in 1853, a copy of which Governor Gandara kindly furnished me before setting out. Colonel
Gray had gone on to Sonoita, about one hundred and
fifty miles above Altar, to which place we continued,
where we learned he had made an exploration of the
coast and gone on to California.

We followed Gray's trail down to the coast, a distance of about fifty miles over the Pinacate Mountains,
and then through about fifteen or twenty miles of sand-
hills to the beach. There is neither fresh water, wood,
grass, nor vegetation of any kind here—nothing but a
desert of sand-hills as far as the eye can reach up and
down the Gulf. The desert extends at least two hundred and fifty miles along the coast by about twenty-five
to thirty miles wide. There is no vestige of a port.
The channel of the Gulf is on the Lower California side.
We travelled along this miserable shore, over these in-
terminable sand-hills—having no grass for our animals,
and nothing but the brackish salty water obtained by
digging wells in the sand along the sea-shore—for a
week, when we reached the mouth of the Colorado
River. We now abandoned all hope of finding a port
in the Gulf or even a location for a town at the mouth
of the river. The mouth of the river is worse than the
shore of the Gulf, if such a thing could be possible, as
the land is subject to overflow for many miles around,
and is all cut up with sloughs and backwater. This
character of country prevails until within four or five

miles of the junction of the Gila and Colorado Rivers, frequently overflowed and consequently sandy and barren. We now turned out to the California Road and returned to Sonoita for the purpose of recruiting, as both men and animals had suffered severely during this horrible expedition, especially from using brackish water.

After recruiting at Sonoita for a week, we travelled through the country of the Papago Indians. This tribe is a branch of the Pima family which formerly inhabited the northern part of Sonora and the country along the Gila River, but having accepted the doctrine of Christianity from the Jesuit missionaries, and received the rite of baptism, they are now called Papagoes—from Bapconia, which in the Pima language means baptized. They cut their hair short and adopt the customs, manners, and costume of civilization. They live in villages, have fine fat cattle, horses, mules, and poultry, and are docile, honest, and industrious ; more so in fact than their neighbors and former teachers, the Mexicans. Their country is barren and unproductive, but so salubrious that they could not be persuaded to leave it for any other part of the world.

Arriving in the Valley of the Santa Cruz, we found the old town of Tubac abandoned by its Mexican garrison and the population which had been dependent upon them for protection against the Apache Indians, the most fierce and barbarous tribe of which we have any account. As the houses in Tubac were in a tolerably good state of preservation, we occupied them for head-quarters during the ensuing winter, and passed the time in exploring the surrounding country for silver mines. The winter season here proved very mild, and our animals were subsisted upon the nutritious grasses which abounded on the hill-sides.

The Valley of the Santa Cruz is a very rich body of land, and with irrigation produces two crops annually— corn in the spring and wheat in the autumn. Wild game in abundance could be procured in the immediate vicinity,

A MOUNTAIN TRAIL.

and by Christmas we had such a store of bear meat, deer, antelope, and fat wild turkeys, that no apprehension of short rations disturbed our enjoyment. We even essay-ed to give an entertainment to our neighbors from So-pori, Tucson, and Magdalena, places distant from twelve to eighty miles, these being the nearest settlements. Old

Colonel Douglass came over from Sopori, booted and spurred in Mexican style, bringing a motley retinue, among them a harper and "fiddlers three." The festivities were continued during Christmas week; and, in order to relieve our guests of any anxiety about the abundant resources of the larder, a dozen fat turkeys were dressed and hung up on the joist over the table in the spacious dining-hall. The best liquid we could place before our guests was a native production from the juice of the maguey, called mescal. It made punches nearly equal to Scotch whisky, and solaced many a winter's evening in this remote lap of the mountains.

In the course of a few months several hundred people had gathered around Tubac and engaged in planting; the mines developed wonderful richness; and traders from Sonora, New Mexico, and California came to supply all our wants with the productions of foreign lands in exchange for the silver bars which we made "current with the merchant."

Thus was formed the first settlement of Americans in this remote region, but it was destined to pass away in a few years, its very history falling into insignificance amid the destruction of civil war, which exposed these remote and feeble settlements to the ravages of the Apaches, the depredations of the Mexicans, and the lawlessness of our own countrymen, leaving no history but the hasty monuments erected over the new-made graves of these brave and hardy pioneers.

END OF POSTON'S NARRATIVE.

EL ARASTRA.

CHAPTER XXV.

REVANTON AND SOPORI.

NO tidings of our wagon, which we had dispatched to Tucson for provisions and forage, having been received, up to the morning of the sixth day, we resolved to leave Tubac and proceed on our journey toward Sopori and the mines of the Cerro Colorado. It was our intention to camp at the Revanton Ranch, eight miles below Tubac, where we hoped to meet the wagon on its way up; nor were we disappointed, for some four or five Papago Indians, of whom the chief was our friend Captain José, came dashing up with the pleasing intelligence that the wagon and detachment were close behind. These doughty warriors were all armed, some with old muskets and others with bows and arrows, and presented something of a stylish appearance in their mixed costume of military coats, serapas, loose pantaloons, rawhide sandals, and straw sombreros. One of them, a very important old gentleman in his own estimation, was peculiarly distinguished for the brilliancy of his uniform. He wore a blue cloth coat with two rows of buttons down in front and the same number on the back; so that, with a tremendous shock of hair, which fell loosely over his face and neck, it was difficult to tell, at a short distance, whether he was riding with his face or his back to the horse's head. Nor was the illusion quite dissipated by the appearance of his legs, which were quite bare, and fortunately so colored by nature that they corresponded exactly with the skin of his horse. We suspected that this doughty old warrior had so fashioned and equipped himself as a decoy for the enemy, whom he doubtless in-

tended to deceive with the appearance of a retreat, when
in reality he was making an advance.

Captain José, although of higher rank, was less osten-
tatiously accoutred, having only a plain blue coat with
brass buttons in front, white cotton pantaloons, buckskin leggings, and moccasins of the same, all a little the
worse for the wear and tear of travel. The rest of the
party were stout young fellows of the tribe, who had
probably distinguished themselves in some of the late
forays against the Apaches. Mr. Poston had written
down to San Xavier, to the Padre Messea, to send up
these chiefs and warriors, in order that they might accompany us on our proposed tour through the region of
the Papago villages lying west of the Baboquivori.
We found their services very useful as scouts, guides, and
interpreters. Captain José speaks good Spanish, and is
a man of excellent character, remarkable for his sobriety
and good sense. Of all the Papagoes he is perhaps the
most reliable and intelligent.

We soon had the pleasure of meeting the wagon and
escort, by which we anxiously expected food both for
body and mind. Only those who have been, as we were,
nearly two months without a word of news from home,
can appreciate the eagerness with which we crowded
around the Sergeant and asked for the letters and newspapers; and only such can appreciate our disappointment, when we found that we had neither news nor
newspapers of a later date than that of our departure
from Tucson. Private letters there were for some of
our party, but nothing that threw the least light upon
the progress of the war. For all the information we
had, we might as well have been in Timbuctoo or China.
I could not but marvel that there existed within the
limits of the United States a spot so completely isolated
from the civilized world. Military expresses are all
that now serve the purposes of communication in Arizona. So far as they go they are a great convenience;
but it is hard for private citizens engaged in business to

be dependent upon such precarious means of intercourse with the outside world. At this moment Arizona is, practically, more distant from San Francisco and New York than either of those cities is from China or Norway. I made the trip from Germany to Iceland and back much more easily, and with much less expense and loss of time, than from San Francisco to Sonora and back. Now that the Governor and his staff have located the capital, and put the wheels of the Territorial Government in operation, it is to be hoped that this great desideratum will attract the attention of Congress. Without mails and newspapers Arizona will never be a thriving country. At the time of our visit there was not a printing-press in the Territory. Mr. Secretary M'Cormick has since established the *Arizona Miner*, a very excellent little paper, edited with spirit and ability. It is the pioneer of a new and more enlightened era, and well deserves the patronage of the public. Newspapers and mails will of course follow the settlement of the country in natural order; but since the Territory of Arizona, with its vast mineral resources, is subject to much greater difficulties of position and settlement than any other within our limits, and has received as yet but little consideration or aid from Government, it seems peculiarly deserving of encouragement from our Federal authorities. So far as I have seen, the people generally are loyal to the Union; the recent election, showing a large Union majority, has sufficiently determined that. Some discontent has heretofore prevailed against the military department for alleged neglect of protection; but measures have been taken to remedy the evils complained of. The recent vigorous and liberal measures taken by the departments in Washington to develop the resources of the Territory will undoubtedly result in a large increase of immigration.

It was our intention to camp at Revanton; but upon our arrival there we found it entirely destitute of water. There was not so much as a pool left in the Santa Cruz

River from which we could satisfy our own thirst, much less water our animals. Thus it is that the rivers of Arizona disappear at the most unexpected points. The oldest Mexicans and Indians of our party had never before known the Santa Cruz to be dry at Revanton. From other causes this fine ranch has been deserted for several years. It was at one time claimed and occupied by Elias Brevoort, who built upon it a fine adobe house, with a large corral and garden, at the crossing of the river, where the road takes off to Sopori and the Cerro Colorado. This palatial edifice occupies a square of several hundred varas, and is perhaps the largest and most imposing private residence in Arizona. Sixteen thousand dollars were expended in the building of the house and improvement of the premises. Mr. Brevoort, as I was informed, had some connection with the Quarter-master's Department of the Army, and was sent down into Chihuahua to recover some absconding wagons and teams belonging to the United States Government. The wagons and teams remained there, and so did Brevoort. Subsequently " old Jimmy Caruthers," a frontiersman, squatted upon the ranch, and cultivated it to some extent, raising a good crop of corn and wheat; but the Apaches stole his cattle and broke him up. The first and last time I saw this eccentric character was on the rise of the mesa near Oatman's Flat, as mentioned in one of the earlier chapters of this narrative.

The Revanton is now a ruin; the house is deserted— a death-like silence reigns over the premises. The grass is crisped, the trees are withered, the bed of the river is dry, the sap of life seems to have deserted the place with its inhabitants, and left nothing but ruin and decay to mark the spot. Yet a more beautiful region of country than that occupied by this ranch it would be hard to find anywhere. It is naturally rich in vegetation; the climate is unsurpassed, and during the season of rain, when the earth is clothed in verdure, it must be one of the loveliest spots in the world. But without water, of what avail are all the advantages of soil and climate? The road by which we travelled on leaving the Revanton had not been much used of late, and was difficult to trace amid the sandy arroyas and patches of mesquit and cactus. Our Mexican vaqueros, however, were never long at fault; their instinct on the subject of roads and trails is equal to that of a dog.

A delightful ride of five or six miles through a broad, rich valley of grass, pleasantly diversified with groves of mesquit and palo-verde, brought us to a narrow pass, on the right elevation of which stand all that remains of the buildings and store-houses of the Sopori Land and Mining Company. Little is now left save ruined abobe walls and tumbled-in roofs. As usual, not a living thing was to be seen. Silence and desolation reigned supreme.

At the time Colonel James W. Douglass lived here the Sopori was one of the most flourishing ranches in the country. He had herds of fat cattle ranging over the pastures; fields of grain and vegetables in the rich bottom that lies just in front of the dwelling-house; domestic animals and fowls of various kinds; and could always afford the traveller a generous reception. In fact the hospitality of " old Jimmy Douglass " was noted even in this country, where hospitality has long been considered one of the necessary virtues of existence. Prior to 1861, in the palmy days of Phil Herbert, Ned M'Gowan, and their confrères, all men who had acquired, by their industry or otherwise, houses and homes, and who had food to eat and blankets to lend, were expected, as a matter of course—indeed, compelled, from the necessity of the case—to lodge and feed (and often to clothe and lend money to) all other men who chose to go drifting about the country without means, and without the desire to procure any by honest labor.

This is the case to some extent in all new countries; but it was especially the case at Tubac, where the private quarters of the chief manager of the " Sonora Exploring and Mining Company " were invaded without ceremony, and their occupant never permitted to enjoy an hour's solitude, except when away from his own house. To feed the hungry and clothe the naked was his legitimate business, since he was one of the few men in the country who had enterprise enough to possess food and raiment; but when, after the exercise of many Christian virtues, in addition to those of patience and hospitality, it became pretty generally understood that "Poston's Hotel" got up about the best dinners and beds in the country, Tubac became a favorite place of resort for the various adjacent communities. Neither board nor lodging cost any thing at this agreeable place, which was a matter of some moment, considering the high price of provisions and the general scarcity of funds. Poston's was famous as the best "hotel" of the kind in Arizona, and being on the public highway to and from Sonora, had by far the largest number of "boarders." It was not a profitable institution in a pecuniary point of view. To be boarded out of one's house is a common calamity, but a few more such boarders as Poston had would have boarded him out of his boots.

The Sopori Ranch, although at present uninhabited, possesses advantages as a mining and grazing region which have long since given it a reputation in Sonora. Embracing over twenty square leagues of mountain and valley, it comprises within its boundaries some of the best silver and copper lodes and cattle-ranges in the country. During the greater part of the year it is well watered, but there are times when the water is scarce, except in the vicinity of the head-quarters, where the supply is never-failing. By means of acequias a considerable extent of bottom-land of a very productive quality has already been cultivated. The usual cereal crops thrive well here, and esculents are especially fine. Wood of many valuable varieties—such as oak, ash, walnut, cotton-wood, willow, and mesquit—grows in the ravines and along the margin of the creek. Lying twelve miles south of Tubac, bordering on the Mission lands of San

Xavier del Bac to the north, and distant but forty-five miles from Tucson, on the highway to the Cerro Colorado, Arivaca, and Sonora, it possesses great advantages of location and a climate unrivalled for its salubrity.

I spent the afternoon rambling over the hills, making sketches of the scenery, which at this season of the year is Italian in its atmospheric coloring. Indeed that land which possesses the "fatal gift of beauty" is fairly outrivalled by the Sopori.

The principal mine, which I also visited, is about two miles from the head-quarters. As yet the lode has been but little explored. A shaft has been sunk, from which some very rich ore has been taken, portions of it in small particles of pure silver.

I do not believe, however, from my own casual observation, that the mother vein has yet been struck. The average of ores taken out, and upon which experiments have been made, demonstrates a yield of $150 to the ton, and this by the rudest process of smelting. Selected specimens have yielded $700 to the ton. Still the vein does not appear to me sufficiently defined, at the point now reached, to warrant the belief that large results can be expected without further exploration. Mr. Bartlett, I believe, has taken a great interest in the development of this region, and has organized a company at Providence, Rhode Island, for the working of the mines on an extensive scale.

The whole country bears strong indications of rich mineral deposits. The Mexicans for many years past have worked some gold placers in the ravines of the neighboring mountains; and we saw the remains of arastras, where these people had formerly ground and smelted silver ores. All this district of country needs development. With capital, energy, and patience it must eventually become one of the most valuable mining districts in the Territory.

It was late when we returned to our pleasant camping-place under the wide-spreading nogales, or walnut-

trees, by the margin of the creek. The grass was luxuriant, and our animals enjoyed it with amazing zest.
A fat deer, which we had killed on the way, enabled us
to recompense ourselves for the fatigues of our tramp
over the hills. When we turned-in upon our soft, grassy
beds, and looked up at the clear star-spangled sky above
us, there were some among us, I have no doubt, who
thought that a home in such a charming wilderness
would not be unpleasant, if one could be assured of
such peace among men as reigned over the quiet earth.
But peace like that is not for the races that inhabit this
world. I lay for hours thinking over the unhappy condition of our country, and a profound sadness oppressed
me as vision after vision of bloodshed and suffering and
death passed like some funeral cortége through the silent watches of the night. Far away, friends were falling in sanguinary strife; everywhere God's beautiful
earth was desecrated by the wickedness of man; even
here, in this remote wilderness, we were not exempt
from the atrocities of a savage foe. We had seen the
recent tracks of an Apache band on the road; and the
cautious manner in which our animals were picketed
and the guard stationed sufficiently manifested the insecurity of life and property in this region.

CHAPTER XXVI.

AN early start enabled us to reach by noon the Heintz-elman Mine—or, as it is more commonly called, the " Cerro Colorado." This celebrated mine belongs to a company of New York capitalists known as the " Arizona Mining Company." The distance by the road from Tubac is as follows: To Revanton, 8 miles; Sopo-ri, 5; Cerro Colorado, 11; total, 24 miles. A much shorter road could be made across the foot-hills of the Atacosa range of mountains, but the work would be at-tended by considerable expense. From Sopori, the road now used is the public highway to Altar, Saric, and oth-er points in Sonora, and will probably form a branch of the projected route to Port Libertad, on the Gulf of California. It runs through a broad open valley abound-ing in groves of walnut, oak, ash, and mesquit, fringing the bed of a creek which is usually dry at this season. Numerous arroyas extending down from the gulches of the neighboring mountains, in which the sands are drifted by the floods of former years, show that the country is not always so destitute of water as it is at present. The valley extends nearly all the way up from the Sopori to the foot-hills of the Cerro Colorado. It is covered with a luxuriant growth of grass, and is one of the finest grazing regions for cattle and sheep I have seen in the Territory. Sufficient water for stock can be had anywhere along the bed of the creek by digging a few feet. On the north side there is a rise of several hundred feet to the level of a mesa, which ex-tends, as far as the eye can reach, toward San Xavier

del Bac. This plateau is dry and rocky, but produces
fine grama grass, and furnishes an inexhaustible range
for sheep. To the southward lie the rolling hills that
join the Atacosa Mountains. These are also covered
with grass, and dotted with palo-verde, mesquit, and
cactus. Deer are abundant in this region, having been
but little disturbed during the past few years. We
killed two as we travelled along the road, and saw
many more. Wild turkeys, rabbits, quails, and other
game also abound in great numbers, so that we had no
difficulty in keeping our camp well supplied.

A prominent landmark for several miles before reaching the head-quarters of the Arizona Mining Company
is the conical hill of reddish-colored rock called by the
Mexicans the " Cerro Colorado," from which the district derives its name. Standing on a rise of rolling
land, isolated from the neighboring mountains, it presents in its conformation and coloring a singularly picturesque feature in the scene. Back of this curious
peak to the north lies a rugged range of mountains, up-
thrown, as it were, out of the earth by some tremendous
volcanic convulsion. In this the strangest confusion of
outlines and colors prevails; it is literally a chaotic
wilderness of rocks, boulders, porphyritic pillars, masses
of lava and scoria; weird and terrible, yet magnificent
in the immensity of its desolation. Well has it been
named by the old Spaniards the *Mal Pais;* yet no part
of God's creation is utterly valueless to man. By that
system of compensation which everywhere prevails,
and of which Arizona furnishes some of the most remarkable examples, this desolate range of mountains
abounds in veins of gold and silver, some of which have
been profitably worked by the Mexicans. As yet, however, it has been but little explored by the Americans;
and it would be difficult to estimate what may be the
value of these deposits of precious minerals. Future
exploration will doubtless develop them.

I was surprised on our arrival at the mine to see the

M

amount of work which had been done at this place. The head-quarters lie on a rise of ground, about a mile distant from the foot of the Cerro Colorado, and present at the first view the appearance of a Mexican village built around the nucleus of a fort.

Scarcely three years ago the hacienda of the Cerro Colorado presented probably the most striking scene of life and energy in the Territory. About a hundred and twenty peons were in the employ of the Company; the works were in active operation; vast piles of ore were cast up daily from the bowels of the earth; wagons were receiving and discharging freights; the puff and whistle of the steam-engine resounded over the hills; herds of cattle, horses, mules, and other stock ranged over the valleys. At the time of our visit it was silent and desolate—a picture of utter abandonment. The adobe houses were fast falling into ruin; the engines were no longer at work; the rich piles of ore lying in front of the shafts had been sacked and robbed by marauding Mexicans; nothing was to be seen but wreck and ruin, and the few solitary graves on a neighboring hill, which tell the story of violence and sacrifice by which the pathway to civilization has been marked in Arizona.

We took up our quarters within the walled fortifications which mark the entrance to the mine. The works are well protected by a tower in one corner of the square, commanding the plaza and various buildings and storehouses, as also the shafts of the mine which open along the ledge for a distance of several hundred yards. We found the steam-engine still standing within the enclosure, but rusty and partially imbedded in the ground. Remains of arastras and "whims," with various massive beams scattered about, showed to some extent the large amount of labor expended upon these works.

The entrance to the mine is close by the tower. The shaft has been sunk to a depth of a hundred and forty feet, and has been for some time partially filled with water. Poston and myself descended by the ladders as

HEINTZELMAN MINE AND WORKS.

far as we could. About sixty feet of water stopped us from going any further. I was surprised at the completeness and durability of the work—the more so knowing with what difficulty every part of it had been accomplished.

Of the quality of the ores in this mine I am not prepared to express any opinion of my own. The best practical evidence I saw of their value was that the Mexicans had been plundering the different shafts which were accessible, just prior to our arrival; and judging from their rude system of reduction I scarcely think they would waste time in stealing ore of little value, and transporting it across the border line through an Apache country. It is well known that the town of Saric, in Sonora, has been built upon the proceeds of ore stolen from the Heintzelman mine. I saw scattered about the premises piles of ore, which had just been broken up ready for packing away; and the fresh tracks of mule-trains and wagon-wheels, on the well-beaten road to Saric, showed how profitable this sort of enterprise must be to the Sonoranians.

Mr. S. F. Butterworth, who visited the Cerro Colorado eight days prior to our arrival, caught a party of Mexicans emerging from the mine. I may here mention that he was accompanied by Mr. Küstel, Mr. Higgins, and Mr. Janin—all gentlemen of learning and experience in mining matters—who assisted him in making a thorough examination of this mine and its resources. In the opinion of Mr. Butterworth and these gentlemen, the lode is one of the richest in Arizona, and will, under a judicious system of working, amply repay the capital invested in its development.

The average product of the Real del Monte mines in Mexico is $52 to the ton.· That of the Gould and Curry, prior to the recent depression of mining interests in Nevada, was about $65. Assays of selected ores form no reliable criterion of the value of a mine. Some of the best ores have been taken from some of the poorest mines. It is the quantity of good average ore, and the facilities for working, that form the true criterion of value in this precarious business. Nothing is more unreliable, therefore, than estimates based upon exceptional tests. What the average of the Heintzelman mine is, has never, I believe, been determined by any systematic calculation, the operations having been of a transitory and progressive character. An assay of selected ore made by Dr. Garnett of San Francisco, in 1857, yielded $8624 of silver to the ton, and $111 20 of copper. The average of eight assays on different ores from the same mine, made by Professors Booth, Torry, Lock, Kinsey, and others, yielded $1424 45 to the ton. Recent assays made by Professor Jackson, of Boston, show 13 to 16 per cent. of silver, and 37 per cent. of copper to the ton. From the best information I can get, the average of ore worked at the Cerro Colorado hacienda, and at the hacienda of Arivaca, where a considerable portion of it was reduced, did not fall short of $250 to the ton; so that there can be no reasonable doubt as to the richness of the vein. It is clearly defined on the surface of the ground for a distance of two miles, and so far as subterranean explorations have gone, increases in width and quality as it descends.

The rich mineral district of the Cerro Colorado was first brought to the notice of Eastern capitalists by Mr. Poston, my friend and travelling companion, who explored it in March, 1856. To his indomitable energy is due the succession of discoveries since made in this and the neighboring districts of Santa Rita, Sopori, and Arivaca. During the summer of 1861, when the Federal troops were withdrawn, the Apaches renewed their depredations, and the barbarous races of Sonora turned loose to complete the work of destruction. Murder after murder followed in rapid succession. Mr. Poston's brother, who was in charge of the Heintzelman mine,

was assassinated by the native employés.   Within a few
weeks every mine in the country, except that of Mr.
Mowry, was deserted.   After a series of hardships and
difficulties almost incredible Poston and a single friend
(Mr. Pumpelly) made their escape to California.

CHAPTER XXVII.

THE ARIVACA RANCH.

SEVEN miles from the Cerro Colorado we reached the Arivaca Ranch, long celebrated for its rich mines and fine pastures. This ranch, called by the Mexicans *La Aribac*, comprises within its boundaries 17,000 acres of agricultural land, 25 silver mines formerly worked by the Mexicans, and numerous gold, copper, and lead mines, as yet undeveloped. It contains a large amount of rich meadow-land, bordering on a never-failing stream; is well wooded with oak, walnut, ash, cotton-wood, and mesquit, and is capable of sustaining a population of five or six thousand souls. The range for cattle and sheep is almost without limit, extending over a belt of grazing country as far south as the Arizuma Mountains; west to the great peak of the Baboquivori, and north and east into the heart of the neighboring mountains. This goes far beyond the boundaries of the ranch; but in Arizona, as in California, the possession of water is tantamount to the possession of the whole surrounding country. The title is held by the Arizona Mining Company, and is derived from Thomas and Ignatio Ortez, who perfected it as early as 1802. It was surveyed by Lieutenant A. B. Gray, of the Boundary Commission, in 1859. Up to the abandonment of the Territory in 1861 it was in a progressive state of improvement under the auspices of the Company's agent. The reduction works of the Heintzelman mine were situated on this ranch for the convenience of wood, water, and pasturage, and were projected on a costly and extensive scale. Little now remains of them save the ruins of the mill and furnaces, the adobe store-houses and offices, and a dilapidated corral.

We camped in the old mill, and spent a couple of days very pleasantly in visiting the mines and exploring the gulches of the neighboring mountains. Game was abundant. Some of our escort, who were good shots, brought in several fat deer, and we lived in sumptuous style during our stay.

A couple of miles below the head-quarters is situated another mining establishment belonging to the same Company, and designed for the use of certain mines in the same vicinity—one of which we visited and found to present very favorable indications of lead and silver ore. Several buildings in a fair state of preservation comprise what is left of the hacienda; also a double corral for horses and cattle.

To this corral hangs a tale. When Arivaca was occupied, great precautions were taken to prevent the loss of stock by theft. The work animals were driven into the corral every evening before dark. A small adobe house, in which the vaqueros slept, stands opposite the entrance, with the door fronting the gate, so that it was supposed nothing could go in or out without attracting the attention of the guard. Watch-dogs were kept in order that the guard might be aroused in case he should happen to fall asleep during his watch, and the vaqueros were obliged to keep their door open. The bars of the gate were fastened with a heavy chain lashed around them, so that the least movement would be likely to make a noise. Besides there were white men in several of the quarters, well armed and always on the *qui vive*.

With all these precautions a band of four or five Apaches came one night and attempted to cut through the wall by sawing a gap in it with their hair riatas; but finding the material too hard they chose the alternative of making an attempt on the gate. To get the bars down without making a noise, they carefully unfastened the chain, and taking it link by link in their serapes as

they moved it, actually succeeded in effecting an opening without even arousing the dogs. The Mexicans in
charge were barely aroused in time to see thirty-nine
valuable mules and several fine horses in full flight for
the mountains. A party of five men was immediately
dispatched in pursuit. The main body of the Apaches
lay in ambush on the trail, and as soon as the pursuing
party approached within a few paces, fired upon them,
killing one, wounding another, and compelling the rest
to fly for their lives. This was the last of the mules
then belonging to the " Sonora Exploring and Mining
Company ;" which respectable body of capitalists will
probably have to explore the mountains of Arizona a
long time before they recover their property.

A still more adroit case of horse-stealing occurred in
Sonora some years ago. A wealthy ranchero built a
stone corral ten feet high, determined that the Apaches
should never get possession of his stock. The gate was
massive and iron-bound, and locked with a strong iron
lock. One night a small band of these dexterous thieves
climbed over the wall and lay down quietly under its
shadow. At the usual time in the morning the vaqueros,
unsuspicious of danger, unlocked the gate, swung it back
to let the animals out as usual, and were profoundly astonished to see them dash forth in a stampede, five or
six of them ridden by yelling devils of Apaches. Before
they could fully realize the state of affairs there was not
an Indian or an animal in sight; nor did the horses ever
come in sight again. This is a well-authenticated incident, and has long been a favorite camp-story in Arizona.

From Arivaca we travelled through a broad open
grazing country, over the proposed route to Libertad, on
the Gulf of California. The first part of our journey,
after passing the boundaries of the Arivaca Ranch, some
five or six miles below the haciendas, lay along a series
of foot-hills to the left, with a fine pasture range to the
right, extending to the Baboquivori Mountains. No

M 2

water is found in this tract of country, but it is well
wooded with mesquit, and the grass is excellent. The
road continues through this valley till it strikes the rise
of an extensive mesa to the right, over which it continues
for twelve miles. A vast plain covered with small stones
and pebbles and a scanty growth of grass and cactus,
bounded in the distance by rugged ranges of mountains,
is all the traveller can depend upon for enjoyment
during the greater part of this day's journey. It becomes oppressively monotonous after a few hours. Nothing possessed of animal life is to be seen, save at very
remote intervals, and then perhaps only a lonely rabbit
or a distant herd of antelope. Even the smallest shrubs
afford relief in this dreary wilderness of magnificent
distances. The road winds, mile after mile, over the
undulations of the mesa, turning to the right or to the
left, like a great snake, often without any apparent reason save to increase the distance. Experience, however, taught us never to leave the main highway in Arizona; for in doing so the traveller is sure, sooner or later,
to encounter an impracticable arroya or some impassable
ridge of rocks. Colonel Ferguson had passed over this
route nearly a year before, and we had the advantage of
his wagon track, which was still comparatively fresh.
This is another peculiarity of the country—the extraordinary length of time which even the slightest indenta-
tion in the ground lasts where the climate is so dry and
equable. We saw wagon and mule-tracks which had
been made, to the knowledge of some of our party, more
than three years before.

Descending from the mesa, as we approached the
mountain range on the right, we entered a beautiful little valley, in which the grass was wonderfully luxuriant;
but as usual there was no sign of water. The country
is well wooded in this vicinity, abounding in fine specimens of cumero, a tree resembling the hackleberry, and
occasionally groves of oak on the hill-sides. Five miles
through the bed of the valley brought us to a sign-board

on the road-side, upon which we found written in Spanish and English :

"WATER 1 MILE."

On referring to Colonel Ferguson's report, we ascertained that the water was to be found at certain seasons about a mile up a cañon to the right, the entrance of which was marked by a cumero-tree. This camp is known as Zazabe, and is distant twenty-four miles from Arizona.

CHAPTER XXVIII.

THE PAPAGORIA.

THE Papago Indians, of whom Captain José, our guide, was the principal Chief, have been driven into the desert area known as the Papagoria, by the hostilities of the Mexicans on the south, and the Apaches on the north and east, yet even now they are not permitted to enjoy the peaceful possession of a country in which it is scarcely possible to sustain life upon the scanty product of the soil. The Mexicans in the pursuit of silver, which abounds in the mountains, drive them from their watering-places, and the Apaches steal their cattle from the limited patches of grazing land, so that they have great difficulty in procuring the means of subsistence. The only place in which they can enjoy comparative security is at San Xavier; and even at this point they are constantly imposed upon by Mexicans and renegade Americans. In a late report of the Commissioner of Indian Affairs (not yet published), Superintendent Poston, speaking of these interesting people, with whom he has been familiar for many years, says: " Their first and principal village is at San Xavier del Bac, a Mission Church erected by the Jesuits in 1668, where they have lived and planted and watched their flocks and herds ever since, resisting the barbarous Apaches, and assisting their Spanish, Mexican and American protectors in many campaigns against the savage Indians. They raise wheat, corn, barley, beans, peas, melons and pumpkins, and are expert in the manufacture of pottery and willow ware. In harvest-time they spread all over the country, as reapers and gleaners, returning with their wages of grain for the winter. They gather the fruit of the *Cereas Giganteus*, which they call *Petayah*, and after expressing the juice for molasses, press the pulp in cakes for their winter stores. The ripening of this fruit is the Papago Carnival, when men, women and children go into ecstasies of delight. They have horses, cattle, sheep, poultry, and great numbers of dogs. As these Indians were found in possession of the soil they cultivate, and have maintained continuous possession ever since, it would seem equitable that their rights should be recognized by the Government of the United States. They have guarded the grand old Church of San Xavier del Bac with religious reverence, and naturally look upon it as their property, held in sacred trust. A square league around the Mission would include all the land they have in cultivation and the water necessary for its irrigation." [The Commissioner of Indian Affairs has since given the necessary authority, and a reservation at San Xavier has been set apart for these Indians.]

The estimated number of the Papago tribe is 6,800 souls, of whom at least three-fourths live in the Papagoria. Their villages are situated around the watering-places. They are a peaceful, simple-minded race, inoffensive in their habits, yet brave in the defense of their families and property against the devastations of their hereditary enemies, the Apaches. A large majority of them are sincere converts to the Catholic faith, which they acquired from the Jesuit Fathers.

In full view to the east, between the Altar and Magdalena roads, lies the group of mountains called the Arizuma, in which the richest discovery of native silver known in the history of mining was made more than a century ago by the Spaniards. We had passed within fifteen or twenty miles of this famous mine on our way down into Sonora, and were now camped on the western side within about the same distance. It was with extreme reluctance that we were compelled to abandon the idea of visiting this interesting place. Our animals were much reduced in flesh, and our supplies of forage and provisions would be exhausted before we could complete our projected tour through the Cahuabia and Papagoria.

Poston and myself, being a few miles ahead of the escort, availed ourselves of the chance to go up the cañon alone in search of the water, thinking we might see a deer on the way. I saw two, and shot one of them; but it did not stop on that account. The trail was marked by Apache tracks, apparently only a few days old. It was possible they were even then looking out for us. We found the water, as stated on the sign-board, about a mile from the cumero-tree. I must confess I kept a pretty sharp eye on the brush thickets and rocky fortresses that lined the sides of the cañon. Poston seemed rather to enjoy the prospect of losing his life than otherwise. I think he was reckless on account of a remark I had inadvertently made in camp the night before, that there would never be peace in Arizona or anywhere else until the whole human race was exterminated; and it was questionable if there would be then, for the animals would keep on fighting and killing one another. This thing of being shot through the body with rifle-balls and arrows, impaled with lances, and hung by the heels to a tree with a slow fire under one's head may be all very well as an adventure, but I am willing to let other people enjoy all the reputation that may attach to it.

A day's travel in Arizona is generally determined by the watering-places. We usually managed to make from twenty to twenty-five miles, but in some places were compelled to make forty or fifty, watering at the last place and dry-camping for the night. Whenever it became necessary to make a long stretch we started in the afternoon, travelled till midnight, camped till day-light, and then made the rest of the *journada* by noon.

Poso-Verde, or Green Wells, was our next encampment after leaving Zazabe. We followed the route to Altar till it intersects the wagon-road from Saric to Fresnal, passing on the way a deserted Indian village and some curious basaltic formations. Twelve miles below the point of the Baboquivori range of mountains we struck the road to Fresnal, which carried us back almost in an acute angle. There was no reason that we could perceive why we should not cut across by the Tucalote trail, except that we were not on a tour of discovery, and could not afford time to experiment in short cuts. Nothing worthy of note occurred during this day's journey. We arrived at the Poso-Verde about two P.M., and found it a good camping-place, rather scarce of wood, but pleasantly sheltered by the mountains. The Boundary Commission spent some weeks at this point recruiting their animals and making explorations in the vicinity. The water is contained in a sort of pit, or natural tank, and has rather a strong flavor of alkali, corn-manure, dead coyotes, Indian sign, and decayed vegetable matter. A few hundred yards from the well is an adobe fort built by the Papago Indians as a protection to their frontier village and grazing range. The remains of a few bacquals are all the evidences of habitation we saw at this point. In former years it was frequented a good deal by Apache bands, but the Papagoes generally came off victorious in the battles that ensued. At this time they rarely appear except in squads of three or four, who descend from the mountains at night and make sudden raids upon the Papago cattle. Captain José, our Chief, evidently felt a good deal of pride in the prowess of his people, though I must do him the justice to say he was quite modest about it.

I took my rifle during the afternoon and rambled up the cañon in search of a deer. About two miles from the well there is a beautiful little valley encircled by rugged mountains. The oak groves which adorn the pastures have much the appearance of apple orchards in a civilized country. The valley abounds in game. In several places near the water-holes the deer tracks were so thick that they reminded me of a sheep corral. Strange

to say I saw but one deer during my ramble, yet this is
not an uncommon experience in Arizona. We all saw
acres of deer tracks and turkey tracks during our journey;
but few of us saw the deer or the turkeys that made them.
Game is exceedingly wild, and difficult to kill when shot.
The tenacity of animal life is extraordinary. Indians
must be riddled with balls before they can be killed. I
know of a deer that ran half a mile without its liver and
lights. As for quail they require about four ounces of
duck-shot, and then they won't die easy. Several that I
killed myself afterward made their escape into the
bushes—a fact that I boldly assert on the veracity of a
hunter.

There was a Californian volunteer in our party, holding
the position of high-private, who declared on his word and
honor as a gentleman that he had shot a large hare four
times and carried away a leg every time, so that the
body of the poor animal had nothing left on it but the
ears and tail; yet with even such limited means of locomotion it actually escaped by whirling over on its ears
and tail, though he ran after it as fast as he could.
Another even more remarkable— But I decline further
revelations on the subject, and for additional information
concerning the natural wonders of Arizona respectfully
refer the reader to Buckskin Alick, a resident of San
Xavier del Bac.

Leaving our camp at the Poso-Verde, we entered upon
the extensive region of country lying to the west of the
Baboquivori, and stretching, with occasional interrup-
tions of detached sierras, as far as the Gulf of California.
This vast tract of territory is for the most part a gravelly desert, intersected at remote intervals with arroyas
and patches of palo-verde, mesquit, suarro, petaya, oquitoia, and choya—the shrubs and cacti usually found in the
desert regions of Arizona. Water exists only in the
" tenagas," or natural tanks, formed at remote intervals
in hollow basins by the action of the sun and rain; yet
so scanty is the supply that men and animals have often

been known to perish in attempting to cross this inhospitable region during the dry season.

A day's journey through the portion of the Papagoria lying along the foot-hills of the Baboquivori brought us to the first of the inhabited rancherias, near which is the small Mexican town of Fresnal, a collection of adobe hovels built at this point within the past two years, on account of the convenience afforded by the Indian wells for the reduction of ores stolen from the Cahuabia mines. There are also some rich silver-bearing veins in the neighborhood, but they have not been developed to any considerable extent.

A curious feature in Arizona mining operations that frequently attracted my attention was here exemplified. The Cahuabia district is situated in a detached range of mountains, distant about twenty-five miles from Fresnal, and although a limited quantity of water exits there, which could be increased by a small amount of labor, the Mexicans steal the ore from abandoned or neglected mines, and pack it across the intervening desert sooner than go to the trouble of digging wells for themselves and reducing the silver on the spot. There is no advantage in the way of wood and other supplies at Fresnal which could not be had by a little trouble at the Cahuabia.

I asked the Padrone, whom we found at work driving a blind horse around one of his arastras, why he went to the trouble of making trips to the Cahuabia mines and packing the ore twenty-five miles to reduce it when he could do it as well on the spot. His reply was, " *Quien sabe ?* " I suggested to him that, from all I heard, water was as plenty in the ground there as it was here, and wood still more so. To this he answered : " Si Señor— *quien sabe*—quisas si—quisas no—*yo no sai.*" I ventured to hint that if the owners of the ore chose to prevent him from stealing it they could do so as well at Fresnal as they could at Cahuabia. " Si Señor," said the Padrone, " *yo pienso co si—yo no sai—quisas si, quisas*

no—quien sabe. Yo son muy pauvera." This was all
I could get out of him, and was as satisfactory as any
thing I had ever derived from a Mexican thief. I think
he was slightly rattled by the formidable appearance of
our escort. Doubtless he thought we had come to raze
the town, or seize the old blind horse that was at work
in the arastra.

Fresnal contains some ten or a dozen rude adobe hovels, roofed and partially walled with the favorite building
material of the country, oquitoia—a kind of hard, thorny
cactus which grows on the deserts. We found here
about twenty vagabond Sonoranians, who were engaged
in grinding and smelting the ores which they had stolen
from the Cahuabia mines. The yield, according to their
own account, was about $300 to the ton. I made a
sketch of the grand old peak of the Baboquivori from
this point. This is one of the most remarkable landmarks in Arizona, and is seen at the distance of sixty or
eighty miles from the surrounding deserts.

We crossed the desert of the Papagoria the next day,
and made an exploration of the Cahuabia district. The
principal mines in this district are owned by the Cahuabia Mining Company. From the report of Mr. Mainzer,
a very able practical engineer, it would appear that the
silver lodes are among the richest in Arizona; and I can
readily believe this to be the case from my own observation. I have seen nothing in Washoe or elsewhere that
presents more favorable indications. Mr. Jaeger, our
Fort Yuma friend "Don Diego," of whose history I gave
a brief sketch in an earlier chapter, owns the "Pecacho,"
a very rich lead, upon which considerable work has been
done. A few Mexicans were engaged in getting out the
ores at the time of our arrival. This mine was leased
to a Mexican during the past two years, who, by the
rudest system of working, managed to get about forty
thousand dollars out of it, over and above expenses. I
apprehend Don Diego is furnishing more silver to his
Mexican friends out of the Pecacho than he is to himself.

THE BABOQUIVORI.

In the hands of a company of capitalists who would properly work the mine, I believe it would be a very profitable investment; but Don Diego is one of those eccentric men who considers himself rich as long as he has a large amount of property. Whether it pays himself or others is nothing to the point. He reminds me of a celebrated gentleman who is ambitious to own fifty millions of acres on the Colorado Desert—it would be such a magnificent piece of property!

Wood and water are scarce in the Cahuabia district, but grazing for animals is good during the greater part of the year. There would be no difficulty in procuring abundance of water by means of artesian wells; which, after all, must eventually be the salvation of Arizona.

We visited the Bahia, a silver lode of extraordinary richness, belonging to the Cahuabia Mining Company. From some Mexicans who were helping themselves to the ore we learned that it yielded an average of $300 to $350 to the ton, and occasionally they struck it in nearly a pure state. There are also very fine copper mines in the vicinity. Mr. Hill d'Amit, who was a member of our party on the trip to Sonora, is largely interested in one of these; and considers it one of the best copper leads in the country—quite equal to the celebrated Maricopa lead on the Gila. Difficulty of transportation is the great drawback to copper-mining in this part of Arizona. I am satisfied, from my own observation and from the concurrent testimony of others, that the Cahuabia is a mineral region of more than ordinary richness. It abounds in almost all the precious metals; but is as yet scarcely known beyond Tucson. No finer field for exploration and enterprise exists south of the Gila.

Our sojourn was necessarily limited. Water was scarce, the grass nearly used up, and our forage entirely out. Provisions, too, were becoming scanty; and we had a long journey yet to make across the barren wastes of the Papagoria.

Leaving our camping-place at the old hacienda of the

Cahuabia Mining Company, we struck across for the next watering-place on the route to San Xavier, called Coyote, where we overtook the escort and baggage-wagons, having sent them on to that point from Fresnal. This is a desolate little spot, under the shadow of the mountains, with a pool of dirty water, the only attraction of the place. We distributed some few trinkets among the poor Indians living in the vicinity, and were kindly furnished in return with three eggs — all their village afforded.

From the Coyote to San Xavier del Bac is a stretch of forty-five miles without water. By starting late in the afternoon, after our animals had fed and quenched their thirst, we were enabled to make a dry camp on the desert, some thirty miles distant, by twelve o'clock at night. Before reaching camp we met a party of three horsemen, one of whom proved to be our friend Hill d'Amit, on the way from Tucson to the Cahuabia. They brought letters from home—the first I had received. Too impatient to wait for a fire, I lingered behind the train and read my letters by moonlight, the only light then available. A curious place to receive and read letters from home—the desert of Papagoria!

CHAPTER XXIX.

ON our arrival at San Xavier we called a gathering of the Papagoes from all the villages of the Papagoria, and had a grand time for the next two weeks, delivering to them the goods and agricultural implements purchased by the Government for their use. There was great rejoicing among the women over their fine calico dresses and fancy-colored beads, and the men seemed much pleased to receive their hoes, picks, and shovels. If the hymns of praise sung by these simple people for the health and happiness of Mr. Commissioner Dole do not favorably affect his standing in the next world, it will not be owing to the ingratitude of his red children, or to the lack of eloquent speeches made in his behalf by Poston and myself.

We lodged in the grand old Mission Church. The good Padre Messea greatly contributed to our comfort and happiness by his unceasing kindness; and we had no reason to regret the time we were obliged to spend at this interesting place.

Sundry complimentary visits from our military friends stationed at Tubac resulted in the withdrawal of our escort and the seizure of our mules. Left on foot, with but scanty means of subsistence, we were compelled to cast ourselves upon the generosity of Captain José, who got us some provisions, and agreed to escort us down to the Pimo villages. By various adroit negotiations Poston secured a couple of private mules and a burro. Mr. J. B. Allen, of Tucson, a most estimable gentleman, to whom we were indebted for the most generous attention on several occasions, furnished us with a team for our ambulance. Thus provided with all the necessaries of life, with Captain José as our Chief and Buckskin Alick as our Adjutant, we made perhaps the grandest sortie out of Tucson ever witnessed in that famous city. In due time we reached the Pimo villages.

OUR BURRO.

Here I was compelled reluctantly to part from my good friend Poston, whose intelligent conversation and unremitting kindness had cheered and encouraged me through the entire tour. He was bound for the North on a political campaign, and I for my cottage home in Oakland, where my presence was rendered necessary by illness in my family. Mr. Allen kindly gave me a seat in his buggy as far as Fort Yuma. There I met an old friend, Mr. Ames, Superintendent of the Military Express, who had just arrived from Camp Drum. In the most generous manner he started on the return trip several days before his customary time, in order to furnish me with the means of conveyance home. We crossed the Colorado Desert and reached Los Angeles without serious accident, and in a few days more I was safely landed in San Francisco.

My impressions of Arizona may be summed up in a few words. I believe it to be a Territory wonderfully rich in minerals, but subject to greater drawbacks than any of our territorial possessions. It will be many years before its mineral resources can be fully and fairly developed. Emigration must be encouraged by increased military protection; capital must be expended without the hope of immediate and extraordinary returns; civil law must be established on a firm basis, and facilities of communication fostered by legislation of Congress.

No country that I have yet visited presents so many striking anomalies as Arizona. With millions of acres of the finest arable lands, there was not at the time of our visit a single farm under cultivation in the Territory; with the richest gold and silver mines, paper-money is the common currency; with forts innumerable, there is scarcely any protection to life and property; with extensive pastures, there is little or no stock; with the finest natural roads, travelling is beset with difficulties; with rivers through every valley, a stranger may die of thirst. Hay is cut with a hoe, and wood with a spade or mattock. In January one enjoys the luxury of a bath as under a tropical sun, and sleeps under double blankets at night. There are towns without inhabitants, and deserts extensively populated; vegetation where there is no soil, and soil where there is no vegetation. Snow is seen where it is never seen to fall, and ice forms where it never snows. There are Indians the most docile in North America, yet travellers are murdered daily by Indians the most barbarous on earth. The Mexicans have driven the Papagoes from their southern homes, and now seek protection from the Apaches in the Papago villages. Fifteen hundred Apache warriors, the most cowardly of the Indian tribes in Arizona, beaten in every fight by the Pimos, Maricopas, and Papagoes, keep these and all other Indians closed up as in a corral; and the same Apaches have desolated a country inhabited by 120,000 Mexicans. Mines without miners and forts without soldiers are common. Politicians without policy, traders without trade, store-keepers without stores, teamsters without teams, and all without means, form the mass of the white population. But here let me end, for I find myself verging on the proverbs.

ARIZONIAN IN SIGHT OF HOME.

N

INDIAN TRIBES OF ARIZONA.

I subjoin also some interesting statistics of the Indian tribes in Arizona, derived from the best authorities:

GILA APACHES.

Mimbrenas	750	Cominos	1500
Chiricahuas	50	Tontos	1500
Sierra Blancas	2500	Mogallones	1500
Pinal Llanos	750		
Coyoteros	3000	Total	12,000

There are altogether about 3000 Apache warriors within the boundaries of Arizona.

PIMOS.

Aqua Baiz	533	Casa Blanca	315
Cerrito	259	Herringuen	514
Arenal	616	Llano	392
Cachunilla	438		
Total			3067

There are 1200 laboring Pimos and 1000 warriors. Farms in cultivation, 604 — containing 1500 acres. Horses and cattle, 1800 head. Annual surplus production of corn, 1,000,000 bushels.

MARICOPAS.		YUMAS.
Huesti Perachi	232	Chiefs: Pasqual Vincente, José Ma-
Sacaton	106	ria, Hauil Eba, Juan, Antonio Chat-
		meka—Total number, 2500.
Total	*338	

MOHAVES.

Chiefs: Iretaba, José Maria, Joaquin, Oré, Manuel, Mescal—600 warriors, 4000 souls.

CHEMEHUEVAS.

300 warriors, 1500 souls.

SEVEN VILLAGES OF THE MOQUIS.

	Warriors.	People.
Oraiba	400	2400
Shu-muth-pa	150	900
Mu-shai-i-na	150	900
Ah-le-la	150	900
Gual-pi	150	900
Shi-nin-na	20	120
Té-qua	100	600
Total	1120	6720

* Productions, farms, and stock included in the above estimate of Pimos, with whom they reside.

PAPAGOES.

San Xavier	500	Mesquite	500
Santa Rosa	400	Perigua	400
Cusbabi	350	Chuba	250
Fresnal	250	Poso Blanca	300
Cobota	500	Quejoton	500
Tecolota	500	Naris	250
Cumera	500	Alcalde	250
Poso Verde	350	Quito Vaqueta	250
San Laida	250	Milpias	250
Sonorita	500		
Total			7050

The following is a rough estimate of the total number of Indians in Arizona, including branches of tribes not hitherto counted and those of the Apaches who make this Territory their head-quarters:

Apaches	5000	Mohaves	5000
Papagoes	7500	Pai Utes	500
Pimos and Maricopas	5000	Hualpais	2000
Cocopas	3000	Moquis	7000
Yumas (Euchas)	5000	Navajoes	15,000
Chemehuevas	2000	Apaches Manzas	100
Yampais	2500		
Total			59,600

Most of these tribes are on friendly terms with the whites, with the exception of Apaches, Navajoes, and those who are intermixed or associated with them, such as the Yampais, Hualpais, etc. I think the estimates are too large, but have no means of arriving at more accurate results. The probability is, 30,000 would embrace all the Indians at present living within the limits of the Territory.

TABLE OF DISTANCES.

For the information of persons intending to visit Arizona, I have compiled the following tables, from various authentic sources; some from reports of official surveys, others from information derived from private parties who have recently travelled over the routes mentioned:

From Los Angeles to	Miles.	From Los Angeles to	Miles.
El Monte	12	Laguna	15
San José	12	Willows	11
El Chino	12	Temecula	10
Temescal	17	Tejunga	14

	Miles.
From Los Angeles to	
Warner's Ranch...............	15
San Felippe....................	15
Vallecito......................	18
La Palma......................	9
Carisa Creek..................	9
Hall's Well....................	16
Indian Well...................	16
Monument.....................	12
Alama Mucho..................	13
Gardner's Wells...............	12
Cook's Wells..................	14
Algadones.....................	14
Fort Yuma....................	10
Total.....................	276

From Fort Yuma to	
Gila City.....................	18
Corunnacion Camp............	11
Antelope Peak................	15
Mohawk	12
Texas Hill....................	11
Stanwick's....................	17
Burke's	12
Oatman Flat..................	12
Kenyon's	14
Gila Bend.....................	16
Desert Station	20
Pimo Villages. { Maricopa Wells......	20
{ Casa Blanca........	10
{ Sacatone Station....	12
Total.....................	200

From Pimo Villages to	
Oneida........................	11
Blue Water....................	12
Pecacho	16
Point of Rocks................	25
Tucson........................	17
Total.....................	81

From Pimo Villages, north, to	
Laguna........................	16
Salinas River.................	18
White Tank Mountain	28
Hasiamp......................	20
Weaverville...................	10
People's Ranch................	12
Kirkland's	8
Granite Ranch................	17
Fort Whipple.................	37
Total.....................	166

From Weaver's to La Paz.......	135
From Weaver's to Walker's Diggings...........	50
From Walker's Diggings to La Paz.......................	185
From La Paz to Los Angeles.....	280
From Tucson to Cienega.....................	36

	Miles.
From Tucson to	
San Pedro.....................	25
Lagune Springs...............	18
Sulphur Springs..............	22
Apache Pass.	25
San Simon....................	18
Stein's Peak..................	17
Barney Station...............	16
Soldier's Farewell............	20
Cow Springs..................	14
Mimbres......................	18
Cook's Springs...............	25
Rio Grande...................	32
Roblaro.......................	14
Doña Ana....................	16
Las Cruces...................	7
Fort Fillmore..:.............	6
El Paso.......................	40
Total.....................	369

From Tucson to	
San Xavier....................	9
Canova.......................	25
Ford's........................	12
Tubac........................	2¼
Total.....................	48¼

From Tubac to	
Sopori........................	10¼
Cerro Colorado..............	11
Arivaca.......................	7¼
Total....................	28¼

From Port Lobos del Sur to	
Picon.........................	24
Pitiquita.....................	50
Altar.........................	14
Padrones.....................	22
Tenaja.......................	7
Zaravi........................	20
Arivaca.......................	18
Total	155

From Fort Yuma to Altar.....	235¼
From Weaver's to Fort Whipple...............	70
From Fort Whipple to Albuquerque (Beale's Route).	395
Santa Fe.....................	76
Total.................	471

From Tucson to	
San Francisco, *via* Fort Yuma	1035
via La Paz...	917
From Tucson to	
Guyamas, *via* Magdalena and Hermosillo...................	367
From Tucson to	
Port Libertad, *via* Altar (Ferguson's Route)...............	226

WASHOE REVISITED.

CHAPTER XXX.

RUNNING THE GAUNTLET.

FOUR years ago a series of papers appeared in a popular periodical descriptive of a visit to Washoe, in which the author related some personal experiences of a very remarkable character. So wonderful, indeed, were many of his adventures, that certain incredulous persons, who have no difficulty in believing any thing except the truth, boldly assumed that the entire narrative was a fiction concocted for speculative purposes.

The simple truth was that the author, an ex-Government officer, found himself one fine morning in San Francisco, with an empty purse in his pocket, and saw no remedy but to visit the newly-discovered silver regions, which were then making a prodigious stir among the gunny-bags of Front Street, and the bummers, bankers, and other men of enterprising genius on Montgomery Street. Aided by a commission to explore some mines which had no existence in this world or in the next, he felt assured that he could, by means of an agency and his own speculative talent, speedily indemnify himself for the unprofitable years which he had spent in the public service. In this hopeful state of mind he set forth on his travels. Unable to procure a conveyance at Placerville short of all the money he possessed or could hope to obtain by borrowing, he sturdily shouldered his blankets, and footed it over the mountains—through mud, and snow, and rain, slush, and scathing storms—to the city of Carson, where he arrived in due time, somewhat battered and wayworn by the hardships of the trip.

It is not my intention to review in detail the wonderful experiences of this adventurer in the land of silver. They will be found in his published narrative, illustrated by authentic wood-cuts. Sufficient is it for my purpose to say that before writing his account of Washoe, and the perils and vicissitudes of life in that region, he deemed it prudent to retire to the continent of Europe. The dreary years of his exile from California he filled up, in some measure, by tours through Spain, Algeria, Germany, Poland, and the regions bordering on the Arctic Circle.

On his return to San Francisco he found, to his astonishment, that the silver mania had taken possession of the entire population, without distinction of age or sex. Washoe and the regions beyond had sprung up into a second California. Gold was nowhere now : it was all silver—above, below, everywhere. Speculation peered into the silvery heavens in search of new lodes ; nay, the genius of enterprise pointed toward the regions of everlasting woe as an appropriate sphere for the smelting interests. Tons of ore were piled in heaps along the curb-stones in the streets ; every office was an emporium for the purchase and sale of feet ; every desk in every store was a stall at which millionaires browsed upon paper ; every window glared and dazzled the sight with gorgeous engravings of stocks ; every man of the hundreds and tens of hundreds that stood at every corner, and in every saloon, and before every bar, carried feet in his pockets and dividends in his eyes ; and every walking thing, save horses and dogs and rats and mice, talked stocks and feet from morning till night, and dreamed dividends from night till morning. Young ladies would hear of no proposition from any gentleman with less than a thousand feet ; and no gentleman, however ardent, would compromise himself without asking, " Is she on the Wild-Cat or Legitimate ? How many pay feet does she offer ? and what assessments are due on her ?" Passing a crowd, " Reese River" was poured into one ear, and " Humboldt" into the other. " Washoe !" " Esmeralda !" " Arizona !" " Sonora !" " Struck it rich !"

NIGHT SCENE IN THE SIERRAS.

"Silver bricks!" and "Pay rock!" hummed and drummed through the air till the brain was nearly addled.

No wonder our adventurer, just from the wilds of Russia and Iceland, was bewildered. Of the various tongues spoken by the various races of the earth whom he had encountered in his travels this was the most difficult to comprehend, and the most foreign to his ear and understanding. The very newspapers which he attempted to read furnished snatches of information that filled him with amazement: "Uncle Sam" was lively; "Yellow Jacket" was scarcely so firm, owing to a difficulty with the Union; "Lady Bryan" was in better repute, at advanced rates, and was still in active demand; "The Savage" was quiet but strong, at rising figures; "Buckeye" was languishing; "Hope" had revived, and sales were made yesterday at $8; "Josephine" was firmer at the close, and much sought for; "Wide West" was drooping and heavy at $80; "Burning Moscow" was unusually brisk; and "Sierra Nevada" had a downward tendency.

How in the world was any sane man to comprehend the state of things when the meaning of terms was changed, and the order of nomenclature wholly disarranged? A few days, however, enabled our adventurer to catch some drift from the general current of conversation. It was evident that fortunes of extraordinary dimensions were to be made over the mountains—made suddenly, certainly, and without capital, which was precisely the most convenient thing in the world for a man who had just scattered his means all over the world. "Yes!" said he, enthusiastically, "I'll go to Washoe! I'll pitch in for feet this time! You bet I'll seize a few of those glittering bricks, and build my castles upon a solid foundation hereafter!"

It was quietly hinted, however, by friends solicitous of his welfare, that he had better not show himself in Washoe again, if he placed any value upon his life or the general stability of his constitution. The reasons assigned for this advice were startling and multifarious. It was alleged that the road was lined with blood-thirsty men armed with pistols, doubled-barrelled shot-guns, clubs, pitchforks, bowie-knives, and axes, every one of whom was on the lookout for a solitary pedestrian who had passed over the mountains three years· before, and

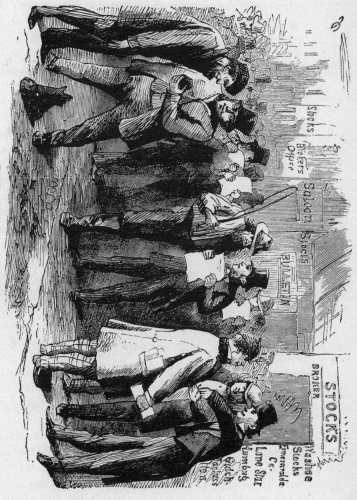

THE SILVER MANIA AT SAN FRANCISCO

damaged their reputation by various slanders in the public prints. Especial mention was made of a ferocious Irishman, by the name of "Dirty Mike," who was watching near the crossing of the American River, with a tremendous shillelah in his right hand and a copy of *Harper's Magazine* in his left; and it was asserted that if the said Michael ever laid eyes upon the author of the Washoe papers he would speedily show which of the two carried upon his person the greater share of his mother earth.

Further on, in Hope Valley, there was a solitary man who lived, like Diogenes in his tub, having only a ferocious bull-dog as a companion. These two—Diogenes and his dog—had been chiefly occupied during the past three years in gloating over the anticipated re-appearance of "the fellow that showed them up in print." The slur upon the cabin might be forgiven; but that villainous likeness of "him and Bull" was only to be wiped out by blood. Yes—he'd offer that fellow fox-skins to eat again—*he* would. You bet he'd spoil his appetite. Ef he didn't you could discount the bill at your own price!

Bad as all this was, it was nothing to compare with the hints of retribution that came floating over the Sierras from Virginia City, the Devil's Gate, and Carson. Here were some thousands of excited men, accustomed to the use of fire-arms from infancy, who had invested largely in the Love's Delight, Sorrowful Countenance, Pious Wretch, Literary Cuss, and other valuable claims of a kindred character—all awaiting, with stern resolution and ill-suppressed rage, the coming of this diabolical quill-driver, who had so basely ruined their mines and blasted all their prospects. Many thousands of people had no other idea of Washoe than what they gathered from these ridiculous caricatures, which were a monstrous fabrication from beginning to end. The tide of capital from the Atlantic States was arrested before it ever got a start from Wall Street. Capitalists in

DIRTY MIKE.

San Francisco were scared out of their boots. Stocks in the most valuable lodes went down a thousand per cent. It may have been a very good joke to perpetrate upon the honest miners, but it certainly gave a back-set to Washoe of more than two years. And now it was hinted that this rattle-brained scribbler, this miserable ink-jerker, was about to become a candidate for Congress from the Territory of Nevada! Let him beware of the vengeance of an outraged public! He had better give Carson, and Silver City, and the Devil's Gate, and Virginia a wide berth in his future travels!

Such were a few of the grave considerations under which I surveyed the prospect of revisiting Washoe—

for you must have already discovered, dear reader, that the writer of these sketches is no other than the disreputable personage above referred to. Held accountable by divers bodies of exasperated men for all the disasters that had occurred on the other side of the mountains during the past three years, and credited by none of the fortunes made, it was due to the great cause of justice that I should go over and set myself right, or gloriously die in the attempt.

With this much in the way of introduction, I shall proceed to give you a detailed narrative of my experiences, in the course of which it will be seen that various and magical changes have taken place in the mining regions of Washoe. Indeed when I look back at what Virginia City was at the time of my first visit—a city of sage-bushes, mud hovels, coyote-holes, gunny-bags, flour-sacks, and tattered blankets, wherein dwelt a population the most motley and incongruous ever gathered together by the force of silver and circumstances—when I think of the multifarious ledges then in the progress of development, and see what has since been done, and what promise there is in the future, I feel precisely as Lord Clive did at the bar of the British Parliament—astonished at my own moderation. The marvel of it is that I carried away so little treasure where there was so much staring me in the face. I wonder how it was I ever told half so much truth, and left so heavy a balance still to be told.

In announcing to certain experienced friends my purpose of revisiting Washoe I was somewhat startled by such questions as these: Is your neck insured by a responsible company? Are you subject to giddiness in the head? How often have your ribs been broken before? Are you accustomed to fractures of the legs and arms? And what provision have you made for the maintenance of your family in case a miscellaneous bullet should strike you through the bowels and lodge in your backbone? Which I understood to mean, in general terms, that a certain percentage of travellers who went over the grade did so head-foremost, with a stage or two on top of them, and that the state of society in Virginia City had not improved in a moral point of view.

CHAPTER XXXI.

I WAS about to hire a private vehicle, when, fortunately, I met a friend who had just come over by the Henness Pass. This gentleman travelled in a buggy for comfort and convenience. At a narrow pass on the way he had encountered a stage, and to avoid being run over had turned out of the grade, but never stopped turning till himself and his buggy, and the horses that pulled the buggy, together with all his provisions, blankets, deeds, mortgages, lists of mines, rolls of assessments, and schedules of dividends were piled in a confused heap at the bottom of a cañon some five hundred feet deep by several thousand feet wide. I say this was a fortunate occurrence, as it afforded me good ground for travelling by the ordinary modes of conveyance, which I have generally found to be about as safe as any other.

Of the trip to Sacramento it is needless to say much. Most people in San Francisco have tried that at least once or twice in their lives. If ever they derived any pleasure from it they accomplished more than I did. Two hours in a chilling wind, during which you partake of a hasty dinner and smoke a cigar, finds you at the Benicia wharf, the steamer fretting and fuming with suppressed steam, crowds pouring in and crowds moving out, and a great many people gathered about the premises, without any ostensible occupation save to be on hand in case something should turn up. When there happens to be no opposition on the line you may escape collision or explosion; but your chances are very small indeed of ever reaching your destination in the event of a rival steamer being on the route. In this country it is a common practice to fight duels with steamboats. Difficulties between captains are settled by steam. The boilers are charged to the bursting point, and the hostile parties, accustomed to the use of steamboats from infancy, manage their weapons with such skill that an effective crash, accompanied by the shrieks of maimed and scalded passengers, is the usual result.

Upon entering the Sacramento River the air becomes softer and warmer, and good-natured travellers who have been up and down a great many times point out the trees in which families of women and children roosted a few years ago when the flood swept away the houses. But many houses still remain, although the effects of the flood are visible all along the banks of the river.

About midnight the steamer, if she be well freighted, as is generally the case, runs aground on the Hog's Back and there sticks fast till morning. Passengers who have secured rooms and berths usually avail themselves of the opportunity thus afforded to lay in a supply of sleep for the journey across the mountains; and passengers who can not procure rooms or berths enjoy the privilege of sitting up in chairs carefully secured to the floors, as a precaution against theft; or spending the night in the lower saloon at a game of sledge or poker, by which means they usually travel with heavy heads and light pockets the next day. The Hog's Back is responsible for a vast deal of trouble. I have seen many hogs in my day, but never so great a bore as this.

Arrived at length in Sacramento, a hasty breakfast of water bewitched and coffee begrudged, leathery beefsteak and saleratus slightly corrected with flour, refreshes the inner man; trunks and knapsacks are vindictively hurled into the baggage-car of the Folsom train; the whistle blows; the passengers rush frantically into the cars and bestow themselves on the seats without regard to order; and the locomotive frets and fizzes on its iron way to Folsom.

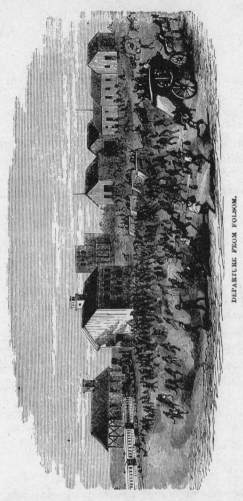

DEPARTURE FROM FOLSOM.

In some respects the progress of California is without parallel in the history of the world. The developments of wealth in the mining regions, the rapid growth of towns and cities, and the wonderful advancement of the agricultural interests, present some of the most remarkable examples of industry, energy and enterprise on record. Yet it must be admitted that if California can challenge the world in these respects, it falls very far short of the general advancement of the times in some others. A stranger coming directly from Europe, or even from the Atlantic States, can not but be unfavorably impressed by the absence of railway communications between the most important points, and the extraordinary apathy manifested in regard to almost every kind of internal improvement. There are few countries in the world so well adapted to railways, and certainly none with a larger amount of trade compared with its population; yet during a period of fourteen years there has been, until within the last few years, but a single railroad in operation in the State, and that a very imperfect one, of very little general use as it stands, extending a distance of only 22 miles from Sacramento to Folsom. It is true there is now a small patch of railroad extending from Marysville to the vicinity of Oroville; also a line between San Francisco and San José; and a few miles of rail attached to the Oakland Ferry; besides some city lines, which can scarcely be estimated in the category of railroads. The total aggregate, exclusive of the Pacific Railroad, does not probably exceed 250 miles. This is but a small advance for a State sprung almost full-grown into existence fourteen years ago, abounding in resources unequalled by those of any other State in the Union.

The truth of the matter is, we are a wonderfully fast people in California, but not a far-seeing people. Even in Europe, where people are proverbially slow, they are not so blind to their own interests on the subject of railways. Within the same period of fourteen years their railway systems have been extended over nearly every habitable portion of the Continent, and the consequence has been a marked revolution in trade, commerce and travel. Property has everywhere increased in value, and the wages of labor have enjoyed a corresponding advance. In the Atlantic States, up to the commencement of the rebellion, the progress of our railways excited the astonishment and admiration of the world. But in California, which abounds in vast tracts of level country, inexhaustible mineral wealth, and the most productive of agricultural lands on the face of the globe, with a population the most energetic and intelligent, we have done comparatively nothing in this respect. A great deal of talk has taken place, and the halls of our Legislature have resounded with magniloquent speeches on the subject, but the rails have not been laid. California has been very much like the unfortunate goose that laid the golden eggs—disembowelled for her treasures, but never cherished for the good that is in her and the treasures she is capable of yielding in the future. Even to this day there is not the interest felt in the permanent welfare of the State which should prevail among her people. Sudden and extraordinary excitements have been the rule rather than the exception. We have had gold manias and silver manias and ranch manias and fruit manias, and all other sorts of manias, till it really seems as if nothing could be done without a special insanity, risking all to the wild excitement of the moment. If our people had risked half as much and displayed half the energy in building up the true and permanent interests of the State, they would now be better off; the rewards of industry would be placed upon a more reliable basis, and the aggregate wealth of the country would stand at a much higher figure than it does now. Such, however, is the character of our people, and no amount of preaching will have any effect. Many years must elapse and many thousands of our citizens must be ruined before the ordinary rewards of industry will be a sufficient incentive to enterprise in this State. So long as individual aggrandizement is the ruling motive of action, so long as every thing is cast aside in the hope of securing sudden wealth without labor, we must be content to live a kind of gambling life, with many ups and downs and but a small average of prosperity compared with our vast and extraordinary resources.

I could not perceive that much improvement had taken

place on the route, unless, indeed, a few additional bar-rooms be accounted in that light. The town of Folsom itself has grown somewhat within the past four years, in consequence of the trade passing through it on the way to Washoe. New brick houses have been built on the main street in the vicinity of the dépôt, and some pleasant little cottages, embowered in flowers and shrubbery, adorn the surrounding slopes. The chief marts of business, as usual in these inland towns, are the express-offices, clothing-stores, and drinking-saloons. Every other house seems to be a house of entertainment, in which the public are feasted on billiards and whisky. Teaming and staging are the grand features of enterprise in this lively little place, and teamsters and stage-drivers the most prominent public characters. The language spoken by this class of the population is a mixture of horse, mule, and ox, with a strong human infusion of blasphemy. Something perhaps in the difficulties and vexations that beset their occupation gives them rather a ferocious expression of countenance, and it is not always an easy matter to mollify the asperities of their nature.

As most passengers desire to get an outside seat, except when it rains, it is highly important that you should proceed at once to secure the favorable consideration of the superintendent, who is a gentleman of great suavity and politeness, considering his position. Should you fail in that, I warn you not to climb up on the fore-wheel with any hope of getting the seat of honor alongside the driver; for whether you be a Minister plenipotentiary or a member of the Common Council he will exercise the right pertaining to his craft—order you down, and then enjoy your discomfiture for a distance of ten miles. I have seen respectable men cling to the front railing of stages, with their feet uneasily balanced on the fore-wheels, for over half an hour—men worth probably fifty thousand dollars in stocks—and then seen them fail—utterly, miserably, and ingloriously fail—to get a seat. I have seen drivers of stages laugh and chuckle by the hour with some sympathizing chum picked up at the last moment; and I have heard these despotic men say they had a good notion to let every body ride on top, for then the stage would be pretty certain to capsize and break a few legs and arms. Why stage-drivers, who are paid a liberal stipend per month for putting passengers over the public highways, should be so vindictively hostile to the travelling community surpasses my comprehension.

The scene on the arrival of the cars is quite inspiring. Stages backed up in a long row; prancing horses in front; swearing and sweating porters, baggage-masters, drivers, and passengers all about and behind; John Chinamen, with long tails rolled up on the backs of their heads, running distractedly through the crowd in search of their lost bundles; anxious ladies, prolific in crinoline and gorgeous in silks and satins (the California travelling costume), fretting and scolding over crushed bandboxes; and stern-looking men of an official cast of countenance shouting, fiercely, "This way, gents! 'Ere's the place for your baggage! Bring it along if you want it weighed; if you don't, it won't go—that's all!" And there is the machine that weighs, and there stands the inexorable gentleman that marks off the weights—ten, forty, sixty, ninety pounds per passenger—thirty pounds allowed; all extra baggage twenty-five cents per pound. "Fifteen dollars for you, Sir." "Twenty-five for you, Sir." "Forty-six for you, Madam." "Seventy-five for you, Miss—heavy trunk that, Miss." "Oh dear! oh goodness gracious! must I pay seventy-five dollars for my trunk?" "Yes, Miss—sorry for it—no getting over it." "Oh!" "Quick, if you please, ladies and gents! Stages behind time—won't get to Placerville before dark!" "Your names, gents." "Smith, Jones, Brown, Johnson." "All aboard!" and off goes stage No. 1. "Pile in, gents. Get down from the front seat, you, Sir—place engaged. All aboard!" and off goes stage No. 2. "Henness? Placerville? Dammit, why didn't you say so?" "Johnson, Brown, Jones, Smith." "Pitch in, Cap—all set!"

and stage No. 3 follows through the dusty clouds that cover the road and the hill-sides. And so on till we are all fairly in and off, and looking back, with fervent thanks to Providence that we are clear of the smoke and trouble and turmoil of the railroad dépôt at Folsom.

It is always pleasant to make a start; yet if any body can

RATHER DUSTY.

say the road from Folsom to Placerville is an agreeable road to travel in the early part of October, before the autumn showers have commenced, he must be fond of dust, and ruts, and hills, and plenty of warm sunshine. As for the dust—whew!

With a gentle breeze behind; the horses' ears dimly

perceptible in front; curling clouds rising up at every step and imbedding the stage with its sneezing, gasping, suffocating human freight as in a chaotic bank of pulverized earth without top, bottom, or sides; your face smeared with red, yellow, and black stripes of sweat and mud; your nostrils stuffed with a pasty conglomerate; your hair turned prematurely gray; your eyelashes blinking with a feathery fringe-work of native soil; your lungs surcharged with gold, porphyry, sulphurets and all the indications that predominate in a mineral region— I say, if you can enjoy this sort of thing, you are fit to travel to Washoe or any other country. You are part and parcel of California, worth very nearly your weight in gold. Put you through the hydraulic process after your arrival at Placerville, and your washings are worth $14 per ounce. Pan you out, and two dollars a pan would be a low estimate of your intrinsic value. In fact I am told the hotel-keepers are growing rich on this single source of profit. Each hotel keeps a kind of sluice or washing arrangement in the back-room, through which the travellers by stage are immediately put on their arrival; and judging by the accumulations in the bottoms of the basins, I should say every man leaves behind him pay dirt of a very rich quality. For my part, I paid my fare, and positively refused to wash. Why should a man impoverish himself in this way for the benefit of tavern-keepers? His dust is worth as much to himself as it is to any other man, and he certainly has the best claim to it.

As we heard the cry of Washoe in early times, so we now heard the cry of Reese River. Every body and his uncle, cousin, brother, and son-in-law was gone or going to Reese. The streets and shops of Placerville were crowded with Reese River goods, Reese River wagons, Reese River croppings, and Reese River notices of various kinds. Nothing was dreamed of in the philosophy of the busy multitude but Reese River.

It was 5 o'clock P.M., just three hours after the usual time, thanks to the Hog's Back, when we took our places

GOLD DUST.

on the stages, and girded up our loins for the trip across the mountains. I was the lucky recipient of an outside seat. The seat of honor, by the side of that exalted dignitary the driver, was accorded me by the "polite and gentlemanly agent."

The driver was Charlie. Of course every body knows Charlie—that same Old Charlie who has driven all over the roads in California, and never capsized any body but himself. On that occasion he broke several of his ribs, or as he expressed it to me, "Bust his sides in." I was proud and happy to sit by the side of Charlie—especially as the road was supposed to be a little undulating even by its best friends. Possibly I may have travelled over worse roads than the first ten miles out of Placerville. If so, they must have been in Iceland; for there are not

many quite so bad on the continent of North America.
I speak of what the road was at the close of summer, cut
up by heavy teams, a foot deep with dust, and abounding
in holes and pitfalls big enough to swallow a thousand
stages and six thousand horses without inconvenience to
itself.   There are places, over which we passed after
dark, where I am sure the road is three miles wide, and
every acre of it a model stage-trap; where it branches
off over hills, and along the sides of hills, and into deep
cañons, and up hills again; dark, dismal places in the
midst of great forests of pine, where the horses seem
to be eternally plunging over precipices and the stage
following them with a crashing noise, horribly suggestive
of cracked skulls and broken bones.   But I had im-
plicit confidence in Old Charlie.   The way he handled the
reins and peered through the clouds of dust and volumes
of darkness, and saw trees and stumps and boulders of
rock and horses' ears, when I could scarcely see my own
hand before me, was a miracle of stage-driving.   " Git
aeoup !" was the warning cry of this old stager.   " Git
alang, my beauties !" was the natural outpouring of the
poetry that filled his capacious soul.

   " Do many people get killed on this route ?" said I to
Charlie, as we made a sudden lurch in the dark and
bowled along the edge of a fearful precipice.

   " Nary a kill that I know of.   Some of the drivers
mashes 'em once in a while, but that's whisky or bad
drivin'.   Last summer a few stages went over the grade,
but nobody was hurt bad—only a few legs'n arms broken.
Them was opposition stages.   Pioneer stages, as a genr'l
thing, travels on the road.   Git aeoup !"

   " Is it possible ?   Why, I have read horrible stories of
the people crushed to death going over these mountains !"

   " Very likely—they kill 'em quite lively on the Henness
route.   Git alang, my beauties !   Drivers only break their
legs a little on this route; that is, some of the opposition
boys did it last summer; but our company's very strict;

they won't keep drivers, as a genr'l thing, that gets drunk and mashes up stages. Git aeoup, Jake! Git alang, Mack! 'Twon't pay; 'tain't a good investment for man nor beast. A stage is worth more'n two thousand dollars, and legs costs heavy besides. You Jake, git!"

"How in the world can you see your way through this dust?"

"Smell it. Fact is, I've travelled over these mountains so often I can tell where the road is by the sound of the wheels. When they rattle I'm on hard ground; when they don't rattle I gen'r'lly look over the side to see where she's agoing."

"Have you any other signs?"

"Backer's another sign; when I'm a little skeer'd I chaw more'n ordinary. Then I know the road's bad."

"Don't you get tired driving over the same road so often?"

"Well, I do—kalklate to quit the business next trip. I'm getting well on in years, you see, and don't like it so well as I used to, afore I was busted in!"

"How long have you driven stage?"

"Nigh on to thirty years, an' I'm no better off now than when I commenced. Pay's small; work heavy; gettin' old; rheumatism in the bones; nobody to look out for used-up stage-drivers; kick the bucket one of these days, and that's the last of Old Charlie."

"Why, you must have made plenty of friends during so long a career of staging?"

"Oh yes, plenty of 'em; see 'em to-day, gone to-morrow! Git alang!"

And so passed the long hours of the night, Charlie and I gossiping pleasantly about the risks and charms, and mysteries of the stage-driving profession. A hard life is that of the stage-driver; a life of exposure and peril, and wear and tear, such as few other men experience in this world. You, my good friend, who cross the Sierras of California once or twice in a life-time, imagine you have done great things—you boast of your qualities as a travel-

ler; you have passed unscathed through the piercing
night air; have scarcely shuddered at the narrow bridges,
or winced at the fearful precipices. You have braved
all the dangers of the trip, and can afford to slap yourself complacently on the leg in proof of the fact that you
are still sound. But think of old Charlie! He has crossed the mountains a thousand times; crossed when the
roads were at their worst; by night and by day; in
storm and gloom and darkness; through snow and sleet
and rain, and burning suns and dust; back and forth;
subject to the risks of different teams and different
stages; his life balanced on the temper of a horse or the
strength of a screw. This is a career worthy the consideration of the heedless world! Who thinks of old
Charlie? Where is the gazette to herald his achieve-
ments? What pen is there to trumpet his praises?

All hail to thee, Old Charlie! Never shall it be said
that ingratitude is one of my vices. Here, in these
illuminated pages your name shall be rescued from oblivion. Sweet and gentle ladies shall pay the tribute of
admiration to your manly features; and honest men shall
award you honor, to whom honor is due. For in the
vicissitudes of my career have I not found brave and
sterling qualities in all classes of men; heroes whose
names are never known; hearts and souls, human affec-
tions, and the fear of God in the bodies of stage-
drivers?

Thus I think and moralize as we approach the grade.
The bad road is at an end. We strike in upon the smooth
broad highway, and dash onward with a feeling of absolute relief. The horses' hoofs clatter merrily on the
hard, gravelly earth. The tall pines form a magnificent
avenue through which the moon begins to glimmer, making a fretwork of silvery light on the backs of our noble
animals.

Yet I must confess the trip to Washoe has, to me at
least, lost much of its original charm. No longer is the
way variegated by long strings of pedestrians, carrying

their picks, shovels, and blankets upon their backs; no longer are the stopping-places crowded every night with two or three hundred adventurers inspired by visionary thoughts of the future; no longer are the wild mountain passes enlivened by grotesque scenes of saddle-trains and passengers struggling through the mud and snow; it is all now a regular and established line of travel; too civilized to be interesting in any great degree, and too convenient to admit of those charming discomforts which formerly afforded us so much amusement. Only think how the emigrants who crossed these mountains in 1848 would have stared at the bare suggestion of a Pioneer stage-line. If we are behind the times in railroads, it is certain there is no such country in the world for feats of horse-flesh as California. The length of our stage routes, the rapidity with which we travel upon them, and the facilities afforded by our expresses, are matters of astonishment to the people of Europe, who have not the faintest idea of the real difficulties to be overcome in carrying such enterprises into effect in a wild country like ours. During my sojourn in Germany I received a letter from California by Pony Express in less than four weeks after it was written; and it was not until I showed the date and express-stamp and carefully explained the whole matter that I was enabled to overcome the incredulity of my Teutonic friends. The idea of such a feat being accomplished by horse-flesh was something they could not comprehend. Nor could they quite reconcile to their notions of the practicable that we had spanned the continent with our stages—crossing deserts and mountains, from San Francisco to Missouri, as they would cross the cultivated plains and well-graded hills of their native country. But their astonishment was still more excited when I read a dispatch received from San Francisco in just fourteen days! The telegraph line had outstripped the ponies, and time was annihilated between the East and the West! "Oh," said they, when convinced there was no joke about it, "you are indebted

to the Germans for that. The magnetic telegraph was invented by a German forty years ago."

" Then, why didn't he put it in operation forty years ago, and let the world enjoy the benefit of it?" was my answer.

"Because," said they, " he was too poor to do it himself, and could find nobody to believe in it who was able to assist him. He presented his plan to the Government, but the idea was ridiculed and Government would have nothing to do with it."

I could not but think that there was very little to boast of in this—even supposing it to be true. It certainly argued poorly for the sagacity of the people in Europe, or the intelligence of the Governments, that an American should be the first to establish in their own country an invention claimed by them, and now indispensable to the civilized world. I must say this much, however—for nothing is further from my thoughts than to depreciate the German character—that the education, skill, and intellect of this people have contributed largely to the progress and prosperity of our country. Indeed, they are now a part of ourselves, and what reflects credit upon them reflects credit upon us all as a nation.

The approach to the crossing of the American River is indescribably grand. Here the grade takes a downward plunge, and here the scenery becomes truly Alpine. Formerly the descent was made on the right side of the ridge. Wonderful improvements, however, have taken place in the grades of this road during the past few years, chiefly owing to the enterprise of Mr. Louis M'Lane, President of the Pioneer Stage Company. In 1860, as already stated, I travelled over this part of the country on foot, in common with some thousands of adventurers, equally independent of horse-flesh. I then enjoyed the scenery of the American River, for I saw it by the early morning, when the mountains were decked in all the glories of spring; when torrents of snow-water burst from every ravine, and fell thundering into the depths below, and limpid springs made a pleasant music over the moss-covered rocks by the way-side; when the sun's rays glimmered through the dripping trees, and the air was fragrant with the odor of wild flowers. But I had never till now been impressed with an adequate sense of its beauties. How calm and still the night was! how exquisitely balmy the air! how sublime the repose of these grand old mountains! I thought of all the scenes I had witnessed in other countries, yet could not recall any thing to surpass this. There is something in the mystic lights and shades, and the profound solemnity of the night, which lends an awful sublimity to these wild regions. The gigantic forest trees standing in bold outline on the opposite sides of the mountains, seem to pierce the sky; and the moonbeams, pouring down into the mysterious abyss through which the river dashes, fringe the tops of the pines, as far down as the eye can reach, with a frost-like drapery. Nothing can be more thrilling than the descent of the grade by moonlight. The road is a magnificent piece of engineering—smooth, broad, and beautifully regular.

Imagine yourself seated in front of the stage, by the side of that genial old whipster, Charlie, who knows every foot of the way, and upon whom you can implicitly rely for the safety of your life and limbs. Holding the reins with a firm hand, and casting a penetrating eye ahead, he cracks his whip, and away go the horses with inspiring velocity—six magnificent chestnuts, superbly adorned with flowing manes and tails. The stillness of the night is pleasantly broken by their measured tread, and the rattle of the wheels over the gravel echoes through the wild rifts and openings of the cañon like a voice from the civilized world telling of human enterprise. Down, and still down, we plunge into the gloomy depths of the abyss; the ghostly forms of trees looming up on our left; to the right, rising far beyond the range of vision, the towering heights of the Sierras; and ever and anon yawning gulfs in front and bottomless pits of darkness still threatening to devour. The road turns and winds like a serpent, sometimes apparently running into a huge bank of granite boulders, then whirling suddenly, and plunging into a shimmering wilderness of rocks and trees, where destruction seems inevitable. Yet onward dash the horses, with an instinct so admirable in its precision that it seems for the time superior to human intelligence. They never swerve from the track; through the fretwork of light and darkness they pursue their way with unrivalled ease and grace; sweeping around the narrow turns; now coursing along on the extreme edge of the precipice, or closely hugging the upper bank as the road winds to the right or the left; now plunging down and whirling with marvellous sagacity over the narrow bridges that span the ravines, often where there is neither rail nor post to mark the way, ever true to the slightest touch of the reins, and ever obedient to the voice of their driver. Is it a wonder that Old Charlie loves his horses and talks of his teams with a kind of paternal affection—that he knows them by heart, and holds converse with them through the long watches of the night as with human friends?

I have attempted to give some idea of the romantic beauties of these mountain regions and the peculiar wildness of the scenery; but it must be conceded that nature has not been permitted to lie wholly undisturbed in the immediate vicinity of the road. There is probably not an acre of ground, possessing a water privilege, on the entire route between Placerville and Virginia City, which has not been taken up and settled upon by some enterprising squatter or speculator, whose views of the present necessities of trade and the future prosperity of Nevada invest this region of country with an extraordinary value. When I travelled over the road in the spring of 1860 there were symptoms of rapid progress. Tents and shanties were springing up all along the way-side; and if the weary pedestrian could get nothing else, he

could at least always be sure of whisky, even where the
houses had neither walls nor roofs. If lodgings were
scarce, bedfellows were plenty; if there was trouble in
keeping the outer man warm, there was abundance of
fuel for the inner man. For this reason, perhaps, it was
not an uncommon thing to see the sturdy adventurers
who were on their way to the silver regions quite elevated by the time they reached the summit; and if they
got sober again, it must have been after they had invested
their last dollar in some of those flourishing leads which
prevail around Carson and the Devil's Gate.

The state of things is now very different. Good and substantial taverns, well supplied with provisions, beds, fleas,
bugs, etc., to say nothing of the essential article of whisky, are to be met with at intervals of every two or three
miles all along the route. Here the stages stop, and here
the horses are watered and changed; and here the drivers
and passengers get down and stretch their legs, but as a
general thing they don't indulge so much in water as the
horses.

A great many able-bodied men, very dirty, and a good
deal oftener drunk than sober, hang about the bars and
front doors of these establishments, conversing in a style
peculiar to a large class of our inhabitants—that is to
say, swearing horribly at things in general. I don't know
why it is that people swear so hard in some parts of
California. Every other word is an oath. In fact, oaths
have become embodied in our language as an essential
part of it. Ordinary words possess no meaning to men
of this class unless accompanied by some profane appeal
to the Deity—so that an unsophisticated traveller like
myself, unaccustomed to such a strong style of language,
is frequently misled as to the purport of the conversation, and naturally imagines that people who indulge in
such a shocking mode of expression must be furiously
angry, and will presently pull out their knives or pistols
and begin to kill each other. I have heard men relate
the most trivial incidents, with such a torrent of impre-

cations, that I looked with amazement to see what there was in the matter to provoke them so unreasonably, or arouse their resentment to such a pitch of ferocity. The other day one of the stage drivers, boasting of a new whip-handle which a friend had presented to him, cursed it in a manner so shocking, as the best piece of hickory he had ever seen, that I was absolutely afraid he would swear the hat off his head. Now, if this vigorous mode of expression is to prevail in California and our new territories—for I notice that men of character and education are adopting it extensively—would it not be well to expunge from our school-books those tame, trite, and meaningless words which have hitherto formed the staple of the English language in civilized communities? Let us have at least one common language in which we can all communicate our thoughts. As it becomes fashionable it will cease to be profane; and then, only imagine the luxury of swearing at our best friends! The lover, instead of whispering honeyed nothings to the object of his adoration, can blast her eyes under the fiery inspiration of his passion; and she, the gentle and the beautiful, can tenderly turn to him and stop the floodgates of his despair with such a soothing little dam of affection as to render him completely happy for the remainder of his days. These hints I throw out especially for the benefit of our public men, who wield an influence in the community, and who seek to obtain popular favor by adopting popular modes of expression. It will be an advantage to ladies in crossing over the mountains and settling down in new territories to have their ears cultivated to the standard of the prevailing language—otherwise they may be a little shocked at what seems to be a general looseness of style. For my part I have long since given up the hope of reaching Congress by adapting myself to the popular taste. I dislike shedding blood —can't drink whisky as a standard beverage, and have no talent for swearing. But there are plenty of men in the country of sufficiently vigorous constitution to stand

O 2

OLD CHARLIE.

these tests of merit, and fully and fairly represent us in
the national councils.

As we approached Strawberry, I am free to admit that
I became somewhat nervous. A lurking suspicion took
possession of me that I was recognized by the driver,
Old Charlie; though I took particular pains to join with

him in abusing that vile slanderer Ross Browne, whose Peep at Washoe had aroused the indignation of every publican on the route. Charlie admitted that he had never read any of this fellow's productions, but he believed him to be the Prince of Liars on general principles; an assertion in which I naturally coincided, with an internal reservation that it was strange how angry it made people to have the truth told about them. "Lord, Lord, Charlie," said I, handing him a cigar, "how this world is given to lying!" By this time we were at Strawberry, and I saw that I had to face the music.

The story goes that there was once upon a time a man named Berry, who located a claim in a pleasant little flat about eight miles from the summit of the mountain. Here he set up his shanty, seeing with a prophetic eye that it would soon become an important point for the accommodation of travellers on the way over to Carson. When the people of California were seized with the silver mania, and began to crowd up the slopes of the Sierras with their teams and pack-trains, their picks, shovels, and blankets, Berry's became a great stopping-place, and his house, which he speedily enlarged, a famous resort for travellers; and this Berry soon became a very rich Berry. His dinners were excellent; his suppers without reproach; his beds as good as any on the road; his whisky as sure to kill at any given range as the best Port Townsend; and altogether he was a popular and a flourishing Berry. But as teams crowded around his premises and supplies of hay were cut off by storms and bad roads, he was forced to offer straw to his customers as a substitute for the regular horse and mule feed. Of course he charged hay prices, for even straw has a hay value under certain circumstances. Now the teamsters when they got straw in place of hay waxed unreasonably wroth, and called this excellent old Berry STRAW-BERRY—a name to which let all homage be rendered. By this honored name goes to this day that famous stopping-place known to the travelling public as Strawberry.

I deemed it prudent, however, not to avow my name on the occasion of my present visit. It was 10 o'clock when we arrived. Covered with dust; beard, eyebrows, and hair a motley gray; hat, coat, shirt, trowsers, and boots the same color; face all striped and piebald, I was effectually disguised. If any body was there who had ever seen me before he could not have recognized me now with a microscope. I walked all about the old room with the fire-place—familiar, yet changed—looked calmly at every body about the premises, and stood with my back to the fire while the horses were being changed, with a delightful consciousness of security. In the darkness of night I had escaped Dirty Mike, and now, amid the curious and penetrating crowd at Strawberry, not a soul knew me!

The improvements at Strawberry are not to be slighted. A fine hotel now adjoins the old building; a tele-graph-office affords conveniences for stock-jobbing and catching thieves; handsome rooms are to be had merely for the asking; spring beds invite the wayfarer to repose; the dining-room, billiard-saloon, and bar would do credit to Virginia City, or any other civilized community, where men eat, gamble, and drink spirituous liquors; the out-buildings are numerous and capacious; the stables fit for the most aristocratic horses; the hay no longer a subject of reproach to man nor beast, the straw as good as ever bore grain—O, Straw-Berry!

"*All aboard!*"—a new voice, a new face, and a new driver. I bade good-bye to Charlie, and hoped we might meet again in the next world, if not in this. Once more we are on our way. The road over the mountain from Strawberry has been greatly improved. It is now a magnificent highway. Formerly the ascent to the summit was difficult and dangerous. The rise is now so beautifully graded as to be scarcely appreciable. Our horses trotted along briskly nearly the whole way. The scenery becomes weird and stern as we approach the highest altitude of the Sierras. The trees are scraggy;

the earth is barren and of a whitish cast; great boulders of rock rear their hoary crests high over the way-side. threatening to topple over and crush all beneath them, Sometimes huge masses of rock seem detached from the main body of the slope or cliff around which the road winds, and balanced on a mere point—thousands of tons of solid stone, ready apparently at the slightest vibration of the earth or puff of wind to come crashing down upon the stage. At some of these points I deeply sympathized with a gentleman from San Francisco, of whom the driver spoke in terms of ridicule.

"He was so 'fraid them rocks 'ud be shook loose and fall on his head, he kept a dodgin' 'em all the time. His hair stood right up like a hog's brussels. Every now and then he was peerin' around for a soft spot of road to jump out on; an' when he seed he couldn't find it, he held on to the railin' with both hands till his fingers wos all blistered. 'D-d-driver,' sez he, 'd'ye think there's any danger?' 'Danger?' sez I—'ov course there's danger! Supposing that 'ere rock was shook loose by the rattlin' ov this 'ere stage—what d'ye think 'ud be the consequences?' 'I r-r-really can't say,' sez he; 'p-p-possibly it would crush the stage!' 'No,' sez I, 'it wouldn't crush it; but it 'ud make sich a d—d squash of it that bones wouldn't count. Your bones an' my bones, an' the bones ov three passengers above an' four behind an' nine down below, 'ud be all squashed, an' the verdic of Corners Inquest 'ud be — "Eighteen men, six horses an' a Pioneer Stage squashed by the above stone!" 'D-d-driver,' sez he—his teeth a-chatterin' like a box o' dice—'is that so?' 'You bet,' sez I; 'the last time I see it done, three ladies an' ten gents from Frisco was squashed.' 'Good gracious!' sez he, turnin' as white as a sheet, 'let me down at the next station!' And sure 'nuff he got down at the next station and made tracks for Frisco. He changed his base—*he* did. Git aeoup!"

"Is that true, driver?"

"True?"—and the indignant look with which my

friend of the whip resented the question satisfied me that it would not be prudent to push my doubts too far—so I qualified the inquiry—"Is it on the square, I mean?"

"Stranger," said he, solemnly, "I don't make a habit o'lyin'; when I lie I kin lie as good as any body; but gen'r'lly speakin' I'm on the square."

"Of course—that's all right; that's just what I mean; you don't usually steer clear of facts when the 'truth is strange—stranger than fiction.' Won't you take a cigar, driver?"

"Don't care if I do."

And thus the dawning difficulty was amicably adjusted.

Owing to our late start we did not reach the summit

DANGEROUS BOULDERS.

before two o'clock. The air at this elevation was sharp, though not unpleasantly so. The altitude is estimated at eight thousand feet above the level of the sea. Frost was on the ground, and there was promise of colder nights soon to come. The moon, which had so kindly befriended us during the greater part of our journey to this point, was still shining brightly, shedding its silvery rays over the wilderness of mountains that loomed up around us. The view over Lake Valley was superb. I have seen nothing to surpass it in Switzerland or Norway. Perhaps the finest feature of the whole journey is the descent of the new grade. For a distance of five or six miles the road winds around the sides of the mountains, crossing ravines and doubling up occasionally in turns so rapid that the stage seems to run one way and the horses another. Some of these whirling turns reminded me of the flight of an Australian bomerang. As we strike the straight road again the driver gives rein to our spirited animals; crack goes the whip, and down we plunge over narrow bridges, along the edges of terrific precipices a thousand feet deep, through dark forests of pine and along frowning banks of granite, hewn from the solid bed of the mountain. Despite the ridiculous stories we had heard of accidents and alarms, every passenger with a nervous system clings tenaciously to the stage fixtures, as if determined to follow the stage wherever it might go, and there were moments when we even held our breath to keep up a balance. I flatter myself I saved the lives of the whole party several times by hoisting at the lee rail, and holding my breath hard, while I leaned over on the weather side. It is not comfortable to look down when you are flying along at the rate of ten miles an hour and see no bottom short of a thousand or fifteen hundred feet. Yet there is a charm in this dashing, reckless journey by moonlight. The danger is just sufficient to give it a relish. The excitement keeps the blood warm; the fresh mountain air invigorates and inspires every faculty; the spirit rises with

the rapidity of the motion, and before you get half-way
to the valley you find yourself in a condition to sing,
shout, or dance. The driver, by whose side I had the
honor to sit, had evidently cultivated his voice for singing ; but unfortunately he knew but one song—and of
that he remembered but one line—

"When this cruel war is over!"

which he sang straight ahead for three hours, commenc-
ing at the top of the grade and ending only when relieved by a new driver. Indeed, I am not sure that he
ended then, for the last I heard of him he was leaning
against a post at the station-house, humming over to
himself—

"When this cruel war is over!"

and it is not impossible he may be at it yet. The only
variety I noticed during the journey was in the form of
an interlude as he spoke to the horses, " Git aeoup, Bummers ! Git alang, Rebs !

"When this—and so forth ; now git !"

The song is not bad when you get the whole of it, with
a strong chorus ; but a single line of it, repeated for a
distance of twenty-five miles without a chorus, becomes
monotonous.

Whether the lack of variety in the poetry had a soporific
tendency, or loss of rest produced a heaviness in the head,
I don't know ; but after the novelty of our flight down
the grade had worn away somewhat, I now and then de-
tected myself in the act of plunging overboard on the
backs of the horses, or bobbing into some frightful abyss.
Once I actually thought I was gone, and received such a
shock when I discovered that I had only been asleep, and
was still on hand, as to keep me wide awake during the
rest of the way to Lake Tahoe.

CHAPTER XXXII.

LAKE TAHOE.

THIS beautiful lake was originally named Bigler, after a distinguished politician, who held the position of Governor of California—John Bigler. It was so named by a gentleman who had a high admiration for the name of Bigler. The beauty of the scenery, the crystal clearness of the water, the inspiring purity of the atmosphere filled the soul of Bigler's friend with poetry, and he called this lovely spot Bigler. It was a just tribute to the popularity of the Governor among his friends; but no governor on earth can enjoy every man's friendship. Bigler had enemies like other governors—some because they wanted office and couldn't get it; others because they wanted a contract and couldn't get it; and many because they wanted to be governor themselves. When this distinguished gentleman ceased to be Governor of California he was made a Minister to South America. It was then discovered by both friends and enemies that the name was inappropriate and lacked euphony; friends had nothing more to hope; enemies nothing more to fear. Who the deuce is John Bigler, said they, that the finest lake in California should be called after him? Let us blot his ugly name off the map and call this beautiful sheet of water Lake Latham or Lake Downey. But here commenced a squabble between the friends of these eminent gentlemen relative to their respective claims. Latham, it was true, had served with honor in the Custom-House—had held the Gubernatorial chair for a few weeks, and subsequently had become United States Senator. But then Downey had vetoed

SCENE IN THE SIERRA NEVADA.

the Bulkhead bill. Pending this difficulty, a hint from some obscure source came very near resulting in the selection of a name that would doubtless have afforded general satisfaction, since it could be claimed by a great many people throughout the State—the name of Brown. It was brief, pointed, and popular—Lake Brown! But what Brown? Jack Brown, Jim Brown, Bill Brown or Ross Browne? There were thirty-six Browns in the Penitentiary, besides several more who ought to be there; and at least forty-four Browns were candidates for the Legislature or inmates of the Lunatic Asylum; so that it was difficult to see what Brown would be specially benefited by the compliment. The name itself scarcely presented sufficient claims over all other names to be selected merely on account of its euphony. So Brown was dropped; and between Latham and Downey it was impossible to come to an equitable decision. The name of Bigler remained unmolested for several years longer. In due time, when Latham and Downey were both thrown overboard, the discussion of the question was renewed —every prominent man in the State claiming that the lake should be named after himself. Finally, as popular sentiment could not fix upon the name of any white man, it gradually settled down in favor of the supposed Indian name— *Tahoe*—which was the first word spoken to the discoverer by a solitary digger, whom he encountered upon its shores. "Tahoe!" cried the digger; and it was at once assumed that "Tahoe" meant "Big Water;" but I am assured by an old settler that "Tahoe" means "Strong Water"—in other words, "Whisky"—so that this magnificent lake, formerly called Bigler, is now literally "Lake Whisky!"

Within the past two years the people of California and Washoe have begun to discover the beauties of this charming region, and its rare advantages as a place of summer resort. Situated in the bosom of the Sierra Nevada mountains, 6000 feet above the level of the sea, with an atmosphere of wonderful purity; abounding in game; convenient of access, and possessing all the attractions of retirement from the busy world, amid scenery unrivalled for its romantic beauties, there can be no doubt it will soon become the grand central point of pleasure and recreation for the people of the Pacific coast. The water of the lake is singularly clear and blue, and during the

warmest months is so cool as to render bathing rather a
lively and stimulating exercise. It abounds in the finest
trout, which supply the markets of Carson and Virginia
City, and occasionally furnish a rich treat to the epicures
of San Francisco. Fishermen are busily occupied with
their nets at intervals along its shores, greatly to the
detriment of gentlemen who follow in the footsteps of
Izaak Walton. An excellent hotel, called the Lake House,
has been established at a beautiful and picturesque point
on the right shore (going toward Virginia), where good
accommodations and " all the luxuries of the season " can
now be had. Two enterprising Americans, Messrs. Dean
and Martin, had recently purchased the premises, with
a view of getting up a splendid watering-place in the
Atlantic style. Already they had bath-houses, pleasure-
boats, riding-horses, billiard-tables, bowling-alleys, and
all the conveniences for health and recreation. At the
time of my visit the house was in process of enlarge-
ment. Martin was one of my fellow-pedestrians on my
first trip across the mountains to Washoe, and I can safely say it would give me great pleasure to hear of his
success in this enterprise. He is a clever, genial fellow,
a first-rate travelling companion, and an upright, honest
man. To dyspeptics, consumptives, and broken-down
stock-brokers I have a word of advice to offer : If you
want your digestive apparatus put in complete order, so
that brickbats will stick to your ribs without inconvenience, spend a month with my friend Martin; if your
bronchial tubes distress you, swallow a few thousand gal-
lons of Lake Tahoe air, and you can blow bellows blasts
from your lungs forever after ; if your nervous system
is deranged by bad speculations in stocks, bowl nine-pins
and row one of Martin's boats for six weeks, and I venture to affirm stocks will rise a thousand per cent. It is
all a matter of health in the long-run ; with good digestion and a sound nervous system there is no trouble in
life ; and for these ends there is no place like Tahoe.

From the first hour after leaving Placerville we pass-

ed along the road-side numerous teams and trains of
wagons, most of which were grouped together under the
trees, or in front of the station-houses, in the old-fashioned camp style. I commenced a rough calculation of the
number of wagons, but soon gave it up as a hopeless
task. It seemed to me that there were enough of them,

JOB.

big and little, to reach all the way over the mountain.
At the least calculation we must have passed two or three
hundred. Every wagon was heavily freighted—some
with merchandise, others with iron castings for the mills,
and quite a goodly number with families, fruit, whisky,
and furniture. There were horse-teams, and mule-teams,
and ox-teams. I never before saw so many teams on one
road. No wonder the dust was pretty deep!

"Are you going back to the States?" said I, to a Pike
County man, with a wagon-load of wife and children,
beds, chairs, and cooking utensils. "No, Sir," said he,
turning the quid in his leathery jaw, "you bet I ain't!
I'm bound for Reese! After I make my pile thar, a
keeping of a tavern, I'll steer for Californy agin—it's
good enough a country for me." "Why did you leave
it?" I asked. "Wa'al," said the poor fellow, wiping the
dust from his face with the back of his hand, "that's
more'n I know. 'Twarn't my fault. The old 'oman was
high for feet. She said we were fools for a tinkerin' on
our little farm down thar, when every body was makin'
fortunes in Reese. She's tolerable peert—the old 'oman
is. Oh, she's on it, you bet!" "Well, I wish you luck!"
"Thank yer," drawled Pike; "what mout yer name
be, stranger?" "My name?—ahem—is—John." The
man looked hard at me; turned the quid once more in
his leathery jaw; squirted out a copious stream of juice,
and, without changing in the slightest degree the gravity
of his countenance, said, "Mine's Job;" and then went to
work unhitching his horses. This was the last I saw of
Job. The camp scenes along the way-side were lively
and picturesque. I enjoyed them with a peculiar zest
after three years of travel through the deserts of civilization in Europe. Here was life reduced to its primary
elements; here were accommodations cheap, roomy, and
gorgeously furnished; here was comfort fit for poet,
artist, or any other man of a naturally healthy and barbarous taste; here were food and fire without stint, and
fresh air to an unlimited extent; and holes enough

through the tops of the trees to let the smoke out; and neither commissioners nor waiters to stand behind and admire your style of eating. Who is there so depraved as not to yearn for the heavenly joys of a camp life in the wilderness? Just take a side-peep at that merry group of teamsters! Uncouth and unsentimental they may be; tired and hungry after their hard day's work they doubtless are; but did you ever see a happier-looking set of vagabonds? Their faces, despite the dust and grime that besmear them, absolutely shine in the cheery light of the big log fire; they sniff the steaming stew that simmers in the pot with sympathetic unction; they sit and loll upon their mother earth in exquisite unconsciousness of dirt; they spin their yarns of the day's adventures with many a merry burst of laughter; and now, as they fall to work and devour the savory mess before them, what need have they for dinner-pills? Hunger is their sauce—fresh air and exercise their medicine. Oh, the jolly rascals! How I envy them their camp life!

On second thoughts I don't know that they are to be envied in every particular. As to the daily part of their occupation—driving ox and mule teams over the Sierras; swallowing dust and alkali on the plains; pushing, pulling, sweating, and swearing at their stubborn animals, and navigating their heavy wagons over bad roads from one month's end to another—I can't conscientiously envy them. Sooner than follow mule or ox driving as a profession, I think I'd profess politics for a living—which I consider the last resort of a worthless man.

Yet I must confess the trip to Washoe has, to me at least, lost much of its original charm. No longer is the way variegated by long strings of pedestrians, carrying their picks, shovels, and blankets upon their backs; no longer are the stopping-places crowded every night with two or three hundred millionaires rejoicing in empty pockets and brimming heads; no longer are the wild mountain passes enlivened by grotesque gangs of saddle-

trains and passengers struggling through the mud and
snow; it is all now a regular and well-established line of
travel—too civilized to be interesting in any great degree,
and too convenient to admit of those charming discomforts which formerly afforded us so much amusement.
The business man who now leaves San Francisco at 4
P.M. is deposited at Virginia City by 10 o'clock the next
night—just thirty-six hours' travelling time. Fancy how
the emigrants who crossed these mountains prior to 1860
would have stared at the bare suggestion of such a feat
as this! If we are behind the times in railroads, it is
certain there is no such country in the world for feats
of horse-flesh as California. The length of our stage-
routes, the rapidity with which we travel on them, and
the facilities afforded by our expresses, would astonish
the humdrum people of the Atlantic States, if they had
the faintest idea of the difficulties to be overcome in carrying such enterprises into effect in a country like ours.

A new road now winds along the shores of Lake Tahoe. This part of the trip will compare favorably with
a journey along the shores of Como. At the Point of
Rocks the scene is equal to any thing of the kind to be
found in Europe. The road is cut through the brow of
the cliff, and for a distance of several hundred feet is
supported by massive timbers. To the left the clear blue
waters of the lake glimmer through forests of towering
pine; to the right is a colossal tower of rocks, presenting a front like some grand old fortress built by an ante-
diluvian race of giants. A rough and very hasty sketch
was all I could get of this remarkable point.

Leaving the lake at the Glenbrook Station, we begin
to ascend the last of the Sierra Nevada " divides," and,
after a heavy pull and long descent, enjoy a fine view of
the pretty little town of Carson. An hour more, and we
are safely landed at the Express office of Wells, Fargo,
and Co., from which point we can diverge to any number of bad hotels. By selecting the worst you will possibly not be disappointed.

POINT OF ROCKS, LAKE TAHOE.

Carson City has enjoyed a very wholesome kind of prosperity since my first visit, if I might be allowed to judge by a casual glance at the new buildings around the Plaza and the many pleasant residences in the suburbs. The plethoric condition of the stock market in San Francisco, and the fact that capital had been pouring through the various passes of the Sierras into Washoe,

P

had led me to expect that wonderful improvements must be the result. Nor was I disappointed. The number of drinking-saloons in Carson City, and in fact all along the route, manifested in a remarkable degree the rapid progress of civilization. The splendid stone Penitentiary, situated a couple of miles from Carson, presented another striking evidence of moral advancement.

STATION ON THE WASHOE ROAD.

CHAPTER XXXIII.

I WAS prepared to find great changes on the route from Carson to Virginia City. At Empire City— which was nothing but a sage-desert inhabited by Dutch Nick on the occasion of my early explorations—I was quite bewildered with the busy scenes of life and industry. Quartz-mills and saw-mills had completely usurped the valley along the head of the Carson River; and now the hammering of stamps, the hissing of steam, the whirling clouds of smoke from tall chimneys, and the confused clamor of voices from a busy multitude, reminded one of a manufacturing city. Here, indeed, was progress of a substantial kind.

Further beyond, at Silver City, there were similar evidences of prosperity. From the descent into the cañon through the Devil's Gate, and up the grade to Gold Hill, it is almost a continuous line of quartz-mills, tunnels, dumps, sluices, water-wheels, frame shanties, and grog-shops.

Gold Hill itself has swelled into the proportions of a city. It is now practically a continuation of Virginia. Here the evidences of busy enterprise are peculiarly striking. The whole hill is riddled and honey-combed with shafts and tunnels. Engine - houses for hoisting are perched on points apparently inaccessible; quartz-mills of various capacities line the sides of the cañon; the main street is well flanked by brick stores, hotels, express-offices, saloons, restaurants, groggeries, and all those attractive places of resort which go to make up a flourishing mining town. Even a newspaper is printed here, which I know to be a spirited and popular institution, having been viciously assailed by the same. A runaway team of horses, charging full tilt down the street, greeted our arrival in a lively and characteristic manner, and came very near capsizing our stage. One man was run over some distance below, and partially crushed; but as somebody was killed nearly every day, such a meagre result afforded no general satisfaction.

Descending the slope of the ridge that divides Gold Hill from Virginia City a strange scene attracts the eye. He who gazes upon it for the first time is apt to doubt if it be real. Perhaps there is not another spot upon the face of the globe that presents a scene so weird and desolate in its natural aspect, yet so replete with busy life, so animate with human interest. It is as if a wondrous battle raged, in which the combatants were man and earth. Myriads of swarthy, bearded, dust-covered men are piercing into the grim old mountains, ripping them open, thrusting murderous holes through their naked bodies; piling up engines to cut out their vital arteries; stamping and crushing up with infernal machines their disembowelled fragments, and holding fiendish revels amid the chaos of destruction; while the mighty earth, blasted, barren, and scarred by the tempests of ages, fiercely affronts the foe—smiting him with disease and death; scoffing at his puny assaults with a grim scorn; ever grand in his desolation, ever dominant in the infinity of his endurance. " Come!" he seems to mutter, " dig, delve, pierce, and bore, with your picks, your shovels, and your infernal machines; wring out of my veins a few globules of the precious blood; hoard it, spend it, gamble for it, bring perdition to your souls with it—do what you will, puny insects! Sooner or later the death-blow smites you, and Earth swallows you! From earth you came—to earth you go again!"

The city lies on a rugged slope, and is singularly diversified in its uprisings and downfallings. It is difficult to determine, by any system of observation or measurement,

VIRGINIA CITY.

upon what principle it was laid out. My impression is
that it never was laid out at all, but followed the dips,
spurs, and angles of the immortal Comstock. Some of
the streets run straight enough; others seem to dodge
about at acute angles in search of an open space, as
miners explore the subterranean regions in search of a
lead. The cross streets must have been forgotten in the
original plan—if ever there was a plan about this eccentric
city. Sometimes they happen accidentally at the most
unexpected points; and sometimes they don't happen at
all where you are sure to require them. A man in a
hurry to get from the upper slope of the town to any
opposite point below must try it underground or over
the roofs of the houses, or take the customary circuit of
half a mile. Every body seems to have built wherever
he could secure a lot. The two main streets, it must be
admitted, are so far regular as to follow pretty nearly
the direction of the Comstock lode. On the lower slope,
or plateau, the town, as viewed from any neighboring
eminence, presents much the appearance of a vast number
of shingle-roofs shaken down at random, like a jumbled
pack of cards. All the streets are narrow, except where
there are but few houses, and there they are wide enough
at present. The business part of the town has been
built up with astonishing rapidity. In the spring of
1860 there was nothing of it save a few frame shanties
and canvas tents, and one or two rough stone cabins. It
now presents some of the distinguishing features of a
metropolitan city. Large and substantial brick houses,
three or four stories high, with ornamental fronts, have
filled up most of the gaps, and many more are still in
progress of erection. The oddity of the plan, and variety of its architecture—combining most of the styles
known to the ancients, and some but little known to the
moderns—give this famous city a grotesque, if not picturesque, appearance, which is rather increased upon a
close inspection.

HAULING ORE TO THE MILLS.

Immense freight-wagons, with ponderous wheels and axles, heavily laboring under prodigious loads of ore for the mills, or groaning with piles of merchandise in boxes, bales, bags, and crates, block the narrow streets. Powerful teams of horses, mules, or oxen, numbering from eight to sixteen animals to each wagon, make frantic efforts to drag these land schooners over the ruts, and up the sudden rises, or through the sinks of this rut-smitten, ever-rising, ever-sinking city. A pitiable sight it is to see them! Smoking hot, reeking with sweat, dripping with liquified dust, they pull, jerk, groan, fall back, and dash forward, tumble down, kick, plunge, and bite; then buckle to it again, under the galling lash; and so live and so struggle these poor beasts, for their pittance of barley and hay, till they drop down dead. How they would welcome death if they had souls! Yet men have souls, and work hard too for their miserable pittance of food. How few of the countless millions of the earth yearn for death or welcome its coming? Even the teamsters that drive these struggling labor-worn brutes seem so fond of life that they scorn eternity. Brawny, bearded fellows they are; their faces so ingrained with the dust and grit of earth, and tanned to such an uncertain hue by the scorching suns and dry winds of the road, that for the matter of identity they might as well be Hindoos or Belooches. With what malignant zeal they crack their leather-thonged whips, and with what ferocious vigor they rend the air with their imprecations! O Plutus! such swearing—a sliding scale of oaths to which swearing in all other parts of the world is as the murmuring of a gentle brook to the volume and rush and thunder of a cataract. The fertility of resource displayed by these reckless men; their ready command of metaphor; their marvellous genius for strange, startling, and graphic combination of slang and profanity; their grotesque originality of inflection and climax; their infatuated credulity in the understanding of dumb animals; would in the pursuit of any nobler art elevate them to a niche in the temple of fame. Surely if murder be deemed one of the Fine Arts in Virginia City, swearing ought not to be held in such common repute.

Entering the main street you pass on the upper side huge piles of earth and ore, hoisted out of the shafts or run out of the tunnels, and cast over the "dumps." The hill-sides, for a distance of more than a mile, are perfectly honey-combed. Steam-engines are puffing off their steam; smoke-stacks are blackening the air with their thick volumes of smoke; quartz-batteries are battering; hammers are hammering; subterranean blasts are bursting up the earth; picks and crow-bars are picking and crashing into the precious rocks; shanties are springing up, and carpenters are sawing and ripping and nailing; store-keepers are rolling their merchandise in and out along the way-side; fruit venders are peddling their fruits; wagoners are tumbling out and piling in their freights of dry goods and ore; saloons are glittering with their gaudy bars and fancy glasses, and many-colored liquors, and thirsty men are swilling the burning poison; auctioneers, surrounded by eager and gaping crowds of speculators, are shouting off the stocks of delinquent stockholders; organ-grinders are grinding their organs and torturing consumptive monkeys; hurdy-gurdy girls are singing bacchanalian songs in bacchanalian dens; Jew clothiers are selling off prodigious assortments of worthless garments at ruinous prices; bill-stickers are sticking up bills of auctions, theatres, and new saloons; newsboys are crying the city papers with the latest telegraphic news; stages are dashing off with passengers for "Reese;" and stages are dashing in with passengers from "Frisco;" and the inevitable Wells, Fargo, and Co. are distributing letters, packages, and papers to the hungry multitude, amid tempting piles of silver bricks and wonderful complications of scales, letter-boxes, clerks, account-books, and twenty-dollar pieces. All is life, excitement, avarice, lust, deviltry, and enterprise. A strange city truly, abounding in strange exhibitions

A BLASTED SCRAPE.

and startling combinations of the human passions.
Where upon earth is there such another place?

One of the most characteristic features of Virginia is
the inordinate passion of the inhabitants for advertising.
Not only are the columns of the newspapers filled with
every possible species of advertisement, but .the streets
and hill-sides are pasted all over with flaming bills. Says
the proprietor of a small shanty, in letters that send a
thrill of astonishment through your brain:

"LOOK HERE! *For fifty cents* YOU CAN GET A GOOD SQUARE
MEAL at the HOWLING WILDERNESS SALOON!"

A square meal is not, as may be supposed, a meal placed
upon the table in the form of a solid cubic block, but a
substantial repast of pork and beans, onions, cabbage, and
other articles of sustenance that will serve to fill up the
corners of a miner's stomach.

The Jew clothing-stores present the most marvellous
fertility of invention in this style of advertising. Bills
are posted all over the door-ways, in the windows, on the
pavements, and on the various articles of clothing hung
up for sale. He who runs may read:

"Now or Never! *Cheapest coats in the world!!* PANTS GIVEN
AWAY!!! WALK IN, GENTS."

And so on without limit. New clothes and clothes
doubtful are offered for sale at these prolific establishments, which are always selling off at cost or suicidal
prices, yet never seem to be reduced in stock. I verily
believe I saw hanging at the door of one of these shops
the identical pair of stockings stolen from me several
years ago at Strawberry.

Drinking establishments being rather numerous, the
competition in this line of business gives rise to a very
persuasive and attractive style of advertising. The bills
are usually printed in florid and elaborately gilt letters,
and frequently abound in pictures of an imaginative
character. "Cosy Home," "Miner's Retreat," "Social-
Hall," "Empire," "Indication," "Fancy-Free," "Snug,"

THE HURDY-GURDY GIRLS.

"Shades," etc., are a few of the seductive names given to these places of popular resort; and the announcements are generally followed by a list of "choice liquors" and the gorgeous attractions of the billiard department, together with a hint that Dick, Jack, Dan, or Jerry "is always on hand, and while grateful for past favors, will spare no pains to merit a continuance of the same. By catering to the public taste he hopes to make his house in the future, as it has been in the past, a real HOME for the Boys!" Nice homes these, and a nice family of boys that will come out of them! Where will they live when they grow to be men? A good idea it was to build a stone penitentiary.

"Oh yes! Oh yes! Oh yes!
"AUCTION SALES EVERY DAY!"

This is another form of advertisement for a very prolific branch of trade. Day and night auctions are all the rage in Virginia as in San Francisco. Every thing that can't go any other way, and many things that can, go by auction. Stocks, horses, mules, boots, groceries, tinware, drugs and medicines, and rubbish of all kinds are put in flaming bills and auctioned off to the highest bidder for cash. "An'af! an'af! an'af! shall I have it?" is a part of the language popularly spoken on the principal streets.

A cigar store not much bigger than a dry goods box must have its mammoth posters out over the town and hill-sides, displaying to the public eye the prodigious assortments of Regalias, Principes, Cheroots, etc., and choice brands of "Yellow-leaf," "Honey-dew," Solace," and "Eureka," to be had within the limits of their cigar and tobacco emporium. If Archimedes were to rush from the solace of a bath and run naked through the streets of Virginia, shouting, "Eureka! Eureka!" it would merely be regarded as a dodge to dispose of an invoice of Fine-Cut.

Quack pills, sirups, tonics, and rectifiers stare you in the face from every mud-bank, rock, post, and corner, in red, black, blue, and white letters; in hieroglyphics, in

cadaverous pictures of sick men, and astounding pictures of well men.

Every branch of trade, every conceivable species of amusement, is forced upon the public eye in this way. Bill-posting is one of the fine arts. Its professors are among the most notable characters in Virginia. They have a specific interest in certain corners, boards, boxes, and banks of earth and rock, which, with the brush and pot of paste, yield them a handsome revenue. To one who witnesses this bill-mania for the first time the effect is rather peculiar. He naturally imagines that the whole place is turned inside out. Every man's business fills his eye from every point of view, and he can not conceive the existence of a residence unless it be that where so much of the inside is out some portion of the outside may be in. With the exception of the silver mines this is, to a casual observer, an inverted city, and may well claim to be a city of anomalies.

I had occasion, during my stay, to avail myself of the services of a professional bill-sticker. For the sum of six dollars he agreed to make me notorious. The bills were printed in the approved form: "A Trip to Iceland," etc. Special stress was given to the word "ICELAND," and my name was printed in extravagantly conspicuous letters. In the course of a day or two I was shocked at the publicity the Professor of Bill-Posting had given me. From every rock, corner, dry goods box, and awning post; from every screen in every drinking-saloon, I was confronted and brow-beaten by my own name. I felt disposed to shrink into my boots. Had any body walked up to me and said, "Sir, you are a humbug!" it would have been an absolute relief. I would have grasped him by the hand, and answered, "I know it, my dear fellow, and honor you for your frankness!" But there was one consolation: I was suffering in company. A lady, popularly known as "The Menken," had created an immense sensation in San Francisco, and was about to favor the citizens of Virginia with a classical equestrian exhibition

entitled "Mazeppa." She was represented as tied in an almost nude state to the back of a wild horse, which was running away with her at a fearful rate of speed. My friend the Professor was an artist in the line of bill-sticking, and carefully studied effects. He evidently enjoyed Mazeppa. It was a flaming and a gorgeous bill. Its colors were of the most florid character; and he posted accordingly. First came Mazeppa on the mustang horse; then came the Trip to Iceland and myself. If I remember correctly, we (that is to say "The Menken" and I) were followed by "Ayer's Tonic Pills," "Brown's Bronchial Troches," and "A good Square Meal at the Howling Wilderness Saloon." Well, I suppose it was all right, though it took me rather aback at the first view. If the lady had no reason to complain it was not for me, an old traveller, to find fault with the bill-sticker for placing me prominently before the public. Perhaps the juxtaposition was unfortunate in a pecuniary point of view; perhaps the citizens of Virginia feel no great interest in icy regions. Be that as it may, never again so long as I live will I undertake to run "Iceland" in the vicinity of a beautiful woman tied to the back of a wild horse.

But I anticipate my story. Scarcely had I descended from the stage when I was greeted by several old friends, who expressed themselves highly gratified at my arrival. Their remarks, indeed, were so complimentary that I hesitate to repeat them. Truth, however, must be regarded, even at the expense of modesty. "Your sketch of Washoe," said they, "was a capital burlesque. It was worthy of Phœnix or Artemus Ward! A great many people thought it was true! Of course we understood it, but you know one-half of mankind doesn't know a joke from a demonstration in Euclid!" Here was glory! Here was a reward for all my past sufferings! An unfortunate gentleman walks all the way over from Placerville to Washoe, with his blankets on his back; endures the most extraordinary privations; catches the

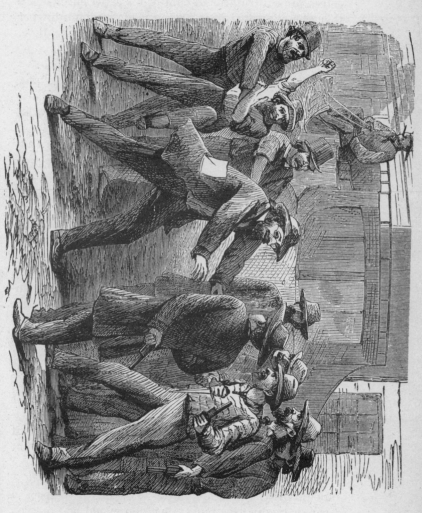

rheumatism, tic-douloureux, and dysentery; invests in the Dead Broke; fails to make an agency pay; drags his weary limbs back again, and writes out what he conceives to be a truthful account of his experiences, and is then complimented upon having made a capital hit, perpetrated a most admirable burlesque, worthy the distinguished humorists of the age! It was a sorry joke for me. I was terribly in earnest about it, at all events.

"You will admit," said these excellent friends, "that the richness of this country surpasses any thing ever known in the world before; that you were altogether mistaken about the silver lodes?"

"No, gentlemen," was my answer, "I can't admit any such thing. I said the Comstock was wonderfully rich, so far as any body could judge from the specimens of ore taken out; but I thought there was considerable doubt as to where the running feet might run. That doubt is not yet removed from my mind. I advised people not to invest in the ten thousand outside lodes that were then in existence. Where are your Flowery Diggings now? What is your Desert worth per running foot? How much will you give me for my Scandalous Wretch, or Bobtail Horse, or Root Hog or Die —all first-class lodes in the neighborhood of the Devil's Gate? Show me a single claim that pays assessments, or pays any thing at all, or is likely ever to pay fifty cents per acre, outside of the main lead in Gold Hill and Virginia City; show me how many of your best mines pay dividends, and I will take back all I said."

At this there was a general look of blankness, as if the facts had not occurred to them before in that point of view.

"But you'll admit that a man can't see much of a mineral district in a few days. You ought to spend a week or two in each mine; then you would be prepared to say something about it."

Strange, isn't it, that people will never get over this

DIVIDENDS.

idea! Wherever I travel I am told that nothing can be seen short of a few weeks or a few months or a few years! If I undertake to look at a potato-patch or a cabbage-garden, it is urgently represented that I can "form no conception how potatoes and cabbages grow in this section" without a month's careful examination of the roots or fibres. I am occasionally so bothered in this way as to feel tempted to offer rather a rude reply, viz.: that one who makes it his business to observe things around him can, with an ordinary share of penetration and some common sense, see as much in a day as many people who live on the spot see in a life-time. It might be effrontery to tell these Virginians, upon so brief an inspection, that I knew more of their city and its resources than they did; but I would even venture something on that point.

"You did us great injury," said they, "by so casual a glance at our mines. For example, you cast contempt upon the whole Comstock lode by representing its dips, spurs, and angles in a sort of burlesque map resembling a bunch of straw."

Alas, poor human nature! These very parties, who complained of my map because it resembled a bunch of straw—illustrating the assertion that every body's dips, spurs, and angles were running into every body else's —were at that very moment, and doubtless are yet, at daggers' points of litigation with other parties who had run into their dips, spurs, and angles. I don't know of a mine on the Comstock which does not infringe upon the alleged rights of some other mine. The results of an actual survey are precisely the same as those produced by a bundle of straw well inked and pressed upon a sheet of paper. To call a map so accurately truthful as mine a burlesque calculated to throw contempt upon the subject, manifests a degree of visual obliquity, if not moral assurance, absolutely refreshing.

ASSESSMENTS.

CHAPTER XXXIV.

A DELIGHTFUL CLIMATE.

THE citizens of Virginia, like the citizens of Timbuctoo in Africa and Reykjavik in Iceland, are enthusiastic admirers of their own place of residence. Not satisfied with the praise usually bestowed upon the city by every stranger who enters it and who desires to maintain friendly relations with the inhabitants, they are exacting to a degree bordering on the despotic. A visitor is required to go into ecstasies over the climate, should there chance to occur, during his sojourn, a passably fine day. He is called upon at every turn to do homage to the wonderful progress of improvement, which they consider far ahead of any thing ever achieved by human beings constructed in the usual form. He is expected to pay the tribute of admiration to the magnificence of the buildings and the sumptuous accommodations of the hotels. If he does not boldly, firmly, and without reservation, express the opinion that the mines are richer by a thousand to one than those of Mexico or South America, he is at once set down as a man whose opinion is worth nothing. Should a stray bullet whiz by his head and kill some equally innocent party within a distance of three paces, he is gravely assured and required to believe that there is as much respect paid to life and limb in Virginia City as there is in any city in the Union. At any hour of the night, when the noise around his lodgings would shame Bedlam, his attention is exultingly directed to the elysian repose of this delectable metropolis. Passing those dens of infamy that abound on every street, he is invited, with an assurance

CLIMATE OF VIRGINIA CITY.

almost incredible, to render homage to the exalted condition of public morals. In full view of the most barren, blasted, and horribly desolate country that perhaps the light of heaven ever shone upon, he is appealed to, as a lover of nature, to admire the fertility of the soil, the luxuriance of the vegetation, and the exquisite beauty of the scenery. Surrounded by an enthusiastic dozen of citizens, most of whom are afflicted with sore throat, mountain fever, erysipelas, bleeding of the nose, shortness of breath, heart disease, diarrhea, and loss of appetite, he is urged to observe the remarkable salubrity of the climate, and to disabuse his mind of those prejudices against it arising from the misrepresentations of interested parties.

"Oh wad some power the giftie gie us—"

But what's the use? It would only make us miserable. We are better off as it is. Men who can see heaven in Virginia City are to be envied. Their condition is such that a change to a better world would not seem materially necessary to their exaltation; and I am sure the worst that could happen them would be borne with as much fortitude as lost sinners are permitted to exercise.

Making due allowance for the atmosphere of exaggeration through which a visitor sees every thing in this wonderful mining metropolis, its progress has been sufficiently remarkable to palliate in some measure the extraordinary flights of fancy in which its inhabitants are prone to indulge. I was not prepared to see so great a change within the brief period of three years; for when people assure me " the world never saw any thing like it," " California is left in the shade," " San Francisco is eclipsed," " Montgomery Street is nowhere now," my incredulity is excited, and it takes some little time to judge of the true state of the case without prejudice. Speaking then strictly within bounds, the growth of this city is remarkable. When it is considered that the surrounding country affords but few facilities for the construction of houses; that lumber has to be hauled a considerable distance at great expense; that lime, bricks, iron-work, sashes, doors, etc., cost three or four times what similar articles do in San Francisco; that much indispensable material can only be had by transporting it over the mountains a distance of more than a hundred and fifty miles; and that the average of mechanical labor, living, and other expenses is correspondingly higher than in California, it is really wonderful how much has been done in so short a space of time.

Yet, allowing all this, what would be the impressions of a Fejee Islander sent upon a mission of inquiry to this strange place? His earliest glimpse of the main street would reveal the curious fact that it is paved with a conglomerate of dust, mud, splintered planks, old boots, clippings of tinware, and playing-cards. It is especially prolific in the matter of cards. Mules are said to fatten on them during seasons of scarcity when the straw gives out. The next marvellous fact that would strike the observation of this wild native is that so many people live in so many saloons, and do nothing from morning till night, and from night till morning again, but drink fiery liquids and indulge in profane language. How can all these able-bodied men afford to be idle? Who pays their expenses? And why do they carry pistols, knives, and other deadly weapons, when no harm could possibly befall them if they went unarmed and devoted themselves to some useful occupation? Has the God of the white men done them such an injury in furnishing all this silver for their use that they should treat his name with contempt and disrespect? Why do they send missionaries to the Fejee Islands and leave their own country in such a dreadful state of neglect? The Fejeeans devour their enemies occasionally as a war measure; the white man swallows his enemy all the time without regard to measure. Truly the white man is a very uncertain native! Fejeeans can't rely upon him.

When I was about to start on my trip to Washoe,

friends from Virginia assured me I would find hotels
there almost if not quite equal to the best in San Francisco. There was but little difference, they said, except
in the matter of extent. The Virginia hotels were quite
as good, though not quite so large. Of course I believed
all they told me. Now I really don't consider myself
fastidious on the subject of hotels. Having travelled in
many different countries, I have enjoyed an extensive experience in the way of accommodations, from my moth-
er-earth to the foretop of a whale-ship, from an Indian
wigwam to a Parisian hotel, from an African palm-tree
to an Arctic snow-bank. I have slept in the same bed
with two donkeys, a camel, half a dozen Arabs, several
goats, and a horse. I have slept on beds alive with
snakes, lizards, scorpions, centipeds, bugs, and fleas—beds

OFFICE AND DWELLING OF THE GOULD AND CURRY COMPANY.

in which men stricken with the plague had died horrible deaths—beds that might reasonably be suspected of small-pox, measles, and Asiatic cholera. I have slept in beds of rivers and beds of sand, and on the bare bed rock. Standing, sitting, lying down, doubled up, and hanging over; twisted, punched, jammed, and elbowed by drunken men; snored at in the cars; sat upon and smothered by the nightmare; burnt by fires, rained upon, snowed upon, and bitten by frost—in all these positions, and subject to all these discomforts, I have slept with comparative satisfaction. There are pleasanter ways of sleeping, to be sure, but there are times when any way is a blessing. In respect to the matter of eating I am even less particular. Frogs, horse-leeches, snails, and grasshoppers are luxuries to what I have eaten. It has pleased Providence to favor me with appetites and tastes appropriate to a great variety of circumstances and many conditions of life. These facts serve to show that I am not fastidious on the subject of personal accommodations.

Perhaps my experience in Virginia was exceptional; perhaps misfortune was determined to try me to the utmost extremity. I endeavored to find accommodations at a hotel recommended as the best in the place, and was shown a room over the kitchen stove, in which the thermometer ranged at about 130 to 150 degrees of Fahrenheit. To be lodged and baked at the rate of $2 per night, cash in advance, was more than I could stand, so I asked for another room. There was but one more, and that was pre-empted by a lodger who might or might not come back and claim possession in the middle of the night. It had no window except one that opened into the passage, and the bed was so arranged that every other lodger in the house could take a passing observation of the sleeper and enjoy his style of sleeping. Nay, it was not beyond the resources of the photographic art to secure his negative and print his likeness for general distribution. It was bad enough to be smothered for want of light and air; but I had no idea of paying $2 a night for the poor privilege of showing people how I looked with my eyes shut, and possibly my mouth open. A man may have an attack of nightmare, his countenance may be distorted by horrible dreams; he may laugh immoderately at a very bad pun made in his sleep—in all which conditions of body and mind he doubtless presents an interesting spectacle to the critical eyes of a stranger, but he doesn't like to wake up suddenly and be caught in the act.

The next hotel to which I was recommended was eligibly located on a street composed principally of grog-shops and gambling-houses. I was favored with a front room about eight feet square. The walls were constructed of boards fancifully decorated with paper, and afforded this facility to a lodger—that he could hear all that was going on in the adjacent rooms. The partitions might deceive the eye, but the ear received the full benefit of the various oaths, ejaculations, conversations, and perambulations in which his neighbors indulged. As for the bed, I don't know how long it had been in use, or what race of people had hitherto slept in it, but the sheets and blankets seemed to be sadly discolored by age —or lack of soap and water. It would be safe to say washing was not considered a paying investment by the managers of this establishment. Having been twenty-four hours without sleep or rest, I made an attempt to procure a small supply, but miserably failed in consequence of an interesting conversation carried on in the passage between the chamber-maids, waiters, and other ladies and gentlemen, respecting the last free fight. From what I could gather, this was considered the best neighborhood in the city for free fights. Within the past two weeks three or four men had been shot, stabbed, or maimed close by the door. " Oh it's a lively place, you bet!" said one of the ladies (the chamber-maid, I think), " an oncommon lively place—reely hexcitin'. I look out of the winder every mornin' jist to see how many dead men are layin' around. I declare to gracious the bullets

LADIES OF THE HOTEL.

flies around here sometimes like hailstones!" "An'
shure," said a voice in that rich brogue which can never
be mistaken, "it's no wondher the boys shud be killin'
an' murtherin' themselves forninst the door, whin they're
all just like me, dyin' in love wid yer beauteeful self!"
A smart slap and a general laugh followed this suggestion. "Git away wid ye, Dinnis; yer always up to yer
mischief! As I was sayin', no later than this mornin', I

see two men a poppin' away at each other wid six-shoot-
ers—a big man an' a little man. The big man he stag-
gered an' fell right under the winder, wid his head on
the curb-stone, an' his legs a stickin' right up in the air.
He was all over blood, and when the boys picked him up
he was dead as a brickbat. 'Tother chap he run into a
saloon. You better b'leeve this is a lively neighborhood.
I tell you hailstones is nothink to the way the bullets
flies around." "That's so," chimes in another female
voice; "I see myself, with my own eyes, Jack's corpse
an' two more carried away in the last month. If I'd a
had a six-shooter then, you bet they'd a carried away the
fellow that nipped Jack!"

Now taking into view the picturesque spectacle that a
few dead men dabbled in blood must present to the eye on
a fine morning, and the chances of a miscellaneous ball
carrying away the top of one's cranium, or penetrating
the thin board wall and ranging upward through his
body as he lies in bed, I considered it best to seek a more
secluded neighborhood, where the scenery was of a less
stimulating character and the hail-storms not quite so
heavy. By the kind aid of a friend I secured comparatively agreeable quarters in a private lodging-house kept
by a widow lady. The rooms were good and the beds
clean, and the price not extravagant for this locality—$12
a week without board.

So much for the famous hotels of Virginia. If there
are any better, neither myself, nor some fellow-travellers
who told me their experiences, succeeded in finding them.
The concurrent testimony was that they are dirty, ill-
kept, badly attended by rough, ill mannered-waiters—
noisy to such a degree that a sober man can get but little rest, day or night, and extravagantly high in proportion to the small comfort they afford. One of the newspapers published a statement which the author probably
intended for a joke, but which is doubtless founded upon
fact—namely, that a certain hotel advertised for 300
chickens to serve the same number of guests. Only one

chicken could be had for love or money—a very ancient rooster, which was made into soup and afterward served up in the form of a fricasee for the 300 guests. The flavor was considered extremely delicate—what there was of it; and there was plenty of it such as it was.

Still if we are to credit what the Virginia newspapers say—and it would be dangerous to intimate that they ever deal in any thing save the truth—there are other cities on the eastern slope of the Sierras which afford equally attractive accommodations. On the occasion of the recent Senatorial contest at Carson City, the prevailing rates charged for lodgings, according to the Virginia *Enterprise,* were as follows : " For a bed in a house, barn, blacksmith-shop, or hay-yard (none to be had—all having been engaged shortly before election) ; horse-blanket in an old sugar hogshead per night, $10 ; crockery-crate, with straw, $7 50 ; without straw, $5 75 ; for cellar-door, $4 ; for roosting on a smooth pole, $3 50 ; pole, common, rough, $3 ; plaza fence, $2 50 ; walking up and down the Warm Spring road—if cloudy, $1 50 ; if clear, $1 25. (In case the clouds are very thick and low, $1 75 is generally asked.) Very good roosting in a pine-tree, back of Camp Nye, may still be had free, but we understand that a company is being formed to monopolize all the more accessible trees. We believe they propose to improve by putting two pins in the bottom of each tree, or keep a man to boost regular customers. They talk of charging six bits."

I could scarcely credit this, if it were not that a friend of mine, who visited Reese River last summer, related some experiences of a corroborative character. Unable to secure lodgings elsewhere, he undertook to find accommodations in a vacant sheep corral. The proprietor happening to come home about midnight, found him spread out under the lee of the fence. " Look-a-here, stranger !" said he, gruffly, " that's all well enough, but I gen'rally collect in advance. Just fork over four bits or mizzle !" My friend indignantly mizzled. Cursing the progressive spirit of the age, he walked some distance out of town, and was about to finish the night under the lee of a big quartz boulder, when a fierce-looking speculator, with a six-shooter in his hand, suddenly appeared from a cavity in the rock, saying, "No yer don't! Take a fool's advice now, and git! When you go a prospectin' around ov nights agin, jest steer clear ov this boulder ef you please!" In vain my friend attempted to explain. The rising wrath of the squatter was not to be appeased by soft words, and the click of the trigger, as he raised his pistol and drew a bead, warned the trespasser that it was time to be off. He found lodgings that night on the public highway to Virginia City and San Francisco.

Q 2

CHAPTER XXXV.

DOWN IN THE MINES.

WHEN you visit a friend in the country he usually displays his interest in your pleasure by inviting you to take a walk in his garden. He shows you his fruit trees and cabbages; dilates upon the productive qualities of his soil; surprises you with the growth of his pumpkins; excites your astonishment by the magnitude of his squashes; and if you happen to be interested in stock, takes you by the arm, conducts you to the back-yard, and shows you his fancy boar or improved style of ram. Some hospitable gentlemen connected with the Ophir, having none of these attractions about their premises, invited me, on the occasion of a visit, to take a ramble through their subterranean garden. This is a compliment paid to visitors from distant parts of the world, and is considered a satisfactory substitute for the civilities available in other places. It was a little trying to the muscles, they admitted, but would amply repay me for the trouble. As to risk, it was trifling. Visitors to other mines now and then got their skulls crushed, or tumbled down shafts and were mashed, or became nervous and fainted into the machinery; but nothing of the kind was common in the Ophir. As a preliminary measure I was kindly furnished with a suit of rough outergarments, somewhat dilapidated by frequent contact with different colored ores, and the drippings of candles and whitewash, but good enough for general protection. Into this ancient suit I speedily dived, and was so disguised that when I looked in the glass my first impulse was to turn round and knock down the miserable satire

VIEW FROM REAR OF OPHIR WORKS.

that stood in my boots. I was next provided with a candle and directed to hold it between my fingers, so as to
reflect the light from the palm of my hand.   Thus accoutred, we climbed a bit of a hill, and entered a hole
somewhere, which we began to descend single file by
means of a ladder.   At the end of the ladder was a small
bit of ground to stand on; and then another hole in the
ground and another ladder. All along the range of
these various ladders was a shaft, in which a ponderous
piece of machinery appeared to be engaged in hoisting
out water from the bottom of the mine. The holes
through which we descended were so narrow that it was
sometimes difficult to tell which was the ladder and
which was the machine; but I continued to keep a firm
grip of the ladder and let the machine look out for itself.
When we got into this last hole, we squeezed through a
trap-door and went down still further by another ladder that led to another, and then another, and so on till
we reached another.   I have no idea how many ladders
there were.   All I know is, they stand very straight up,
and keep fearfully close to the machinery that drags up
the water.   I saw a good deal of rock and earth by holding the candle close to the sides of the subterranean excavations through which we passed.   Whether the rock
contained the silver, or whether the silver was contained
in the loose earth, or whether they both contained it together, is a matter not to be recklessly or inconsiderate-
ly divulged.   The interests of this mine are so extensive
and multifarious that no man who values his reputation
will jeopard it by disclosing facts which must either elevate stock to the detriment of purchasers, or depress it to
the detriment of sellers.   I therefore keep my own counsel.   This much I may state : that the scientific gentleman who accompanied me was continually holding his
candle against the dripping rocks and banks of earth and
ejaculating: " There ! you see it ; hornblendic, feldspathic — graniferous !   Casings distinctly marked — Dip
forty-five degrees.   Here again—very rich !   Don't you

see it ? And here ! and here again—eh ?" I certainly
saw something. The reader will kindly consider me
speechless with amazement. What I did see in those
subterranean tunnels; the gloomy passages through
which I navigated in pursuit of the scientific gentleman,
whose motions were frightfully rapid; bobbing my head

A SHAFT.

against timbers and sharp points of overhanging rock; doubling up and twisting around corners; and piles of ore, more or less valuable, that I stumbled over in striving to catch up with my learned friend; the color of the veins that dazzled my vision under the inspiration of his disquisitions on the feldspathic and hornblendic; the prodigious quantity of something in that line that darkened the highways and by-ways, must remain at the present writing a profound secret.

A memorable tour that was. Never in this world can I forget the Ophir! Once when I was at the bottom, creeping through the bowels of the earth, some cars laden with ore came rumbling along. "Stand aside, gents!" cried somebody, and I tried to stand aside. But who in the world can stand aside when there is scarcely foot-room for a goat? Here was a passage about five feet wide, at least three of which was taken up by railway and cars, and the rest by heavy timbers. I hugged a dark, wet wall; it was not near so comfortable as other substances I have hugged in my day. The cars scraped by; my bones were not crushed, and that was just all. Pleasant place that for a promenade! To be rolled out, squashed, or cut in segments may be a very trifling contingency to scientific gentlemen and experts; but I prefer the contemplation of the heavenly bodies from the surface of the earth.

I really can not remember how many dismal passages we went through. We explored the sixth story, the fifth, and several others, which had the same general aspect of mud and mineral. In one shaft the workmen above were pitching down loose earth and rocks to be run out through a tunnel. This we climbed by means of a very long ladder. It was good exercise for body and mind. The ore came tumbling down more or less all the time, and I had faint hopes some large mass would not fall on my head before I reached the top and carry me to the bottom. The accidents that occur in this way are numerous. Recently two miners, ascending a shaft in one of the mines, were struck by a dog and crushed to atoms. They were 175 feet from the bottom, and were going up in a tub. The dog tripped in attempting to run across the mouth of the shaft, and struck them at a distance of over 100 feet from the surface, carrying all before him. In another place we enjoyed a view of the wreck caused by the caving in of the Mexican. Here, to be sure, was a crush of matter! Timbers shivered and wrenched to splinters; rocks and masses of earth tumbled into chaos! Even where we stood the massive beams that supported the tunnel were imbedded in each other by the tremendous weight of the mass above, which never ceases to bear down upon them. It appeared to me that it settled as I gazed upon it. Beams of timber eighteen inches square seemed to offer but a feeble resistance to such a crushing weight. That this whole tunnel must cave in sooner or later is my deliberate conviction. Miners, like sailors, grow to be indifferent to danger.

When the Mexican caved in there was a concussion of air in the Ophir that knocked down several of the workmen. One man, in the confusion of the moment, rushed frantically through the falling mass of earth and timber, and, strange to say, escaped with a few scratches and bruises. He must have passed through 100 feet of this chaotic mass. The spot was pointed out to me, and I must say had my informant not been a scientific gentleman, given to mathematical demonstrations, I must have doubted the story. Timbers, rocks, and earth are crushed together in one vast conglomerate of rubbish. It is scarcely conceivable that even a rat could creep through it; yet this man escaped and is now boring into more earth for a living.

Having seen all the wonders of the Ophir, I was kindly permitted to select three modes of reaching the upper crust of the world: to climb up the ladders again, or be dragged up the "incline" by a steam-engine; or be hoisted up a shaft in a wooden bucket by means of a hand-windlass. The ladders I had already enjoyed; the

"STAND ASIDE, GENTS."

incline I did not incline to, from a vague notion that the
machinery might keep on turning after I got to the top
and drag me into it, or snap the rope and send me whiz-
zing to the bottom again; so I elected to be hoisted out
by the hand-windlass. Dispensing with the bucket, I
put my foot in a noose of the rope; was hoisted away;

bobbed against the sides of the shaft; scraped through a trap-door, and deposited on the landing-place. It was an interesting tour, and I was thankful to my friends, but more thankful still to Providence, when I breathed once more the fresh air and enjoyed the pleasant sunshine of the outer world.

Every city has its chronic nightmare, whether in the shape of flood, fire, earthquake, or pestilence. Every community is, or deems itself liable to some special calamity. The citizens of Virginia are troubled with a one-ledge theory. It is the nightmare of property-owners—the special calamity that threatens ruin to the speculators in Wild Cat. Naturally enough it is unpopular among the masses. No man who aspires to public honors can by any possibility succeed on the one-ledge theory. He must believe in a multiplicity of ledges; he must be sound on the Comstock as a basis, and sound on the great family of ledges supposed to exist in its neighborhood. The owner of feet in the Comstock can afford to be a one-ledge man, provided he has been successful in quieting the rival claims of squatters who have dipped into his spurs; but he is interested in the prosperity of the city, and therefore will best consult his interests by being a many-ledged man. The editor of a newspaper may have doubts on the subject—if editors ever have doubts on any subject—but he can have no doubt about the policy of retaining his subscribers and his advertising patronage. The more ledges the more companies, and the more companies the more notices of assessments. Hence it is the interest of the majority to put down and demolish the one-ledge theory; and hence it is popularly considered absurd, anti-democratic, monstrous, and diabolical. Nevertheless, although there are few so daring as to violate the general sentiment on this subject, the question, with the vitality of a seven-headed dragon, is continually springing up as much alive as ever, and can't be burned or flooded out either by fires of invective or oceans of vituperation.

CAVE-IN OF THE MEXICAN.

As an interesting feature in human nature, I may be permitted to say that, in general, you may determine a man's status by his views on this subject. Original owners in Comstock are one-ledgers by nature and instinct, whatever they may be by policy. Owners of outside claims, proprietors of building sites, merchants, shopkeepers, traders, and speculators are many-ledgers under the all-powerful stimulus of interest. For myself, I have my private views, but my public sentiments assimilate with those of the many-ledgers. It is the best policy for a man who doesn't own a foot in a single ledge. If the mines in Mexico and South America are confined to one well-defined vein, as geologists contend, what does that prove? Simply that nature adopts certain specific laws in Mexico and South America. If trees grow there with their branches and fruits in the air, is it any reason why trees should not grow in Washoe with their branches and fruits in the ground? Silver mines in Mexico and South America may have one way of doing things, and silver mines in Washoe another. I am disposed to go it strong, therefore, on the many-ledge theory. I believe there are many ledges in Washoe. At all events there are many companies based upon ledges.

This complication of adverse interests gives rise to endless litigation. The records of the courts are crowded with suits, and every suit breeds another brood of suits. The halls of justice are crammed with litigants. Companies are pitted against companies, and individuals against individuals. Uncle Sam, who owns all the mines, magnanimously stands aloof and enjoys the fight over his own property. The whole district is racked with litigation. It is sapping the vitals of the community. There is money enough spent in law to build the Pacific Railroad. The whole trouble arises from the superabundance of legal counsel. Whenever a lawyer in California, from misfortune, incompetency, whisky, or any other cause, falls into a depression of finances, he straightway gathers up his books and starts for the silver regions.

GOULD AND CURRY COMPANY'S REDUCTION WORKS.

Acute by profession, he scents the remedy from afar. These gentlemen must have silver: they can't help it—must have it; and to have it must have litigation. Two evils therefore beset the Washoeites—many ledges and many lawyers. Either they must be everlastingly in court and submit to final exhaustion of all their precious ores, or pay these needy members of the bar what the world owes them, and let them travel. I don't doubt they will go somewhere else in the vicinity of silver. Pay them fifty thousand dollars apiece, and then raise a fund for the subsistence of absentees, and pay them for staying away. I venture to say such a course would obviate the first grand trouble. After that a court might be organized consisting of three Digger Indians. Keep them from fire-water, and my word for it, their decisions would be as satisfactory as any rendered by the most learned judges. It is true they might be corrupted by whisky; red blankets and cotton shirts might cause them to waver from the paths of rectitude; a string of beads to some favorite squaw might affect the eye or the understanding of the most stolid Digger; a bucketful of "hogadie" might confound the perceptive faculties of the great Winnemucca himself; but human nature must be taken as it is. The highest dignitaries in the land are subject to temptation. The Washoeites complain that their Bench is corrupt; they abuse their judges; hint in pretty strong terms that when a judge receives a heavy bonus of feet for services in the great cause of justice, other parties give more and get it all; in short, they raised such a hubbub last year that the judges resigned in disgust. I don't blame them. It would be impossible for them to satisfy every body. If they are honest men—and I have no reason to doubt it—they could render no decision which would not make them unpopular with the disappointed party. What the Washoeites need most is, judges who will be faithfully dishonest and honestly faithless.

CHAPTER XXXVI.

THE ROUGHS AND THE SMOOTHS.

S O bitter are the feuds resulting from conflicting claims, under the one-ledge and many-ledge theories, that a summary method of settling disputes not unfrequently usurps the functions of the Judiciary. An enterprising class of the community, known as the "roughs," may be relied upon in any emergency. For a reasonable consideration these accommodating gentlemen will espouse any cause, however hopeless in the eye of the law. Their habits of life are such that no conscientious scruples, touching questions of right and wrong, have the slightest influence over their acts. Most of them have killed from ten to a dozen men each in bar-room affrays, gambling difficulties, or murders of a general character; and to be "quick on the trigger" is their greatest boast. Without any particular line of business, save to frequent public places and look up casual jobs, they are recognized as Professional Blood-letters, and treated accordingly with great consideration by the peaceful members of the community. It is regarded as something of an honor to be intimately acquainted with the most noted of these sanguinary Professors. I am on terms of friendship with several of them myself, and regard the leader, who lost his nose in a recent bloody fight, as a gentleman of great personal suavity. I take special care, however, not to irritate him by any difference of opinion touching the various subjects that come under discussion during our social intercourse. It usually costs me four bits to remove a shadow from his brow, and a dollar or more to get him enthusiastic in his reminiscences of human butchery.

During my third visit (last year) there was considerable excitement about town in consequence of the resignation of the judges, and an expected collision between the "roughs" in the service of two rival companies. One company squatted upon the premises belonging to another. The case did not admit of question, so far as I could see. It was an unjustifiable trespass without the shadow of right. But lawyers saw difficulties, and while they were busy concocting briefs and making learned speeches the squatter company was digging into the bowels of the earth and extracting precious ores that belonged to the other party. On the very day, and at the very hour, when it was confidently expected that two hundred men would come in collision, far down in the gloomy cavities of the earth, it was my fortune to be a visitor at the principal mine. The Superintendent invited me to explore it—adding, as an inducement, that his "roughs" were all ready, and there was momentary prospect of a bloody subterranean battle. His life had been threatened the day before by one of the squatter "roughs," but it was probably insured: at all events, the prospect of losing it did not seem to give him much concern. I must confess the proposition to go down a hundred and fifty feet under the earth and witness a bloody fight within the limited space of a drift or tunnel was novel if not attractive. There was no getting over it—I had to go.

The expected battle-ground, on our side, was occupied by as imposing a body of "roughs" as I had ever seen assembled together. They sat loosely and pleasantly on the dripping rocks, smoking their cigars, gossiping about the last free fight, and evidently enjoying the prospect of the business in hand. A gang of miners was picking and hammering into the disputed portion of the ledge. Another gang, backed by another body of "roughs," belonging to the squatter company, was picking and hammering on the other side. About three feet of rock separated the rival factions. I could distinctly hear the

THE SMOOTHS.

noise of the picks through the thin layer of rock. It was a very curious and impressive scene on our side ; and doubtless was equally so on the other. The whole available space was not over six or eight feet in width by the same in height, and what range there might be through the adjoining tunnels or drifts which were wrapped in darkness. A faint flickering halo from sundry candles, pasted with sticky mud against the rocks, dimly lighted the walls and casings of the mine, and shed a ghastly hue over the faces of our fighting men, to whom I was personally introduced by the Superintendent. Their features were in admirable keeping with the place and the occasion. One man had the end of his nose bitten off ; another was ornamented with a magnificent scar across his cheek ; a third had lost three fingers ; a fourth was pitted with buck-shot ; and so on. All men of mark ; all notoriously crack fellows in their way, which was evidently, from the variety of pistols and knives with which they were garnished, a very bloody way. I was especially pleased with a wax-faced gentleman, with a square chin, a pig-eye, and a stovepipe hat. He was "on it" or I greatly misjudged his countenance.

"Gentlemen," said I, with all the deference due to such famous characters, "I see you're on it."

"You bet," was the answer.

"When do you expect the fight to come off ?" I ventured to inquire.

"Oh, any time when they bust through that there wall. Guess they ain't eager for it. Likely as not they'll fizzle."

I made no comment upon this suggestion ; but personally had no objection to the fizzle. It was not a pleasant place to be caught in a bloody affray. Balls fired through a tunnel only six or eight feet square, or into a drift with a solid bank of rock at the end, would be likely to hit something. I was not interested to the extent of a leg or an arm, much less a foot.

As if to keep up a pleasant state of expectancy, blasts

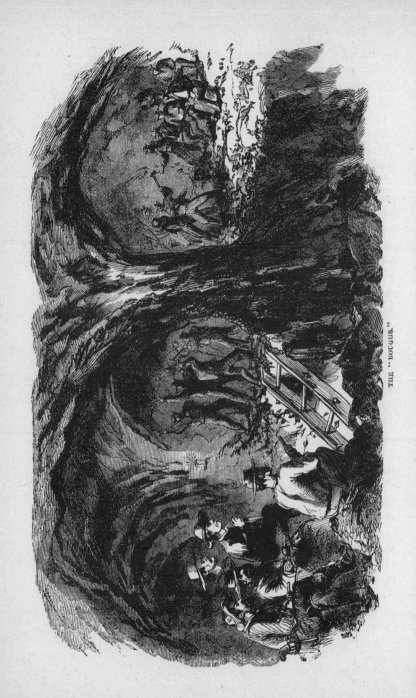

THE "ROUGUE."

were let off now and then, causing a startling concussion of the air and a perceptible tremor of the earth. It is due to the cause of humanity to say that the rival factions always notified each other by certain signals when they were about to let off a blast, having no desire to take a snap judgment upon their enemies.

Between the picking and blasting, darkness and gunpowder, pistols, knives, and bloody conversation, unkempt miners and ferocious roughs, with a sprinkling of grit from overhead and the plashing of water underfoot, I think the most rigid casuist will hold me blameless for whispering to the Superintendent, "This is a devil of a queer place; let's get out of it. Don't you smell brimstone?"

Unfortunately for the interest of my sketch the fight did not come off. The difficulty, I believe, was referred to one of those honest gentlemen in whom every body has confidence until his decision is made known. He may be a member of the bar or a member of the church; his character stands unimpeached before he makes his report. As a referee he is bound to decide according to the law and the evidence. But his report makes an explosion. Law and evidence suit some people and don't suit others, and referees have different modes of interpretation. It is a thankless, though it may be a profitable business. I will not say that the decision in the present case was not according to the law and the evidence; but it surprised me nevertheless. A friend of mine, who claimed to be in the Legitimate, sold out after he heard the decision. He would have made money had he sold out before.

CHAPTER XXXVII.

CHINESE VS DIGGERS.

THE American is not the only race subject to trouble in the various operations of mining. Even the Celestials, who occupy the neglected nooks and corners of the mineral regions, have their share of adversity and disaster in the pursuit of wealth. Whenever they strike a good claim it belongs to some white man. He may never have seen or heard of it, or may have abandoned it and gone elsewhere; but if " John Chinaman" strikes it rich he comes back or sends his partner to take possession. The Digger Indians are learning the great lesson of civilization from their American benefactors. Driven from gulch to cañon in their own country, they see that "Melican man" claims mines and minerals on general principles, and, like him, they despise an inferior race. They hate the Chinese because " Chinaman squaw ; no kill Injun like Melican man !" They seem to look upon the Celestials as a base imitation of the Indian race, without the redeeming quality of bravery. Hence the Diggers are singularly bitter in their hostility to these miserable interlopers, and tax them without mercy, or kill them whenever they get a chance. One Indian chief and his band made several thousand dollars last summer by following up the Chinese and compelling them, by force of arms, to pay taxes for the privilege of working the mines. Poor John is taxed by the State, by the Government, by every white pilgrim who jogs along with pick and shovel, by his own people, and finally by the Digger Indians. Sometimes he rouses himself up to a spirit of resistance against the exorbitant claims

DIGGERS COLLECTING TAXES.

of the latter, and then ensues a scene to which no pencil save that of Hogarth could do justice.

The aboriginal tax-collectors come along stealthily—one, two, or three at a time, till ten or a dozen of them are gathered about the camp of the Celestials. Their arms consist of a bow and arrow, and a rude club or a spear; and their costume is seldom more than a deer-skin, or a ragged old blanket, with the merest pretense of a cincture round the loins. A wretched tatterdemalion set they are—poor, thriftless, and dirty; in no respect like the warrior chiefs of Mr. Fenimore Cooper, or the braves of the Hon. Augustus Murray. Still there is fight in them if pushed to the bank. Their contempt for the Chinese is sublime. Having no knowledge of the Mongolian language, it becomes necessary that they should speak English, which is the available means of communication with the trespassers.

"Say, John!" says the Digger Chief, "what you do here?"

"Me workee. Who you?"

"Me Piute Cappen. Me kill plenty Melican man. Dis my lan'. You payee me, John. No payee me, got-tam, me killee you!"

"No got — velly poor Chinaman; how muchee you want?"

"Fifty dollar."

"No got fifty dollar—velly poor. Melican man he catchee Chinaman; he makee Chinaman pay; no got fifty dollar. Melican man—"

"D—n Melican man! me no sabbe Melican man! Me Piute Cappen. S'pose you no payee me fifty dollar, me killee you!"

Generally the money is paid, after many protests and various lamentations; but where the Digger force is small, and the Celestials numerous, the cry of battle is raised, and then comes the tug of war. When Greek meets Greek the spectacle may be very impressive; when Chinaman meets Digger it is absolutely gorgeous! Negotiation has been prolonged without issue ; the English language has been exhausted ; the fight is inevitable. From every hole in the earth the valiant Celestials rush forth, armed with picks and shovels, tin pans, platters, gongs, and kettles—every thing that can be made available for warlike purposes in the emergency of the moment. They beat their pans, blow their wind instruments, shriek, shout, laugh, make horrible faces, and perform the most frightful antics, in the hope of striking terror into the ranks of the foe. In every conceivable way they tax invention to make themselves hideous ; poke their tongues out ; double themselves up ; hop on one leg ; squat on the ground like frogs ; rush furiously toward the enemy, and furiously retire. The hills and forests resound with their barbarous cries and the deafening clatter of their tin kettles and gongs. Meantime the Diggers are not idle. Adepts in the artifices of barbarian war, they are in no degree intimidated by the ferocious demonstrations of the enemy. A pistol or a shot-gun has its terrors, but they are up to the flimsy substitute of loud noises and empty threats. While the foe is thus wasting his vital powers upon the air, Digger goes in with his clubs, spears, or bows and arrows. A few pricks of the barbed instruments generally ends the battle—save when the Celestial party can muster up an old shot-gun or a pistol, in which case they fight with heroic desperation, and sometimes come off victorious. But a pistol or gun in the hands of the enemy brings them to terms very speedily—and thus are they forced to pay the tax that breaks the camel's back. It ought to be a consolation to them to know that they do it for the benefit of civilization. Every dime they pay benefits some white whisky-dealer in Virginia City or Carson, or some other civilized place.

I have mainly confined myself in the foregoing sketches to a delineation of the characteristic features of Virginia City and its surroundings, during the excitement which prevailed in the latter part of 1863 ; reserving for another and more serious report a detailed account of the mines and mills.   The progress of Washoe has been unexampled in the history of mining.   No country of which I have any knowledge has made so rapid an advance, and with so little benefit to capitalists or individuals.   That there is great wealth of mineral in the country is beyond question; that a very bad use has been made of it, so far, is equally undeniable.

Allow me now, as the result of careful observation and grave deliberation, to whisper a word in your ear, gentle reader.   Do you own stocks in the Ophir, the Savage, the Chollar, the Gould and Curry, the Potosi, the Yellow Jacket, or other prominent leads, and would you like to know what you had better do with them—whether sell them or hold on to them?   I will tell you candidly; if the stocks were mine, I'd—think about it !   Are you the possessor of a few thousand dollars which you'd like to invest to good advantage, and would it be a promising speculation to invest in one of the three companies on the Comstock ledge, that pays dividends at the present writing?   Now, I'll tell you candidly what I would do if I had a few thousand dollars to spare—I'd start on a foot tour through Tartary, and wind up with a camel-ride through Persia !

BODIE BLUFF.

CHAPTER XXXVIII.

TO BODIE BLUFF.

I HAD enjoyed to my heart's content the amenities of social life in Aurora; had witnessed a Sunday procession to the badger fight of Mr. T. Jefferson Phelan, a high-toned European; had barely missed seeing a man shot dead in front of the Sazerac Saloon for throwing brickbats at another man's house; had taken a general view of the country from the top of Mount Brayley and the bottom of the Real del Monte. I was now prepared to vary my experience by a trip to Bodie Bluff and Mono Lake, the "Dead Sea of the West."

Of the Bodie district I had heard the most enthusiastic accounts. It was represented to be a region of peculiar interest in a mineralogical point of view; and the scenery was reputed to be as barren as any thing I had enjoyed during my recent tour through Arizona. For the matter of comfort, I was assured that if an utter lack of accommodation for man or beast, and a reasonable chance of suffering from chilly nights and dusty roads, could be accounted among the luxuries of travel, I would not be likely to regret the trip.

A friend politely offered me the use of his buggy, and agreed to drive the horses himself—a proposition which I gladly accepted for two reasons: first, because I knew nothing of the road; and secondly, because I had no confidence in horses ridden or driven by myself. Up to

HO! FOR BODIE!

that period of their lives they had always been very good horses; but they invariably underwent a radical change upon discovering that they had fallen under my control.

My friend was called the Judge, though I believe he claimed to be of no higher rank than an attorney at law. All popular lawyers, however, are judges in Nevada, whether they practice at the bar or sit upon the bench. He was a gentleman of good sense and genial manners, and although bred to the legal profession, took no mean advantage of me during the entire trip. No outfit beyond a few cold chickens, a ham, some crackers, and a bottle of medicine to use in case of snake-bites, would be necessary, the Judge assured me, unless I contemplated spending some time in the mountains. There was snake-medicine to be had on the way; but he advised me not to trust to it, as it was more poisonous than the virus of the snakes. I inquired if these vicious reptiles, of which I had heard so much in Aurora, were of the rattle or copperhead species; to which my friend replied that both of these were very prevalent in the country; but the greatest damage was done by a venomous reptile scarcely known to naturalists, of which a specimen dead or alive had never yet been caught.

On a fine morning in September we set forth on our expedition. The rugged cliffs along the road cropped out at every turn like grim old castles of feudal times, and there were frowning fortresses of solid rock that seemed ready to belch forth murderous streams of fire upon any enemy that might approach. I was particularly struck with the rugged grandeur of the scenery in the neighborhood of Fogus's quartz-mill; and on the occasion of a subsequent visit made a sketch of the mill and principal bluff.

At Haskell's toll-gate, about a mile from the town, we halted awhile to enjoy the hospitality of the worthy toll-keeper and his wife, who cordially invited us to stop and dine with them. I found here what I had not unfrequently before met with in the course of my travels through this wild region—refinement and intelligence. The cabin was a mere frame shanty of the rudest kind; yet it was clean and neat; nicely carpeted, and prettily ornamented with water-colored sketches, very cleverly executed by Mrs. Haskell. The tables were covered with books and periodicals, among which I observed a Magazine that takes the lead in civilizing new countries, but of which special mention would be superfluous. The readers of *Harper* will understand, of course, that good taste, good order, intelligence, pretty children, and domestic happiness are the necessary consequences, even in a mountain cabin, of a few years' subscription to a Magazine, which, according to the advertisement, contains in itself a library of useful and entertaining knowledge.

We stopped awhile at the foot of the grade to visit the magnificent quartz-mills of the Real del Monte and Antelope Mining Companies, of which I had heard much since my arrival at Aurora. Both of these mills are built of brick on the same plan, and in the Gothic style of architecture. Nothing finer in point of symmetrical propor-

tion, beauty and finish of the machinery, and capacity for
reducing ores by crushing and amalgamation, exists on
the eastern slope of the Sierras. These mills were in
operation at the time of our visit, but were not working
to their full capacity, owing to the want of a sufficiency of
ore. I had little expected to find in this out-of-the-way
part of the world such splendid monuments of enterprise.
The Real del Monte contains a battery of thirty stamps ;
thirty-six Wheeler pans, and other machinery in proportion ; the Antelope a somewhat smaller number of stamps
and pans. Steam is the motive power, and the machinery works with the neatness and perfection of clock-
work.

Passing several other mills, as we proceeded up the
cañon, one of which was burned a few days after, we entered a singularly wild and rugged pass in the mountains,
where it seemed as if the earth had been rent asunder by
some convulsion of nature for the express purpose of
letting people through. The Judge was of opinion that
this curious piece of engineering was performed by the
bursting through of a river or flood in by-gone times. It
reminded me of the Almannajau in Iceland, which was
evidently produced by the contraction of the lava as it cool-
ed and dried. Whatever way it happened, the road thus
formed is a great convenience to the travelling public.

Several fine valleys, now used as hay and cattle ranches,
lie between Aurora and Bodie. They are small, but rich
in soil and well watered by the springs that course down
from the neighboring ravines, and produce some fine
grass. The ranch-men were at work hauling the hay
to the Aurora market, where it brings from $40 to $60
a ton. Hay ranches are as good as silver mines almost
anywhere on the eastern slope—better, in some respects,
for they are certain to yield something for the labor expended upon them. A scrubby growth of pine relieves in
some measure the sterile aspect of the surrounding
mountains, which, as we advanced on our way, seemed to
become more and more barren. Some eight or nine

FOGUS'S MILL.

miles from Aurora we reached the base of a conical hill, surmounted by a range of reddish-colored cliffs, very rough, jagged, and picturesque; a capital-looking place for a den of robbers or a gold mine. This was the famous Bodie Bluff. The entire hill, as well as the surrounding country, is destitute of vegetation, with the exception of sage-brush and bunch-grass—presenting even to the eye of a traveller who had just been surfeited with the deserts of Arizona a wonderfully refreshing picture of desolation.

We revelled in dust along the road that skirts the Bluff; it was rich and unctuous, and penetrated us through and through, so that by the time we arrived at the Judge's cabin, where he had some workmen employed, we were permeated with the precious metals of Bodie. A fine spring of water, aided by a little snake-medicine, set us all right; and a good lunch prepared us for a tour of exploration over the mountains.

I must here introduce the reader to the interior of a miner's cabin. The Judge had some ten or a dozen men employed, who lived in a frame shanty close by a fine spring of water, surrounded by the most luxuriant natural garden of sage-brush, weeds, wild flax, and other ornamental products of the earth which seemed to rejoice in the prolific soil of this region. These jolly miners were the happiest set of bachelors imaginable; had neither chick nor child, that I knew of, to trouble them; cooked their own food; did their own washing; mended their own clothes, made their own beds, and on Sundays cut their own hair, greased their own boots, and brushed their own coats; thus proving by the most direct positive evidence that woman is an unnecessary and expensive institution which ought to be abolished by law. I have always maintained, and do still contend, that the constant interference, the despotic sway, the exactions and caprices of the female sex ought no longer to be tolerated; and it is with a glow of pride and triumph that I introduce this striking example of the ability of man

REAL DEL MONTE AND ANTELOPE MILLS.

to live in a state of perfect exemption from all these trials and tribulations. True, I must admit that the honest miners of Bodie spent a great deal of their leisure time in reading yellow-covered novels and writing love-letters; but that was probably only a clever device to fortify themselves against the insidious approaches of the enemy.

A miner's cabin in any of the outside districts is a very primitive specimen of architecture. Most people have some general idea of mining operations; but there are few who know any thing about the way in which the miners live. I do not speak of the laboring classes of Virginia or Austin, who herd together in boarding-houses, or take their meals at restaurants. They are seldom seen in their characteristic aspect as working-men—the true heroes of the pick and shovel. Men who work in gangs and spend their leisure time in varied metropolitan pursuits are apt to lose their individuality. To know what a genuine miner is, and how he lives, you must visit the remote interior districts, and partake of his hospitality; but lest you should form an erroneous idea in regard to the accommodations, I must tell you as nearly as possible what a miner's cabin is made of and what it affords in the way of entertainment.

Usually it is constructed of the materials nearest at hand. Stone and mud answer for the walls where wood is scarce; but if wood be abundant, a kind of stockade is formed of logs placed close together and upright in the ground. The roof is made of clap-boards, or rough shingles, brush-wood covered with sod, canvas, or any thing else that may be available. I have seen roofs constructed of flour-sacks, cast-off shirts, coats, and pantaloons, all sewed together like a home-made quilt. Rawhide, with big stones on the corners, is very good in dry countries, but it is apt to become flabby and odorous in damp climates. The chimney is the most imposing part of the house. Where the location permits, the cabin is backed up against a bluff, so as to afford a chance for a substantial flue by merely cutting a hole through the bank; but where such natural facilities do not exist, the

INTERIOR OF A MINER'S CABIN.

BODIE BLUFF.

variety of material used in the construction of chimneys is wonderful. Stone, wood, scraps of sheet-iron, adobe-bricks, mud, whisky-barrels, nail-kegs, and even canvas, are the component parts. Think of a canvas chimney! How an Insurance Agent would stare at it!

These primitive habitations are to be found wherever any valuable ledges are in progress of development; perched up among the rocks, out on the arid slopes, in the narrow cañons, down under shaking earth-banks—the locations being chosen as the convenience or fancy of the occupants may dictate. Externally they are rural and picturesque, like the wigwams of the Digger Indians. Internally the triumphs of civilization are apparent. Push open the rough board or slab door, and you have before you the social and domestic life of the honest miner. If the walls are a little rough, and somewhat smoked in the vacant spots, what matters it?—they are abundantly ornamented. The chinks are stopped with gold and silver croppings; pegs project from convenient crevices, from which hang old boots, shirts, flitches of bacon, bunches of onions, and sundry other articles of apparel and subsistence; rough clap-board shelves heaped with books, hardware, crockery and groceries abound at convenient intervals; a bedstead made of pine logs, with blue or red blankets over it, occupies one corner, or there may be a row of bunks ranged along a side-wall, ship-fashion, to accommodate straggling or casual inmates. Frying-pans, tin cups and a coffee-pot hang over the fire-place, by way of pictures. But even pictures are no rarity in the miner's cabin. The battle-scenes in *Harper's Weekly* form the most artistic collections in the mining community. Entire walls are covered with them —whole houses are papered with them. You can sit on a three-legged stool in any of these cabins and see the great rebellion or the impeachment of President Johnson acted over from beginning to end.

I spent three days at Bodie, during which, owing to the kindness of the Judge, who was determined that I should see every thing, my time was very fully occupied. In fact, it is a little remarkable that I am now alive to tell the story of my adventures. I penetrated more shafts in the earth, was dragged through more dangerous pits and holes in wooden buckets, was forced to creep over more slippery ledges, rich in mineral deposits, and to climb up a greater number of rickety ladders than I would like to undertake again for less than a thousand shares in the " Empire Gold and Silver Mining Company." But as I design these papers rather for information than amusement, I will state the results of my observations in as matter-of-fact a way as it is possible for a man of my temperament to write.

CHAPTER XXXIX.

A STARTLING ADVENTURE.

IN the undeveloped condition of the mines, which are yet but partially opened, much is left to conjecture; but from the direction of the various lodes I should judge them to be ramifications from some great principal vein, or Veta Madre, as the Mexicans call it. Loose quartz in disconnected masses is found on the surface of the hill, within the limits assumed as belonging to the mother vein; and the probability is a rich deposit of mineral lies at the point of junction, which is estimated to be from three to five hundred feet below the surface of the earth.

I descended several of these shafts rather to oblige my friend the Judge than to satisfy any curiosity I had on the subject myself. This thing of being dropped down two hundred feet into the bowels of the earth in wooden buckets, and hoisted out by blind horses attached to "whims," may be very amusing to read about, but I have enjoyed pleasanter modes of locomotion. There was one shaft in particular which left an indelible impression upon my mind—so much so indeed that I am astonished every hair in my head is not quite gray. It was in the San Antonio, a mine in which the Judge held an interest in connection with a worthy Norwegian by the name of Jansen. As I had travelled in Norway, Jansen was enthusiastic in his devotion to my enjoyment —declared he would go down with me himself and show me every thing worth seeing—even to the lower level just opened. While I was attempting to frame an excuse the honest Norwegian had lighted a couple of candles, given directions to one of the "boys" to look out for the old blind horse attached to the whim, and now stood ready at the mouth of the shaft to guide me into the subterranean regions.

"Mr. Jansen," said I, looking with horror at the rickety wooden bucket and the flimsy little rope that was to hold us suspended between the surface of the earth and eternity, "is that rope strong?"

"Well, I think it's strong enough to hold us," replied Jansen; "it carries a ton of ore. We don't weigh a ton, I guess."

"But the bucket looks fearfully battered. And who can vouch that the old horse won't run away and let us down by the run?"

"Oh, Sir, he's used to it. That horse never runs. You see he's fast asleep now. He sleeps all along on the down turn. It's the up turn that gets him."

"Mr. Jansen," said I, "all that may be very true; but suppose the bucket should catch and drop us out?"

"Well, sometimes it catches; but nobody's been hurt bad yet: one man fell fifteen feet perpendicular. He lit on the top of his head."

"Wasn't he killed?"

"No: he was only stunned a little. There was a buzzin' about among his brains for a few days after; he's at work down below now, as well as ever."

"Mr. Jansen, upon the whole I think I'd rather go down by the ladder, if it's all the same to you."

"Certainly, Sir, suit yourself; only the ladder's sort o' broke in spots, and you'll find it a tolerably hard climb down; hows'ever I'll go ahead and sing out when I come to the bad places."

With this the Norwegian disappeared. I looked down after him. The shaft was about four feet square; rough, black, and dismal, with a small flickering light, apparently a thousand feet below, making the darkness visible. It was almost perpendicular; the ladders stood against the near side, perched on ledges or hanging together by means of chafed and ragged-looking ropes. I regretted that I had not taken Jansen's advice and committed myself to the bucket; but it was now too late. With a hurried glance at the bright world around me, a thought of home and the unhappy condition of widows and orphans, as a general thing, I seized the rungs of the ladder and took the irrevocable dive. Down I crept, rung after rung, ladder after ladder, in the black darkness, with the solid walls of rock pressing the air close around me. Sometimes I heard the incoherent mutterings of voices below, but could make nothing of them. Perhaps Jansen was warning me of breaks in the ladder; perhaps his voice was split up by the rocks and sounded like many voices; or it might be that there were gnomes whisking about in the dark depths below. Down and still down I crept; slower and slower, for I was getting tired, and I fancied there might be poisonous gases in the air. When I had reached the depth of a thousand feet, as it seemed, but about a hundred and forty as it was in reality, the thought occurred to me that I was beginning to get alarmed. In truth I was shaking like a man with an ague. Suppose I should become nervous and lose my grip on the ladder? The very idea was enough to make me shaky. There was an indefinite extent of shaft underneath; black, narrow, and scraggy, with a solid base of rock at the bottom. I did not wonder that it caused a buzzing of the brain to fall fifteen feet and light on the top of the head. My brain was buzzing already, and I had not fallen yet. But the prospect to that effect was getting better and better every moment, for I was now quite out of breath, and had to stop and cling around the ladder to avoid falling. The longer I stood this way the more certain it became that sooner or later I would lose my presence of mind and topple over. With a desperate effort I proceeded, step after step, clinging to the frail wood-work as the drowning man clings to a straw, gasping for breath; the cold

sweat streaming down my face, and my jaws chattering
audibly. The breaks in the ladders were getting fearfully common. Sometimes I found two rungs gone, sometimes six or seven ; and then I had to slide down by the
sides till my feet found a resting-place on another rung
or some casual ledge of rock. To Jansen, or the miners
who worked down in the shaft every day, all this of
course was mere pastime. They knew every break and
resting - place; and besides, familiarity with any particular kind of danger blunts the sense of it. I am confident I could make the same trip again without experi-
encing any unpleasant sensation. By good fortune I at
length reached the bottom of the shaft, where I found
my Norwegian friend and some three or four workmen
quietly awaiting my arrival. A bucket of ore, containing some five or six hundred pounds, was ready to be
hoisted up. It was very nice-looking ore, and very
rich ore, as Jansen assured me ; but what did I care
about ore till I got the breath back again into my
body ?

"Stand from under, Sir !" said Jansen, dodging into a
hole in the rocks ; " a chunk of ore might fall out, or the
bucket might give way."

Stand from under ? Where in the name of sense was
a man to stand in such a hole as this, not more than six
or eight feet at the base, with a few dark chasms in the
neighborhood through which it was quite possible to be
precipitated in to the infernal regions. However, I stood
as close to the wall as it was possible without backing
clean into it. The bucket of ore having gone up out of
sight, I was now introduced to the ledge upon which the
men were at work. It was about four feet thick, clearly
defined, and apparently rich in the precious metals. In
some specimens which I took out myself gold was visible
to the naked eye. The indications of silver were also
well marked. This was at a depth of a hundred and
seventy-five feet. At the bottom of this shaft there was
a loose flooring of rafters and planks.

STAND FROM UNDER!

"If you like, Sir," said Jansen, "we'll go down here and take a look at the lower drift. They've just struck the ledge about forty feet below."

"Are the ladders as good as those above, Mr. Jansen?" I inquired.

"Oh yes, Sir, they're all good; some of the lower ones

may be busted a little with the blastin'; but there's two men down there. Guess they got down somehow."

"To tell you the truth, Mr. Jansen, I'm not curious about the lower drift. You can show me some specimens of the ore—that will be perfectly satisfactory."

"Yes, Sir, but I'd like you to see the vein where the drift strikes it. It's really beautiful."

A beautiful sight down in this region was worth looking at, so I succumbed. Jansen lifted up the planks; told the men to cover us well up as soon as we had disappeared, in order to keep the ore from the upper shaft from tumbling on our heads; and then, diving down, politely requested me to follow. I had barely descended a few steps when the massive planks and rafters were thrown across overhead, and thus all exit to the outer world was cut off. There was an oppressive sensation in being so completely isolated—barred out, as it were, from the surface of the earth. Yet how many there are who spend half their lives in such places for a pittance of wages which they squander in dissipation! Surely it is worth four dollars a day to work in these dismal holes.

Bracing my nerves with such thoughts as these, I scrambled down the rickety ladders till the last rung seemed to have disappeared. I probed about with a spare leg for a landing-place, but could touch neither top, bottom, nor sides. The ladder was apparently suspended in space like Mohammed's coffin.

"Come on, Sir," cried the voice of Jansen far down below. "They're agoing to blast!"

Pleasant, if not picturesque, to be hanging by two hands and one leg to a ladder, squirming about in search of a foothold, while somebody below was setting fire to a fuse with the design, no doubt, of blowing up the entire premises!

"Mr. Jansen," said I, in a voice of unnatural calmness, while the big drops of agony stood on my brow, "there's no difficulty in saying 'Come on, Sir!' but to do it without an inch more of ladder or any thing else that I can see, requires both time and reflection. How far do you expect me to drop?"

"Oh, don't you let go, Sir! Just hang on to that rope at the bottom of the ladder, and let yourself down."

I hung on as directed, and let myself down. It was plain sailing enough to one who knew the chart. The

"COME ON, SIR."

ladder, it seemed, had been broken by a blast of rocks; and now there was to be another blast. We retired into a convenient hole about ten or a dozen paces from the deposit of Hazard's powder. The blast went off with a dead reverberation, causing a concussion in the air that affected one like a shock of galvanism; and then there was a diabolical smell of brimstone. Jansen was charmed at the result. A mass of the ledge was burst clean open. He grasped up the blackened fragments of quartz, licked them with his tongue, held them to the candle, and constantly exclaimed: "There! Sir, there! Isn't it beautiful? Did you ever see any thing like it?—pure gold almost—here it is!—don't you see it?"

I suppose I saw it; at all events I put some specimens in my pocket, and saw them afterward out in the pure sunlight, where the smoke was not so dense; and it is due to the great cause of truth to say that gold was there in glittering specks, as if shaken over it from a pepper-box.

Having concluded my examination of the mine, I took the bucket as a medium of exit, being fully satisfied with the ladders. About half-way up the shaft the iron swing or handle to which the rope was attached caught in one of the ladders. The rope stretched. I felt it harden and grow thin in my hands. The bucket began to tip over. It was pitch dark all around. Jansen was far below, coming up the ladder. Something seemed to be creaking, cracking, or giving way. I felt the rough, heavy sides of the bucket press against my legs. A terrible apprehension seized me that the gear was tangled and would presently snap. In the pitchy darkness and the confusion of the moment I could not conjecture what was the matter. I darted out my hands, seized the ladder, and jerking myself high out of the bucket, clambered up with the agility of an acrobat. Relieved of my weight, the iron catch swung loose, and up came the bucket banging and thundering after me with a velocity that was perfectly frightful. Never was there such a subterranean chase, I verily believe, since the beginning of the world. To stop a single moment would be certain destruction ; for the bucket was large, heavy, and massively bound with iron; and the space in the shaft was not sufficient to admit of its passing without crushing me flat against the ladder.

But such a chase could not last long. I felt my strength give way at every lift. The distance out was too great to admit the hope of escape by climbing. My only chance was to seize the rope above the bucket and hang on to it. This I did. It was a lucky thought— one of those thoughts that sometimes flash upon the mind like inspiration in a moment of peril. A few more revolutions of the whim brought me so near the surface that I could see the bucket only a few yards below my feet. The noise of the rope over the block above reminded me that I had better slip down a little to save my hands, which I did in good style, and was presently landed on the upper crust of the earth, all safe and sound, though somewhat dazzled by the light and rattled by my subterranean experiences.

It was not long before Jansen came up, looking as cool as a cucumber. He blew out the candle, and remarked to the men generally, "Boys, they've struck it rich in the new drift! We must pitch into it to-morrow !"

After my pleasant little adventure in the "San Antonio" I took the down track over the western side of the bluff, with my pockets—so to speak—full of rocks, which I caused to be pounded up in a mortar and washed out at one of the springs in the valley. The "San Antonio" is on the same ledge with the "New Mexico," one of the Empire Company's mines. My specimens were obtained at a depth of 175 and 215 feet. I had some doubts as to their value until I saw the result of the washing process, which settled the matter satisfactorily. There was as nice a little deposit of pure gold in the bottom of the horn as ever I saw taken at random from any mine in

California, Washoe, or Arizona. The quartz at this depth is decomposed, and runs in thin layers, between which, adhering to the surface, the gold is found. Silver exists in the bluish veins which permeate the quartz, but is not found in such abundance as the gold. The bullion rates at about ten dollars to the ounce. There seems to be very little difference in the quality of the ores in any of the lodes extending through Bodie Bluff. I subsequently explored most of them, as far as they were excavated, and made several tests, which produced a similar show of gold. Judging by actual results derived from the working of some two or three hundred tons in the Aurora Mills, where the waste was evidently great, it would be safe to estimate the average yield at from thirty-five to forty-five dollars per ton; though I am informed that during the past fall and winter the yield was sixty dollars and upward. With increased care and more perfect system of reduction it is not improbable a higher yield could be obtained.

For speculative purposes this is low; but there is a satisfaction to stockholders in knowing exactly what they possess, and upon what basis to found their calculations of future profit. The best paying mines on this coast are those that yield a moderate average. This is especially the case in the districts of Nevada and Grass Valley, California, which now, after having as it was thought been worked out, yield better average results than they ever did before. I speak of the quartz ledges, of course, not of the placer diggings. The Real del Monte in Mexico, according to the estimates of Baron Humboldt and Mr. Ward, yielded for a series of years, during a period of high prosperity, an average of fifty-two dollars to the ton. It is the certainty and abundance of the precious metals, and the facility with which the ore is obtained, that constitute the true criterion of excellence and give permanent value to the mine.

The history of some of the Washoe mines, which have yielded extraordinary results under a heavy pressure of

WHAT'S THE MATTER?

expense and labor, and which are now suffering a depression resulting from exhaustion of the upper strata,
presents the most striking examples of this fact.   Had the
inferior ores been properly economized, and the mines
worked with a view to the future, stockholders in these
mines would now have no cause to regret their invest-

ments. I do not wish to be understood as advancing the idea that the Comstock ledge is exhausted or likely to be; for I have always regarded it, and do still, as the richest silver lode yet discovered in our mineral territories. But I think the world can present no such example as we find in the history of that ledge, of mismanagement, extravagance, and fraud. It would almost seem, indeed, as if the American people, owing to some inherent characteristic—an impatient, speculative, prodigal spirit, perhaps—were incapable of conducting the business of mining upon any principle of reason, honesty, or common sense. Why is it, otherwise, that, with the richest mines in the world—with untiring enterprise, inventive genius of the highest order, a larger average of intelligence than any other people possess, we have never yet made mining a permanently profitable business to all concerned? The truth is, we are too impatient and too exacting, and expect to make fortunes as we live—by telegraphic speed. We must tear out the entrails of the earth by novel and expeditious applications of steam, and turn our capital by galvanic speculations, or give it up in disgust.

In respect to the article of provisions, the proximity of the Big Meadows, Mono Lake, and Walker's Valley, where vegetable products of all kinds are now abundantly raised, is a great advantage to this district. Until within a year or two miners suffered much from the want of vegetables; scurvy was a common disease; but during the past summer the supply has been quite equal to the demand. Farms are being located and cultivated in all the adjacent valleys, where the altitude is not too great for agricultural purposes; and it is found that the land, though apparently barren, is extraordinarily rich, owing to deposits of fertilizing matter from the surrounding mountains. Of course every thing which has a tendency to reduce the cost of living must reduce the cost of mining in this country—a very important consideration. No mines, however rich, can be profitably worked for any great length of time where the wages for ordinary labor are four dollars a day. Ores worth fifteen or twenty dollars a ton are necessarily cast aside, and only such as yield over thirty or forty dollars can be made to pay. There is always more poor ore in every mining district than rich; hence the preponderance of wealth is lost where the inferior ores can not be made available. The period is not very distant when the ores now discarded will be the source of permanent wealth in Nevada. It is to a general reduction of expenses, and not to the discovery of richer leads, that we must look for that high state of prosperity which I think, despite all the losses and drawbacks which have attended the investment of capital in Nevada, is the ultimate destiny of that region.

Whether or not the Bodie mines will be worked profitably on a large scale depends very much upon the system of operations introduced by the owners. As a general rule, large companies are less successful in the working of mines than small parties and private individuals. The cause of this may be found in the fact that mining,

MINING AT BODIE.

INTERIOR OF THE BODIE BUNKER.

like any other business, requires judicious and econom-
ical management, and strict personal attention, to be permanently profitable.   Indeed the risks are so much greater than in any other business, that those maxims of economy and accountability which apply to the ordinary transactions of life possess still greater force as applied to the
business of mining.   Unnecessarily expensive mills, a
loose system of disbursement, incompetent managers, and
inefficient experts, have effected the ruin of many mines
and many stockholders in the Territory of Nevada.   The
same causes would produce similar results in any other
business.   Exorbitant and unreasonable demands for high
dividends have been a fruitful source of failure.   Capitalists are not satisfied unless they receive from two to
five per cent. a month upon their investments; and superintendents work under a heavy pressure, and assume
great hazards to produce that result.   Now I am very
confident that no ten mines in Virginia City have ever
yet yielded an average of one per cent. a month over and
above expenses, and I venture to assert that no mines in
South America, Mexico, or Nevada have continued to
pay such high dividends for any great length of time.

S 2

Permanency and extraordinary dividends are incompatible. Where the yield is evidently reliable, a reasonable percentage, regularly paid, is better than a larger amount which must necessarily involve greater risk and increased expenditure.

At the head of the Bodie Valley, where I spent a day very pleasantly among the miners, is a beautiful natural location for a town, sheltered by surrounding hills from the chilling winds that sweep down from the snow-capped peaks of the Sierras. There are now some fifteen or twenty small frame and adobe houses erected for the use of the workmen; a boarding-house is already established; lots and streets are laid out by means of stakes; new houses are springing up in every direction, and speculation in real estate is quite the fashion. It was amusing to witness the enthusiasm with which the citizens went into the business of trading in lots. Groups of speculators were constantly engaged in examining choice locations, and descanting upon the brilliant future of the embryo city. A pair of boots, I suppose, would have se-

BROWNE STREET, BODIE.

cured the right to a tolerably good lot; but having only one pair, and that pretty well worn, I did not venture upon an investment. Some of the city dignitaries, however, duly impressed with the importance of having a view of their town appear in the illuminated pages of *Harper*, paid me the compliment to attach my name to the principal street; and thus, in future ages, I confidently expect my memory will be rescued from oblivion. Opposite is the promised view of the town.

Although the altitude is greater than that of any inhabited spot within the limits of the United States, and only surpassed by those of Potosi, which is 13,330 feet, and Quito, 9540 feet, the climate is exceedingly healthy; never too warm in summer, and rarely rigorous in winter. This, at an elevation of nearly 9000 feet, is remarkable. Water is abundantly supplied from a fine spring distant a few hundred yards from the centre of the town; wood, for mining purposes and for the use of the inhabitants, can be obtained from a pine-forest situated on the side of a hill about four miles from the camp. The supply of this latter article, however, is limited, and can not be depended upon for more than a few years; but the ravines in the main range of the Sierra Nevadas, bordering on Mono Lake, are clothed with inexhaustible forests, suitable for lumber as well as fuel. A good road is now open to the shores of Mono, the nearest part of which lies about fourteen miles from Bodie. A view of the lake from the eastern side of the bluff presents one of the finest specimens of scenic grandeur to be found in the whole range of the Sierra Nevadas. Mountain after mountain rolls off in the distance, like the waves of an angry sea. Perpetual snow covers the highest peaks of the Sierras. Dark forests of pine stand in bold outline on the inferior ranges, and vast chasms and rocky cañons open out upon the shores of the lake, which lies dead and still apparently within a stone's-throw of the beholder. Circling deposits of alkali and drifts of wood mark the barren plains that lie on the eastern shore of the lake, showing that in by-gone centuries it covered a vast extent of country from which it has now receded.

A direct communication from the valley of the San Joaquin, *via* Sonora, has recently been opened by the citizens of Mono and Esmerelda; thus saving in transportation, from the head of navigation at Stockton, at least four or five days of wagon travel from the usual time required by the old route from Sacramento *via* Carson Valley. This will greatly reduce the cost of transporting supplies of machinery and provisions from San Francisco.

THE DEAD SEA OF THE WEST.

CHAPTER XL.

A BADGER FIGHT.

AT the town of Bodie I witnessed one of those impressive Sunday exhibitions which seem to be the popular mode of recreation in this country—a badger fight. Some Indians from Mono Lake came in during the forenoon with a remarkably large badger, which they offered for sale to the miners. The price demanded was ten dollars. As that amount of ready cash did not seem to be within the resources of the multitude, the Diggers, upon consultation, agreed to take three, which was finally made up by some enterprising members of the community. The usual mode of digging a hole in the ground, as a fortification for the badger, was deemed unnecessary, owing to the formidable proportions and ferocious temper of the animal on hand; and it was decided that there should be a pitched battle in the open valley. All who had dogs were invited to bring them forward and enter the ring gratis. In about ten minutes there were about half a dozen dogs brought to the scratch, and the battle opened cautiously on both sides. The badger was fresh and vigorous. Long experience in the noble art of self-defense had taught him skill in the use of his natural weapons. He lay close down to the ground, flattening himself as the rattlesnake flattens his head prior to the fatal dart. With a keen and wary eye he watched the dogs. First a large, ill-favored,

BADGERING THE BADGER.

yellow cur was let loose upon him. The badger never
moved till the mouth of his enemy was within an inch
of his tail, when, with a motion as quick as lightning, he
had him by the under-lip, and a fierce struggle ensued.
The dog howled, the badger held on, the dust flew up
from the dry earth, over and over the combatants rolled ;
the spectators crowded in, laughing, shouting, clapping
their hands, and urging on the yelling cur, whose grand
object seemed to be to get away. A favorable turn enabled him to break loose. Panting, whining, and with
bleeding mouth, he sneaked off amid the jeers of the
crowd.

"Here's a dog that'll settle his hash !" said the owner
of a bull-terrier ; "let him in !"

"No, no !" cried a chorus of voices. "Hold back !
Don't kill him yet ! Try the other dogs first !"

A vicious-looking black dog, part wolf, was next let
loose. The badger had meantime crept close up to a
bank of earth, against which he fortified his rear. The
wolfish cur surveyed the prospect warily, smelled the

badger at the distance of a few feet, peered into his eyes, and quietly walked away. The crowd drove him back. "Fight, you durned coyote!" shouted his master, catching him by the back of the neck and dragging him close up to the badger. "Now fight!" Wolf looked as if he'd rather not; but there was no help for it. With hair erect and a wolfish bark he flew savagely at the enemy; jumping first to one side and then the other; back and at him again; snapping, barking, snarling, and howling; but to no purpose. The badger seemed to be all head; there was not a vulnerable point about him that did not show a head and a sharp row of teeth the moment it was assailed. During some of the dog's gyrations Mr. Badger got him by the hind-leg, and then there was a very pretty scene of howling and running. Wolf flew all over the ground; badger held on; dust, shouts, shrieks, yells, oaths, and clapping of hands were the natural consequences of this achievement. Badger-stock ran up fifty per cent.; dog-stock was rapidly declining.

"Tell you what, gents," cried the Committee on the Badger, "we'll fight him agin all six of yer dogs for ten dollars!"

"No, no!" shouted every body; "give him a fair show; his mouth's full of dust; 'tain't fair—six to one."

"Then come on with yer bull-terrier!" cried the Committee, exultingly; "here's the boy for him!"

Bull was let loose—a white, clean-made little fellow, with massive jaws, thin flanks, and a sharp, hard tail, that stood out from his body like a spike. There was neither growl nor bark about him; it was all serious work, in which he evidently delighted; and he went at it with a will—straight, quick, fierce, like a well-trained bruiser who meant blood. He had been accustomed, as was evident from the many scars on his head and face, to enemies of his own species. He could get hold of a fellow-dog, however large, and throttle him. Getting hold of a badger was quite another thing. Both animals were nearly of the same size. The dog perhaps had the

advantage in muscular strength; but the badger was
the quicker with his head and teeth. The moment Bull's
mouth was within reach the badger had him by the under jaw, fast and firm as a vice. Now commenced the
grand tussle—teeth against teeth, neck against neck.
Thick dust covered the combatants; to and fro, over and
over, they rolled, in their scarce visible struggle; the
crowd pressing close in; not a word spoken; for this
was a genuine fight at last — earnest and thrilling —
a fight to the death. Sunday as it was, I could not but
push in closer and look on. I was getting profoundly
interested in the fate of the badger. In fact, I don't
know but I might have made a bet had any body ban-
tered me at the moment. I would have bet on either
side, no matter which, as many a man does who gets
excited and has no definite opinion on the subject at
issue.

"Stand back! give him a chance!" shouted some of
the men in front.

"Take him to water! he's choking with dust!" cried
others; and I must say a pang of regret shot through
me at what I supposed to be the fate of my badger
friend.

But it was not the badger that suffered most. The
dog was dragged out, his mouth full of hair and dust,
gasping for breath. I looked again when the dust
cleared away. Bleeding and torn, but dauntless as ever,
with the same fixed and wary eye, the badger awaited
the next assault.

"Too bad! too bad!" remonstrated several voices.
"That's murder in the first degree!" Sympathy seemed
to lean toward the side of the poor animal which was
making so gallant a struggle for life. "Kill him! kill
him with a club!"

"No ye don't, gents!" shouted the exultant Committee, who had paid their three dollars for a Sunday forenoon's sport. "We'll fight him against all the dogs
first; if he don't whip 'em, then you can kill him."

Incredible as it may seem, the six dogs, large and small, were next let loose, and for over an hour they fought that poor badger without doing him any material damage. While some attacked him in front, others picked him up behind, gave him a shake, and then dropped him. He seemed to possess more lives than a cat. He bit back a dozen bites for every one he received ; and at every respite faced his enemies with that peculiar fixed and indomitable eye which had at first attracted my attention. It was almost human in its expression, and seemed to say, "Shame ! shame ! Cruel as you are, you can not make me quail : I die game to the last !"

Some such thought must have entered the heads of the by-standers, two or three of whom now rushed in with clubs and attempted to batter his brains out. Even then he fought fiercely, biting at the clubs, and in his dying throes glaring with undaunted eyes at his assailants. I am free to confess that I turned away with a strong emotion of pity. The fight had lasted two hours. When I next looked back and saw the crowd move away, dragging after them the dead body of the badger, I could not but feel that there was something about the whole business very much like murder.

My friend the Judge was obliged to return to Aurora from this point. I was committed to the charge of a very pleasant and intelligent young man, one of the owners of the Bodie Bunker, who kindly volunteered to procure horses and accompany me on my proposed expedition to Mono Lake. The horses were ranging in the hills, and there was some difficulty in finding them. In due time we were mounted and on our way.

CHAPTER XLI.

THE road crosses a hill back of Bodie, and thence down through a cañon into Cotton-wood Valley. For a distance of some five or six miles the country is rolling and barren. Rocks and sage-brush, with desolate mountains in the distance, are the principal features. During the trip my companion entertained me with many interesting reminiscences of his experience in the country, his adventures as a police-officer during the Vigilance Committee excitement at Aurora, his mining speculations, and many other matters which to me possessed all the charms of romance. From him also I obtained the particulars of a very singular and tragical occurrence which had taken place about two months previously on the road to the Big Meadows, not far from where we were travelling. I had heard of this on my first arrival at Aurora, and had seen some account of it in the newspapers. Subsequently I crossed the cañon in which the disaster occurred, and made a sketch of it.

Some time in the month of July two men, with their wives, and three children belonging to one of the parties, started from Aurora in a small wagon for the Big Meadows. The distance is twenty-eight miles. When about half-way, as they were passing through a rocky cañon, unsuspicious of danger, they observed some signs of rain, but thought it would be nothing more than a casual shower. Suddenly the sky darkened, and they heard a loud roaring noise behind them. Mr. Glenn, one of the men, and his comrade, who were sitting on the front seat, finding the horses become unmanageable from

BURSTING OF A CLOUD IN THE CAÑON.

fright, jumped out to see what was the matter. The lead horses had swung round, and were making frantic efforts to break loose from their traces. Scarcely had the two men touched the ground when they saw sweeping down toward them a solid flood of water about six or eight feet high, presenting a front like a prodigious wave of the sea as it breaks upon the beach in a storm. They attempted to force the horses up on one side, so as to haul the wagon out of the channel. Before any thing could be done the torrent burst upon them, carrying all before it. The wagon was capsized and dashed to pieces among the rocks. The screams of the women and children rose high above the wild roar of the flood ; and for a moment they were seen struggling amid the shattered wreck of the wagon, but were soon dashed out and whirled against the rocks. One of the men, by superhuman efforts, succeeded in getting a foothold a short distance below, and, grasping an overhanging bush, caught his wife as she was swept along on the raging current. He had dragged her nearly out of the water when she was struck by a heavy piece of drift-wood and torn from his grasp. The next moment she was whirled away beyond reach, and her body, maimed by the jagged rocks, was buried in the current a shapeless mass. Meantime the other man was disabled by his struggles amid the wreck, and barely escaped with his life. The shrieks of the poor children were heart-rending. " Oh, father ! father ! save me ! Oh, mother, save me !" were all that could be heard ; but soon their tender limbs were crushed amid the boiling surges of drift and flood, and they were swept beyond all human aid. In less than a minute nothing was left to mark the tragedy. Women, children, wagon, horses, all had disappeared. Such was the force of the torrent that rocks and trees were carried away like feathers. I saw myself prodigious boulders of solid stone, six or seven feet in diameter, which had been rolled for miles through the cañon.

When the news of this sad event reached Aurora the most intense excitement and sympathy prevailed. Parties went out immediately to afford what assistance they could. The unfortunate men who had suffered so strange and sudden a bereavement were provided with such aid as their suffering condition required. Search was made for the bodies of the women and children.

Their mutilated remains were found scattered among the rocks from one to three miles below the scene of the disaster, and were taken in and buried amid the sympathizing tears of relatives, friends, and strangers.

An interesting circumstance connected with this sad event was mentioned to me by Mrs. Voorhies, a highly intelligent lady from Oakland, who happened that day to be out riding on horseback near Aurora, accompanied by her husband and a party of friends. They had reached the summit of Mount Braley, when the attention of the party was directed by Mrs. Voorhies to the peculiar appearance of a cloud which appeared to hang over the earth like a huge black funnel in the direction of the Big Meadows. It had a dark-greenish tinge around the edges as if charged with sulphur or electricity. Other clouds were in the sky, but the weather was warm and pleasant. The attention of the whole party was fixed upon the black cloud. Suddenly it changed its form, and disappeared almost like magic. Apparently the attraction of the earth had scattered it or absorbed its contents. This was doubtless the same cloud which had burst and swept all before it in the Rocky Cañon. The time and direction corresponded precisely with the tragic event above recorded.

The only other instance known to me of the bursting of a water-cloud with such disastrous consequences occurred about four years ago in the San Francisquito Cañon between Los Angeles and Fort Tejon. I have frequently passed through this cañon, and can readily conceive how disastrous a sudden flood would be anywhere between the points of entrance and exit. It is some ten or twelve miles through, and closely bounded on each side by precipitous hills and mountains. Within this distance the road crosses a small stream that courses through it eighty-seven times. In this cañon a family belonging to Los Angeles, who were on their way home from the valley of the San Joaquin, were overtaken by a heavy rain-cloud, which burst close behind them. The man jumped out of his wagon and strove to urge his animals up a steep bank; but the flood came upon them so suddenly that the wagon was swept away, dragging with it the animals. The women and children were all drowned.

I have been told of similar instances of water-spouts, or, more properly, the bursting of rain-clouds, in the cañons of the Colorado, and in other parts of Arizona. Owing, perhaps, to the fact that few people travel through the mountainous parts of that country in wagons, they have not often been attended by any loss of life, though Governor Goodwin, of Arizona, recently gave me an account of an entire mining camp that was swept away. Two lives were lost and much property damaged.

Proceeding some fourteen miles on our journey, we turned the point of a hill overlooking the lake. It seemed to be just at our feet. We had to travel twelve miles further before we reached Lawrence's Ranch.

Down in the cañon on the right of the road we passed some placer diggings, which attracted considerable attention two years ago. White labor could not make it pay, and the usual herd of Chinese had crowded in and taken possession of the abandoned huts and sluices. They seemed to be doing well, if one might judge by their noisy jargon and barbarous gesticulations.

CHAPTER XLII.

MONO LAKE.

A FEW miles beyond we passed the town of Mono, consisting at present of three or four shanties, one of which only was inhabited.

A ride of twenty-five miles over the rough mountain trails gave me such an appetite as I had not experienced for many months. The atmosphere is wonderfully clear and bracing in these elevated ranges. An ecstatic glow of health pervades the system; the sight becomes keen; the blood flows freely through the veins; the digestion is perfect; and the world-worn traveller feels something of that elasticity and freshness with which he set forth in early life to put a girdle round about the earth. I was well disposed to enjoy the hospitality of Mr. Lawrence, the owner of the ranch at which we proposed stopping for the night. It was a pleasant, home-looking place, with hay-stacks, wagons, and lowing cattle about the farm-yard; and the honest watch-dog bayed a deep-mouthed welcome as we rode up to the house. The worthy settler came out on the grassy slope in front and greeted us with the hearty cordiality of a frontiersman.

"Get down, gentlemen; get down and come in. We haven't much in this wild country, but what we have is at your service."

It was a pleasant surprise, when I was introduced to him, to find that we were old fellow-travellers.

"Bless my soul!" he exclaimed, grasping my hand with the grip of a vice; "is it possible you have arrived here at last? I have been expecting you for over two years. I knew you'd visit Mono Lake some time or oth-

TOWN OF MONO.

er. Why, my dear fellow, we are old friends! I have travelled with you all over the world—in print."

And here let me say, in all humility, that some of the happiest moments of my life have been derived from just such meetings as this in the wild regions bordering on the Pacific. To find myself known where it was least to be expected; to receive a cordial greeting as a friend where I could only hope for the ordinary civility due to a stranger; to feel that a few trifles of travel cast adrift upon the world in the pages of a Magazine, without a thought of their fate beyond the current month, had inspired, far away from the haunts of civilization, a friendly personal interest in the writer—these, I say, affected me with no ordinary emotions of pleasure; for they proved in some degree that my wanderings in lonely countries had not altogether isolated me from the great brotherhood of man.

The house was a snug frame shanty, containing three or four rooms, roughly but comfortably furnished, and decorated with some curious specimens of colored engravings, which evinced at least a leaning toward the Fine Arts. Beds were plenty—deep, full feather beds, in which the sleeper was luxuriously buried for the night. I found that feathers were a staple product here. In truth, I had a dream, after my burial in the deepest of these beds, that nature had gifted me with wings, and that I was flying about among the pine-trees pursued by some adroit sportsmen, who amused themselves peppering me with snipe-shot. But this might have been owing to the supper prepared by the skillful hands of the good housewife. It is but simple justice to that lady to say that such a supper would have done honor to the best hotel in New York. For where else but in the mountain regions of the Pacific is there such delicately-flavored mutton, such rich yellow cream, such pure fresh milk and sparkling butter? The biscuits, too, were delicious; and there were preserves of wild mountain berries, and jams and tarts and pies that must have taxed the

T

ingenuity of the inventor.   As for vegetables, there was
any variety; and the potatoes were as rich and mealy as
the best Irish murphies.   I never tasted any thing in the
potato-line superior to them.   Upon warmly expressing
this sentiment to our kind host he was naturally elated,
and offered to take me at once to his potato-patch.
" You shall see for yourself," said he; " I rather calculate
you never saw such a patch."

I was pretty stiff, however, after my long ride, and suggested that the morning sunshine would be the best light
perhaps in which to view this remarkable potato-patch.

It was a pleasant scene that evening at Lawrence's
Ranch.   A gentleman and his wife from Aurora were
stopping at the house for the enjoyment of the lake air;
and their conversation contributed greatly to our enjoyment.   We sat on the front porch, overlooking the whole
magnificent panorama outspread before us.   The glowing
atmosphere hung over the lake like a vast prismatic canopy.   Myriads of aquatic fowl sported on the glassy surface of the water, which reflected the varied outlines and
many-colored slopes of the surrounding mountains.
Trees, rocks, islands, and all visible objects were dupli-
cated with wonderful clearness and accuracy.   The white
mountains of Montgomery fifty miles distant stood out
against the horizon in their minutest details, every rock
and furrow as if seen through a telescope.   A soft, delicious air, fragrant with the odors of wild flowers and
new-made hay, made it a luxury to breathe.   High to the
right, tipped by the glowing rays of the sun, towered the
snow-capped peaks of the Sierra Nevadas.   To the west
and south, grand and solitary—monarchs among the
mountain kings—stood Castle Peak and Mount Dana, as
if in sublime scorn of the puny civilization which encir-
cles their feet.   These mighty potentates of the wilderness, according to the geological survey of Professor
Whitney, reach the altitude respectively of 13,000 and
13,500 feet above the level of the sea.   Still higher
mountains have been found to the southward, during a

LAKE SHORE.

recent expedition of the survey, of which very interesting reports by Professor Brewer, Mr. Charles F. Hoffman, Mr. King, Mr. Gardiner, and others, are now in progress of publication. A new and most interesting region between Kern River and Owen's Valley was explored by these gentlemen during the past summer, of which a brief notice has recently appeared in Silliman's *Scientific Journal*.

The shores of Lake Mono, in the vicinity of the water, have a whitish color, arising from the prevalence of calcareous deposits. It well deserves the name suggested by an early visitor—the " Dead Sea of the West." Not even that wondrous sea, whose bitter waters wash the ruined sites of Sodom and Gomorrah, presents a scene of greater desolation. Fourteen years had passed—how short a time it seemed !—since my trusty guide, Yusef Badra, pointed out to me from the St. Saba road the shores of the Dead Sea. I could almost imagine myself there again. Yet for grandeur of scenery, and for interesting geological phenomena, this lake of the Western Sierras is far superior to the Oriental Sea. Here the traveller, whether artist, geologist, botanist, or poet, might spend many months, and find ample occupation for every hour of his time.

Lake Mono was visited in 1852 by Lieutenant Moore, whose adventures in that wild region, during the Indian war, gave him a high reputation on the Pacific coast. I am not aware whether any official report of his visit to Mono has been published. It would doubtless be most interesting; for few men have seen it under such novel and interesting circumstances.

The lake is eighteen miles in length by about ten or twelve in width. On the western side are distinct water-marks, showing that in former years it attained an elevation of 800 to 1000 feet above its present level.

This would indicate a superficial area of such vast magnitude that it must have resembled a great inland sea. On the eastern side is a gap or depression in the hills, through which it must have flowed, covering an immense area of the great Walker River basin. It is not improbable that it was once a continuous sea to Walker's Lake. But I will not hazard any conjectures on this point; for when one goes beyond the bare facts, as he sees them, in such a country as this, the imagination is bewildered. A vague idea possesses the mind that all the great interior basins, including that of Salt Lake, might have formed a grand intermediate ocean, stretching from the far north to the Gulf of California, between the great parallel ranges of the Cascades and Sierra Nevadas to the west, and the Rocky Mountains to the east.

On the Sierra side of the lake there are points of woodland which extend some distance into the water. Back from the shore deep cañons, rocky and precipitous, with ridges of pine on each side, cut their way into the heart of the mountains; and huge boulders, hurled down from the dizzy heights, stand like castles on the beach. From innumerable ravines fresh-water springs and streams pour their tribute into the lake. There is no visible outlet; yet the bitterness of the water is retained, and there is seldom a perceptible rise. Even in the great flood of '62, when every ravine poured down a roaring torrent, the rise did not exceed a few inches; and during the continuance of the flood, after the reception of the first volume of water, the level of the lake remained unchanged. It would seem that there must be a subterranean outlet; yet there is no evidence that the surplus water again reaches the surface. The probability is it becomes absorbed in the dry sands of the desert.

On the eastern shore low plains or alluvial bottoms, incrusted with alkali, show in distinct curvicular rims, composed of calcareous deposits, the gradual retrocession of the lake to its present level. The beach is strewn with beautiful specimens of boracic or alkaline incrustations. Weeds, twigs, stones, and even dead birds and animals, are covered by this peculiar coating, and present the appearance of coral formations. Some

MONO LAKE.

specimens that I picked up are photographic in the minuteness and delicacy of their details. When broken open, the fibres of leaves, the feathers of birds, the grain of wood are found impressed in the calcareous moulding with exquisite perfection. Almost every conceivable variety of form may be found among these incrustations. White columns and elaborate façades, like those of the ruined temples of Greece, stand on the desert shore to the north. Archways and domes and embattlements are represented with astonishing fidelity. It is commonly supposed that these are formations of white coral; but there can be no doubt that they are produced by the chemical action of the water, which at frequent intervals is forced up through the fissures of the earth by subterranean heat. These springs are numerous, and probably form around them a base of calcareous matter, which by constant accretions rises above the surrounding level.

A curious and rather disgusting deposit of worms, about two feet high by three or four in thickness, extends like a vast rim around the shores of the lake. I saw no end to it during a walk of several miles along the beach. These worms are the larvæ of flies, originally deposited in a floating tissue on the surface of the water. So far as I could discover most of them were dead. They lay in a solid oily mass, exhaling a peculiar though not unpleasant odor in the sun. Swarms of small black flies covered them to the depth of several inches. Such was the multitude of these flies that my progress was frequently arrested by them as they flew up. Whether they were engaged in an attempt to identify their own progeny, or, cannibal-like, were devouring the children of their enemies, it was impossible to determine. The former seemed to be rather a hopeless undertaking amid such a mixed crowd. The air for a circle of several yards was blackened with these flies, and their buzz sounded like the brewing of a distant storm. My eyes, nose, mouth, and ears were filled. I could not beat them off. Wherever they lit there they remained, sluggish and slimy. I fain had to rush out of reach and seek a breathing-place some distance from the festive scene.

It would appear that the worms, as soon as they attain the power of locomotion, creep up from the water, or are deposited on the beach by the waves during some of those violent gales which prevail in this region. The Mono Indians derive from them a fruitful source of subsistence. By drying them in the sun and mixing them with acorns, berries, grass-seeds, and other articles of food gathered up in the mountains, they make a conglomerate called *cuchaba*, which they use as a kind of bread. I am told it is very nutritious and not at all unpalatable. The worms are also eaten in their natural condition. It is considered a delicacy to fry them in their own grease. When properly prepared by a skillful cook they resemble pork " cracklings." I was not hungry enough to require one of these dishes during my sojourn, but would recommend any friend who may visit the lake to eat a pound or two and let me know the result at his earliest convenience. In fact, I don't yearn for fat worms as an article of diet, though almost any kind of food is acceptable when my appetite is good. There must be hundreds, perhaps thousands of tons of these oleaginous insects cast up on the beach every year. There is no danger of starvation on the shores of Mono. The inhabitants may be snowed in, flooded out, or cut off by aboriginal hordes, but they can always rely upon the beach for fat meat.

No other insect or animal that I could hear of exists in the waters of the lake. The concurrent testimony of the settlers is, that nothing containing the vital principle is indigenous to the water. It is possible, however, that scientific research may develop various forms of animalcule. Fish are not found in any of the streams that fall into it, even high up in the Sierra Nevadas. Yet in adjacent streams that form the sources of supply to Owen's and Walker's rivers there is a great abundance of fish.

No analysis, I believe, has yet been made of the water of this lake. It is strong and bitter to the taste, and probably contains borax and soda. To the touch it feels soft and soapy ; and indeed has much the effect of liquid shaving soap. Upon being rubbed on the skin or any foreign substance, it makes an excellent lather. For washing purposes it is admirable. I washed my head in it, and was astonished at the result. To quote the language of a patent advertisement—it removes the dandruff from the hair, purifies the skin, causes a healthy glow, takes the grease out of cloth, and is especially successful as a general expurgator. The only difficulty I found about it is that it shrinks up the flesh when steeped in it for any great length of time, like a strong decoction of lye, and is hard to get rid of without a subsequent application of fresh water. I think it would extract all the flesh, blood, and muscular tissue out of the human body, and form the usual calcareous deposit over the bones in a very short time. Its buoyant properties are even more remarkable than those of the Dead Sea. To sink in it requires the strongest efforts of a strong swimmer. But one might almost as well sink as float in a case of wreck ; for in either event his chance of life would be slender.

There are two islands situated a few miles from the northern shore, one of which is about two miles in length by one and a half in width ; the other is smaller. Detached rocks extend around these for some distance into the water.

The larger island has a singular volcano in the interior, from which issues hot water and steam. Within a few yards of the boiling spring, the water of which is bitter, a spring of pure fresh water gushes out of the rocks. This is justly regarded as the greatest natural wonder of the lake. Fresh water bursting up from the very depths of a volcanic pile, surrounded by a sea of soda and borax, is surely one of the most striking anomalies of which we have any record.

The smaller island is evidently an extinct crater. Lava formations abound upon it. No springs, either hot or cold, are found upon this island.

Immense swarms of gulls visit these islands during the spring of the year and deposit their eggs on every available spot. Myriads upon myriads of them hover over the rocks from morning till night, deafening the ear with their wild screams, and the water is literally covered by them for a circle of many miles. It is a common practice for the settlers to go over in their boats, and in the course of a few hours gather as many eggs as they can carry home. In some parts of the main island the open spaces between the rocks are so thickly covered with eggs that the pedestrian is at a loss to find a vacant spot for his foot. The Indians, until recently, derived a considerable portion of their subsistence from this source; but the white man, having a better right, of which gunpowder is the proof, has ordered the aboriginal egg-hunters to keep away. I have heard that a Yankee speculator now monopolizes the trade. The eggs are strong in flavor, but good for hotels and restaurants, those of the Farraleones are much esteemed. A few go a long way in giving flavor to an omelette. The miners seem to relish them.

During the winter months the waters of the lake are literally covered with swans, geese, brant, ducks, and smaller aquatic fowl. It is incredible the number of these birds that appear after the first rains. Sportsmen find it a laborious job to carry home their game. A regular gunning expedition in this region results in nothing short of wholesale slaughter. Twenty or thirty teal duck at a single shot is nothing unusual.

Frequent and violent storms visit the lake in autumn and winter; and during the summer the sudden gusts of wind from the mountains render navigation in a small boat somewhat perilous. A visit to the islands is attended by considerable risk and uncertainty. Only a few small skiffs have yet been built, and these are generally in a dilapidated condition. The tourist must calculate upon spending a night on the bare rocks, and go well prepared with blankets and provisions, otherwise he may suffer more than he bargains for. I would suggest June, July, and August as the best months in which to make the trip.

At the southern extremity of the lake are three remarkable volcanic peaks, of a conical form, the sides of which are covered with loose pumice-stone and obsidian. Regular craters are found in these peaks, showing signs of volcanic eruptions at no very remote date. The highest is 1500 feet above the level of the lake. It is extremely difficult to ascend, owing to the loose stratum by which it is covered; but there is a consolation in the facility with which the descent is made. At the base the ground is covered with various specimens of lava, of the most fanciful shapes and beautiful colors. I saw some that would be an ornament to any cabinet of curiosities in the Atlantic States. Unfortunately I had no convenient way of packing them on my horse.

There are some twenty settlers living on the shores of Lake Mono, most of whom are engaged in stock-raising and hay-cutting. The best ranches and farms are owned by Mr. Lundy, Mr. Van Read, and Mr. Lawrence. Most of the lands available for cultivation have been taken up. These are timbered, or adjacent to timber, and are well watered by springs. A saw-mill has recently been erected, and now that there is a chance of getting lumber it is probable a number of new houses will be built during the next summer.

The country is not strictly agricultural. The amount of arable land is small; but the mountains abound in mineral veins, and gold mining and prospecting for gold occupy considerable attention. Within a year or two, when the facilities for crossing the Sierra Nevadas are increased, visitors from the Yo Semite Falls will doubtless pay their respects to Mono Lake by the way of the Bloody Cañon. A rough trail now crosses from that point by which the falls of Yo Semite may be reached in something less than two days. I have known the trip to be made in thirty hours on a good mule.

In this isolated region, abounding in grand primeval forests, magnificent scenery, natural curiosities of the most remarkable kind; deer, sage-hens, quail, rabbits, and water-fowl; a fine bracing climate, and entire exemption from the petty annoyances of crowded communities, how peacefully and contentedly life might be passed! And yet the settlers have their troubles, their quarrels about landmarks and cattle, and the usual bickerings of frontier communities. I suppose man is born to trouble everywhere as the sparks fly upward.

My friend Lawrence was very anxious that I should spend a month with him, and make a detailed exploration of the country. He offered to get up his horses and travel with me entirely round the lake; through Bloody Cañon, across to Yo Semite, anywhere for variety and adventure. Pleasant as the prospect was, I was compelled to decline it. My time was limited. I had the Walker River Country to visit, and the season was getting advanced.

Next day, after a hard ride of thirty miles over the mountains, I reached Aurora. Hurried and unsatisfactory as my trip had been, I had seen a good deal in so short a time; and if the reader has derived any pleasure from the recital, I certainly have no cause to regret my visit to Bodie Bluff and the "Dead Sea of the West."

THE WALKER RIVER COUNTRY.

CHAPTER XLIII.

A SMASH-UP.

MY preparations for the Walker River expedition were on a scale of more than usual grandeur. On this occasion I was resolved to travel in a dignified style, according with the gravity and importance of the undertaking. Certain coal and iron mines, recently discovered in that region, had aroused in me that spirit of speculation which had received so disastrous a check in Washoe. I was resolved, since gold and silver ignored my friendly advances, to try what sympathetic virtue there might be in coal and iron. Scouts were sent out all over the town of Aurora to secure the best wheeled vehicle the community could afford; preference to be given to a thorough-braced ambulance of Concord manufacture. If that was beyond the resources of enterprise, an ordinary furniture wagon might be made available, or at the worst a butcher's job-cart.

It so happened that a heavy drain had been made upon the livery-stables by the recent exodus of citizens to the Montgomery district. Wagons of all sorts were in great demand for the transportation of goods, wares, and honest miners to the argentiferous paradise; and the long-continued drought, high price of forage, and constant demand for animals had nearly exhausted the whole horse-creation. Skeleton emigrant horses, scrag-tailed mustangs, galled mules and burros, were in requisition at prices that inspired in the owners sentiments of profound affection for their property.

My scout-in-chief, one Timothy Mason, was a man of unlimited genius in his way. Though small in stature he carried a large nose, which enabled him to scent out horses with unerring instinct. He penetrated the wigwams of the Aurorians; dodged into the back-yards and by-ways; smelled every spot where there was a suspicion of hay, grain, or horse-flesh; and in due course of time announced the glad tidings that he had succeeded in securing a conveyance worthy of the President " or any other man."

It was a wagon which had crossed the plains during the summer, and could therefore be recommended as thoroughly dried and not likely to fall to pieces by the action of the sun's rays. The bed was somewhat shattered; the springs broken here and there; a few spokes out of the wheels; the hubs cracked, and the tires gone in at occasional intervals; but it was a remarkably tough wagon nevertheless, capable of being stretched or contracted at pleasure without materially injuring its appearance or powers of locomotion. I rather liked Timothy's description of the wagon. There was something pleasant in the idea of travelling in such a wagon as that.

" You are sure it won't break down, Timothy?" said I, somewhat dubiously.

" Well, 'tain't likely a wagon that's just come all the way from Iowa with a family of women and children in it 'll be taken with a breakin' down between this and Walker."

Thus was every doubt removed. Horses were the chief trouble. Timothy had secured a couple of very fine bloods, rather mortifying in appearance, but of wonderful endurance, since they had lived throughout the entire drought of summer on nothing but sage-brush and alkali and were not yet dead. If I had any pride about the matter of appearance he would borrow a pair of shears and clip their wool a little before we started.

BOUND FOR WALKER RIVER.

" On the contrary, Timothy," said I, " it would be a downright sin to disfigure such noble animals as you have described. I am addicted to the picturesque in nature. I like starved, galled, and woolly-skinned horses. What they lack in flesh and symmetry they will doubtless make up in spirit and variety of outline. So fetch along your nags, Timothy—and don't forget the wagon !"

When, in due time, my remarkable equipage appeared in the main street of Aurora, ready for a start, I was not surprised that the entire population, without distinction of age or sex, crowded out from every door to enjoy the spectacle. Timothy sat perched upon the remains of the front seat with undisguised triumph beaming from every feature. Sooth to say, I enjoyed the sight myself as much as any body. It was a source of infinite satisfaction to me to be able to travel in such distinguished style, after having roughed it on horseback over in the Mono country. Above you have both wagon and horses —nothing extenuate nor aught set down in malice.

In addition to Timothy I had secured the services of one Dr. Fanning as guide, caterer, and purveyor-general to the expedition. An overflowing, generous, genial soul was the Doctor; an experienced mountaineer, who had roughed it all over the gold regions of Idaho; a man of intelligence, and withal as unsophisticated as a child. I liked him from the beginning. Whatever he did he did with all his heart and soul. He purveyed and catered without regard to reason, expense, or the everlasting fitness of things. When the wagon was ready to receive its cargo I found my friend Fanning up to his neck in business at one of the principal grocery stores. He was diving into pickles, wallowing in clams and sardines, luxuriating in jellies, revelling in spiced sauces, and rejoicing in various bottles, jugs, and demi-johns of brandy and whisky of the most famous brands.

When I surveyed his list of purchases I was glad my English friends, whose outfit in Iceland I had attempted to describe a few years ago, were not present. Here was a pretty catalogue of comforts and conveniences for a week's journey! Boxes of cigars, pipes, bags of to-bacco, preserved meats, jellies, desiccated vegetables, brandy, wine, vinegar, and crockery without limit. I was about to ask the Doctor how many years he expect-ed me to be absent, and what he meant by this reflection on my powers of endurance in a rough country, when I perceived, from certain undulations in his motion and an extravagantly benevolent expression in his features, that it would be no use. The fact is, his arduous labors as caterer had proved a little too much for his equilibri-um. He had tasted too many strong mixtures, and his mind was becoming a little bewildered by the multitude of his responsibilities. So that when the wagon was freighted to its utmost capacity, the driver on his seat cracking his whip, and the horses fast asleep, the Doc-tor had taken a new kink, and was off about town in search of an additional brick to put in his hat. "Never mind," quoth Timothy, the whipster, "he will overtake us on the road. He is only taking a parting smile at the snakes. Wake up, Abe! Git along, Ulyssus!"

Up the hill of Aurora we toiled and tugged, till, by the united efforts of Timothy, myself, and the two horses, we reached the summit; from which we enjoyed a parting view of the town while we stopped to regain our breath. A little below to the right, in a pleasant green flat, stands the quartz-mill of the famous pioneer, speculator, miner, and prospector, once chief owner in the Comstock ledge, John D. Winters. The mill was busily at work crushing quartz, and presented a very lively and picturesque scene.

A splendid turnpike has been made within the last two years from Aurora to the valley stretching along the base of the Sierras. Stunted pine grows on the sides of the mountains, which are otherwise exceedingly barren. A mile or two from the summit the road passes some curious lime formations, and several lime-kilns have been established close by. The rugged cliffs on each side of the cañon are diversified by a remarkable variety of colors, indicating mineral deposits of various kinds.

About a mile beyond the end of the cañon we reached the Five-mile House, a pleasant rural station, conveniently situated as a watering-place for man and beast. Here, in a desert flat, the effects of irrigation have been made apparent. It is difficult to conceive that a blade of grass could be made to grow in so barren a spot; yet, by the introduction of a small stream from the neighboring hills, the enterprising proprietor has succeeded in making quite a thrifty little farm. His vegetable garden is really a curiosity. Cabbages, beets, potatoes, and greens of various sorts flourish with a luxuriance that would do credit to California. I had seen before, in the neighborhood of Aurora, and mention it now as one of the anomalies of this strange country, some very remarkable examples of the natural fertility of this sage-desert soil. All it requires is irrigation to make it as productive as the best soil in any country. The climate seems highly favorable to vegetable products; and the time is approaching when Nevada will prove not only a rich mineral country, but be noted for its agricultural resources.

At a point called the Elbow, four miles beyond this station, we reached another oasis in the desert, where we concluded to camp for the night. A good and substantial frame house, with stables, corrals, and various out-buildings, has been erected here for the accommodation of travellers; and the scene, upon our arrival, was lively and characteristic. Freight trains were drawn up in front of the tavern, the teams tied to the wagon-poles, with piles of hay before them which they were devouring with great relish; groups of dust-covered teamsters sitting around the glowing camp-fires; an emigrant family a little to one side, weary and way-worn, but cheered by the prospect of soon reaching the end of their journey; a stage just arrived from Wellington's, with a noisy delegation of politicians from Carson; some half a dozen stray miners on broken-down horses, from unknown parts, and bound to unknown districts; while here and there dust-covered pedestrians, whose stock in trade consisted of a pick, shovel, pan, and blanket, were scattered about on the ground, taking their ease after their dreary walk across the deserts.

While my trusty man Friday was engaged in un-hitching the horses I selected a pleasant little grassy slope near some running water, fringed by willows, as a suitable place for our tent. The next thing was to gather up some dried willow-wood and make a big fire, which presently blazed and crackled with a cheerful glow, illuminating our camp in the most picturesque and satisfactory manner. At this altitude the evenings are always cool, notwithstanding the heat of the day; and a good fire after sunset is one of the chief comforts of life. We pitched our tent without delay, and then went to work and cooked such a supper of oysters, potatoes, coffee, and other luxuries as would have made old Nestor smile. I was sorry for the Doctor. At

every pause in the feast we sighed for his genial presence. It was evident he had lost his way—or his equi-
librium, which amounted to the same thing. He did
not make his appearance during the night, nor had we
the satisfaction of seeing his familiar countenance in the
morning. What could have happened?

Bright and early we struck our tent, hitched up our
team, packed our wagon, and set forth on our journey
across a broad desert valley stretching to the eastward.
It was eight miles of a dreary drag through sand and
gravel to the first pass in a range of mountains which
separates this district from the Walker River Country.
Our poor animals, jaded and starved, had a very hard
time of it. I walked most of the way rather than im-
pose my weight upon them. Timothy laughed at my
scruples of conscience, and assured me the horses were
not near dead yet; that they could travel across the
plains on sage-brush. Going asleep and giving out was
only a way they had.

After a long and heavy pull we ascended the divid-
ing range, and had a fine view of the surrounding country. To the right stands, in towering grandeur, a peak
of the Sierras appropriately named Mount Grant, after
our distinguished General. Passing over the divide
we entered a cañon through which the road winds for
a distance of five miles. The sides are rocky, barren,
and evidently of volcanic formation. Very little timber is to be seen, save here and there a gnarled and
stunted pine. If ever there was a mineral country
rendered attractive by a pervading spirit of desolation
this was one. Every rock and tree, every ledge and fissure, looked the impersonation of strife between heaven
and earth. The rich and varied colors of the mineral
strata that cropped out in seams and ledges gave the
whole country a strangely variegated aspect, and filled
the mind with vague notions of undiscovered treasure
beneath the earth's surface. Yet wild and rugged as it
is, Nature seems to have formed this country with some

regard for the convenience of man. In the midst of withering barrenness that sternly forbids his approach, natural roads open out through the mountains, in many places so well defined and so perfectly graded as to resemble the best turnpikes.

Slowly descending the cañon—for our load was heavy and our wagon not the strongest—we entered upon the dried bed of a stream, which formed our road during the principal part of the way through. The towering walls of rock on each side converge till they form a winding pass, almost like an irregular street of some old city in the interior of Germany. There were breaks here and there, where we had to plunge over precipices that sorely tried the shattered frame-work of our wagon. At one place we had to take out the horses and lower our precious vehicle down a rocky pitch about ten feet deep by means of ropes. It broke away from us when half-way down, and never stopped running till it came in contact with a point of rocks about fifty feet below, where it wound up in a crash of matter that caused us the most profound concern for our absent

A WRECK.

friend, the Doctor. Demijohns were smashed; brandy, whisky, match-boxes, and powder poured together in fearful conglomerate; salt and sugar, paper and ink, boiled shirts and molasses, pickles and preserves—all mixed up in the general amalgamation. I had secured a sketch of Mount Grant under the cushion of the seat. Cushion, seat, and all were pitched overboard. When I dragged forth my sketch from the wreck I was struck with its changed appearance. A bottle of whisky, a can of oysters, some lucifer matches, and the contents of a loose powder-flask had been mixed over it. Timothy was knocked speechless at the immensity of the disaster. He had the most profound respect for my genius as an artist, and evidently regarded the whole expedition as ruined.

"Never mind, Timothy, my boy," said I, assuming a cheerfulness which I did not feel—"never mind. This accident is doubtless Providential. So far from ruining my sketch, I think it increases the spirit. Don't you see the indomitable Grant is now blazing away at Richmond? Look at the clouds of smoke! Here's Richmond—this crushed box of lucifers; and here's Jeff Davis —a smashed oyster!"

I don't know whether he felt the force of the remark, but my trusty whipster brightened up after this, and went to work cheerily to get the horses hitched to the wagon. No material damage was done, after all—only a few small stores sacrificed to the great cause of human progress. By the same skillful system of navigation we at length reached the turning-off point, where we left the cañon, and ascended a hill to the right, from the summit of which we had a grand view of Walker's Valley and the Bullion Range of mountains to the south.

CHAPTER XLIV.

FOUR miles below we reached the first crossing of Walker River. Contrasted with the barren slopes of the surrounding mountains the verdure of the bottom lands was peculiarly refreshing. Even at this dry season—the dryest known for many years—the river contained an abundance of water, pure, fresh, and sparkling, from the snowy heights of the Sierra Nevadas. It was a rarity, in these hot and desert regions, to stand by the water's edge and see the generous flood dash over the rocks and flow in eddying currents over the clear gravelly bottom — so rare to me, indeed, that I quickly divested myself of my dust-covered habiliments and took a plunge in the deepest pool I could find. Talk of your Russian baths — your baths of Constantinople and Damascus! What could equal the luxury of a plunge in this mountain stream after a day's journey through scorching sands and crackling sage-brush and cañons that held the air like a bake-oven! This was luxury beyond description, bought by sweat and toil, such luxury as the indolent lounger in the Orient never dreamed of. And there were houris too; and they came and sat upon the bank, and enjoyed my sportive motions in the water; copper-colored, flat-nosed, thick-lipped houris, of the Pi-Ute race, with red blankets over their bodies and fat babies in their arms. My man Timothy, without regard for the illusions of romance, or the tender influences of beauty, remarked that they were Pi-Ute squaws, on a "hogadie expedition"—"hogadie" signifying muck-a-muck, or food. There was but one way of making my escape from the water to that part of the bank upon which I had left my clothes.

" Give them hogadie, Timothy, and tell them to leave."

He gave them crackers and meat, and motioned to them to be off; but they only laughed and sat down on the bank again. It was sociable, to say the least.

" *They* don't care, Sir," said Timothy, with an encouraging smile; "you needn't be afraid to come out !"

"I know *they* don't care, Timothy; but what would Mrs. Grundy say ? Deuce take it, why don't they go ?"

While Timothy was casting about him for a suitable answer to this question, it occurred to me that I heard strange voices in the distance.

"What's that—who's coming ?" I asked, with some anxiety.

Timothy looked up the road on the opposite side of the river. " Oh, that's only an emigrant family," said he, quietly, " two or three men and some women and children. Guess they're bound for California."

It mattered very little to me where they were bound. They had to cross the river where I was blockaded ; and a painful consciousness took possession of me that there could not be a more unbecoming spectacle for an emigrant family than that of a middle-aged gentleman, with a bald spot on his head, disporting himself in the water before a bevy of Pi-Ute squaws.

" Timothy, my boy," said I, in extreme consternation, " can't you run up the road and engage the enemy while I make an effort to get my clothes on or hide in the bushes ?"

" Oh, Sir," answered my trusty whipster, with a surprised look, as if he had not previously suspected me of any unusual depravity, " if you wish to be left alone here of course I'll go."

Before I could guess his meaning he had driven the horses across the river, and the last I saw of him, as he disappeared on the other side, he was shaking his head in a sorrowful manner—having evidently lost all confidence in human virtue. To rush out, grasp up my scattered clothing, and retreat into a thicket of thorny bushes, was the frantic achievement of a moment. Of course the bevy of Pi-Utes laughed. It was natural enough they should enjoy so novel a scene—a white man hopping, in a nude state, over rocks and thorns, as if for his life, with a bundle of rags under his arm. I never knew a female in my life who didn't laugh at the discomfiture of man in this its most aggravated form.

As soon as possible I emerged from the bushes, somewhat excoriated but not altogether disheartened, and proceeded on foot after my wagon and driver. I found Timothy engaged in a pleasant conversation with some ladies who had just crossed the plains. They were on their way to California. It was refreshing to meet with such enterprising females; and I was nothing loth to join in the conversation. The male members of the party occupied themselves in hunting up some of their laggard stock.

It was getting late, however, and we were forced to push on in order to reach Lawson's Ranch by night.

A few farms had been started on the bottom lands, and we passed some very cozy little farm-houses and thrifty gardens. The river is fringed with willow, sycamore, and a species of cotton-wood, resembling balm of Gilead. We followed its course about seven miles through a series of narrow valleys, on the left side, till we reached a gorge in the mountains through which it passes. At this point there is a good ford, over which we crossed. Lawson's Ranch commences here. A drive of half a mile took us to the house; a frame shanty pleasantly situated near the road. Mr. Lawson was at home, and kindly offered us the accommodations of his place. He has an excellent farm, well cultivated, and a garden abounding in luxuries. Corn, beets, melons, potatoes, and many other kinds of vegetables seem admirably adapted to the soil and climate.

Lawson's Ranch may be considered the beginning of

the main East Walker River Valley.   The bottom gradually widens.   On the right lies a sloping plain, barren
in appearance but abounding in some of the finest lands
east of the Sierras.   A survey of this country has recently been made by Major E. A. Sherman, under the auspices
of a company of Aurorians, with a view of opening it up
for settlement.   It is in contemplation to make a canal
or acequia from Lawson's Ford for the purpose of irrigating the extensive tract of land now lying waste between the foot-hills and the river bottom.   There can be
no doubt that the project is feasible and would repay
the expense.   The descent of the river is sufficient to
give a fall of water at every point.   At least a hundred
thousand acres of the finest valley land could thus be redeemed.   A similar system of irrigation has been successfully practiced by the early Spaniards in Sonora and
Arizona : and there are now in the vicinity of Salt Lake
and other parts of Utah many hundred thousand acres
of sage-desert brought under successful cultivation by
the introduction of water.   People living on the eastern

EMIGRANT FAMILY.

U

slope of the Sierras are beginning to understand that water is all they require to make the most unpromising parts
of the country highly productive.

The general appearance of the Walker River Valley
is barren.   Very little timber is to be seen, except on
the distant spurs of the Sierras.   The everlasting sage-
bush is the staple product of the country.   A farmer
from the Western States, accustomed to luxuriant pastures and endless forests, would turn away in horror from
such a desolate scene ; and his first impulse would be to
set down any man who suggested the idea of cultivating
it as a fit subject for a lunatic asylum.   Still more absurd
would he regard the assertion, often made by the old
settlers in Nevada and firmly believed, that this very
land, apparently so barren, is more productive than the
best land in the Western States.   It is a well-established
fact that no such yield can be obtained in any of the
Atlantic States.   This is partly attributable to the difference of climate, and partly to the natural fertility of
the soil in Nevada.   Owing to the mineral discoveries
in this Territory, and the absorption of capital and labor
in the development of the mines, agriculture has been almost entirely neglected.   Yet nothing has paid so certainly and so well—not even the best mines and mills.

The opening out of so large a tract of arable land to
settlement and cultivation, in a country where agricultural products are in such demand, would be a most profitable and beneficial enterprise.   A ready market for all
the cereals and for vegetables of every kind may be
found in the adjacent mining districts.   At present all
the fruits and most of the grain used in Nevada are imported from California at a heavy expense for transportation.   The few farmers in Carson Valley have made
handsome fortunes.   Barley raised anywhere on the
eastern slope has an advantage of three to five cents a
pound over the imported article ; in other words, the
cost of freight may be added to whatever can be produced in this region.   Hay seldom rates at less than $40

a ton—often at $60 and $100; and this of a very poor and coarse quality. Few, if any, flour-mills have yet been established in the country, owing to the scarcity or high price of wheat. In short, it may be emphatically stated that no part of the world offers greater inducements to farmers; and the quantity of land subject to irrigation is so small, compared with the population and area of territory, that there will always be a remunerative market for agricultural products.

Other considerations claim attention in looking to the future of Nevada. The high price of labor in the mines, arising chiefly from the great expense of living, is a serious drawback to the prosperity of the country. The best mines are exhausted in paying expenses. Capitalists can not understand why it is that, with such enormous gross yields, the net results are so small. Fraud and mismanagement are of course prolific causes; but under the most favorable circumstances the mines can never be profitable where labor is so high. To remedy this the expense of living must be reduced. Agriculture must be encouraged. The heavy percentage now paid to teamsters for hauling provisions across the Sierras must be saved, or so applied as to develop the resources of the country.

Indirectly other advantages must follow the encouragement of agriculture. Schools and colleges will be established; an improved condition of society will take the place of that lawless state of things which always exists in a new country where the male population largely predominates; and employment will be furnished to that surplus of adventurers who now live upon the industry of others.

CHAPTER XLV.

A WARLIKE LADY.

CONTINUING our journey down the valley from Lawson's, after a good night's rest, we encountered during the day several large bands of American horses, which had been recruiting for some time past on the luxuriant pastures of the river-bottom after their dreary journey across the plains. This was the first good grazing country on the route after passing Salt Lake and Ruby Valley. Here the way-worn emigrants and their jaded teams found rest and plenty, and here we found them, from time to time, in the full enjoyment of the abundance that surrounded them. Wagons were drawn up by the river-banks in pleasant groves of willow; the lowing cattle gathered on the green pastures near by; the camp-fires sending up cheerful clouds of smoke, and the merry voices of children making a sweet accord with the lively strains of flute and violin. At one point, where the grass was luxuriant and the willow abundant, we came upon an encampment consisting of some ten or a dozen families. About twenty wagons were drawn up in lines, and several tents were scattered along the banks of the river in cozy little nooks, some of them decorated with flags. It was evidently a Union camp, which I regret to say was not the case in every instance that came under our observation. I was attracted by the merry strains of music and shouts of laughter that greeted our arrival; and soon perceived that the young men and women were enjoying a dance on the green flat in front of the wagons. A group of older members of the party were sitting on the bank, looking on with a pleased yet a thoughtful interest. Their dancing days had passed, and they were drawing toward their journey's end. There were among them some elderly ladies, who seemed to derive a sober sort of comfort from their pipes, which they smoked in the good old-fashioned style of the back-woods. To these, as the responsible members of the party, I addressed myself—hazarding the conjecture that they were just across the plains.

" Yes—been here nigh onto four weeks," said one of the ladies, puffing off a suppressed cloud of smoke from her pipe. " Our men has mostly gone across to Californy to see what's the chances for fodder. Folks tells us it's powerful dry over there."

" I'm sorry to say its rather dry just now, ma'am ; but California is a fine country when it rains."

" Wa'al, I don't know what to think," replied the talk-ative lady. " Some folks told us we'd better stop at Reese, and folks tell us here we'd better stop at Walker, and then again folks say Californy's the best country. I don't know. It ought to be a good country, for it takes a dreadful long time to get to it, and costs a pile of money."

I respectfully inquired if the families had enjoyed good health on the journey across the plains.

" Wa'al, only tolerable. Me and my man has been ailin' considerable. Betsy Jane, she had a spell of ager, Lowysee, she was took with a spindle-fever till her legs warn't no thicker than your thumb ; Zeke, he fell out of the wagon and like to a busted his head ; and the baby, he's troubled with a diary. Some of the families is wuss an' we are ; and some again get along pretty peert con-siderin'. I tell you, stranger, 'tain't no easy trip across these sage-deserts. What with Injuns an' alkali an' dust an' one thing or 'nother, it's a powerful hard road to travel."

I consoled the old lady by telling her what a glorious country California was, and how much better the climate was than that of Missouri. Besides, it was a strong Union State, and gave every body a fair chance to live in peace and plenty.

"Stranger," said the old lady, brightening up, "what's the news about the war?"

"Good news, ma'am—good news. The Union army triumphant everywhere. The rebellion caving in. There won't be a fly-speck for the rebels to hang a hope on in six months."

"Hooray! durn 'em! This camp is all Union. We started pretty well mixed, but split on the way. Secesh took one road—we took t'other. Pop, he's Union to the hub. Folks told us before we came to a little town t'other side of Austin we'd better look out. Every body was secesh there. Our wagon was two days ahead of the rest. We was all alone. Pop he stuck out his flag, an' sez he, ' I'll stake my chances on that!' Just outside of town a fancy-looking fellow rides up an' sez he, ' Cap, take a fool's advice an' haul down your dish-rag. We don't tolerate your breed here. This is a secesh camp.' Pop, he fires up and says, ' Stranger, if your spilin' for a diffikilty you kin hev it. The first man that lays a hand on that flag *I'll drop him sure!*' Chiv he looked black, but Pop had his turkey-buster well in hand; and Chiv changed his base and fell back on the town. Pop cracked his black-snake, and we all rid in with flying colors. The gals jined in a chorus, and all of us, big an' little, peeked out of the wagon and giv 'em, as we rid along the main street, ' Rally round the flag, boys, rally round the flag!' which stirred 'em up considerable."

"Did they molest you?" I asked, with much interest.

"You bet they didn't. They looked mighty hard at Pop as he sot with his rifle in one hand an' his black-snake in t'other; but something in his eye didn't please 'em. 'Let him rip!' said they, and we ripped. We gave them a partin' stare as we left the town, ' Hurrah for Abe Linkeln?' Oh, you bet the country's all safe so far as we're concerned."

I thought it was, and having expressed my satisfaction, gave Timothy the wink to drive on.

CHAPTER XLVI.

WE stopped for the night at a comfortable farm-house belonging to a Mr. Shimmens, an emigrant, who on crossing the plains last year was so much pleased with the Walker River Valley that he determined to locate a claim and try what he could do at farming and stock-raising in this isolated part of the world. Nothing can be more characteristic of American enterprise and the progressive spirit of the age than the daring hardihood with which families from the Western States settle themselves down amid the wilds of Nevada, surrounded by sage-deserts and Indians. Often they go to work ploughing the land and putting in crops before they have so much as a shanty to cover their heads, or even the slightest assurance that the climate is suitable for farming purposes. The risk of the undertaking seems to give it a charm, and they go ahead with an easy confidence that would astonish the people living in older and more settled countries. Is is no uncommon thing to see men in this part of the world turning up the virgin soil and whistling cheerily at their work, while their wives and children are dwelling in all the luxury of unlimited freedom under a bunch of willows or a brush-wood wigwam. A few cows, a sack or two of beans, a small supply of flour and groceries, and such other remnants of their original outfit as may be left, constitute the bulk of their worldly possessions; yet they are hopeful and happy. It is seldom they fail to make a good living. I have met families just from the Western States with no better outfit, who in the course of a year or two were as

comfortably situated as any reasonable people could desire; having good houses, thrifty farms, plenty of stock,
and all the accessories of civilized homes.   It was thus
we found Mr. Shimmens.   His dwelling is pleasantly situated at the base of Lookout Mountain, with a broad alluvial valley in front, beautifully watered by the river and
its numerous "sloos" and branches; and although this
was only his second year, he has now a fine farm, well
fenced, and a garden abounding in vegetables of the best
quality.   His pastures yield excellent hay, and afford an
unlimited range for his cattle.   It was altogether a pleasant scene—this homestead in the wilderness; and I shall
not readily forget the kindness and cordiality with which I
was greeted by this worthy family.   For here again, to
my surprise and gratification, I found that *Harper's
Magazine* had preceded me, and paved the way to a very
pleasant acquaintance.   At the hospitable board of Mr.
Shimmens I enjoyed many a luxurious meal; and the
evenings were rendered delightful by the reminiscences
of our host, whose adventurous career across the plains
would furnish material for a romance.   Nor were we

GRANITE BLUFF.

without the refinements of music and song. A melodeon, slightly cracked and somewhat wheezy after its long journey, was one of the institutions of the house. The daughter of our host, a young lady of sweet sixteen, favored us with several popular airs, such as " Lucy Long," " Old Dan Tucker," the " Arkansas Traveller," etc., and a number of patriotic songs of more recent origin.

One of the notable features of the country is the Gold Hill Range, situated about two miles from Shimmens's Ranch. Some very promising auriferous veins were discovered here in 1862, and there was, as usual, a great rush to the Walker River country. Claims were staked off for a circuit of ten miles, and companies were organized without regard to reason, facts, or possibilities. Several hundred veins were opened ; most of them yielding a fair show of gold and silver. Assays were made rating at $50 to $100 to the ton. A worthy Professor of my acquaintance living in Oakland was attracted thither by the noise of the discovery. It was his ambition to make a fortune, and devote the remainder of his days to the study of Plato and Aristotle. He knew nothing about quartz-mines or quartz-mills ; but he was a classical scholar and a gentleman of varied scientific attainments. Of what avail was all this knowledge if he could not build a quartz-mill ? He was poor, but he had friends and credit. Like a brave man he went to work, and by dint of algebraic equations, trigonometry, geometry, and an occasional reference to Plato and Aristotle, he built a quartz-mill. On the banks of Walker River the wreck of that mill stands to this day. I saw it myself, and made a sketch of it from the Granite Bluff.

I refer to that mill as a solemn warning to Professors. There was no trouble about getting the ores. Wagonloads came pouring down from the Gold Hill Range. The Professor was in ecstasies. His mill-wheels flew around with a tremendous clatter ; his battery battered up the quartz at an amazing rate ; his amalgamating pans made the finest of suds ; all went ahead smashingly—only the

U 2

machinery was new and required grease. The Professor greased it—greased the water-wheel, the battery, the amalgamating pans, every thing that was worried by friction. Then the machinery worked to a charm ; then the Professor gazed admiringly through his spectacles at the result of his skill, and was pleased to think that he would soon be able to retire into the quiet shades of his Academical groves. Well, the Professor is a kind friend and a good neighbor. I must deal gently with him. When the great day came to determine the result of all this working—to test the wonderful advantages of education and intellect over vulgar prejudice in matters of this kind—the wheels were stopped, the pans were cleaned up, and the result was—I would be sorry to hazard a conjecture where it was. People said it was in the tailings. Back of the mill was a sluice which was found to be rich in gold. At all events the gold was nowhere else. Some hinted that grease and quartz have no amalgamating affinities, that the grease carried the precious metals with it ; but this I consider a thoughtless fling at the Professor. The trouble was in the machinery. A few thousand dollars would remedy it. But thousands of dollars were getting scarce.

Then came the disastrous flood of '62. It swept down the valley from the gulches and cañons of the Sierra Nevadas, carrying with it hay-stacks, cabins, and even farms. I knew a man whose entire farm was swept clean off— soil, house, barns, hay-stacks, fences and all. There was nothing left of it but a desert sand-bottom. The honest miners were nearly starved out. The roads to Aurora and Carson were cut off by impassable torrents and lagoons. There was no such thing as travel, except on the rugged ridges of the mountains. The Professor was forced to abandon his mill and seek refuge in a hole which he and his friends burrowed in a neighboring hill. Here a happy coterie of hardy adventurers lay blockaded nearly all the winter. Sometimes the Professor read his beloved Plato, or philosophized to his fellows like Diog-

IRON MOUNTAIN.

enes in his tub; sometimes he looked out upon the
dreary expanse of water, and saw with sorrow his mill
and his hopes of the Academical groves vanish day by
day.   Spring came at last; the country dried up; the
Professor cast a long lingering look at the wreck of his
mill, girded up his loins, and with a heavy sigh wended
his way homeward, serious but not subdued.   He is still
an enthusiastic believer in that mill and the Walker River country.   All he wants now to make it a grand success is capital.   And, indeed, to do strict justice to his
discernment, nobody questions the richness of the lodes
in the Gold Hill Range, though many doubt whether they
can be successfully worked by mills built on the Profess-
or's plan.

In the mean time attention was attracted elsewhere by
new discoveries, and before any thing could be done in
this district it was abandoned.   It fell by default rather
than from any want of confidence in its resources.

Upon a somewhat cursory view of the lodes in the
Gold Hill Range, which I visited with Mr. Shimmens and
some of his neighbors, I am inclined to believe there is
good ore in them.   Some of the specimens I saw taken
out present very fair indications.   The lodes are not
wide, but they are numerous, and easy of access either
from the surface or by means of tunnels.   Curious chim-
ney-like formations of quartz crop out all over the Gold
Hill Range.   Flag-staffs had been erected in the most
prominent of these by Major Sherman, who had recently
made a survey of the district.

I had erected my tent on a pleasant little flat by the
river-side, within a few hundred yards of Shimmens's
house.   Here, with my man Timothy, I kept a sort of
bachelor's hall, entertaining all visitors in the most hospitable style.   On the second morning after our arrival
I was rejoiced to see the familiar face of my friend Fanning peering through the willow-bushes.   He had walked all the way from Aurora.   It was a source of genuine
happiness to me to find him well and sprightly after his

heavy siege in Aurora. Not a word was said on the subject. The Doctor shook hands as kindly and cordially as if we had never deserted him. He had lost all the bricks out of his hat, and was now clear of head and steady of hand.

Among the wonders still to be seen was the Iron Mountain—a discovery recently made by the Doctor, upon which, in common with myself and others, he founded his most sanguine hopes of future wealth. I was to have a share in it. I was to be the owner of feet—none of your flimsy gold and silver feet, but rough, hard, honest feet of iron. Henceforth I would spurn the grovelling world with the iron heel of despotism ; I would rule my fellow-beings with an iron rod ; I would enjoy the best books of travel and romance till seduced to repose by the iron tongue of midnight.

On a bright, glowing morning—a morning such as the unhappy dwellers in the Atlantic States rarely see ; when the sun rises from his couch of gold, and fills the universe around him with a flood of glowing light; on such a morning I arose from my blankets by the willow-shaded banks of the Walker, and listened to the music of cooing doves and rippling waters, till my soul was touched with inspiration. I called aloud to my trusty followers—"Ho, merry men of Walker ! Up, my brave fellows, and shake off the feathers of sleep ! Arouse thee, Timothy, my boy, and strike the culinary fires ! Get thee up, Fanning, my beauty, and let us prepare for triumph ! Rejoice, and ho ! for this very day we visit the Iron Mountain—that wonderful work of Nature, wherein lies your wealth and mine, and that of our children's grandchildren !"

" You bet !" said the Doctor, slowly unwinding himself from his blankets, and gazing at me with an affectionate smile. " Bet your life on that lay-out !" And I " betted " internally—not my life, but an old horse down in Oakland, which I was anxious to dispose of at ·some approximation to cost.

Happy is he who can breakfast with relish by the rays

of the rising sun; whose only bitters are sound sleep and fresh air; whose sense of the beautiful in nature has not been blunted by the vexations of business or the frivolities of life in crowded communities! By the banks of the Walker, to the sweet harmony of running waters and singing birds, we enjoyed our morning repast. When all was ready the Doctor and I set forth in fine spirits on our expedition to the Iron Mountain.

I was sorry to be obliged to leave Timothy in camp. Some Pi-Ute Indians had been prowling about since our arrival, and, although harmless and inoffensive otherwise, it was evident they were not scrupulous about the means of satisfying their appetites. We gave them food and tobacco, which of course attached them to us by the strongest ties of friendship. It would not do to leave them alone in camp, and thus Timothy had to stand as a rear-guard over our precious "hogadie."

Fanning knew the country well. He had spent two years in exploring it, and was familiar with every rock and gulch. To his guidance I committed myself, confident that he would never lose his way so long as we had nothing but water as a beverage.

Crossing the river a little below our encampment, we made a bee line for the Iron Mountain, which is clearly visible from Shimmens's Ranch; standing out like a huge cone, isolated from the adjacent mountains, and easily recognized by its reddish color.

The first part of our journey lay across Walker's Valley. At this point the arable lands embrace a width of about two miles, gently sloping from the river to the foot-hills. To all appearance the earth is utterly barren. No sign of vegetation, save the everlasting sage-bush, greets the eye; yet upon a close inspection the soil is found to be composed of a rich alluvial deposit, which only requires irrigation to make it highly productive. Dry as the season now is, the sage-bushes are green, indicating the proximity of water. This is the valley claimed and surveyed by the Walker River Company.

We soon reached the first of a series of foot-hills, or rather a rolling plain, which extends all the way to the Bullion range of mountains, distant about ten miles from the river. Following a deep winding arroya for several miles, we ascended upon a ridge where we struck an Indian trail. The whole surrounding country was fearfully wild and barren—nothing but gravelly deserts and rugged mountains ahead, and deep gorges in the desolate plain around us. I noticed along the trail projecting carboniferous strata indicating coal, and unmistakable evidences of the proximity of iron. The earth in many places was covered with rust. Boulders of ferrugiferous stone cropped out at intervals; and at one point of our journey we travelled nearly a mile over broken beds of iron, resembling pot-metal. It was light and porous, but strongly metallic, and jingled under our horses' hoofs like the waste fragments of cast-iron lying about a foundry yard.

Seven miles from the river we reached the foot of the Iron Mountain—a rough, barren, conical peak, rising about five hundred feet above the level of the surrounding hills. Deep gorges and ravines render the approach somewhat difficult; but Fanning knew the way, and we encountered no serious obstacle. Rusty boulders and broken masses of iron grew more and more abundant, till we merged into a complete labyrinth of iron ledges. Evidences of floods and drifts and volcanic fires lay around us in chaotic desolation. A few hundred yards back of the main cone we came upon a black ledge, cropping out of the earth to the height of several feet, in sharp points, presenting a smooth, polished surface that glistened in the sun like glass.

Now I beg the reader to understand that I am prejudiced in favor of this magnificent enterprise. I am a thousand feet, more or less, in this mine, but will endeavor to tell as much truth as can be expected under the circumstances. When I saw the pure iron thus crop out of the earth and stare me in the face, I returned thanks to Providence that the Apaches had spared my life in Arizona; that I had survived all the disasters of travel in that region to see this blessed day. For here surely was a substantial reward for all my sufferings; here was iron enough to make any reasonable man jingle along merrily through the remainder of life's journey.

I dismounted; fastened my horse to a solid boulder; took a pick, and went to work vigorously to dislodge a mass of the ore. Aided by the energy and muscle of my friend Fanning, it was not long before I had a specimen that would astonish the iron-men of Pennsylvania. There was no room for doubt. It was the purest kind of magnetic iron. I crushed a portion of it with my hammer, and found that it adhered to the face of the hammer in flakes like feathers. A shingle nail which I had in my pocket furnished the next test. The mass of ore bore the weight of the nail without difficulty. I believe this is considered a very valuable quality of iron, but requires to be mixed with inferior ores before it can be made available for use.

The vein is about four feet thick where it crops out. From its dip on each side I should judge it must rapidly increase as it descends. I traced it over the surface of the earth for a mile or more, and do not know how much further it may run. At the top of the mountain it assumes a broken form, appearing over an area of several hundred feet. The probability is the chief deposit lies in the depths of the main cone. As yet no excavations have been made.

We gathered up as many specimens as we could pack on our horses, and, having concluded our inspection, ascended the peak of the Iron Mountain for the purpose of enjoying the view, than which nothing can be finer. Mount Butler lies to the east; Mount Grant to the west. To the south stretches a rugged range of sierras, dotted with pine-trees; and to the north the rich alluvial bottom of Walker River. A fine spring of water is seen about two miles distant, in the Gold Cañon range; rich outcroppings of gold and silver quartz ledges mark the face of the hills; but this part of the country has been but little explored. The day must come when it will be thickly settled by an industrious community of miners.

Should the iron and coal veins of Walker River prove valuable, no estimate can be formed of their importance to the industrial interests of Nevada. The cost of freight across the mountains is now a serious drawback. Machinery must be transported at enormous expense. The price of labor is high, owing to the cost of provisions, and it is clear to my mind that mining will never be profitable in Nevada until it can be carried on with greater economy. At present " it costs a mine to work a mine." The products of the best mines are consumed in expenses.

Having seen the principal objects of interest in this part of the country, I returned to Oakland, a wiser if not a richer man.

DEMONSTRATING THE VALUE OF LEDGES.

THE REESE RIVER COUNTRY.

CHAPTER XLVII.

JOURNEY TO AUSTIN.

I WILL not subject the reader to the perils of another trip across the mountains. The road is familiar to him by this time. He has seen it in winter, spring, and summer—by day-light and by moonlight—on foot and from the front seat of a pioneer stage.

On a pleasant morning in the month of May, 1865, I took my seat in the stage for Austin. My fellow-passengers were a couple of Israelites in the ready-made clothing line; three honest miners, deep in ledges; and a motherly female, with five small children, including one at the breast. We were not to say crammed, but there were enough of us for comfort, considering the heat of the weather and the length of the journey. I do not wish to convey the idea that there is the slightest inconvenience in sitting bolt upright on a narrow seat between two heavy men, one of whom persists in telling you all about a patent amalgamator; and the other in smoking bad cigars, going to sleep at brief intervals, punching you with his elbows, and butting you with his head; or any thing to complain of in the boots of your opposite neighbor, which have a propensity for resting on your toes, ranging over your shins, getting up on your seat, and airing themselves on the adjacent window-sill; or cause of mental disquietude in the suspicion of being greased all over the back of your only coat by a numerous family of

children, whose hopeless attempts to appease their appetites by means of sausage, bread and butter, and mince-
pies, are constantly impressed upon you; or any thing
short of agreeable sensations in breathing clouds of al-
kali-dust, and fighting whole armies of gnats. With
special reference to stage-passengers who travel along
the banks of the Carson in the early part of summer
the afflictions are of too serious and complicated a nature to fall within the range of ordinary comprehension,
unaided by an enlarged practical experience.

A trip to Austin is something to look back upon with
pleasure in after-life. It is always a source of happiness
to think that it is over; that there. are no more gnats
and alkali-clouds to swallow; no more rickety and for-
lorn stations to stop at; no more greasy beans and bacon to pay a dollar for; no more jolting, and punching,
and butting of heads to be endured on that route at
least. And yet it has its attractive aspect; the rich
flood of sunshine that covers the plains; the glorious atmospheric tints that rest upon the mountains, morning
and evening; the broad expanse of sage-desert, so mournfully grand in its desolation. The whole journey of a
hundred and seventy miles from Virginia City may be
summed up thus: Forty miles along the Carson, picturesque and pleasant, though rather dusty and somewhat
obscured by gnats; station-houses built of boards, posts,
and adobes where the horses are changed; occasionally
bars and bad whisky; bacon and beans, with a strange
dilution of coffee three times a day; excellent drivers and
the best of pioneer stages; sage-deserts and alkali-deserts,
varied by low barren mountains; teams with heavy wagons, heavily laden with machinery and provisions for
Reese River, slowly tugging through the dust; emigrant
wagons filled with women and children, wending their
way tediously toward the land of gold, and empty freight
wagons, coming back from Reese, such are the principal
features of the journey.

Of the country I shall only add that it is the most bar-

CITY OF AUSTIN.

ren, desolate, scorched-up, waterless, alkali-smitten patch
of the North American continent I have ever yet seen—
a series of horrible deserts, each worse than the other.
Parallel ranges of naked mountains running nearly north
and south, with spurs or foot-hills running east and west,
form a continuation of valleys through which the road
winds. These valleys sink in the middle, where there is
generally a dry white lake of alkali in which even the
sage refuses to grow. Very little wood is to be seen
anywhere on the route—none in the valleys, and only a
few dwarfish nut-pines on the sides of the mountains. I
know of no reason at all why any human being should
live in such a country; and yet some people do, and
they seem to like it. Not that they are making money
either, for very few are doing that, but they get a sort
of fondness for alkali in thei. food and water, and seem
to relish flies, gnats, bacon, and grease as standard articles of diet.

After two days and a night of concentrated enjoyment in this kind of travel, our last driver cracks his whip, and our stage makes a dive into a little rut and out again. There is a faint show of water on the wheels, "What's that?" cries every body in astonishment!

"Gents!" says the driver, "I didn't like to alarm you; but that's REESE RIVER, and there's Jacobsville!"

No wonder we were startled, for Reese River is a source of astonishment to every traveller who passes over the road to Austin for the first time. It derives its name from an emigrant, who must have had a humorous turn of mind when he called it a river. That it is not so long as the Missouri or so majestic as the Mississippi is very generally understood; but when the expectant traveller comes to a sort of ditch in the desert about six feet wide, with the slightest glimmering of a streak of water at the bottom, he is naturally astounded at the frolicsome audacity of Reese. A jolly old Reese he must have been, to embark his name on the smallest river in the world, which sinks in the desert a few miles below the crossing, and thus undertake to float down the stream of life into an enduring fame! May you never be forgotten, Reese, while Reese River flows through the sage-deserts of Nevada! May you never be thirsty, even in the thirstiest region of futurity, when you think of that noble stream which bears your name forever onward over the upper crust of earth!

Seven miles more in the pleasant glow of a sunshiny afternoon takes us rattling up the slope of a cañon, near the mouth of which stands the famous city of Clifton, or rather its ghost; for Clifton was the father of Austin, and died a sudden death about two years ago. All that remains of it now is a broad street flanked by the wrecks of many frame shanties, whose lights are fled and whose garlands must be dead, for they are nowhere seen, unless the everlasting bunches of sage that variegate the scene should be regarded in that metaphorical point of view.

It is said of the citizens of Clifton that they were

blind to their own interests when they started the city. With florid imaginations in reference to the future, they established florid prices for town-lots, and thus drove honest miners higher up the cañon. The nucleus of a new town called Austin was formed; but the way to get to it was hard—like the way of the transgressor—and the Cliftonites chuckled much, believing they had the thing in their own hands; when lo! the Austinites suddenly went to work and built a magnificent grade, and down went Clifton, as if stricken by the fist of a mighty pugilist, with a cloud of mourning around its eye!

But we anticipate history. It behooves us first to explain why Clifton and Austin ever came to be built at all, there being nothing in the general aspect of the country to encourage settlement from any indication it presents of social, agricultural or commercial advantages over other parts of the world.

The present site of Jacobsville, seven miles from the mouth of the cañon, was an overland station prior to the discovery of the silver mines. Its principal feature was then, and still is, a fine spring of water, which is a notable attraction in that dry country. The town of Jacobsville was started on speculation after the Reese River excitement commenced; it being the only place within a hundred miles where whisky could be had in any considerable quantity. Like Clifton, however, it received a black eye when Austin was started; and now stands a melancholy monument of human hopes frustrated.

THE KEYSTONE MILL.

CHAPTER XLVIII.

DISCOVERY OF THE SILVER LEDGES.

IN May, 1862, William Talcott, an employé in the Pony Express service, went to look for his ponies in the nearest ranges of mountains, which, as fortune ordained, was the Toyabe range. He took with him an Apache boy, purchased by James Jacobs in Arizona for a jack-knife and pair of blankets. Talcott and the Apache thus became the pioneers of civilization. They struck for the nearest cañon—and they struck up this cañon in search of the ponies—and while they were looking about them they struck a streak of greenish quartz, which Talcott thought resembled some quartz he had seen in Gold Hill. It was of a bluish green color, with a strong suspicion of mineral in it, but what kind of mineral nobody knew up to that date—not even the Apache who was born in a mineral country, and whose range of observation had been confined almost exclusively to mineral deserts from the time he was born up to the date of his purchase by Jacobs for a jack-knife and pair of blankets.

It is a remarkable fact that Frémont might have distinguished himself by this discovery, many years before, had he not passed a little too far to the south. His route lay through Death Valley and the southern rim of Smoky Valley, crossing by Silver Peak to Walker's Lake, and thence up the Walker River Valley. He left some of his men at Owen's Lake and crossed the Sierras into California. The great Pathfinder, unfortunately for himself, took the wrong path and missed the Reese River Mines by about 170 miles. Of course no blame

V

can be attached to him for that, though there are people in Central Nevada who, having availed themselves of other people's discoveries, rather incline to the opinion that Frémont ought to have gone the Reese River route and opened up the mines. If mining speculations be a test of merit, is it not enough to have opened up and sold out the great Mariposa estate? And yet there may be people in New York who could wish that the famous Pathfinder had missed the Mariposa trail by 170 miles north or south, east or west—so it seems quite impossible to select a path that will suit every body.

On the 10th of July, 1862, the first miners' meeting in the Reese River country was held, and the district of that name was established. William Talcott, James Jacobs, Wash. Jacobs, and a Mr. O'Neill located a claim on a ledge, which was called, in honor of the pony express, the "Pony Ledge." It is a mooted question whether Talcott or the Apache boy can justly claim so much as the ponies they were in search of, which were thus summarily disposed of with a name and the four feet they happened to carry about them. This company located three other claims in the lower foot-hills, but none of them turned out very well. The ores first discovered were chiefly antimonial. Mr. O'Neill had a ranch on Truckee River, where he lived when he undertook to live in any particular locality. On his return from Reese River he took home with him some of the ores from the newly-discovered mines.

Mr. Vanderbosch, an intelligent Hollander, who had some knowledge of minerals, happened to see these specimens at the house of O'Neill, and immediately pronounced a favorable opinion as to the " indications of silver " contained in them. They consisted, in great part, of the metals usually found in connection with silver—copper, iron, antimony, and galena. The traces of silver were but slight; still sufficient, with the indications mentioned, to encourage the idea that there were deposits of rich silver ore in the vicinity. Specimens were subse-

quently taken to Virginia City and tested by assay, with
such results as to attract immediate attention.

In October, 1862, David E. Buel, an enterprising miner and frontiersman, who had spent much of his life
among the Indians of California, started for the Reese
River country with two friends, William Harrington
and Fred Baker. Buel was a man of indomitable spirit,

CAÑON CITY—BUEL'S MILL.

great energy of character, and superior intelligence. He had served in various official capacities in California—for several years as Indian Agent in charge of the Klamath Reservation, where I first met him. And here let me say, as Ex-Special Agent of the Government, that I found Buel a remarkable man in more respects than one. He was an honest Indian Agent—the rarest work of God that I know of.

This party prospected about two miles south of the present city of Austin, in the foot-hills. Nothing that could be properly denominated a ledge had been found at that time above the Pony Ledge. The only work done was the running of a tunnel, called the Highland Mary, which failed to strike any thing except a good place for burying money. San Francisco parties, I believe, were engaged in this.

Buel and his friends made several locations, some of which turned out well. They had a hard time of it, without shelter and with but little food. The town of Austin was named by Buel, who, if not its only father, was at least its biggest and ablest father.

As an independent historian I am greatly at a loss on this point. During my stay of nearly three months in the Reese River country I think I saw the first man who started Austin (according to his own account) in fifty different aspects. Sometimes he was tall and sometimes short; sometimes thick and sometimes thin; occasionally old and occasionally young; sober by turns and drunk by turns; always with a different name, and never concerned about his own fame, but merely desirous of setting me right and preventing interested parties from imposing on me. As a stranger, of course I could not be expected to know who built the first house—there it was, built by my informant; which accounts for the fact that fifty different houses were pointed out to me as the nucleus around which the famous city of Austin sprang up.

Mr. Vanderbosch, having satisfied himself as to the

value of the ores, started over from Virginia, and arrived in December, 1862, with a small party. Up to that date little had been done except in the way of prospecting. Wherever blue rock was found locations were made; but their value had not yet been determined.

OREGON LEDGE.

The first locations of importance were made by Vanderbosch and his party. On the 19th of December the Oregon Ledge was discovered and located, near the upper end of the cañon, where now stands that part of the town called Upper Austin. Ten days later the "North Star" and "Southern Light" were located. These were the first true discoveries of rich silver ores in the Reese River district. All that had previously taken place was uncertain and conjectural. Six miles south, in the so-called but now abandoned district of Simpson's Park, Andrew Veatch, an enterprising explorer, who had been all through the Humboldt country, had discovered and located a claim called the "Comet," which attracted some attention. Veatch and his party went vigorously to work to develop their ledge. It went up like a rocket, and then came down like its stick.

THE PRINCIPAL MINES

Vanderbosch obtained his first specimens of ore from the Oregon Ledge. They were found in a quartz vein three feet wide, with granite casings, showing silver chlorides, fahlertz, antimonial, and ruby silver. These specimens were sent to Virginia City to be assayed. The yield was so extraordinary—several thousand dollars to the ton—as to cause the most intense excitement.

Nothing so rich had yet been discovered in our mineral possessions. Numerous as the frauds and disappointments had been in mining speculations, there could be no doubt as to the wonderful richness of these ores. There were the ores and there were the assays to speak for themselves. What if the veins were narrow? Nobody wanted a very wide vein, when a narrow one yielded six

THE PARROTT MILL.

or seven thousand dollars to the ton. The Comstock was prodigiously big and wide, but it looked poor in comparison with this. These assays were made in the latter part of December. Immediately the news spread— it flew on the wings of the wind, north, south, east, and west.

Then came the great rush of January, 1863—the Washoe excitement over again! I flattered myself I had helped to put an extinguisher on these crazy mining speculations; but when will people learn any thing from experience? Kern River, Gold Bluff, Frazer River, Washoe—these were not enough! Time misspent and money misapplied only whetted the public appetite for the precious metals. Failure never yet disheartened the American nature, or quelched its individual members. General Grant was no more defeated by numerous repulses at the siege of Vicksburg than these hardy adventurers were by suffering, loss of means, loss of time, and constant failure to realize their expectations. Ever cheery, ever hopeful, they were up and at it again after every knock-down — knowing no such thing as defeat.

I am sorry for this trait in my fellow-countrymen. It is so annoying to our neighbors across the water. Englishmen can't understand it, and won't believe it; and yet we do these things in our own self-confident style, as if the British Lion were of no consequence whatever. Even the London *Times* never stopped us from winning a battle or opening up a new country, or emptying our pockets in any new speculation that offered the slightest symptom of a " pay-streak."

Ho, then, for Reese River! Have you a gold mine? Sell it out and go to Reese! Have you a copper mine? Throw it away and go to Reese! Do you own dry goods? Pack them up for Reese! Are you the proprietor of lots in the City of Oakland? Give them to your worst enemy and go to Reese! Are you a merchant, broker, doctor, lawyer, or mule-driver? Buckle up your

THE GREAT MAGNIFF LEDGE.

blankets and off with you to Reese, for there is the land of glittering bullion! — there lies the pay-streak! So, at least, every body thought in the winter of 1862–3. The weather was cold; the mountains were covered with snow; neither food nor shelter was to be had at Reese; but what of that? Did lack of food or lack of houses ever stop a Californian from going anywhere he pleased? Sage-brush was plenty, at all events, and bunch-grass; and if horses and mules and cows could live on sage and grass, men could live on meat. The only house in the cañon was a small stone cabin, situated near the Pony Ledge. Vanderbosch and party, Buel and party, and other leading pioneers, camped all the winter in open tents; and I am told they had a jovial time of it. Every body was wonderfully rich—in feet. Tents and wigwams of all kinds soon began to sprinkle the hill-sides. Then came great freight-wagons with lumber, and whisky, and food and raiment, which brought fabulous prices; and up went Clifton and Austin like magic. About five thousand people gathered in and around Austin during the spring and summer of 1863. They came from California, from Washoe, from Idaho, from Salt Lake, from every quarter of the compass—some with money, most without, but all with the brightest hopes of sudden wealth. Speculation soon reached a pitch of extravagance to which all previous mining excitements were tame. Lander Hill, Central Hill, and Mount Prometheus soon became riddled with claims, looking like naked giants, lying on their backs, sprinkled with small-pox. Every man who had a pick or a shovel dug a hole two or three feet in the ground, and called it the " Grand Magniff," or the " Great Stupendous Ledge;" and thereupon he took to speculation. It was all feet— but little or no mining. Every body wanted to realize the grand result without delay.

This was the memorable period to which I alluded in a former chapter, when lodgings in a sheep-corral had to be paid for at the rate of fifty cents per night in ad-

SHEEP-CORRAL LODGINGS.

vance; when no man could safely undertake to sleep under the lee of a quartz-boulder, in consequence of that claim being guarded by a prior occupant armed with a six-shooter; when it was a luxury to sit all night by a stove, or stand against a post behind a six-feet tent. I have heard of men who contrived to get through the coldest part of the season by sleeping when the sun was warm, and running up and down Lander Hill all night; and another man who staved off the pangs of hunger by lying on his back for an hour or so at meal-times with a quartz-boulder on his stomach. Of the wild speculations in mineral ledges it is needless for me to speak in detail. The subject is a sore one for some of my friends in San Francisco. A notable instance was re-

POST LODGINGS.

lated to me as characteristic of the spirit of the times. An adventurer, with nothing to sustain him but his own sanguine anticipations of the future, was one day engaged in digging a post-hole, when he struck something blue. It was a ledge—rich in mineral. He at once perceived that the ore was the best kind of chloride silver; and he staked off his ledge, putting down himself and numerous friends as locators. But speculation was too keen and too grasping for him to profit by the working of his mine. An immediate offer of $60,000 was made

MIDAS MINE.

him for his discovery, and he was fool enough to sell out, pocket his money, and retire from the mining business. At least every body thought he was a simpleton, till an assay of the ore was made. It was not chloride of silver, it was only chloride of lead—which may be valuable some day, when lead rises to a dollar a pound. The "Post-hole Ledge" attracted much attention at the time. I am told the purchaser does not place much confidence in the honesty of the discoverer, whom he at first regarded as a singularly verdant man to sell out at such a price, but now considers a cunning rogue.

Foreseeing that mills would be necessary to work the ores, Messrs. Buel and Dorsey took time by the forelock, and in June and July, 1863, erected a five-stamp mill in the cañon, which is now known as the California Mill. During the same summer the Rhode Island, Union, Pioneer, and Clifton mills were built. The Oregon Mill was commenced in May, but not finished and in running order till January, 1864. This and the Pioneer

OREGON MILL, UPPER AUSTIN.

were ten-stamp mills. All the rest had but five stamps each.

The work of building mills in this new country was attended with enormous labor and expense. Suitable timber for joists and beams was exceedingly scarce. Labor of every kind was high. Lumber was from $250 to $500 a thousand. The cost of transportation from California was a heavy item—freight being eighteen cents a pound from Sacramento. To get the necessary machinery across the mountains was a most laborious and expensive undertaking. There was scarcely any thing in the country but the stones upon which to build the foundations. The mines had produced comparatively nothing as yet, and the greatest difficulty was to procure the capital for the prosecution of these enterprises. Besides, little was known of the quality of the ores or the proper manner of treating them. It was a mere experiment—but a very bold one. By the rude process of crushing and amalgamation the wastage was great, and the result by no means encouraging.

Mr. Vanderbosch, finding from the working of the first ores that it would be a losing business, and that a different plan must be adopted, erected a roasting furnace in March, 1864, which was a perfect success. It was the great event in the history of Reese River. Many had begun to despair of getting any thing out of the ores; but the roasting process proved at once that they could be successfully and profitably worked. The experiment was made under the most discouraging circumstances. The weather was so cold that the bricks of the furnaces had to be covered with blankets to keep any heat in them; and the machinery was of the most primitive kind. Still it was a success. The yield was remarkable considering all things—ranging from $150 to $1750 to the ton. The first class chlorides averaged from $300 to $500; second class from $150 to $300; and the third class would have yielded from $100 to $150; but it was not considered profitable to work them

ABORIGINAL CITIZENS.

so long as there was an abundance of superior ores. The cost of working was about $80. It is now, as announced, somewhat less.

During the latter part of 1863 the natural result of the wild speculations which had been going on during the year became apparent. Little or no work had been done on the ledges. Miners had expended all their means, and nothing was coming in to keep them in food and raiment. Outsiders began to feel their pockets and wonder if there was any thing in this Reese River country. The success of the Vanderbosch mill, and the development of the Oregon ledges during the ensuing spring, had an encouraging effect. Things began to brighten up; and San Francisco capital began to flow in. About $2,000,000 were invested in mines, mills, etc., during the year 1864.

Before the close of 1864 a panic took place in the Reese River stocks. Some of the leading mines, which had been opened to the depth of sixty or seventy feet, had reached poor or barren rock, and a general impression prevailed that the ledges were not permanent. A fearful state of depression followed. Money was scarce, and it was impossible to go on working without capital. The supplies from San Francisco stopped. Those who owned stocks became tired of paying assessments; and now that there seemed no hope of returns in the future, many allowed themselves to be sold out.

The miners themselves remained confident—never for a moment losing faith in the mines. Such of them as were able continued to work on the ledges, hoping in time to get through the barren streak.

THE MIDAS MILL.

CHAPTER XLIX.

THE IMMORTAL GRIDLEY.

IT is a leading peculiarity of the American people that they carry with them into every new territory their municipal and political institutions. A "city" of two houses and half a dozen inhabitants must have its Mayor and Common Council, its primary meetings, and election excitements. An American could no more live without making speeches or hearing them, holding office or voting somebody else into office, participating in a torch-light procession or flourishing his hat over it, than he could without his newspaper or his daily "tod."

Austin was not exempt from this notable feature in American life. The city charter was passed with due solemnity in April, 1864. Public rejoicings followed as

MR. RANKIN'S HOUSE, AUSTIN.

a matter of course. There was immense excitement at this time touching the political issues of the day. Republicans and Copperheads were pretty evenly divided; and the state of feeling between them was exceedingly lively, if not hostile. A great deal of betting took place on the test questions, the chief of which was the election of Mayor. Every man felt not only a local and personal but a national interest in the result. The two candidates were well matched. On the Democratic side was my friend David E. Buel—" Uncle Dave," as his fellow-citizens familiarly called him—a man of imposing presence, six feet four, and large in proportion, without a fault save that of being always on the wrong side, and with a frank, generous, off-hand way about him that was wonderfully attractive to the honest miners. Buel was a miner himself, and enjoyed a high reputation for energy and honesty. A more popular candidate could not have been chosen to give strength and respectability to a bad cause. It was expected that he would carry a large portion of the Republicans, and doubtless he would have done so at any other time. The other candidate was Charles Holbrook, a young man of excellent character and fine business capacity. Holbrook had just erected a handsome store, built of cut granite, and was one of the leading merchants. His integrity was undoubted, his intelligence of a superior order, and his political faith ultra-Union. The gladiators went heart and soul into the fight. Betting was the order of the day. Each party was perfectly confident of success. Among the bets made was one of a somewhat eccentric character. Dr. H. S. Herrick entered into an agreement with R. C. Gridley to the following effect: If Buel was elected, Herrick was to carry a sack of flour from Clifton to Upper Austin, the distance being about a mile and a half, and the grade up-hill all the way. If Holbrook was elected, Gridley was to carry a sack of flour from Upper Austin to Clifton, having the advantage of the down-hill grade.

ONE OF THE CANDIDATES FOR MAYOR.

The battle was exciting, but it was bravely and honorably fought on both sides. Holbrook, the Republican candidate, was elected by a fair majority. The sentiment of the people was sound when it came to the great question of maintaining the Union.

Gridley, true to his engagement, was on hand at the appointed time with his sack of flour. An immense concourse of people had assembled in Upper Austin to witness the novel performance. Laughter and good-humor prevailed on all sides. The best feeling existed between the victorious and the defeated candidates. Winners and losers enjoyed the scene with equal gusto. A grand procession was formed, headed by an excellent band of music. The newly-elected officers, including his Honor the Mayor, followed the musicians, mounted on horseback. Next to them came the hero of the day, the redoubtable Gridley, with a sack of flour on his back. On each side marched a standard-bearer, carrying high in the air the flag of the Union. Gridley stood up to his task like a man, never flinching before the glorious emblem of liberty. If the truth were known he worshiped it in his heart, though he had an eccentric way of showing it. Friends, citizens, and strangers followed. Never was there seen such a lively crowd in Austin. " Go it, Gridley !" " Stick to it, Gridley !" " Never say die, Gridley !" were the encouraging words that cheered him on all sides.

Arrived at Clifton, it was suggested by some enterprising genius, whose speculative spirit kept pace with his patriotism, that the sack of flour should be sold for the benefit of the Sanitary Commission. The proposition was received with unbounded applause. In a moment an empty barrel or a dry-goods box was found, and an auctioneer mounted upon it. The bidding was lively; but the crowd were not quite warmed up to the joke, and the flour only brought five dollars.

It was then determined that there should be another auction held in Austin. The sack of flour was taken up again, and the procession started back with it—this time marching to the tune of " Dixie." The most uncompromising Copperhead was won over ; and all united in common sympathy for the suffering soldiers. It was a clever stroke of policy for the Republicans. The procession halted in front of the store owned by his Honor the Mayor. By this time the crowd was immense. Every body turned out to see the fun: miners from their holes in the ground; Reese River capitalists from their shanties; business men from their stores; women and children from their cottages and cabins.

The sack of flour was once more put up at auction with a general hurrah. This time the bidders were in earnest. They bid by the hundred, and by fifties and by twenties, many bidding against themselves. Republicans and Democrats bid without distinction of party. The best feeling prevailed; and $3000 was the grand result! The last purchaser always donated his purchase back to the Sanitary Fund. A third auction was held on the following day. The result on this occasion was $1700. The nucleus of so large a fund thus formed aroused the patriotic fire in the soul of Gridley. It was a glorious cause that could thus win the sympathies of every party. Henceforth Gridley was with it body and soul. He would make an institution of this sack of flour. He would immortalize it—make a magnificent donation to the sick soldiers and a reputation for himself. So Gridley set forth with his sack of flour. It was sold at Virginia City for $8000; at Sacramento for $10,000; and at San Francisco for about $15,000. I was witness to the procession in San Francisco. It was the memorable event of the times. Never did Montgomery Street present a more imposing appearance. The beauty and fashion of the city were there; and so was Gridley, decked out in glorious array, the observed of all observers. Who would not have been Gridley then—gazed at as *the* great man of the age? What would Grant or Sherman have amounted to when Gridley was in view? Thus did Gridley draw the surplus cash from the pockets of the generous public; and thus did he do good service in the cause of freedom. All honor to Gridley!

Of the career of this distinguished gentleman on the Atlantic side I have read wonderful newspaper accounts. He was fêted, and gazed at, and admired, and hurrahed, and printed in weekly pictorials, and puffed, and joked

—was the irrepressible Gridley; and the grand finale was $100,000 to the Sanitary Commission! Ever praised, ever sung in song be Gridley! It was a noble specula-tion, based upon a sack of flour and the popular sympathy for a noble cause. It commenced in Austin and ended with a net profit of $100,000 to the suffering soldiers, and immortality to the name of Gridley.

On the strength of his fame Gridley became interested with Mr. John W. Harker and other experienced finan-ciers, and raised sufficient capital in New York to return to Austin and start a bank. The great banking estab-lishment called the "First National Bank of Nevada" is now one of the prominent institutions of the country.

Buel, after his defeat for the Mayoralty of Austin, concluded to run for the Governorship of the State. He was nominated by the Convention at Carson—alas for Buel! The State was Republican. My worthy friend was sanguine to the last; he had many votes, but failed for want of votes enough. May he have better luck in his choice of party next time! He is a good fellow, and deserves to win in a good cause. Morally, he still lives; politically, he is a dead Buel.

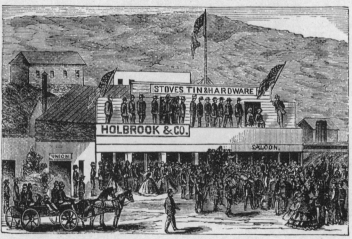

THE GRIDLEY SACK OF FLOUR AT AUCTION.

NEW YORK SPECULATORS.

W

CHAPTER L.

A GENERAL impression seems to prevail in these new mineral regions that every visitor who makes his appearance for the first time is a capitalist, or a gentleman of profound scientific attainments, or the representative of some heavy moneyed corporation, or a person who in some way possesses extraordinary influence over public opinion. The worthy citizens of Austin are proverbial for their hospitality. Not only do they feast every new-comer of any pretensions whatever with a prodigal hand, but extend to him all manner of invitations to explore their ledges and fill his pockets with specimens of chlorides, bromides and sulphurets.

I fear there is something scientific in the expression of my countenance. For three months I lived principally underground. My travels were through drifts and tunnels and shafts and inclines—tracing ledges and probing veins rather to oblige the mining community than from any expectation of individual profit. When I come to reflect upon the number of times I have gone down hundreds of feet under the earth in rickety buckets, the bumps and jams and alarms I have had in being conducted through dismal subterranean passages and hoisted out like a bag of ore, the damage to my clothes and disfigurement to my person, it really strikes me that there is some inconvenience after all in having a scientific reputation. Scarcely a day passed, during my sojourn at Reese, that I was not beset with invitations to explore mines varying from ten to a hundred and fifty miles distant. The prevalent idea was that I was en-

gaged in the preparation of elaborate works for Messrs.
Harper & Brothers; and every man who had a mine or
a ledge or the shadow of a claim appeared to think it
would never do to leave the country without seeing that
particular property, inasmuch as by that alone the wonderful richness of the mineral belt could be fairly appreciated. Never was there any thing so fabulously rich!
—ledge forty feet wide—outcroppings three hundred
dollars to the ton!—the virgin silver everywhere visible! It was quite useless to urge that I was merely engaged in jotting down some general notes on the country, and could not well spare the time to go into such
minute details. How was it possible to form any idea
of the country without seeing the " Carotid Artery,"
or the " Great Umbilical," or the " Mammoth Siwash?"
One active and enterprising little fellow with a bull-terrier face dogged me for three days, insisting upon it that
I should climb a rugged mountain about five or six
thousand feet high and take a look at the " Smiling Jane,"
in which he had a half interest. It was by all odds the
best thing in Reese. All it wanted was development.
The ledge was forty feet wide and nearly pure silver.

" Why don't you work it?" said I, somewhat annoyed
at his pertinacity.

" That's just what we want to do," answered my friend,
briskly. " But you see me and my pardner is bust. We
must have capital, and to have capital we must sell out
an interest in the Smiling Jane."

" What do you ask for the whole mine?"

" Well, it ought to be worth two hundred thousand
dollars—that would give us a hundred thousand apiece."

The cool audacity with which this was said gave me
rather a favorable impression of the man's speculative
genius.

" Really," said I, " that's a ledge worth owning. But
I don't see what profit it is to me whether your ledge
is worth two hundred thousand dollars or two cents."

" Oh, you're on the make, are you?" suggested my

shrewd friend rather indignantly—as if he thought there was a large amount of moral turpitude in my being " on the make " while he, an honest miner, had no predilections at all in that way.

" Why, yes, to be candid, I'd like to make fifty thousand or so. I think that amount would quicken my interest in the Smiling Jane."

The bull-terrier didn't see it in that point of view. He thought it rather a hard case that men who had worked, and starved, and suffered all sorts of hardships for two or three years should be obliged to give away half their claims before they could realize any thing on the other half. There was Professor Silliman and Professor Jackson and a dozen other professors who wouldn't express an opinion short of $500 to $1000.

" Well," said I, " it probably cost these gentlemen something to obtain an education. You don't expect men of reputation to visit such a country as this for amusement."

No—he didn't expect that, but the miners were poor. They had no spare cash. For his part, he was not disposed to be mean. He would give a liberal contingent to have the " Smiling Jane" examined, and a report made upon it.

" Very well," said I; " lead the way, and I'll see what can be done."

We climbed mountains and scaled precipices for the next two hours, till we came to a barren spot of earth, which seemed to be rooted up by squirrels or gophers to the depth of about three feet. I confess the effort had somewhat exhausted me, and I sat down on a stone to wipe my forehead and gain breath.

" The ledge, as you see, is not yet developed," remarked my companion—" all it wants is development."

" Where is it?" I asked, looking about in every direction, for I was unable to see any thing in the shape of a ledge.

" Here—right here under your feet! Don't you see

the chlorides cropping out? Look at them casings, Sir! Cast your eye on that virgin deposit, Sir! Did you ever see finer surface ore? Here's a chunk would go a dollar to the pound!"

In vain I looked; in vain I picked up little bits of earth and rock; in vain I pounded them up and gazed at the fragments; by no possible effort of imagination could I make a ledge out of the "Smiling Jane."

"Well, Sir!" said the Terrier, a little impatiently, "what do you make of it?"

"I should call it A PROSPECT," was my answer.

"True, the ledge is not yet developed—all it wants is capital to bring it out."

"Have you had any of these ores assayed?"

"Not yet. We don't go much on assays. Assays isn't worth shucks. I know men in the assay line that keeps blank certificates, and fills 'em up accordin' to order—five dollars for five hundred and ten dollars for a thousand to the ton. Assays is nothing."

The Terrier having thus expressed himself, lighted a pipe and stood with the jaunty air of a proprietor—his hands in his pockets, his legs spread like a pair of dividers across the supposed ledge—awaiting my opinion.

"Friend," said I, "it would be impossible for me to make a satisfactory report on that mine in its present state of development. But this much I will say. You ought to be able to get a million of dollars for it in New York. The New York capitalists seem to have a fancy for mines of this kind."

"I'll tell you what," said the Terrier after some deliberation—"if you'll go on to New York and sell the 'Smiling Jane' for a million, I'll give you my personal obligation for fifty thousand dollars."

Want of time compelled me to decline this flattering offer. The Terrier did not give it up so easily. Every time I met him for some weeks after he renewed the proposition, with various tempting additions in the way

of future prospects.   The last I heard of him, he had
"made a raise" of three hundred dollars and was on
his way to New York with several elaborate reports
done by friendly hands, and numerous certificates of assay purchased at the prevailing rates, showing the wonderful resources of the "Smiling Jane."   I warn the
citizens of New York that there are town-lots for sale
in the City of Oakland in which capital may be invested
with less risk and quite as good a prospect of speedy
returns.   Still, if they want to go into the "Smiling Jane,"
I will say this much : There is no telling the amount of
wealth that may be in it.   At all events, there is ample
room for speculation on the premises.

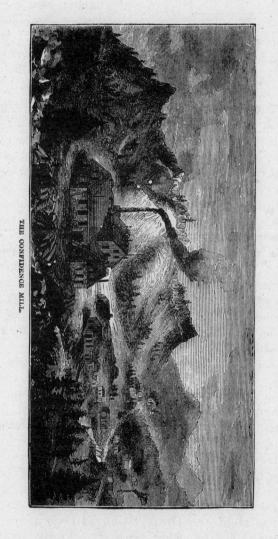

THE CONFIDENCE MILL.

CHAPTER LI.

THE LOST LEDGE.

THERE is a class of men peculiar to our new mineral territories to whom the world has not yet done justice. In truth they are but little known individually, though in the aggregate they have accomplished wonderful things. I speak of those vagrant spirits, commonly called "prospectors," who never make any thing for themselves, but are always on the move to make fortunes for other people. Regular miners, traders, and speculators belong to an entirely different genus. They come in after the way has been opened; but with them the spirit of adventure is not a controlling power. They are no more to be compared with the genuine "prospector" than the motley crowd of merchants and artisans who flocked over to the new world in the tracks of the great Columbus are to be named in the same day with that renowned discoverer.

The prospector is a man of imagination. He is a poet—though not generally aware of the fact. Ragged and unshaved, he owns millions, yet seldom has two dimes to jingle in his pocket—for his wealth lies in the undeveloped wilds. The spirit of unrest burns in his blood. He scorns work, but will endure any amount of hardship in his endless search for "rich leads." There is no desert too barren, no tribe of Indians too hostile, no climate too rigorous for his researches. From the rugged cañons of the Toyabe he roams to the arid wastes of the Great Basin. Hunger, thirst, chilling snows, and scorching sands seem to give him new life and inspiration. It matters nothing that he discovers "a good thing"—a nest of ledges, worth say a million apiece—this is well enough, but he wants something better; and after a day or two spent in "locating his claims" he is off again—nobody knows where—often with scarcely provision enough to last him back to the settlements. He travels on mule-back, when he happens to own a mule; on foot, when he must; with company, when any offers; without, when there is none; any way to be driving ahead, discovering new regions and locating claims. He locates so many claims that he forgets where his possessions are located. If he discovered a ledge of pure silver, six feet thick, he would die in a week if he had to work it on his own account. His industry runs in another direction. Variety is the spice of his existence, the motive-power of his life.

By no means do I intend to depreciate the services of this class of men. They have done more to open up our vast interior territories to settlement and civilization than all the scientific expeditions ever sent across the Rocky Mountains. The indomitable courage, the powers of endurance, the spirit of enterprise, the self-reliance and the fertility of resource exhibited by this class of men under circumstances of extraordinary difficulty, have no parallel in the annals of daring adventure. Where is there a desert so barren or a mountain so rugged that it is not traversed or explored by the irrepressible Prospector? In the wild declivities of the South Pass, in the desolate wastes of Colorado and Utah, in the alkali plains and sage-deserts and rugged mountain ranges of Nevada, you find him with his pick and shovel—ever hopeful, ever on the strike for "a new lead." He is the most sanguine of men—the most persistent of explorers. Neither disappointment nor the vicissitudes of climate can check the ardor of his enthusiasm. As privation is his lot in this world, it is to be hoped he will strike "a better lead" in the next.

Early in the summer of 1852 a train of sixty wagons left the Mountain Meadows for San Bernardino. The

W 2

party consisted chiefly of Mormons, but among them were some Gentiles who availed themselves of the protection afforded by the train against the attacks of hostile Indians. The road taken was that known as the old Spanish trail between Salt Lake and San Bernardino. It was the intention of the emigrants to cut off a bend in the road running by Las Vegas Springs, which approaches within thirty or forty miles of the Rio Colorado, and considerably increases the distance. At the Armagosa a difference of opinion arose as to the proper direction to be pursued—some being in favor of striking straight across the desert, while others, who knew the terrible sufferings likely to be encountered from want of water in those arid wastes, thought it more prudent to keep within range of the river. As usual in such cases, the discussion ended in a quarrel. Fifty-one of the wagons started down the Armagosa, determined to gain the old road again and follow the beaten track. The remaining nine crossed the range of mountains between the Armagosa and Death Valley. On reaching Furnace Creek another dispute arose. The weary wanderers were in the midst of a wilderness, with nothing in sight but barren mountains and desolate plains save the wretched little water-hole at which they were camped. Seven of the wagons finally started to explore Death Valley for an outlet to the north-west. The other two struck out to the south-west; but were soon lost in the rugged declivities of the mountains bordering on Panamint Valley. On their route they discovered the skeletons of three men, at a point called Poison Springs —the waters of which are supposed to cause death. The bones of cattle and of various wild animals were found scattered about in the vicinity. From the train that went down the Armagosa there was a further division of three men, named Farley, Cadwallader and Towne; who, tired of the slow rate of progress and the constant dissensions that prevailed, determined to strike out for themselves. Providing themselves with some

jerked beef and such other articles of subsistence as
they could carry on their backs, they left the wagons,
taking a route a little north of west. For several days
they wandered about in the wilderness, suffering greatly
from thirst and heat. At Day-light Springs they found
water. Thence they crossed Death Valley and ascended
the range of mountains lying between that desolate region and the Valley of Panamint, at a point called Folly's Pass. In the course of their wanderings they saw
many wonders in the way of mineral ledges; but were
unable to examine them carefully owing to their sufferings from thirst and the necessity of reaching some
spring or water-hole while they had strength. At one
place, supposed to be in the foot-hills of the Panamint
range, they discovered a silver-ledge of such extraordinary richness, that in the language of one of the party
the "virgin silver glittered in the sun." Weary as they
were, and precious as their time was, they stopped long
enough to break off a few masses of the ore and locate
a claim. The ledge cropped up boldly out of the earth,
showing a well-defined vein of four or five feet in thickness, and so rich that the virgin ore was visible all over
it.

After great hardships and terrible suffering from
thirst, the three men found water at a place called the
"Last Chance Springs," where they camped for several
days. While resting there, the two wagons that separated from the nine at Furnace Creek, came in with the
small party accompanying them. They had been many
times lost; their stock was nearly broken down with
fatigue and thirst, and they were now seeking to get on
some known trail that would lead them to California.
A Methodist minister named King, with his wife, occupied one of these wagons. The three men, Farley, Cadwallader and Towne, told King of the wonderful discovery they had made, and showed him the ore they had
obtained from the ledge. King knew but little of mining practically, but he was an intelligent man and saw

no reason to doubt the representations made to him. Provisions were getting short, however, and there was a long journey before them. It was not possible to go back to the ledge and make any further examination of it without a strong chance of perishing in the attempt. The party then joined together and pursued their way in a south-westerly direction till they struck the San Bernardino road and entered California. King and his wife had relatives in the Santa Clara Valley, and settled there. Accounts given by them of the great silver ledge attracted considerable attention, though not so much, probably, as would have been the case after the discovery of the Washoe mines. The people of California were not prepared to attach any great importance to discoveries of silver while their attention was so fully occupied in the development of the gold mines. The Kings had with them a specimen of the ore presented to them by the discoverers, which of course tended to authenticate their statement; but they were not skilled in getting up speculations, and consequently the matter soon died out, so far as they were concerned.

Farley, Cadwallader, and Towne separated on their arrival at San Bernardino. Cadwallader went on a prospecting expedition to Sonora. Farley and Towne roved about the southern country for some time, finally stopping at Los Angeles. While there they talked freely about their great silver ledge near Death Valley. The attention of some practical gentlemen in Los Angeles was attracted by the specimens of ore which these two men carried with them. A company was organized and capital paid in to make the necessary tests and fit out an expedition to work the ledge. Some of the ore was taken to San Francisco by a member of the company and assayed. The yield surpassed their most extravagant anticipations—being eighty-five per cent. of silver. Such a yield from croppings, taken at random from the surface, by travellers hurrying along on a journey of life or death, was well calculated to inspire confidence in the

richness of the ledge. Provisions and mining implements were purchased, and a party fitted out, under the
guidance of Farley, to find this wonderful deposit and
work it. On the approach to Folly's Pass, Farley got
into a quarrel with a member of the party named Wilson, in the course of which Wilson shot him dead.
There was no hope of finding the ledge after this unfortunate event without the aid of one of the remaining
discoverers.

Not knowing what else to do, and none being willing to stay behind upon an uncertainty, the members
of the expedition returned to Los Angeles, where
they procured the services of Towne as a guide. Another start was made, and all went on successfully till
they reached Owen's Lake, on the eastern side of the
Sierra Nevada Mountains. There Towne was taken
with a fever and died. It seemed as if fate were against
the enterprise. Compelled once more to return to Los
Angeles, the company next set to work to find Cadwallader, the only surviving member of the party by whom the
ledge was discovered, and who knew of its location.
Without his guidance the whole enterprise must prove
a failure. A reliable agent was sent down into Sonora
to search for him, and make him such propositions as
would secure his services. The search was successful,
in so far as Cadwallader was found; but he was in such
a condition from habits of intemperance into which he
had fallen, that it was almost impossible to get him sober. When he became sober enough to listen to any
proposition understandingly, he died.

All attempts to find the ledge having thus failed
through a strange fatality attending the discoverers,
the company was compelled to abandon the enterprise.
Other parties, however, undertook to find it from the
general descriptions given of the locality. Three years
after the death of Cadwallader a new company was
formed under the leadership of a Lieutenant Bailey, who
professed to be well acquainted with the country. This

gentleman had explored Death Valley and the Pana-mint, and even claimed to have discovered the "Lost Ledge." He brought with him to San Francisco some extraordinarily rich ore, and had no difficulty in pro-curing from capitalists a large amount of money for the purpose of developing the ledge. Some say he collect-ed as much as $70,000. He refused to sell any portion of the original ledge, but got up subscriptions on a con-tinuation or extension, which was rich enough to satisfy the sagacious men of San Francisco. A party was fit-ted out, with wagons, provisions, implements, etc., and started from Los Angeles. Bailey was to overtake them in a few days at some point near Owen's Lake, and conduct them to that wonderful deposit of virgin silver which was to make them all rich. The expedi-tion reached the point designated, and halted according to agreement. Days passed, and weeks passed, and months passed. No Bailey came. I tell the story as I heard it. If that gentleman be among the living, he will greatly oblige his San Francisco friends by account-ing for his absence. The party left at Owen's Lake are under the impression that there would be no difficulty whatever in finding the "Lost Ledge" if they could only find the lost Bailey.

But if any body supposes such a mining population as we have on the Pacific coast can be disheartened by disaster and failure, he greatly mistakes the character of our people. No sooner was the Reese River country opened up to settlement and enterprise than prospecting parties started out in every direction to find new ledges. My old friend, Dave Buel, of whom I have so frequent-ly made honorable mention, having located all the claims he wanted in the neighborhood of Austin, became in-spired with the grand idea of discovering a new route to the Colorado River. Such at least was the ostensible object of the famous expedition made by him in the winter of 1855. But I strongly suspect the "Lost Ledge" formed a prominent feature in the enterprise.

Buel had obtained some valuable information respecting
its supposed locality from one of the men who had accompanied the train of wagons in 1852.   He had carefully studied the whole subject, and thought he could
" spot the treasure."   Certainly if any man living could
do it, Buel could.   Of gigantic frame, great powers of
endurance, unerring sagacity, and indomitable perseverance, he was well fitted by nature for such an enterprise.   The history of that memorable expedition remains yet to be written.   The party consisted of six—
all chosen spirits—hardy and sanguine.   They left Austin on mule-back—they came back on foot.   Of their
sufferings from thirst in the burning wastes of Death
Valley; the loss of all their animals save one little pack-
mule; the dreary days they spent in " prospecting"
for the ledge while death stared them in the face;
their escapes from roving bands of hostile Indians, and
miraculous preservation from starvation, I can not now
give a detailed account.   Gaunt and haggard, blackened by the sun, ragged and foot-sore, they returned to
Austin after an absence of two months.   Buel lost thirty-five pounds of flesh, but he gained a large amount of
experience concerning lost ledges generally.   He thinks
he was on the right track and could have found the
identical ledge discovered by Farley, Cadwallader, and
Towne had the provisions held out.   The indications
were wonderfully encouraging—mineral everywhere—
nothing but mineral—not even a blade of grass or a drop
of water.   At one time the party lived for three days on a
little streak of snow which they found under a shelving
rock.   Buel considers it a fine country for horned frogs.
From the skeletons of men and broken wagons that he encountered near some of the water-holes, he is disposed
to think that there may be better routes to the Colorado.

Inspired by the disasters of the Buel expedition, which
were deemed rather encouraging in a mineral point of
view, another company was formed during the past
summer, of which a Mr. Breyfogle was a prominent

member. I knew Breyfogle in former years. He was tax-collector of Alameda County, California; and seemed to be a man of good sense, much respected by the community. During the Washoe excitement he departed for that region, and was engaged for several years in mining speculations. Like many others, he had ups and downs of fortune. It was during a down turn that he became infatuated with the idea of discovering the "Lost Ledge." The failure of all attempts hitherto made he attributed to want of perseverance, and he announced it as his determination "to find the ledge or die." That was the only spirit that would lead to its discovery. He would "come back a rich man, or leave his bones in Death Valley." Every body said that was the way to talk, but nobody knew how much in earnest was Breyfogle.

Some five or six enterprising spirits united their resources and started with this irrepressible prospector, full of glorious visions of the Lost Ledge. They travelled to the southward, following the Toyabe range till they struck into the dreary desert of Death Valley. There they wandered for many days, probing the foot-hills of the Panamint range. They crossed and recrossed Buel's trail; they camped at the Poison Springs, and saw the skeletons of dead men; they went through Folly's Pass, and ranged through the Panamint Valley. North, south, east, and west they traversed the country, till their mules broke down and their provisions fell short. Breyfogle urged them to continue the search. "Stick to it, boys, and we'll find it yet," he would say. "Never give up while there's a ghost of a chance." But they were all ghosts by that time, and were rapidly becoming skeletons. Their only hope of saving their lives was to strike for the nearest mining camp—San Antonio—which was distant over a hundred miles. Breyfogle had been getting more and more excited for several days. He begged his companions to try it a little longer—only two days—even a day—as Columbus did in the days of yore. But here was certain death; or so, at least, it appeared; for what could they do without food in this fearful desert, remote from any point where they could obtain human aid, and already so weak that they could scarcely drag their limbs over the heavy sand? Breyfogle's eyes were bloodshot and had a wild and haggard expression. When it was announced to him that it was the determination of the party to abandon the search, he said: "Then I will continue it alone. I have sworn to find the Lost Ledge or leave my bones here, and I intend to do it." His comrades entreated him not to stay behind—they had scarcely provision enough to last them to San Antonio, and could not spare him more than two days' supply at the furthest. What if he found the ledge? the discovery would be of no use to him or any body else, for he would be sure to die. These arguments fell without effect upon the excited brain of the visionary. Too weak and weary to take him by force, Breyfogle's comrades reluctantly bade him good-bye and left him to his fate. With great difficulty they reached San Antonio. There they recruited till they were able to pursue their journey homeward to Austin. In the mean time Breyfogle wandered about searching the deserts and the mountains for the Lost Ledge. When his provisions gave out he lived on frogs and lizards; but became very weak. It is probable his reason had been affected for some time. How long he wandered in this crazy condition would be difficult to say without a more accurate knowledge of dates. While thus helpless, a party of two or three Indians who had been watching him for several days, came upon him suddenly, beat him with their clubs, robbed him of his clothes, and ended by scalping him. One might think this rigorous course of treatment would have put an end to the poor wanderer; but such was not the case. Two days after the attack upon him by the Indians, a wagon-train, on the way from Los Angeles to Salt Lake City, picked him up and carried him to the City of the Saints. The injury to his scalp seemed to restore his faculties. He gave a graphic narrative of his adventures from the time his companions left him. At Austin it was reported that he was dead; but he turned up at Salt Lake City a few weeks after, as much alive as ever, and still determined to find the Lost Ledge. My visit to Salt Lake was shortly after his arrival. Hearing that he was there, I was about to hunt him up, when an attack of mountain fever laid me on my back, so that I lost the chance of seeing him before his departure on a little side-expedition to Idaho and Montana.

CHAPTER LII.

I NOW come to a stand-point, from which I think we may take a general view of the country with special reference to its resources and future prospects. The elaborate reports of Professors Silliman, Jackson, and Adleberg, who visited Reese River during the year 1865, leave me but little to say, even if I were competent, in relation to its geological features; and the admirable detailed reports of Mr. Clayton on the individual ledges have quite exhausted that branch of the subject. A summary of what I saw myself in my unlearned way, with what I gathered from practical miners and experts, may enable the general reader to form a more vivid and comprehensive idea of the country than could be derived from purely scientific reports.

The district of Reese River lies on the western slope of the Toyabe range of mountains, and is distant from Virginia City, by the Overland Mail Route, 170 miles. It embraces a track of hilly country some eight miles in length by four in width, bounded on the north by the Yankee Blade Cañon, on the west by the Reese River Valley, on the south by Simpson's Park, and on the east by the summit of the Toyabe range. Within these limits are situated, in close proximity to the main cañon which runs from Reese River Valley to the summit, those spurs or hills of the Toyabe range known as "Lander Hill," "Mount Prometheus," and "Central Hill," in which the principal discoveries of silver-bearing veins have been made. Austin, the chief town and county seat of Lander County, lies high up in the cañon, extending along it for a distance of more than a mile, with a broad main street, intersected by cross streets running up to the left over the lower slopes of the hills. It contains at the present time (January, 1866) a permanent population of about five thousand. The buildings are principally frame, well constructed, and ornamented in front by rows of scrubby pines stuck in the ground. Among them are some pretty cottages, evincing a growing taste for the comforts and even the luxuries of life. The best private residences, such as Mayor Hanson's and Mr. Rankin's, are substantially built of stone.

In the business part of the town, on the main street, are many fine brick houses; also several handsome stores and saloons built of stone. The general aspect of Austin is cheerful and picturesque. During the period of my sojourn — from May to August — it presented every indication of prosperity. The population is one of the best I have seen in any mining town—active, industrious, hospitable, and orderly. In point of morals I do not believe there is a better condition of society in any community of equal number on the Pacific coast. This is mainly attributable to the fact that a larger proportion of the population consists of women and children than in most new mining towns; and in part to the prevailing scarcity of surplus means. Every man has to labor for a living. There is not much chance for gamblers or idlers; consequently there are few of them.

The Toyabe range of mountains, in which most of the discoveries of silver ledges now attracting attention have been made, commences near the Humboldt River, about 100 miles north of Austin, and extends in a southerly course, trending slightly to the west, a distance of 175 miles, where it terminates in the high desert plateau, which forms the southern rim of the Great Basin. Formerly the Overland Telegraph and Mail Routes crossed it a few miles to the north of Pony Cañon; but since the building of Austin both telegraph line and overland stages pass directly through that city and across the head of Big Smoky Valley.

The characteristic appearance of the Toyabe Mountains is that of extreme barrenness. The cañons and a few of the open slopes are dotted with a scrubby growth of nut-pine, juniper, white-pine, and a hard, scraggy kind of timber called mountain mahogany. In the vicinity of Austin most of the wood has been cut away for fuel and other purposes in the progress of mining; but north and south, from eight to ten miles distant, there is still a sufficient supply to last for several years, probably five or six. In the Smoky Valley districts the quantity of wood is much greater; and it will probably be many years before any difficulty will be experienced on that score. The barren aspect of the mountains arises more from the extreme dryness of the climate than from any want of fertility in the soil. During the rainy season bunch-grass flourishes all over the hill-sides, affording a fine pasturage for stock; and wherever there is water for irrigation the land is highly productive. The valleys are entirely destitute of timber, presenting a singularly desert-like appearance, except in those portions which are sufficiently moist to give a tinge of green to the everlasting sage-bushes by which they are covered.

One of the advantages claimed for the ledges near Austin is the facility with which they can be worked. The granite formation in which they lie is soft, and blasting is but little required in getting out the ores. They are all true fissure veins, with well-defined casings. The clay seam between the quartz and the casings renders the excavation of the ores comparatively easy.

The chloride ores reach from the surface to a depth of 60 or 70 feet. Then comes a lean or barren streak, extending down from 20 to 30 feet to what is called the water-level. It was this unproductive stratum which caused the extraordinary depression of mining stocks in 1864. But experience has demonstrated, in every case where the excavations have extended below the water-level, that the vein continues unbroken, and with every promise of permanency, to an unknown depth. Insufficient machinery for pumping and hoisting has hitherto been the great drawback to the profitable working of the mines. The miners, who have held on to their claims through all the fluctuations and alarm of the past two years, are now reduced to the necessity of calling in the aid of capital. This, in part, accounts for the extraordinary number of claims now flooding the markets of New York.

Of the vast number of mining properties offered for sale in New York, it is scarcely necessary to say that the great majority are valueless. Every adventurer who possesses the shadow of a claim takes it or sends it East in order that he may realize a fortune. There is no difficulty in obtaining an imposing array of evidence to demonstrate its value. Scientific reports and certificates of assay are cheap—considering the prices for which worthless claims are sold. I do not mean to say that no really valuable mining properties are offered for sale; but it is certain they form an exception to the rule. Capitalists show a want of judgment in their investments, scarcely to be expected in men who are so shrewd in the ordinary transactions of business. I like this in them. It is pleasant to find a weak spot in the character of a class noted for sharp practice and hard dealings. It gratifies one's self-love to think that men who would deliberately refuse to lend him five dollars on his individual note at three per cent. a month, are susceptible of being imposed upon by the shallowest tricks of speculation. For myself, I have no taste for financial business—on the contrary I rather scorn that sort of business as a waste of valuable time which might be profitably employed in visiting remote and unknown countries. The consequence is, my most intimate friends in the business community are apt to regard me as rather a visionary and erratic character, unfitted by nature for the serious transactions of life. Sometimes I fancy they look upon me with an eye of pity, because I lose so many good opportunities of making a fortune. Be this as it may, I protest it would mortify me exceedingly to be guilty of such acts of verdancy as I have seen perpetrated by the sagacious business men of New York.

In the course of my Reese River experience I think I must have read a dozen pamphlets devoted to enthusiastic descriptions of mining properties purchased by New York companies, which to the best of my belief exist only on paper. A common error is to suppose the truth can be ascertained by a telegraphic dispatch to some confidential friend. Let us suppose a case: An immensely valuable property, comprising five hundred silver ledges, forty thousand acres of woodland, one hundred mill-sites, and twenty-five town-sites, is offered for sale at the moderate sum of two million five hundred thousand dollars. So confident of its value are the proprietors that they are willing to take two hundred and fifty thousand dollars in cash, and the remainder on mortgage at one per cent. or in stock, as may be agreed upon. Half a dozen sagacious capitalists take a fancy to this magnificent enterprise — not an unlikely supposition considering the number of ledges, water-privileges and town-sites. As business men, and on business principles, they offer the round sum of two hundred thousand dollars cash, and the balance in stock—provided, upon the transmission of a telegraphic dispatch to a reliable gentleman of their acquaintance in Nevada, the response should be favorable. The terms are accepted. The dispatch is sent. The reliable gentleman, if not one of the owners, knows the value of his opinion. He is not spending his time in a desolate mining country merely for pleasure. He must be a rarely reliable gentleman, indeed, to refuse an offer of twenty thousand dollars and a heavy contingent for recommending the purchase of a valuable property. If he examines it, he does so through the highly-colored spectacles of interest; he sees a magnificent prospect all over it, and reports accordingly. Neither you nor I would do so, dear reader, unless we conscientiously believed it to be a good thing; but the majority of men are not so scrupulous in their morals. Mining speculations, like transactions in horse-flesh, have a tendency to blunt the moral perceptions. Nine-tenths of the frauds committed in the sale of mining stocks have their origin in misplaced confidence. Surely no sensible man would purchase a horse from his father, uncle, or brother without strong collateral testimony from a disinterested party as to the value of the animal. Why then should he purchase a mine, or a ledge, or a mill-site, without taking similar precautions to ascertain its value? In this case, where the amount risked is so great, the chief trouble is to find a disinterested party. Your friend may not be interested in the particular property offered for sale, but it is quite probable he has a nice little enterprise of his own that he would like to submit to your consideration. Is it any wonder, then, that when the grand purchase is consummated, superintendents and experts appointed, machinery shipped, and every thing under way to develop the vast resources of the company's possessions, that the five hundred ledges are found to be merely conjectural, the forty thousand acres of woodland a patch of scrubby pines in some inaccessible mountain region, the hundred mill-sites scattered over a sage-desert where there is not water enough to run a grindstone, and the twenty-five town-sites agreeably situated in the middle of an alkali lake!

Now, if I had the honor of a personal acquaintance with a company of millionaires who had just engaged in a magnificent enterprise like this, do you know what I would recommend them to do? Issue a pamphlet at once, with maps, diagrams, etc., showing the extraordinary value of their possessions; rent a fine office at two hundred dollars a month; appoint a Board of Trustees who never saw a silver ledge; elect a President famous for his operations in shoddy; appoint all the younger

sons, cousins, and nephews belonging to the most influ-
ential members of the company, and notorious for stu-
pidity or dissipated habits, and send them out to carry
on the business; then invite the credulous and unsus-
pecting public to take stock; and then in view of the
dividends likely to accrue at an early day from this judicious course, I would modestly suggest that the author
of this article having incurred considerable trouble and
expense in qualifying himself to give this advice, would
not object to a slight testimonial of appreciation on the
part of the company.

It would be a source of great regret to me if any in-
ference prejudicial to the interests of Nevada should be
drawn from these observations. I am satisfied that
great injury has been done to the State by fraudulent
speculations. The mineral resources of the country are
sufficiently wonderful, without exaggerated statements
and ridiculous misrepresentations. No visitor who has
carefully examined the ledges in and around Austin, or
in the districts of Amador, Yankee Blade, Smoky Valley, Bunker Hill, Twin River, Washington, Marysville,
Union, Mammoth, and other well-known mining localities,
can fail to be impressed with the extraordinary richness
and permanency of the mineral deposits. It is a great
detriment to the country that the true character of its
resources is so little known. The official reports on the
Mineral Resources of the States and Territories West
of the Rocky Mountains, recently published by Congress,
will it is hoped do some good by disseminating correct
information on this important subject. Every fraud
committed in the sale of worthless mining stock has a
tendency to shake the confidence of capitalists in really
good investments.

That many swindles have been perpetrated, and many
worthless claims palmed off on a credulous public, is beyond dispute; but it is both unreasonable and unjust to
condemn the whole country because dishonest men engage in nefarious speculations detrimental to its inter-

X

ests. If there are no good mines in the Reese River country, where can we look for them? The man who is cheated in a horse would be laughed at if he complained that there are no good horses. Mining speculations are much on a par with speculations in horse-flesh. Brokers and horse-jockeys generally make their profits from the credulity of their fellow-men. If every purchaser personally examined the mines offered to him, or availed himself of the services of an experienced agent, there would be less disappointment in the investment of capital.

The general direction of the veins in the Toyabe range is north-northwest and south-southeast, with a dip to the east. The pitch is from 30° to 70°, the average inclining from 35° to 45°.

From May to October the climate is mild; seldom too warm, and the sky almost invariably bright and clear. The extreme rarity of the atmosphere at this elevation, 6500 feet above the level of the sea, and the absence of moisture, give rise to a peculiar form of intermittent fever, called by emigrants and miners the mountain fever. Otherwise it would be difficult to find a more healthy climate. The winters are cold, though sometimes open and pleasant. On the north side of the hills the snow usually lies from November to May. In the valleys it seldom remains more than a few days at a time, and rarely interrupts communication by the public highways.

Some idea of the wonderful progress of Central Nevada may be formed from a glance at the number of mining districts which have been established since the discovery of the Reese River mines. Austin may be considered the central point from which these districts radiate. Mills have already been erected in many of them, and active operations in the way of developing the mines are now going on in most of them. The following are the principal districts, located within the past three years, with the distances from Austin, viz: Yankee

Blade, 4 miles; Amador, 6; Big Creek, 12; Geneva, 15; Santa Fé, 22; Bunker Hill, 30; Summit, 20; Ravenswood, 20; Washington, 35; Marysville, 45; Union, 63; Twin River, 65; Mammoth, 63; Diamond, 80; Cortez 60; San Antonio, 100; Silver Peak, 125; Ione, 75; E. Walker River, 120; Egan Cañon, 160.

These do not by any means comprise all the valuable districts which have been opened throughout the interior and on the confines of Nevada. I refer to them as having intercourse with Austin, and contributing in a great measure to the importance of that place as a market for the trade of the mines.

The high cost of reducing the ores has hitherto been a great drawback to the prosperity of the mining interests. While the Washoe mills can make handsome profits on ores ranging from $20 to $100 per ton, the Reese River mills are compelled, in consequence of the additional cost of roasting, to charge from $80 to $100 per ton. None but very rich ores can bear such costly working. A large amount of the labor and expense of working the mines is lost. Mills that could reduce $40 and $50 ores, with advantage to themselves and the miners, would soon make handsome fortunes. There is plenty of that grade of ore now lying waste over the hills.

CHAPTER LIII.

REDUCING THE ORES.

IN this connection a brief description of the process of reduction, under the improved system, may not be uninteresting.

When the ore is delivered at the mill it is placed in a kiln and the moisture evaporated. It is then crushed dry in the batteries and taken from them in cars, upon a railway leading to a series of hoppers in the furnace room. From the hoppers it is shaken down into the ovens, where it is roasted. While the process of roast-

BATTERY AND AMALGAMATING ROOM.

INTERIOR OF BUEL'S MILL.

ing is going on, it requires to be constantly stirred so that the most minute particles may be subjected to the action of the heat. This is continued from four to eight hours at a charge, according to the quality of the ore. Rich ores and heavy sulphurets require a longer time than poor or light ores. Salt is added, according to the greater or less amount of sulphurets to be reduced to chlorides. The percentage of salt used is from eight to twenty, varying with the quality of the ore. Its effect is to develop through the heat a chlorine gas, which has a strong affinity for silver, and forms after desulphurization a chloride of silver. The base metals are mostly volatilized, and thus separated from the silver. As soon as the ores are sufficiently roasted they are removed from the ovens to the cooling and screening-room, where they are sprinkled with water to prevent wastage in the transportation to the amalgamating room. The next process is to collect the silver by amalgamation. Some of the mills use the Freiberg or barrel process, which is conducted by means of revolving barrels. Wheeler pans are also extensively used. Differences of opinion exist as to the relative advantages of the various methods of amalgamation. A common practice is, to precipitate the chloride of silver by means of copper arms revolving in tubs. Steam is injected through small holes in the bottom of each tub, disseminating the quicksilver through the revolving mass. The silver chlorides, by contact with the copper arms, are precipitated in the form of metallic silver, leaving as a residuum a chloride of copper, which flows off into the tailings when the tubs are discharged. This process usually lasts from three to four hours. The silver thus collected is then placed in retorts and smelted. The best mills produce bullion ranging from 900 to 1000 fine.

ROASTING CHAMBER OF MIDAS MILL.

After nearly three months of hard experience, during which I scarcely passed a day without exploring one or more of the mines, I am thoroughly convinced this is a very rich mineral region. Whether all the mining enterprises now in progress will pay is another question. I think Eastern people are too easily imposed upon by specious representations, and have too great a tendency to expend large sums of money in the erection of mills and offices before they fully develop their ledges. This evil will cure itself in time. Undoubtedly there will be heavy losses in individual cases; but I am fully satisfied there will be a large average of success where capital is judiciously invested, and mills and mines economically managed.

THE END.